Page 1: Nootka mask used during Wolf Dance, collected by Livingston Farrand among the Quileute of Washington, 1898

Right: The country around Urtyn Obo, Mongolia, is especially rugged, with many exposures ideal for fossil prospecting. The nearby Baron Sog strata yielded fossil bones so large that the expedition labeled them "the monster of Baron Sog." Photograph by James Shackelford

Pages 4–5: Eight exposures, at twenty-minute intervals, of the midnight sun at Sunrise Point, in Smith Sound, Greenland, 11 P.M. July 25, 1916, to 1:20 A.M. July 26, 1916. The slight curve of the sun increases as one travels to the south, while at the North Pole the line of suns is parallel with the horizon. From a hand-colored lantern slide

Page 6: "The Monuments" of Canyon de Chelly, Arizona, 1925. In a 1917 letter to the Museum, archaeologist Earl Morris wrote, "Getting around is more difficult than it used to be. In 1912 there were livery stables and though horses were slow you could get there. Today it is mostly car service and it seems, if the car is not busy, it is busted."

Page 7, above: The nineteen-foot Hesperus, sailed by archaeologists Junius and Peggy Bird through the islands of Chile and Tierra del Fuego, in the Western Channels of Chile, 1935. Photograph by Junius Bird

Page 7, below: Chinook canoe on the beach near Fort Rupert, Canada, 1894. Photograph by O. C. Hastings

AMERICAN MUSEUM OF NATURAL HISTORY

125 YEARS OF EXPEDITION AND DISCOVERY

Lyle Rexer and Rachel Klein

Foreword by Edward O. Wilson

Harry N. Abrams, Inc., Publishers,

in association with the

American Museum of Natural History

For our children, Raisa, Norah, and Jonah

Editor: Harriet Whelchel
Designer: Dirk Luykx

Page 8: In the forest of central Sulawesi, June 1975.
Photograph by Guy Musser

Library of Congress Cataloging-in-Publication Data
Rexer, Lyle.
American Museum of Natural History : 125 years of expedition and
discovery / Lyle Rexer and Rachel Klein.
p.   cm.
Includes bibliographical references (p. 248) and index.
ISBN 0–8109–1965–6 (hardcover)
1. American Museum of Natural History—History.   I. Klein,
Rachel.   II. American Museum of Natural History.   III. Title.
QH70.U62N488   1995
508'.074747'1—dc20   95–6108

Published in 1995 by Harry N. Abrams, Incorporated, New York
A Times Mirror Company
All rights reserved. No part of the contents of this book may be
reproduced without the written permission of the publisher

Printed and bound in Japan

Contents

Preface

WHERE HAVE THEY COME FROM, the dinosaur skeletons, elephants, totem poles, and whales that are so much a part of every New Yorker's—and millions of other visitors'—childhood iconography? How have they arrived at Seventy-seventh Street and Central Park West, and why have they been gathered?

The archives and photographic collections of the American Museum of Natural History provide fascinating answers. They represent a kind of virtual reality within the Museum, one that parallels its vast collections of specimens and artifacts. Indeed, a new branch should be added to mammalogy, paleontology, and the other museum sciences, one that seeks to unearth the evolutionary history of a great institution in its accumulated images.

The images in this book tell the story of scientific field study and the people who pursue it. Regardless of how the American Museum of Natural History began 125 years ago—as civic showpiece or cosmic cabinet of curiosities—it soon became a scientific leviathan and has remained so. The volume of its scientific publications, most based on the work of Museum staff in the field and laboratory, is unsurpassed for a research institution based outside a university. Like the symphony orchestra and the novel of manners, the natural-history museum may have outlived its historical moment, yet the sheer weight of this museum's intellectual achievements has made it indispensable. Indeed, after 125 years, the American Museum of Natural History is entering what may be one of the most important periods of its history.

The delight of photography is that every image reveals more than the taker intended, and, over time, like some rich deposit of fossils, photographs accumulate layers of irony and poignancy. Even a reader with no interest in science (is there such a person in the age of the double helix, rain-forest destruction, and *Jurassic Park*?) will be riveted by symbols, struck by the mystery of places still little known to most of us. Stories within stories emerge: the physical danger of fieldwork, for instance, which is usually masked by the nonchalance of the subjects but present at the margins, in the encroaching tangle of vegetation, the unending ice, the emptiness of a desert landscape. We track, too, the progressive defeat of those dangers by the ascending technology of travel,

Artists William Leigh and A. A. Jansson making studies for the Klipspringer Group diorama, Lukenia Hills, Kenya, Eastman-Pomeroy-Akeley Expedition, 1926–27. From a hand-colored lantern slide by Carl Akeley

from dogsleds to freight cars filled with dinosaur fossils to automobiles in the Gobi Desert, to wings over Africa and on the rivers of New Guinea to helicopters on the Venezuelan plateaus.

The period of the Museum's growth also witnesses the replacement of the adventurer-scientist by the scientist-adventurer. In his autobiography, *Ends of the Earth,* Roy Chapman Andrews, of Gobi-expedition fame, relates an encounter with the Museum's African explorer Carl Akeley, just before the latter's final, fatal expedition to his beloved East Africa. Both were on layover between exotic destinations—a rare coincidence during their careers with the Museum. At the time of this encounter, the expeditionary tide was still rising, not to crest until 1930, when some thirty-five Museum expeditions occupied the field; yet both men seemed to recognize that their time was passing:

We often talked of the difficulties of financing our respective work and of the obligations we incurred to those who made it possible. I remember that he said one day: "Roy, sometime before I die I'm going on my own. I'll build my little camp-fire in Africa and I'll sit there and smoke my pipe and do nothing and be happy because I won't have to make good to anybody."

"Yes," said I, "you will *not.* You know darned well you'll have to make good to yourself. . . . We're all like that or we wouldn't be here. It's the only way we can be happy."[1]

Around the same time, Museum ornithologist Robert Cushman Murphy wrote the epitaph for the age: "The haphazard age of discovery is over, and exploration is no longer an end but a means."[2] It is not just that the clothes have changed, and today's paleontologists no longer resemble Baden-Powell protégés packing sidearms. Before the rise of molecular biology, the gap between scientist and amateur was not so apparent—at least, not at museums and not in the so-called naked-eye sciences, such as paleontology. Some of the Museum's most illustrious fossil discoverers, including Roland T. Bird and Walter Granger, had no academic credentials. The Museum's collections—and some of its most dramatic achievements—rest on the work of often wealthy amateurs. The sportsman Colonel J. T. Faunthorpe and trustee Arthur Vernay traveled from Mongolia to Central Africa to enhance the Museum's collections. So did Theodore Roosevelt, Jr., trustee Suydam Cutting, and Richard Archbold, to name only a few. Yale dropout and Museum trustee Lincoln Ellsworth flew the Poles, and Childs Frick, a gifted and dedicated student of the ancient earth, funded and led a series of expeditions that helped the Museum write the record of mammalian life in North America.

Today there is little room for the amateur naturalist, the "sportsman," and the patron on a modern expedition. It is too expensive, for one thing, and the contributions the gifted amateur might make are small, indeed. Courage, physical strength, and a steady shooting hand are no longer required. Geographical discovery, which is well-nigh exhausted, is not science, nor is the collecting of specimens, per se. Science is systematic investigation of phenomena, organized ideas about experiences and things, not things and experiences themselves. Increasingly, the investigation takes place in a laboratory and at a computer terminal. In the field, collecting and observation have become so specialized that their provinces are closed to those without rigorous training. As Museum ornithologist George Barrowclough remarked, "All the easy questions have been answered. The only ones left are difficult."

Yet why is it that the modern field teams, such as those that returned to the Gobi of Mongolia to renew the search for fossils, look even more devil-may-care (although somewhat less martial) than their predecessors? Perhaps it is because the world has become a smaller and more crowded place, and these scientists, unlike those who spend their careers entirely in the laboratory, are in search of boundlessness and solitude—commodities almost as precious as any new species they might discover. "Out here," Michael Novacek, the Museum's provost, has said about the Gobi, "you are away from telephones and fax machines. You have the time just to think."

The expeditions of the American Museum of Natural History are inner journeys toward understanding as much as they are physical journeys of discovery.

A final note: a great scientific museum pursues durable insight, but it lives in time. The methods and assumptions of an institution so centrally positioned in its culture move with that culture and rarely far ahead of it. Many of the images in this work depict relations with animals and with native peoples and their artifacts. The character of such relations has changed a great deal over the last several decades. The need to take specimens, for example, has put the Museum in a potentially paradoxical position vis-à-vis the conservation of species. Yet even this practice, which is fundamental to the ability to describe the distribution and evolution of species, is undergoing revision.

The need for more precise bio-geographic data has made it more selective, and DNA analysis has, in some cases, eliminated the need for taking whole animal specimens.

In a different way, the Museum's relations with native peoples have undergone a profound shift, altering the terms of exchange between those who seek knowledge and those who are the subject of study. For one thing, the two groups are increasingly one and the same. The world has grown too small to respect the isolation of any culture or permit the fiction of cultural "purity" and timeless stasis. Errands in an unchanging Eden are no longer possible—and never were. In 1910 the Mangbetu of Africa built a ceremonial house to match the one Museum collector Herbert Lang had read about in a book. Today there are motorcycles, revolution, plastic sandals, and public relations in the rain forest of Chiapas, where the last of the Maya-speaking people still live. Anthropology—the objective study of humankind—increasingly fosters complex collaborations in real time to understand, preserve, recover, and even enhance cultural history. Franz Boas, the Museum's first great student of humankind, understood the spurious connotations of the word "primitive." He was in love with human diversity and felt that it and its works were certain to be lost in a shrinking world. He also felt that diversity might be preserved in artifact and story, to enrich future generations' sense of human possibility. So he collected in what he felt was a race against time. A century later, it turns out the race is by no means over, and here, again, the Museum may be more important than ever.

A work this broad, however cursory the treatment of its themes, must have many assistants. Among the writers who have done service to the Museum, and by extension to this project, are Aldona Jonaitis, Douglas Preston, and John Michael Kennedy, whose dissertation on the Museum is probably the most consulted unpublished work in existence. Ronald Rainger has recently offered a bitter but salutary pill about the rise of vertebrate paleontology. The most searching and inspiring commentary comes from the curators themselves. Since the Museum's founding, they have taken their role as educators seriously and have published a truly enormous body of work for popular and scientifically literate audiences. Most of it is still interesting and some of it, including books by Roy Chapman Andrews, Roland T. Bird, Clark Wissler, Colin Turnbull, and Margaret Mead, to name only a few, is downright inspirational. The tradition continues, and this work is indebted to it.

Above all, however, face-to-face conversations with the Museum's scientific staff have given this project its direction and whatever ballast it carries. In particular, thanks are due to dean of science Craig Morris; provost Michael Novacek; chairman George Barrowclough (Ornithology); curator Robert Carniero (Anthropology); curator Niles Eldredge (Invertebrates); chairman David Grimaldi (Entomology); curator Laurel Kendall (Anthropology); chairman Ross MacPhee (Mammalogy); Archbold Curator Guy Musser (Mammalogy), who convinced us that the world is, indeed, ready for the story of the giant rat of Sumatra; curator Norman Platnick (Entomology); Lamont Curator Lester Short (Ornithology); chairman Ian Tattersall (Anthropology); curator David Hurst Thomas (Anthropology); associate curator Melanie Stiassny (Ichthyology); associate curator Charles Spencer (Anthropology); and associate curator Robert Voss (Mammalogy). Curator Enid Schildkrout (Anthropology) provided special help and the title of her book for the chapter on Africa.

The Museum is uniquely fortunate in harboring many people who have made it their business to know the institution's history and keep it alive. Director of the library, Nina Root, and head of special collections, Joel Sweimler, are the most prominent. Curator Stanley Freed (Anthropology), research associate Mary LeCroy (Ornithology), chairman Charles Myers (Herpetology), associate curator Mark Norell (Vertebrate Paleontology), chairman Richard Tedford (Vertebrate Paleontology), and scientific assistant Laila Williamson (Anthropology) offered knowledge and candor in equal amounts. Senior secretary Patricia Brunauer (Mammalogy) and Thomas Miller provided assistance and encouragement; Martha Graham (Cultural Resources Program), Shari Segal, and Elizabeth Chapman read portions of the manuscript; Jeff McCartney and Eric Chait (Development) negotiated; Scarlett Lovell (Special Publications) facilitated; Arnold Klein and David Bergman provided bibliographic resources, and Erin Cornell offered help when help was needed.

At Abrams, our thanks to Dirk Luykx for his skillful design. A final note of appreciation is reserved for editor Harriet Whelchel. Her extensive contributions to this book are best summed up by saying that she is what editors used to be.

Message from the President

FOR NEARLY ALL of its 125-year history, the American Museum of Natural History has undertaken voyages of discovery across seven continents, mapping the origin and progression of life on this planet and exploring the richness and variety of world cultures. This book provides a unique opportunity to view our institution from the perspective of those men and women—scientists, adventurers, visionaries, and artists—who have taken up the challenge of exploration. Their search to understand the extraordinary, the unusual, and the unknown is our priceless legacy.

The expeditions detailed here reflect the great tradition of exploration and research at the heart of this museum. Each fosters a deeper appreciation for, and understanding of, our unrivaled collection of natural-history artifacts, of the explorers who brought them back, and of the times in which they were discovered. They also reveal the wonders and mysteries of life.

Early exploration of the North Pacific challenged the bodies, minds, and spirits of those who set out to preserve a record of changing cultures. The Central Asiatic Expeditions of the 1920s, which began as a search of humanity's dawn, became instead a turning point in the Museum's understanding of dinosaurs. Ambitious journeys to both poles, to the uncharted regions of South America, and to New Guinea's rugged interior succeeded in bringing the world's frontiers closer. Expeditions of discovery, however, are not merely a component of the Museum's past but also a vital aspect of our work today as we initiate one of the most active programs in field exploration in decades.

Expeditions are the embodiment of this Museum's mission of discovery and understanding, throughout its illustrious past and in its continuing role at the forefront of scientific research. More than the sum of its twenty-three buildings, forty exhibition halls, and 30 million specimens, this is a place born of dreams and built on a solid foundation of intellectual inquiry. Through the tireless efforts of its scientists and explorers, both past and present, we see our world through a wider lens.

This book is a wonderful celebration of that vision.

Barosaurus lentus, the world's largest freestanding dinosaur display

Ellen V. Futter
President, American Museum of Natural History

Foreword

Edward O. Wilson

THE AMERICAN MUSEUM OF NATURAL HISTORY: This is a museum that has thought big about the world. In conversation, scientists and scholars most familiar with the institution call it the American Museum for short, or the AMNH, the letters slurred together into a single word and respectfully spoken, as though the initials were engraved upon some imperial standard. Indeed, the emissaries of the Museum during its golden age, from the late 1800s to the mid-1930s, when the Depression dried up most private support, thought of the whole planet as theirs to explore. They wanted to know what lay on and around the poles. They were determined to find out how the New World was first peopled, how culture evolved, how dinosaurs lived. They set out to find unknown creatures dwelling in central Africa, the interior of New Guinea, and other still unexplored reaches of the world, the more remote and mysterious the better. They lived the spirit of Kipling's explorer:

> Something hidden. Go and find it.
> Go and look behind the
>   Ranges—
> Something lost behind the Ranges.

They rejoiced in perseverance and in the ethic of drive and resourcefulness needed to succeed against daunting odds. It was natural for Roy Chapman Andrews, we learn in this volume, to say to an ageing Carl Akeley, who thought he might retire to Africa just to relax, "You will *not*. You know darned well you'll have to make good to yourself." The ability to go alone and stay at the edge of the world was central to the character of such men: "We're all like that or we wouldn't be here."

Andrews, Akeley, and their colleagues were heroes for me and other field researchers of my generation. Reading this book of AMNH expeditions and discoveries, I was reminded as never before of the intellectual debt I owe them. Using fossil remains and living species, William Diller Matthew discovered the phenomenon of faunal dominance, in which waves of species emerge from one continent to spread across the world while replacing others. Later, George Gaylord Simpson documented the process in epic detail for the New World. Because of these paleontologists, I spent part of my life analyzing the nature of dominance and equilibria and the causes of extinction. Ernst Mayr, pondering the birds he assembled from New Guinea, formulated the modern concept of the species. His ideas, summarized in his 1942 classic, *Systematics and the Origin of Species*, were the guidebook that took me into the study of evolution as a college undergraduate. William Morton Wheeler, the great entomologist who left the AMNH to join the Harvard faculty in 1908, assembled the nucleus of the world's largest collection of ants, on which I have spent a lifetime of study. He went around the world to collect specimens, and so have I, following in his footsteps. I am proud to have succeeded to his position at the Museum of Comparative Zoology and have taken care to use the same massive fawn-colored desk. For years I left untouched the pipe and tobacco pouch abandoned by him in the lower right-hand drawer.

Has the expeditionary spirit so well exemplified in the AMNH vanished? No, and I assure you it never will. Specialists have estimated that when insects and other smaller organisms are considered alongside the more familiar birds, mammals, and other vertebrates, fewer than 10 percent of all species in the world are known to science. Only a minority of habitats have been thoroughly studied for the life they contain, and many of the most remote remain to be visited for the first time. The fossil record is still largely uncovered, and expeditions continue to add wondrous new creatures every year, from Greenland to South Africa to Asia. Anthropology also continues to grow as a science, especially as it adds new techniques from linguistics, psychology, and biology. There is a desperate need to study more closely than before the dwindling roster of preliterate tribes and ancient ethnic groups.

Modern museums like the American Museum of Natural History and Museum of Comparative Zoology may focus more on science than raw collecting—curators today spend much of their time over microscopes and in chemical analysis—but the exploration of the world continues as never before, in the field and in the laboratory. The promise of a new golden age is implicit in the task this great museum has set itself.

How Science Came
to a Science Museum

O N THE FIFTH FLOOR of the American Museum of Natural History runs a corridor longer than any outside the Pentagon—nearly three city blocks. At one end is the office of the Department of Anthropology, whose current chairman is an expert in the physical evolution of primates, including human beings. At the other end is the office of the Department of Invertebrates—the earliest living things, which appeared on the Earth as early as 3.5 billion years ago. Off this corridor branch others—the departments of Mammalogy, the study of mammals, and of Vertebrate Paleontology, the study of fossils, including dinosaurs. It is lined with cases full of human artifacts and nature's artifacts—specimens of life forms. In short, the Museum contains the elements of a fascinating narrative. Although you must walk down other corridors to find the study collections of birds and insects, and into another building to find reptiles and fishes, the plot is clear: it is the rise and diversification of life on Earth. To comprehend and present that story is the mission of the American Museum of Natural History.

The Museum was not born to this task but had to grow into it, often in some very remote places—literally "the ends of the earth," in the words of Museum explorer Roy Chapman Andrews. The Museum discovered its mission in the sands of Mongolia and on uncharted rivers in Brazil; on the mist-shrouded plateaus of Venezuela and jungles of New Guinea; on the Red Deer River of Canada and in the Copper Canyon of Mexico; among dead cities and living people. Where the Museum has traveled and what it has learned in 125 years are the subjects of this book.

A Prospect "Most Desolate and Forbidding"

The American Museum of Natural History, from Central Park, 1917

The Museum was established in 1869, and, in its earliest years, perhaps the only person who could have imagined such a role for it was its

"Stroll for an hour or two across this hall so thick with 'living pillars.' . . . Even now, one would have to make an effort to recognize the dead tree trunks within the pillars and to remain deaf to their stifled voices; just as it would be difficult not to perceive, here and there behind the showcase glass, a sombre face, the 'Cannibal Raven' clapping its beak like wings, or the 'Master of the Tides' summoning forth the ebb and flow with a wink of its ingeniously articulated eyes."

—*Claude Lévi-Strauss*

founder, Professor Albert S. Bickmore. In the early 1870s, as he sat atop a huge rock in the midst of the site that was to be the fledgling institution's permanent home, he saw little to encourage him: "The prospect was most desolate and forbidding. . . . As I sat on top of this rock the surrounding view was dreary and my only companions were scores of goats. Only the temporary shanties of squatters could be seen on the north, except two or three small cheap houses. . . . On the west were only shanties perched on the rough rocks, and south of us there was no building near, except the 'Dacotah.'"[1] The site, at Seventy-seventh Street and Central Park West, then called Manhattan Square, was so remote that even grand quarters could rarely induce the Museum's first two presidents, John David Wolfe and Robert Stuart, to make the trip uptown. An initially curious public soon lost interest. But broad directing forces were at work that would insure the Museum's success, and they had found their agent in Bickmore.

There seems to be a need to tell

the story of the Museum's founding, like the recitation of an origin myth, for it has been repeated frequently, in many memoirs and publications.[2] As with any myth, we can pick our place and time of origin somewhat arbitrarily.

We need not go back as far as Aristotle, whose collections took advantage of a widely traveled field man named Alexander the Great. The Ashmolean Museum —the model for nearly all art *and* natural-history museums—was formed in 1686, the British Museum in 1753, the Musée National de l'Histoire Naturelle, with its twelve curators, in 1793. In the early decades of the nineteenth century, some fifty natural-history museums were established in Europe.[3]

Closer to home, the growth of natural-history studies was bound up with a nation's emergence. In 1795, Thomas Jefferson described with great national pride the fossil remains of an ancient creature discovered in Virginia, which he called *Megalonyx,* just as the U.S. Corps of Discovery was being planned under Lewis and Clark and events were setting in motion the Louisiana Purchase. America was discovering, in Jefferson's words, "what a field we have at our doors to signalize ourselves."[4] The new nation possessed not only a boundless future, but an ancient past as well. By 1842, the U.S. Exploring Expedition, sponsored by the federal government, had returned from circling the globe with tens of thousands of specimens and

artifacts and no place to put them.[5] The first of four regional geological surveys that would describe the flora, fauna, and indigenous cultures of the United States was launched. In 1869, the Golden Spike was driven, connecting both coasts by rail. The nation had just ended the Civil War, whose outcome had depended on industrial production. J. P. Morgan, the most prominent of the Museum trustees, had grown wealthy from that conflict, and in New York, capital, including his, was accruing to a degree unprecedented in human history. There were other currents at work as well, including the staging of massive expositions in St. Louis and later Chicago, based on London's Great Exhibition of 1851, featuring the Crystal Palace. Forerunners of the modern world's fair, these extravaganzas brought together art, commerce, and technology, as well as natural history. They were occasions for displaying the wealth and wonders of an expanding world.

This summary is not a comprehensive history of the museum movement, although its broad outline describes a path: science, especially natural science, but also archaeology and anthropology, which as yet had no names, accompanied economic and territorial expansion on both sides of the ocean. The growth of knowledge was linked intimately with geographical ambition. The United States was late in catching up, but it must have seemed to the capitalists and museum builders such as Morgan, Marshall Field in Chicago, and Andrew Carnegie in Pittsburgh that their commercial enterprises sanctioned knowledge of the world. This sense helps explain why, uniquely in America, philan-

thropy could support institutions that often had no immediate practical issue and that in other countries required governments to back them.

Bickmore's Calling

Into this pageant, humbly enough, came Professor Albert S. Bickmore. Bickmore was born in 1839 and grew up on the wild coast of Maine at a time when the Penobscot Indians still sailed their birchbark canoes along the coast to summer fishing grounds. He was fascinated with nature, delighting in birds and butterflies. With few books available, Bickmore's "sacred relic" was not Shakespeare or the Bible but a copy of *Goldsmith's Natural History, Abridged.* He went to college at rural Dartmouth, itself an errand in the wilderness. There he began collecting specimens and never stopped. When he arrived in Cambridge in 1860, his first vision of Professor Louis Agassiz set his course for good: "I found him in the basement amid a great array of bottles and alcoholic specimens and the first words I heard him speak, when asking for 'the Professor,' was his reply, 'Dis is me,' an illustration of his occasional use of the French idiom. . . . He said to me 'gather what specimens you can on the shores near your home, and when you return with them, I will assign you a lesson and in six weeks you will either become utterly weary of the task or you will be so completely fascinated with it as to wish to devote your whole life to the pursuit of science.'"[6]

The world was a mighty maze, but not without a plan; nature, yes, but nature systematized—this seems to have been the powerful attraction of the figure of Professor Agassiz. The meeting was as fateful for the Museum as Henry Fairfield Osborn's with Charles Darwin and T. H. Huxley two decades later. The Swiss-born Agassiz was probably the most important scientific figure in America, carrying the rigor and authority of European methods to a savage and untutored land. A scientist who gave the coelacanth its name, denounced evolution, and believed in a divine plan for creation, Agassiz was at the height of his fame when Bickmore arrived. He was also in the midst of establishing his monument and workplace, the Museum of Comparative Zoology. Only a year later, to the distinguished Sir Henry Wentworth Acland, visiting from Oxford University, Bickmore presented his idea for a museum in New York: "I also remarked, in substance, that as science does not appear to create wealth directly, but only to use for the higher and nobler purpose of promoting original research, it seemed to me natural that an institution, which must depend on the interest which rich and generous men may take in it for its existence and prosperity, should be located in the immediate vicinity of their homes."[7] That vicinity was New York City.

This is a remarkable piece of rhetoric, not the least because it completely reverses the familiar relation of business and science. It is also wholly practical at the same time that it is high-minded. As much as anything, this shrewd high-mindedness explains how the American Museum of Natural History came to be.

Bickmore learned well from watching his mentor Agassiz build his museum, but there would be a critical difference. Agassiz's museum was associated with a great university. It was a Noah's ark with at least two of everything, for scientific study. Bickmore's would be public, educational, and scientific, too—if rhetoric could prevail over reality.

Bickmore nursed the idea for his museum through a harrowing tour of duty as an infantryman in the Civil War. He carried the physical plans with him on a six-thousand-mile collecting expedition in the Malay Archipelago. When he came to New York for good in 1867, he carried with him more than plans. He had the example of Agassiz's world-famous museum and an introduction to financier William E. Dodge. From Dodge's Wall Street office, he would wage his campaign to build a museum.

Dubious Ancestors

The creation of Central Park in 1856 had given tangible form to ideas of broad social improvement that easily accommodated both a natural-history museum and The Metropolitan Museum of Art. The attitude of the New York City Park Commissioners is succinctly captured by controller Andrew Heiskell Green's agreement to accept the collections, and the responsibility for their storage, of the new American Museum of Natural History, which had no quarters at its inception in 1870: "These deposits are such as will, I think, secure the object that the Museum and the Park Commissioners equally desire, to wit, an establishment that shall afford the opportunity for popular instruction and amusement, and for the advancement of the Natural Sciences."[8]

Note well the second *and*, for that afterthought would give birth to more than a thousand expeditions. The word is a conjunction, not a logical connective, and the Museum would meet—and still meets—its greatest challenge in reconciling its tripartite goals: research, education, and exhibition. In truth, the commissioners and the trustees of the new Museum did not know what they were getting into.

They might have had an inkling from the Museum's closest relatives. The earliest direct New York ancestors include a small museum opened by the Tammany Society in 1790 and Delacourt's Cabinet of Natural History, opened in 1804. Neither survived long. Of far grander ambition was the natural-history museum planned for Central Park by the energetic Englishman Waterhouse Hawkins. He went as far as to secure collections and make casts of a fossil *Hadrosaurus*, the first dinosaur excavated in America. He planned spectacular tableaus of giant reptiles in combat. A foundation was laid in the park, but Hawkins ran afoul of the newly installed state senator, William Marcy "Boss" Tweed. Seeing no opportunity in the project for political or personal gain, Tweed used his influence to block approval and even ordered Hawkins's studio ransacked. In contrast, a year earlier in 1869, when Professor Bickmore had come calling in Albany, he carried a list of supporters' names that included railroad lawyer Samuel Tilden. "Well, well, what can I do for Mr. Tilden?" asked Tweed. The charter was passed directly and without emendation.[9] In spite of its name, the American Museum of Natural History, unlike the Smithsonian Institution, which became a federal museum from private origins, would develop an intensely local character, with its fate and fortune bound up in New York politics, society, and finance. This has given it a pronounced public profile unlike that of any other museum save one—The Metropolitan Museum of Art, its neighbor across the park, with whom it shared many original trustees.

In its environment, the American Museum of Natural History could not be "a machine that would go of itself," and Bickmore, the scientist, would find himself increasingly preoccupied, almost until his death, with the single role that would assure the Museum's civic standing and funding—public education. He virtually invented the modern slide lecture. At the same time, the trustees learned they needed deep pockets to be the benefactors of a natural-history museum. This, too, would not have come as a surprise had they considered the history of the first American Museum of Natural History. In 1796, the artist Charles Willson Peale purchased a private collection of disparate specimens known as the American Museum and transformed it into the Philadelphia Museum. In its own way, Peale's museum helped put American natural history on the international map.

Peale, a friend of America's naturalist president, Thomas Jefferson, acquired the bones of a mastodon unearthed in 1801. Reassembled in his museum without regard for anatomical plausibility, they formed a thirty-foot wonder that drew paying customers. The leftovers were later assembled and provided the setting for a grand promotional dinner, with tables under the ribcage. When Peale took his mastodon on a tour of Europe, the eminent French naturalist Georges Cuvier bowed to it as a treasure Europe could not match.

But others could assemble collections of curiosities rapidly and maintain them more easily than Peale, who, like Waterhouse Hawkins, had genuine scientific ambitions. By 1822, Peale was reduced to providing entertainments of varied sorts to attract dwindling crowds. Neither Bickmore nor the nineteen worthies who signed the Museum's act of incorporation kept this cautionary tale in mind. Nor did Bickmore fully consider the success of P. T. Barnum, who had sent him on a collecting expedition to Bermuda in 1862. Barnum knew that the public craved not education but "amusement," as controller Green put it; nature was to be considered as promotional material.

"If no one saw them, what good are they?"

What, after all, was a museum that existed only in the signatures of nineteen of New York City's most prosperous self-made men and in the paper promises of the city's park commissioners? And what was it for? It was not a building, for the new Museum could only secure the partial and temporary quarters of the Arsenal building in Central Park. Nor was it a home for adventure, discovery, or even thought. The Museum was, first of all, collections of life forms, a repository of facts—tangible, visible evidence of a world beyond New York City that many of the visitors would never see. Somehow, the Great Auk would make them better citizens, more diligent workers. For a few of the founders, especially William Haines and Jackson Steward, who were amateur naturalists, the Museum represented an extension of their own collecting activities. For decades, Europeans had been making natural-history collections in the United States. Now it was America's turn to acquire specimens from Europe—with money. With the trustees leading the way, the first subscription for the purchase of collections was accomplished in under two weeks.

The collections provided for by early subscriptions put the Museum on the map. The first, in 1869, was that of Madame Edouard Verreaux of Paris, which was one of the largest of mounted birds and mammals. The second was the "cabinet" of Prince Maximilian of Neuwied. These cabinets were essentially private museums, or collections, usually hodgepodges of artifacts and specimens. The prince's, however, contained many South American rarities. "All lovers of the beautiful agree in taking pleasure in the varied plumage of rare birds," wrote Bickmore later, "and we felt confident from the beginning of our movement that we would be generously supported in our efforts."[10] The language was that of the showman and the compromiser. How different he was from his mentor Agassiz.

The trustees took Bickmore's

ball and ran with it. They went to Europe to inspect and pass judgment on the various collections for sale, while Bickmore unpacked the specimens and wrote labels. They lobbied the city for a spacious new building and for funds to maintain and expand it, while Bickmore took the modest title of superintendent. There were a lot of labels to write, for the collections poured into the Arsenal and later the new building on Manhattan Square. At the outset, Bickmore's academic colleagues had advised him that he had a great opportunity to advance American science. He replied, "It will be years before we can undertake research at the American Museum."[11]

On one key matter, however, Bickmore did use his influence, bringing about a crisis that changed the Museum's direction. James Hall, former director of the New York State Geological Survey, had amassed during his tenure a collection of one hundred thousand invertebrate fossils. From it, he had established the sequence and nomenclature for the geological periods of North America—a monumental achievement. Considering how important that sequence would be to evolutionary studies, acquisition of this collection constituted one of the definitive acts of the new Museum. Agassiz himself was attempting to secure it for his museum at the time of his death in 1873. The price tag was a whopping $65,000. Bickmore and a few sympathetic trustees convinced the rest to buy it.

The cost of the Hall collection could not be covered by subscription, and it put a dent in the budget for years. It also cast in stark relief the problem of a mission that had never been carefully articulated or coherently pursued.

The trustees were buying collections not for study but for display. The small, often drab *mollusca* couldn't compare in crowd appeal with the life-size tableau of a lion attacking an Arab on a camel, which trustee William Blodgett bought on his own for the Museum.

Further, with collections backing up, the result was a triage problem. A new building, designed by the leading architect of the time, Calvert Vaux, opened to great fanfare in 1877, with plans in reserve for a truly grand expansion. Reluctantly, trustee Joseph Choate used all his influence to convince the commissioners to increase funding. And only a few hundred visitors a week visited. "No matter how fine the exhibits are, if no one saw them, what good are they?" queried trustee James Constable.[12]

Jesup Surprises

Today, we would organize a trustee retreat and call in the facilitators and the financial consultants. In 1880, the trustees passed a balanced budget resolution and called on one of their own, Morris Ketchum Jesup, to sort out the Museum's finances and priorities.

It is always tempting to place the entire burden of the past, good and bad, on the shoulders of individuals. This is misleading, of course, but Jesup's shoulders are big enough to carry it. Jesup, at that time chairman of the executive committee, surprised everyone, and history as well. A self-made railroad man whose education extended only to the sixth grade, he was expected to curb the extravagance of the naturalists on the board and the staff. Instead, he called for the creation of an endowment to finance the Museum's scientific

and educational work, began to articulate what education meant, and gently suggested the museum ought to be dedicated to "something that cannot be measured in the scales of the merchant."[13]

No one quite recognized the direction Jesup was suggesting, and it may not have been obvious, even to him. He was most concerned that the exhibits be spruced up and that collections be acquired with potential visitors in mind. Unlike almost everyone else, however, Jesup was able to look at the Museum objectively. He saw great collections, an open field with little immediate national competition, the prospect of a new elevated train line to bring more visitors, and a practical need to press the Museum's educational mission. He and Bickmore set about the last task and, with the hand-colored lantern slide, initiated a program of teacher training in the natural sciences that eventually reached across the state of New York. They also established a relationship with the public schools of New York City that continues today.

Jesup looked still deeper. To find out how other museums operated, he went to Europe. He discovered museums committed to the collecting and study of specimens never intended for public viewing. This planted a seed that was nurtured by one of the Museum's curators and its first notable scientist, Joel Asaph Allen. Allen, also a student of Agassiz, and one of the founders of the American Ornithologists Union, came to the Museum in 1884 after a nervous breakdown ended his field studies. He published many scientific papers in the 1880s even as he advocated more attractive displays at the Museum. He borrowed an idea from British Museum taxidermists who had come over to train Museum staff: mount the birds and mammals in settings that resemble their natural habitats. This simple idea revolutionized the display of museum specimens. Today the American Museum of Natural History is the world's greatest monument to Allen's insight.

A Museum Takes to the Field

With a small mount of a nesting robin, collecting, study, and exhibition began to come together. Exhibits had to be based on broader, up-to-date knowledge, and the best way to ensure that the Museum got precisely what it needed was for it to develop its own collections. In 1888, Jesup persuaded several trustees to sponsor the Museum's first collecting expedition, to North Dakota. Headed by the naturalist Daniel Giraud Elliott, the group made several trips to secure bison specimens for a dramatic new mammal hall. The end result was a bison display that still appears quite compelling in photographs, in spite of the primitive taxidermy methods and the arbitrary glass case. Jesup continued to insist on the priority of spectacular displays, but by 1890 he told the trustees that they should "make plans for the future scientific development of the Museum."[14]

Those plans included assembling an outstanding scientific staff, whose goal increasingly became answering questions about the natural world. Collecting and study were the process, expeditions the necessary means. Up through the turn of the century, under Jesup, the Museum hired a truly remarkable group of scien-

The Museums that Almost Were

As grand as the American Museum of Natural History appears today, it pales in comparison with a plan drafted by architects Calvert Vaux and J. Wrey Mould in 1871. As Robert McCracken Peck has revealed in an article for Natural History *magazine, "The Museum that Never Was," they envisioned a Gothic edifice, in the form of Greek cross, that would have occupied all of Manhattan Square. Less than half that building was realized, for the Museum simply did not have the money after the Depression to continue construction on such a grandiose scale and, in any case, had already modified the plans with the addition of the Hayden Planetarium in 1935.*

More extravagant was a plan conceived by the artist William Holbrook Beard in the late 1860s. A friend of influential artists Albert Bierstadt, Frederic Church, and Winslow Homer, Beard proposed a gigantic domed structure with underground entrances in Central Park. Visitors at one entrance would be met by two stone figures representing Ignorance and Superstition, at the other by twenty-foot-high lions, tigers, and bears. A walkway would lead them past "grotesque antediluvian animals of immense size," as Scribner's Monthly *described it at the time. They would ascend a flight of stone stairs and experience "the gradual progress from barbarism to civilization." The culmination of this evolutionary journey was a gallery filled not with fossils but with depictions of famous and ennobling characters—from recent times, of course.*

Fanciful view of the proposed museum

The Museum's final decisive step into the field came when Jesup himself became interested in a scientific question—whether the first North Americans originally migrated across the Bering Strait from Siberia. This led directly to his sponsorship of the Museum's first large-scale expedition, the Jesup North Pacific Expedition (see pages 31–42). In 1908, when Jesup stepped down due to failing health and Henry Fairfield Osborn was named president, the Museum and its trustees had sponsored expeditions across America, to the North Pole, and to China. Museum curators were collecting specimens, fossils, and artifacts in South America and Africa, and the story of expeditions, not to mention the Museum's scientific contributions, was just beginning.

tists. They included ornithologist Frank Chapman, who taught America how to watch birds; Henry Fairfield Osborn, who would make the Museum the world center for the study of dinosaurs and mammal fossils; paleontologists Barnum Brown, William Diller Matthew, and Walter Granger; Frederic Ward Putnam and Franz Boas, pioneers of anthropology; archaeologist Adolph Bandelier, whose name now graces one of America's national monuments; and entomologist William Morton Wheeler, the world's leading expert on ants.

Jesup, the man who fought to keep the Museum closed on Sundays, had become "convinced that discovering the laws of nature is one of the great tasks of our age."[15] He forged connections to Columbia University, saw the first dinosaur skeleton (a brontosaur) assembled, and built a museum that would make significant contributions to the understanding of evolution and the web of life on Earth. "He had an intuitive sense of what kind of scientific work would be most profitable for the Museum to pursue," said Bickmore.[16] Jesup also put his money where his heart was. Every year he made up the Museum's deficit, and when he died, he left it a million dollars.

The Children's Room at the Museum, 1910

The End of Expeditions?

The golden age of field expeditions at institutions not dependent on government funding lasted until the mid-1930s, when the full effects of the Wall Street financial disaster were felt. By 1935, the Museum had suspended most of its field activities and closed many exhibition halls. Curators were forced to secure their own funding from dwindling private resources. Throughout the 1940s, 1950s, and 1960s, the federal government came to play an increasing role in funding scientific research, but it never restored Museum studies to their previous prominence. In the biological sciences, attention shifted to cellular and molecular studies and, more specifically, to medicine. Cataloguing species, describing their distribution, and enumerating their familial relations and physical evolution—the primary scientific tasks of the Museum—had lower priority.

To some extent, that remains true, yet growing awareness of the loss of biodiversity has brought the Museum's work out of the scientific shadows. "It is more important than ever to know what living things the world contains and to understand their interrelations, at both the genetic and species level," says provost Michael Novacek. "Otherwise, we can't make truly far-sighted decisions about how we

manage human impact on the environment." Museum scientists have been recording and warning of the loss of the Earth's species for a century. The combination of research, education, and activism that reached the apex of its influence under Henry Fairfield Osborn has been reembodied in such initiatives as the Center for Biodiversity and Conservation, established in 1993.

In a final irony of sorts, the very genetic studies that seemed in the late 1970s about to render many evolutionary and anatomical studies, and much fieldwork, obsolete have been incorporated into the descriptive repertoire of the modern biogeographers: the Museum now maintains its own molecular laboratory, and its scientists are consulted on questions as diverse as the genetic designation of endangered species and the possibility of cloning a dinosaur.

The nearly prohibitive cost of large-scale expeditions has perhaps also been a blessing in

disguise, because it has made international collaborations a necessity. Throughout its history, the Museum has forged close ties with the governments and peoples of areas where it has taken to the field. More recent collaborations—with scientists in Mongolia, Venezuela, Cuba, and Vietnam, to name a few—are true partnerships of discovery, enabling the teams to achieve a productivity otherwise impossible. There is simply not enough time for this Museum, and all the museums and universities in the United States, for that matter, to understand fully the potential impact of species loss and what to do about it. Nor can they, on their own, begin to draw the lineages that will reveal how species have adapted and continue to adapt to changing environments. Perhaps, just in time, an adventure that began for this Museum with a crowded collection of marvels has become a truly global errand into a new and chastened Eden.

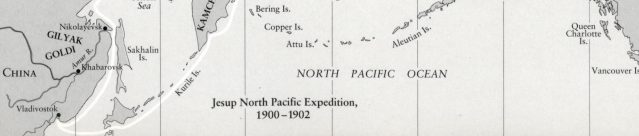

Jesup North Pacific Expedition, 1900–1902

The End of Expeditions?

The golden age of field expeditions at institutions not dependent on government funding lasted until the mid-1930s, when the full effects of the Wall Street financial disaster were felt. By 1935, the Museum had suspended most of its field activities and closed many exhibition halls. Curators were forced to secure their own funding from dwindling private resources. Throughout the 1940s, 1950s, and 1960s, the federal government came to play an increasing role in funding scientific research, but it never restored Museum studies to their previous prominence. In the biological sciences, attention shifted to cellular and molecular studies and, more specifically, to medicine. Cataloguing species, describing their distribution, and enumerating their familial relations and physical evolution—the primary scientific tasks of the Museum—had lower priority.

To some extent, that remains true, yet growing awareness of the loss of biodiversity has brought the Museum's work out of the scientific shadows. "It is more important than ever to know what living things the world contains and to understand their interrelations, at both the genetic and species level," says provost Michael Novacek. "Otherwise, we can't make truly far-sighted decisions about how we

manage human impact on the environment." Museum scientists have been recording and warning of the loss of the Earth's species for a century. The combination of research, education, and activism that reached the apex of its influence under Henry Fairfield Osborn has been reembodied in such initiatives as the Center for Biodiversity and Conservation, established in 1993.

In a final irony of sorts, the very genetic studies that seemed in the late 1970s about to render many evolutionary and anatomical studies, and much fieldwork, obsolete have been incorporated into the descriptive repertoire of the modern biogeographers: the Museum now maintains its own molecular laboratory, and its scientists are consulted on questions as diverse as the genetic designation of endangered species and the possibility of cloning a dinosaur.

The nearly prohibitive cost of large-scale expeditions has perhaps also been a blessing in

disguise, because it has made international collaborations a necessity. Throughout its history, the Museum has forged close ties with the governments and peoples of areas where it has taken to the field. More recent collaborations—with scientists in Mongolia, Venezuela, Cuba, and Vietnam, to name a few—are true partnerships of discovery, enabling the teams to achieve a productivity otherwise impossible. There is simply not enough time for this Museum, and all the museums and universities in the United States, for that matter, to understand fully the potential impact of species loss and what to do about it. Nor can they, on their own, begin to draw the lineages that will reveal how species have adapted and continue to adapt to changing environments. Perhaps, just in time, an adventure that began for this Museum with a crowded collection of marvels has become a truly global errand into a new and chastened Eden.

East Siberian Sea

ARCTIC OCEAN

Beaufort Sea

Wrangel Is.

Verkhoyansk

YUKAGHIR

TUNGUS

Yakutsk

Verkhne-Kolymsk

Siberia

Kolyma R.

CHUKCHI

RUSSIA

Kolodon R.

KOLYMA MOUNTAINS

Anadyr R.

Bering Strait

USA
(Alaska)

YAKUT

KORYAK

Markovo

Anadyr
Bay

Nayakhan R.

Gizhiga

Kuel

Kamenskoye

Mariinsky
Post

St.
Lawrence
Is.

CANADA

TUNGUS

Kushka

Penzhina
Bay

TUNGUS

Sea of
Okhotsk

YAKUT

British Columbia

Nunivak Is.

Shelikot Strait

Karaginsky Is.

KAMCHATKA

Yellow
Sea

Bering Sea

Kodiak Is.

Baranof Is.

Bering Is.

Copper Is.

Aleutian Is.

Queen
Charlotte
Is.

Nikolayevsk

GILYAK

GOLDI

Amur R.

Attu Is.

Sakhalin
Is.

Vancouver Is.

CHINA

Khabarovsk

Kurile Is.

NORTH PACIFIC OCEAN

USA
(Washington)

Vladivostok

**Jesup North Pacific Expedition,
1900–1902**

The North Pacific:
In the House of the Raven

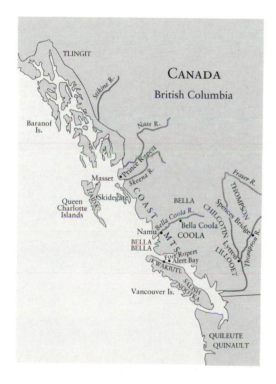

A spring encampment of the Reindeer Koryak, with Jochelson's tent in the middle. The herd of four hundred reindeer were rounded up in anticipation of a search for new pastures. Photograph by Waldemar Jochelson

A Question of Origins

My friend, George Hunt, will read this to you. . . . It is good that you should have a box in which your laws and your stories are kept. My friend, George Hunt, will show you a box in which some of your stories will be kept. It is a book that I have written on what I saw and heard when I was with you two years ago. It is a good book, for in it are your laws and stories. Now they will not be forgotten. Friends, it would be good if my friend, George Hunt, would become the storage box of your laws and of your stories.

—Franz Boas to George Hunt[1]

WITH THESE WORDS written in April 1897, Franz Boas, assistant curator of anthropology at the American Museum of Natural History, sent his field assistant George Hunt as an emissary to the Kwakiutl people of the Northwest Coast of North America. Hunt was to pave the way for the Jesup North Pacific Expedition, the first major field expedition mounted by the Museum. The expedition's scope was the most comprehensive of any museum expedition of its day, both in terms of the sheer area to be covered and the questions it sought to resolve. Working under arduous conditions among native peoples who were often beset by starvation and disease, Museum field assistants assembled an unparalleled record of the life and culture of the peoples of the North Pacific.

Boas and Frederic Ward Putnam, head of the anthropology department at the Museum, had successfully persuaded the president of the Museum, Morris Ketchum Jesup, to sponsor a costly expedition largely to solve a single riddle: whether or not America was first populated by migratory tribes from Asia. "The opportunities for solving this problem are rapidly disappearing," announced Jesup, "and I would be deeply gratified to learn that some friend or friends of the Museum may feel disposed to contribute means for the prosecution of systematic investigations."[2] No "friend or friends" stepped forward, so Jesup, who had made a fortune in banking and railroad finance, provided the money for the expedition himself. This bold statement indicates how strongly the idea had seized his imagination. He was not alone.

The question of the origins of native Americans was of great import at the turn of the century. The writings of the anthropologist Edward Tylor and others had focused attention on how cultures developed. Could they arise and evolve independently, or were they related by geographic diffusion? At the same time, the increasing prominence in museum collections of artifacts from the Northwest Coast spurred questions about the roots of this culture. *The New York Times* described "Mr. Jesup's Explorations" as "alive with human and historic interest" and summarized the issues the expedition hoped to resolve as "about the biggest of the unsolved anthropological and ethnological problems."[3]

Boas had other ideas in mind as well. He took it as a given that native American peoples had first arrived in North America in migrations across the Bering Strait and had long-standing cultural ties to the Old World. For him, the Jesup Expedition was an opportunity to study in depth the peoples of the North Pacific—to determine their physical char-

acteristics, observe their ceremonies, record their myths, and collect their artifacts—in short, to provide a written history of a people whose culture, Boas believed, was in imminent danger of disappearing.

By 1897, the Museum was already deeply involved in collecting Northwest Coast materials. In 1881, when Jesup was named president, the Museum's Northwest Coast collections were insignificant, and the new president was interested in obtaining striking objects, in part to increase flagging Museum attendance. The Smithsonian Institution already boasted a substantial collection, which it had displayed at the 1876 Centennial in Philadelphia (eliciting a generally negative response from the crowds). Not wanting to be outdone by other museums in Europe and the United States that were buying everything they could get their hands on, Jesup felt that it was time for the Museum to undertake its own collections.

In 1880, Heber Bishop, a trustee of the Museum, had offered to purchase a collection of art of the Northwest Coast and Alaska. Bishop enlisted the help of Israel Wood Powell, superintendent for Indian Affairs in British Columbia, and, over the next five years, Powell sent 791 objects to the Museum, including the largest war canoe of its kind. Then, from 1888 to 1893, the Museum purchased upwards of 4,000 Tlingit artifacts from Lieutenant George Thornton Emmons, who had assembled his collection while on duty with the navy in Alaska.

When Boas came to the Museum in 1895, he found the basis of a truly outstanding collection, but with glaring omissions. The inland Bella Coola tribe and

those of Vancouver Island, the Kwakiutl, Salish, and Nootka, where his own interests lay, were not represented at all. In addition, the collections emphasized beautiful pieces at the expense of articles of everyday life, necessary, in his opinion, to record a culture faithfully.

Boas was also throwing down a gauntlet to the cultural evolutionists of the time. Cultural evolutionists believed that so-called primitive peoples occupied lower rungs, physically and culturally, on an evolutionary ladder that led upward to Western society. In his 1896 presidential address to the American Association for the Advancement of Science, Daniel Brinton, one of the most influential anthropologists of the time, proclaimed: "The black, the brown and the red races differ anatomically so much from the white, especially in their splanchnic organs, that even with equal cerebral capacity, they could never rival the results by equal effort."[4]

Boas found these views racist and unscientific. Evidence to the contrary was right in front of him, in the masks, totem poles, canoes, and other objects of an artistically accomplished people.

"*The sculptor of Alaska and British Columbia is not only the sorcerer who confers upon the supernatural a visible form, but also the inspired creator, the interpreter who translates into eternal chefs d'oeuvre the fugitive emotions of man.*"
—Claude Lévi-Strauss

Franz Boas (1858–1942)

Perhaps it was the difficulties that he encountered in his own rigid society that enabled Franz Boas to appreciate the native peoples among whom he lived during his life. Born to a liberal Jewish family in Prussia in 1858, he received a doctoral degree from the University of Kiel in physical science. His thesis dealt with the color of seawater. While a student at Kiel, he was the butt of anti-Semitic remarks, for which he fought duels. He carried the scars from those duels on his face for the rest of his life.

Boas's first anthropological fieldwork was among the Eskimos of Baffin Island in the Arctic Ocean. After immersing himself in their society in 1883–84, he came away with a great admiration for their egalitarian way of life. When he returned to Germany, he found it increasingly difficult to live in a country that was extending its imperial control over the natives of New Guinea and Africa. His social and political views assured he would never be able to secure a university professorship in Germany. Boas's introduction to the peoples of the Northwest Coast came when he prepared an exhibition for the Royal Ethnological Museum of Berlin. He was soon determined to visit the Northwest Coast himself to make his own collections, and in 1886 he made the first of many trips.

In the ensuing years, the British Association for the Advancement of Science sent him on five field trips to study the linguistics and the physical anthropology of the tribes of British Columbia. Then in 1894 Boas went to the Northwest Coast to collect information for life groups at both the Smithsonian Institution and the American Museum of Natural History. In 1895, he was appointed assistant curator of anthropology at the Museum.

Boas left the Museum in 1905 to teach at Columbia University, where he trained a new generation of anthropologists, many of whom became involved with the Museum. Margaret Mead, Robert Lowie, A. L. Kroeber, and Ruth Benedict, among others, established anthropology in the United States. Although Boas wrote extensively on diverse subjects, he reserved his deepest appreciation for the people of the Northwest Coast. Boas and Hunt continued to work together until 1930–31, when Boas, in his seventies, made his last trip to the Northwest Coast. There was still more to learn. In January 1931, Boas wrote in a letter to his children: "This is probably the last time I will see George Hunt. He is seventy-six years old and quite frail. I still had a few questions on the last morning!"

Franz Boas posing for a figure in the Kwakiutl Hamatsa exhibit at the Smithsonian Institution, 1895. In the Kwakiutl Winter Ceremonial, the dancer's head appears through the mouth of the raven spirit, represented here by a hoop.

He offered a radically different vision, which he hoped to confirm through fieldwork: "We are still searching for laws that govern the growth of human culture, of human thought; but we recognize the fact that before we seek for what is common to all culture, we must analyze each culture . . . as the biologist examines the form of living matter. We see that the growth of human culture manifests itself in the growth of each special culture."[5]

Having studied physics and geography at university, Boas was especially appalled by the unscientific methods of his contemporaries. He carefully instructed his field assistants to obtain information on where each artifact came from, its native name, what it was used for, the name of its original owner, and any oral texts that would explain the traditions associated with the object.

Boas was convinced that if he were able to establish definitively the relationship between the American and Asiatic races,

George Hunt and his wife, Francine, Fort Rupert, 1930. Photograph by Franz Boas

and the relationship between the two cultures, the rest of the pieces of the migration puzzle would fall into place. In the end, however, the goals of the Jesup Expedition, so ambitiously imagined and confidently stated, proved difficult to achieve. The difficulty was great enough to drive a wedge between Boas and his patron Jesup and to spark a controversy that still burns. Almost a century later, the question of exactly when people first migrated to the New World from northeast Asia still begs a definitive answer.

To the Land of the Totem Poles

Preparations for the Jesup Expedition progressed rapidly, and in early June of 1897, Boas arrived in Spence's Bridge in the interior of British Columbia, accompanied by a self-trained archaeologist, Harlan Smith, and Livingston Farrand, a professor of psychology at Columbia. They joined forces with James Teit, who, along with George Hunt, was responsible for the bulk of the collecting on the Northwest Coast. Boas was particularly dependent on these two men because of their close ties to the native peoples. He was lucky to have chosen two extraordinary individuals.

Teit, a Scotsman who had emigrated to Canada in 1883, was married to a Thompson Indian woman named Lucy Artko. When Boas first met him in 1894, he was impressed by Teit's intelligence and hired him on the spot. Although Teit had received little formal schooling, his linguistic

abilities were remarkable. He was so fluent in the dialects of the Salish people that even the Indians could not detect an accent when he spoke. Much of the information he gathered was later published under his own name in the Jesup North Pacific Expedition Memoirs. Teit was deeply committed to the people among whom he worked, a people who had suffered much from diseases introduced by the white man. He worked in defense of Indian rights well into the twentieth century, often serving as translator when he accompanied Indians to official meetings in Victoria and Ottawa. On these trips, he always dressed in native clothing.

George Hunt was the child of an English immigrant and a Tlingit noblewoman from Alaska. He spent his entire life in Fort Rupert, British Columbia, with some stays in Alert Bay. Centers of Kwakiutl culture, these two communities had increasing inter-

action with whites. As a child of a mixed marriage, Hunt moved freely from one culture to another. He was, however, raised as a Kwakiutl, and his first language was Kwakwala. In 1854, his Tlingit grandfather came to Fort Rupert to visit his daughter and her baby and to ease the long-standing acrimony between the Kwakiutl and the Tongass Tlingit: "So the old chiefs say that through me that the war stoped. and in there feasts I use to go and listen to them telling Each other there *nEmemot* stories. and that is How I know all there old ways."[6] At the age of nine, Hunt was initiated into Kwakiutl ritual. He also gained ceremonial privileges from his marriages to two Kwakiutl women.

Hunt was well aware of the effects of the influx of white settlers in his community: population decline among natives, the introduction of a cash economy, and the adoption of Western ways.

The Silent One

When one's heart is glad, he gives away gifts. It was given to us by our Creator, to be our way of doing things, we who are Indians. The potlatch was given to us to be our way of expressing joy. Every people on earth is given something. This was given to us.

—a Kwakiutl defendant in the 1922 trial for violating the potlatch law, speaking in the 1980s

Although the Canadian government had already outlawed the potlatch when Franz Boas traveled from his native Germany to British Columbia for the first time in 1886, he attended a potlatch given by the Kwakiutl of Newitti at which he gave the following speech: "I am a chief and no one may command me. . . . I do not wish to interfere with your celebration. My people live far away and would like to know what people in distant lands do, and so I set out. I was in warm lands and cold lands. I saw many different people and told them at home how they live. And then they said to me, 'Go and see what the people in this land do,' and so I went and came here and I saw you eat and drink, sing and dance. And I shall go back and say: 'See, that is how the people live there. They were good to me and asked me to live with them.'"

Boas's speech helped allay the fears of the Kwakiutl, who initially suspected him of being a government agent. The Kwakiutl admired his skills in oration, an important component of the potlatch ritual, and agreed to perform their dances for him at a potlatch that Boas gave. At the end of the meal, a great chief made the following speech to Boas: "This chief has come to us from a distant land, and all our hearts are glad. He is not like the other whites who have come to us. His heart is pure and kind toward us Indians. None of the King George men or the Boston men gave us . . . festival. But his people must be good and he shows that he has the heart of a chief. Whoever of us shall meet him, will be glad and recognize him as a great chief. We are glad he came and hope he will return. My heart is friendly toward him and if he wants anything from us we shall do our best to do what he asks." In response to the Newitti chief's speech, Boas distributed tobacco to all the men.

When Boas returned to the Northwest Coast in 1894, he gave a feast for all the residents of Fort Rupert. The two hundred and fifty Kwakiutl who attended received hardtack and molasses. At a potlatch several weeks later, Boas distributed apples to the Indians. The residents of Fort Rupert accepted Boas in their midst, inviting him to their ceremonies and even bestowing on him a Kwakiutl name, He'iltsakuls, which means "the silent one," because Boas was unable to speak their language.

Against this background, he supported traditional Kwakiutl practices. In 1885, when he was a young man, the Canadian government enacted laws banning the potlatch festival. The potlatch was a ceremony central to the spiritual and social life of the Kwakiutl, at which powerful chiefs distributed gifts to guests, and even destroyed their own property, in order to display wealth and establish status. This law brought the Kwakiutl into conflict with the white authorities, and in 1900 Hunt himself was arrested by Canadian government officials at a Kwakiutl winter ceremony. He wrote immediately to Boas, asking for assistance and money to pay his lawyer. Boas, furious with the officials for interfering with native customs, sent to the court one of his books that acknowledged the assistance of Hunt. In the end the charges were dropped.

When George Hunt first met Franz Boas in 1888, Hunt already had a decade of experience working as a collector of Indian artifacts for such whites as Israel Powell. Boas's reliance on and confidence in a field assistant who was a member of a native tribe was highly unusual for his time. He taught Hunt basic ethnographic techniques and how to write Kwakwala in phonetic characters.[7] During the years of the Jesup Expedition, Hunt compiled a huge number of texts in Kwakwala, for which he was paid at the rate of fifty cents per page, and purchased twenty-five hundred Kwakiutl artifacts for the Museum's collections. Thus, a

Opposite: Kwakiutl chief Holelide thanking Boas for the feast he gave in November 1894 at Fort Rupert. Photograph by O. C. Hastings.

self-taught Kwakiutl field assistant came to play one of the most significant roles in the Northwest Coast portion of this monumental expedition.

That summer of 1897, Harlan Smith remained in the Spence's Bridge area, where he began extensive archaeological excavations. Meanwhile, Boas, Farrand, and Teit started on an arduous journey northward, traveling along Indian trails. With a train of ten horses, the party crossed the mountains to Lillooet. Along the wagon road to Caribou, they stopped at numerous villages and compiled anthropometric mea-

surements of the inhabitants. Anthropometric measurements, which included measurements of the distance between the eyes, of the shape of the skull, and of the lengths of the arm and the leg, were used by physical anthropologists to establish a biological description of a people. In order to answer the questions posed by the Jesup Expedition, Boas had to establish a physical relationship between the tribes of northeastern Siberia and those of North America. Before the advent of genetic studies, this was the only means available.

After about a week, the group

crossed the Fraser River and traveled into the territory of the Chilcotin. The Chilcotin, who had come into contact with whites comparatively recently, were considered the most "primitive" of the tribes of British Columbia. Although many had adopted the ways of the white men, settling in log cabins on reservations, farming and raising cattle and horses, some continued a nomadic existence in the mountains.

Boas's ultimate goal on this leg of the expedition was to study the Bella Coola, one of the major inland tribes, but just getting there was an ordeal. The horses were

continually mired in the swamps on the plateau north of Tatla Lake. Torrential rains soaked the party and their supplies, and immense fallen trees blocked their path.

The Coast Range was the final hurdle. After reaching the summit and crossing over wide snowfields, Boas beheld a breathtaking vista. Five thousand feet below ran the Bella Coola River, "and on the opposite side of its deep and narrow valleys rises the high peak, Nuskulst, which plays a most important part in the mythology of the Bella Coola. Enormous glaciers flank the sides of the mountain. A little farther down the river other snow-clad mountains of beautiful form come into view."[8]

In the past, the Bella Coola lived in villages all along the river, but their numbers had been so decimated by the time of the Jesup expedition that the villages had been abandoned. There was only one left.

They arrived at the village thoroughly exhausted, after enduring nearly a month of heavy rains and swarms of mosquitoes and flies. Waiting for them was George Hunt, who had been collecting myths and artifacts in anticipation of their arrival. Boas was overjoyed at the prospect of sleeping in a bed. Yet, from the letters he wrote to his family during his stay with the Bella Coola, it is clear that things were far from easy there: "Life is very uncomfortable. I sleep very well in Clayton's bed, surrounded by fruit jars, axes, patent medicines, bullets, and what not. I get up at 6 A.M. and George Hunt has breakfast ready in the filthy Indian House. The house is on stilts, and in the middle a place for the fire is built up. Previously the privy, if I may mention it, was in a corner so that all the filth went under the house. Nowadays a platform is built for this purpose behind the village. The weather is cold and unfriendly, and all this makes it not too nice here."[9] He found fieldwork to be a lonely task, and he missed his wife and children terribly.

Rivals in the Field

After leaving the Bella Coola, Boas descended the Bentinck Arm. At Namu he planned to catch the steamer northward to Skeena River. Unfortunately, on the steamer dock he ran into his rival from the Field Museum in Chicago, George Dorsey. Boas disliked both Dorsey and the institution he worked for. Boas had been Frederic Putnam's assistant at the 1893 World's Columbian Exposition in Chicago. He had expected to be offered a position in the museum that was being formed, but neither he nor Putnam was hired. Instead, in 1897, Dorsey was appointed as curator of ethnology, the position that Boas had sought. Both Boas and Putnam were eager to upstage the new Field Museum, which in response launched its own expedition to the Northwest Coast. In 1897 field teams from both institutions were traveling up and down the coast, competing bitterly with one another in an attempt to collect increasingly rare and important artifacts.

Boas also objected to Dorsey's methods and his lack of respect for the Indians and their customs. Boas felt that Dorsey traveled at too rapid a pace and bought indiscriminately without acquiring adequate information about his purchases. Far worse, the Anglican missionary in Masset charged that Dorsey plundered Indian grave sites on the Queen Charlotte Islands, collecting bones and other objects, leaving what he did not want strewn about the ground and not even bothering to cover the excavations.[10]

Boas was already seething before he encountered Dorsey. In a letter to his wife, he wrote, "What makes me so furious is the fact that these Chicago people simply adopt my plans and then try to beat me to it. . . . When I was in Chicago they assured me that Dorsey would not be here at the same time as I. I don't really think his trip will interfere with my work, but this treacherous way of acting makes me awfully angry."[11] The encounter only strengthened his resolve. At the Skeena River, he met up with Smith, and together they collected material on the graphic arts of the Haida. Then they moved on to the Bella Bella, a Kwakiutl tribe, where Farrand joined them. By mid-September, Boas and Farrand were on their way back to New York. Smith traveled to southern British Columbia to study shell mounds on the Fraser River and prehistoric stone monuments on southern Vancouver Island.

"Bloodthirsty Customs and Weird Ceremonies"

When Boas returned to New York City, after the expedition's first year, he discovered that the general public was not ready to accept his views on racial equality. He gave an interview to the sensationalist *New York Herald* and soon saw the Kwakiutl transformed into bloodthirsty savages:

Dr. Franz Boas, of the American Museum of Natural History, has just returned from an expedition along the extreme western coast of British Columbia, close to Alaska, where dwell the Kwakiutl, a race of anthropophagi, man eating savages, who, uninfluenced by the encroachments of civilization and isolated from the rest of the world, still practice the bloodthirsty customs and weird ceremonies instituted when America was unknown to the Old World. They are fond of festivals, and devote a large portion of their time to weird dances and feasts and orgies of the wildest sort, during which terrible tortures are imposed on members of the tribe.[12]

For the rest of his life, Boas devoted himself to educating people about the art and culture of the tribes of the Northwest Coast.

In 1899, Boas once again ran into problems with the press. This time the Kwakiutl were drawn into the dispute, and the repercussions were far more serious. In Victoria, one of the chiefs from Fort Rupert had been told that Boas had made a speech in which he disparaged the Kwakiutl. Harlan Smith was also creating problems. An article criticizing the Kwakiutl, attributed to Smith's wife, appeared in a Victoria newspaper. In response to these two incidents, the Kwakiutl informed Hunt that neither he nor Boas would be allowed to view their ceremonies. Boas managed to convince a disturbed Hunt that the newspaper account was distorted. Then he asked Hunt to invite the chiefs to a feast that he wished to give for them, at which Hunt would read from Boas's book on the Kwakiutl, so

Right: Haida village of Masset. Edward Dossetter was the professional photographer whom Indian agent Israel Powell brought with him on an official tour of villages in 1881. Photograph by Edward Dossetter

that they could see how he portrayed them. Hunt also read the following letter:

I have learned that somebody told you of a speech that I made: that I have been all around the world, and seen everything changed for the best, except the Kwakiutl tribe; that they are still living on dead people. I think, Chief, that you do not believe this. I never made a speech of that kind. I do not say what is not true. . . . The Kwakiutl

Chief Wiah's Monster House, with boardwalk to the beach; Israel Powell; and natives of Masset, 1879. The Edenshaws were an old, illustrious Haida family. Traditionally, the family inhabited the village of Kiusta and owned much land in the interior of the Queen Charlotte Islands. During his lifetime, Chief Edenshaw held seven huge potlatches, a symbol of his substantial wealth and standing. The village of Kiusta was abandoned in the latter part of the nineteenth century, and Chief Edenshaw was forced to move to Masset. In Masset he had to submit to the authority of Chief Wiah, who had been established as chief there since 1840. At that time Chief Wiah had built an enormous house, generally referred to as Monster House, which was more than sixty feet wide and had nine large totem poles. When Chief Edenshaw came to Masset in the 1870s, he brought with him a totem pole that had belonged to his ancestors. He carried this pole into Monster House. First he danced before it; then he had it burned. Photograph by O. C. Hastings

have no better friend than I. . . . I have told to the chiefs in Ottawa and to the chiefs in England many times, that the potlatch and the dance are not bad.[13]

Boas successfully restored his ties with the Kwakiutl, but he kept a tight rein on Harlan Smith.

Although fieldwork along the Northwest Coast continued until the end of 1902, by 1899 the main focus of the North Pacific Expedition had shifted to Asia. Beginning in September of 1900, however, another expedition member, John Swanton, spent more

than a year studying the Haida of the Queen Charlotte Islands. The Haida had once inhabited numerous villages along the coasts of these islands. They built and decorated huge longhouses, sailed in sixty-foot canoes, and carved and erected forests of totem poles. Now they were concentrated in two major villages, Masset and Skidegate. A small-pox epidemic in 1862 had reduced the population by as much as one-third. Swanton attributed the subsequent abandonment

A Haida Raven Creation Tale

Now Raven went farther north, and came to a big river called Gunā'xᵒ. There he saw a house floating out in the sea, with salmon living in it. They lived in one place then. This house was called Abundant-House (T!ā'-inañ na-i). Then he came to a house just behind the last on shore, in which a man lived who had a walking-stick covered with the suckers of the octopus along the sides from top to bottom. Raven wanted to borrow this stick in order to reach the floating house, and after much urging the man let him have it. He laid the stick down pointing towards the house, and it stretched itself out until the suckers fastened upon it. Then he tried to pull the house to land, but in vain. Now he cried to the rocks around him, "Get up and help me!" The stones began to move, but they could not get up; and he said, "You shall lie like that on the ground forever." Then he went up from the beach to some hard-wood trees which grow along the beaches and are called k!as . . . which he shook, telling them to get up and help him; but while he was shaking them, the leaves fell off, after which they all got up like men. Since the leaves fell off, men cannot live long, and die like leaves. He brought these people down to the end of the walking-stick, and let them all take hold along the sides, while he seized the end. Then he began to sing a song while they were pulling, and finally they pulled the house ashore. Jumping into it, he found there spring salmon, silver salmon, cohoes, humpback salmon, and olachen, which he told to go up the different rivers he had made—different fish up different rivers.

of Haida villages to the work of missionaries, who had discouraged the Haida from preserving their customs and who had played a significant role in the destruction of the old houses. Swanton immersed himself in the recording of Haida texts, and by March 1901 his manuscript had reached seventeen hundred pages. He wrote to Boas, "It would break my heart to feel there was a story left I had failed to gather."[14]

Siberia: A Bridge Between Worlds

On the 2d of January I started by dog-sled northward. This journey was exceedingly difficult, and sometimes even dangerous. At one time I narrowly escaped drowning when crossing the ice at the foot of a steep promontory. I broke through the ice, which was much weakened by the action of the waves. Fortunately my guide happened to upset his sledge at the same moment when I broke through. Thus it was that he saw my situation, and extricated me with his staff.

—Berthold Laufer[15]

Right: Tungus cradle with child on reindeer, 1901. Because of the unwieldy size and slow speed of the cameras used by members of the Jesup expedition, taking photographs was an elaborate encounter between cultures. Many of the photographs have a staged, unnatural quality, perhaps reflecting the subjects' suspicion of the strange contraption, which the Yukaghir referred to as "three-legged white stone on man's shadow drawing one." Indoor subjects had to pose because the dim light necessitated a slow shutter speed. Most of the photographs were taken outside, under somewhat better conditions. These photographs also reflect the photographer's desire to structure the shot and arrange his subjects in an attempt to portray the varied aspects of native life. Photograph by Waldemar Jochelson

Opposite: Horns and the god of the village

This journey was the most difficult one that it was ever my fate to undertake. Bogs, mountain torrents, rocky passes and thick forests combined to hinder our progress. Part of our provision consisted of bread and dried fish. A heavy rain which fell during the first few days of our journey soaked the loads of the pack-horses and caused the provisions to rot. Therefore we had to cut down our rations from the very beginning.
—Waldemar Jochelson[16]

At one time, indeed, my illness became so alarming that the Cossack, who also felt responsible for the success of the expedition, asked me for instructions as to which way to carry my body and my "official papers" in case I should die on the route.
—Waldemar Borgoras[17]

While Franz Boas was in New York City dealing with museum rivalries and tabloid journalism, the expedition team on the far side of the Bering Strait faced problems of a different order: famine, measles epidemics, near death from drowning and influenza, primitive living conditions, lice, bitter cold, extreme isolation. To complete the tasks Boas had assigned them, they were expected to cover vast distances, traversing rugged terrain that had never before seen European travelers on horseback, only native Tungus and Koryak on reindeer. They carried out their work almost without complaint, matter-of-factly discussing both their brushes with death and the difficulties of daily life.

Because of the enormous territory to be covered in Siberia, Boas chose to divide the fieldwork into three sections. In the south, Berthold Laufer was placed in charge of operations. He was accompanied into the field by archaeologist Gerald Fowke. Waldemar Borgoras and Waldemar Jochelson were in charge of the two northern teams,

with Jochelson assuming overall responsibility.

Like Boas, Berthold Laufer was a product of the German university tradition. He had written a thesis for the University of Leipzig on a Tibetan text and studied ten Asian languages, but he had never before been in the field. Boas offered him five hundred dollars per year, in addition to his expenses, and Laufer accepted readily. Because Laufer was a Jew, he was unable to obtain a Russian visa to work in Siberia. Jesup appealed to the U.S. Department of State for help. Complicated negotiations followed, and only special permission from the Russian emperor allowed the visa to be issued.

A Box of Spirits

After months of delay, in June 1898 Laufer and Fowke arrived in Vladivostok and from there made their way to Khabarovsk on the Amur River, which formed the border between China and Russia. There Laufer and Fowke parted company. Fowke went

down the Amur by boat, studying archaeological remains along the river, while Laufer proceeded by steamer to Sakhalin Island, northwest of Japan in the Sea of Okhotsk, where he collected artifacts and texts and made recordings of the Gilyak, Tungus, and Ainu tribes. He spent the fall among the Gilyak and Tungus of the northeast, but in October, while visiting a Gilyak village twelve miles inland, he became ill with influenza, which developed into pneumonia. He was incapacitated for two and a half months. When he was barely well enough to travel, he began his journey southward along the east coast of the island, first on horseback, then on reindeer. His first visit was to a Gilyak village, where a celebration of the bear festival was in progress: "I was welcomed with much delight," he wrote, "since I met several of my acquaintances of last summer. For five days I assisted in the ceremonial, and was even permitted to witness the sacrifice of the dog, which is kept secret from the Russians."[18]

Laufer continued to travel

among the Tungus and Ainu of the central and southern parts of the island, but, on New Year's Eve, his journey came to a halt. The Russian governor warned him that bandits in that area had built a fort and were terrorizing the local inhabitants. Before returning to the north, however, he made records of Gilyak songs, using wax cylinders. This new technology amazed the Gilyak as well as the Russians. "'It took me so long to learn this song,'" said a young woman who sang for Laufer, "'and this thing has

learned it at once, without making any mistakes. There is surely a man or a spirit in this box which imitates me!' and at the same time she was crying and laughing with excitement."[19]

Although he was forced to cut short his studies of the Ainu because of his illness and the threat of bandits, Laufer did spend some time among them. They did not speak Russian, so he resorted to Japanese. Their knowledge of that language was limited, but they liked the Japanese people and were thus well disposed to

Laufer. Like the Chilcotin of the Northwest Coast who had refused to be measured by Boas, the Ainu did not allow Laufer to take anthropometric measurements. "The people were afraid that they would die at once after submitting to this process. Although I had their confidence, I failed in my efforts in this direction, even after offering them presents which they considered of great value. I succeeded in measuring a single individual, a man of imposing stature, who, after the measurements had been taken, fell prostrate on the floor, the picture of despair, groaning, 'Now I am going to die to-morrow!'"[20]

Just after the new year, Laufer started north by dogsled. It was on this journey that he nearly lost his life on the ice. He had to travel rapidly to reach Nikolayevsk before the end of March, when spring thaws would make crossing to the mainland impossible. On March 21, he left the island; his destination was Khabarovsk, where there was a large population of Goldi (Nanai).

Once it was navigable in late May, Laufer traveled down the Amur, along the way studying Goldi and Gilyak villages. In the fall he left Siberia to return to New York, via Japan. In a letter written to Franz Boas in November of 1899, Laufer graphically summed up his experiences in Siberia: "Nobody who has not been there can have an idea of the dreadful horrors one has to undergo on account of the insect-pest combined with heat and sixteen months' loanly [sic] life in wilderness, which resulted into an extraordinary state of nervousness I never experienced before."[21]

Despite tight funds and strong competition from Russian dealers, Laufer was able to follow Boas's instructions and to make a comprehensive collection, albeit one that reflected his own fascination with ritual objects and the embroidered work of the Goldi. His monograph, *The Decorative Art of the Amur Tribes*, was not the ethnography Boas had expected; rather it was an appreciation of the decorative motifs that had so enchanted him. Gerald Fowke, on the other hand, turned out to be one of Boas's few mistakes. The self-educated American adventurer spent the summer and fall of 1898 on a large boat, exploring the Amur River, with the help of a German sailor and a Tungus. He found the swamps, tall grasses, and swarms of mosquitoes and flies to be thoroughly unpleasant and discovered nothing of interest along the river. Boas did not have him continue.

Exiles' Return

Unlike Berthold Laufer, the Russian revolutionaries Waldemar Jochelson and Waldemar Borgoras had spent considerable time among the Siberian people. In their student days, each had been exiled to Siberia for involvement with Narodnaya Volya, a radical populist organization. They made good use of their time, however; they undertook linguistic and ethnological studies of the native peoples.

In attempting to enter the field, they, too, ran into official roadblocks. Czar Nicholas II wrote letters to Borgoras and Jochelson, stating that they were to receive all the help necessary to complete their mission. At the same time, because of their political ties, a confidential document was circulated to the chiefs of district police of the Yakutsk Province, instructing them to undertake secret surveillance of the men and render them no assistance.

Despite all this, in the summer of 1900, Borgoras and Jochelson, accompanied by their wives, arrived in Vladivostok. The women's work was to be considered part of the expedition, although they were not to receive additional payment. Their contributions to the expedition were significant. Mrs. Jochelson, who was studying medicine at the University of Zurich, did all the anthropometric work and most of the photography. Mrs. Borgoras did most of the collecting of artifacts for the Museum, while her husband gathered scientific information. At Vladivostok, the expedition split into two parties. The Borgoras party headed for their headquarters at the mouth of the Anadyr River. The Jochelsons planned to make their headquarters in Kushka, at the mouth of the Gishiga River.

Upon their arrival in Kushka, the Jochelsons were greeted by dismal news: the district had been ravaged by a measles epidemic the preceding winter, which had killed a third of the population of five hundred in only two months. Most of the inhabitants were now sick with the grippe. The Reindeer Koryak, who usually spent the winter nearby, had fled to the mountains with their herds. In order to reach the Maritime Koryak, located on Penzhina Bay to the east, Jochelson would have to cross rough seas or go overland across the tundra. The seas were impassable without adequate boats, while the tundra could be negotiated only in the winter months by reindeer and dog teams. Jochelson had no choice but to attempt to cross the tundra by packhorse. Of the sixty-five horses available in the region, most were being used by an American engineer working for a Russo-American gold-mining company. Jochelson was able to obtain only twenty horses, most of which he felt were too young to make the arduous journey.

The trip across the boggy tundra was a nightmare. Progress was extremely slow, no more than ten miles a day. The horses became mired in the mud and had to be pulled out. At one point, Jochelson and his wife lost the trail and wandered for two days without food or shelter from the cold. At last they started a huge fire and were discovered by their men. At the foot of the last pass, the group encountered the first snowstorm of the season, which delayed them for three days. In early October, they arrived in Kuel to begin their winter among the Maritime Koryak. The guides were sent back to Kushka with the horses. This return journey also was full of misadventure:

six horses were lost in a snowstorm in which the men themselves almost died, and another six horses died of exhaustion after their return.

Conditions among the Maritime Koryak were primitive and trying. They lived in underground dwellings reached by ladder through the smoke hole:

It is almost impossible to describe the squalor of these dwellings. The smoke, which fills the hut, makes the eyes smart. It is particularly dense in the upper part of the hut, so that work that has to be done in an upright position becomes almost impossible. Walls, ladder and household utensils are covered with a greasy soot, so that contact with them leaves shining black spots on hands and clothing. The dim light which falls through the smoke-hole is hardly sufficient for writing and reading. The odor of blubber and of refuse is almost intolerable; and the inmates, intoxicated with fly agaric, add to the discomfort of the situation. The natives are infested with lice. As long as we remained in these dwellings we could not escape these insects, which we dreaded more than any of the privations of our journey.[22]

After several months, the Jochelson party, with twenty dog sleds, started for Kamenskoye to study the Reindeer Koryak of the interior. They found conditions there only slightly better. The native winter huts were so cold that the Jochelsons were unable to work in them. They put up their own tent and furnished it with a

"All that exists, lives. The lamp walks around. The walls of the house have voices of their own. Even the chamber-pot has a separate land and house. The skins sleeping in the bags talk at night. The antlers lying on the tombs arise at night and walk in procession around the mounds, while the deceased rise and visit the living."
—Waldemar Borgoras, quoting a Chukchi shaman

Opposite: Koryak shaman performance

Right: Waldemar Jochelson, his wife, Dina Brodsky, and their field party at the start of their raft trip down the Korkodon River en route to Verkhne-Kolymsk, 1901

small iron stove, which provided sufficient heat, but at night, in the extreme cold, they slept in bags made of wolfskin.

In May, the party returned to Kushka, where they catalogued and packed up the collections they had made the previous winter. During June they made an extremely dangerous journey to the mouth of the Nayakhan River to visit the nomadic Tungus gathered there. On the return trip, the seas drove them into the Bay of Atykyna, where they were stranded without any food. They averted starvation only when, on the fourth day, they managed to kill two seals.

The Tribe Without a Future

The Jochelsons departed Kushka in August 1901 to spend another year in Siberia with the Yukaghir of Kolyma. (About Kolyma's physical hospitality it is necessary only to say that, when Joseph Stalin established his penal system of gulags, Kolyma was chief among them.) The journey across the Kolyma Mountains to Verkhne-Kolymsk on the Yassachna River, a tributary of the Kolyma, took a grueling fifty-six days. They were the first whites ever to cross the mountains. This journey Jochelson described as "the most difficult one it was ever my fate to undertake." When they finally reached the other side, they and their horses were

exhausted. The increasing cold, however, made it necessary to proceed quickly if they wished to reach their destination before the river froze over. They built a strong raft and set off down the Korkodon River to a camp of the Yukaghir, while the three Yakut returned to Kushka with the horses. Expecting a trip of two or three days, Jochelson had left most of the provisions with the Yakut. Instead, the journey lasted nine days, and provisions had to be stretched to the limit.

After four days with the Yukaghir, the party continued down the Korkodon and the Kolyma in a boat. On the seventh night, however, the river froze, while they were still forty miles from their destination. They abandoned the boat and walked two days to reach the village of Verkhne-Kolymsk.

Conditions among the Yukaghir were not much better than those among the Koryak. The people were in the grip of a famine. Both their hunting and fishing had failed and they were starving to death. They were re-

duced to killing their own dog teams because they could not feed them. After assisting them as much as he could, Jochelson sent a messenger to Sredne-Kolymsk in a fruitless plea to the government for some assistance for the Yukaghir.

He had already spent much time among the Yukaghir and was aware of the dire problems that they faced. Their population had been drastically reduced to just a few hundred, spread out over a vast area. Much like Boas on the Northwest Coast, Jochelson felt that his mission was to record all aspects of native culture and language while it was still possible. In the introduction to his study of the Yukaghir, Jochelson wrote: "The study of a tribe which to a great extent has lost its original ethnic peculiarities—a tribe insignificant in numbers and having no future—was a difficult, and, from a practical point of view, a thankless task. But the science of ethnology recognizes that a knowledge of small tribes is equally as important as that of great peoples. In fact,

A Siberian Love Letter

On an earlier expedition, undertaken in 1895–96 for the Russian Geographical Society, Waldemar Jochelson had spent considerable time among the Yukaghir. He had ample opportunity to observe the free sexual relations among Yukaghir men and women before marriage. On several occasions, Jochelson unwittingly embarrassed or offended young women when he rejected their sexual offers. Two of these girls wrote Jochelson a love letter on birchbark, in which they referred to their disappointment with him. In his writings on the Yukaghir, Jochelson describes these two incidents:

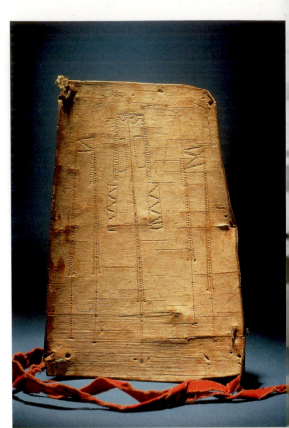

I traveled alone, without my wife; and the Yukaghir, as I learned to understand later, felt obliged to be hospitable to me in every respect. Once I was in the house of the elder of the Yassachna Yukaghir. . . . The elder had no children, and, besides his old wife, had with him only an adopted daughter, a distant relative, a girl of seventeen or eighteen years. I noticed that, as soon as I settled in the house, the nightly visits of the young men were discontinued. Afterwards I learned from my interpreter, Dolganoff, that the girl was offended at my indifference to her, and that her girl friends and the young men made fun of her. Once the hostess said to me, "It seems that among you, men can live without wives." I told her that among us, if a married man loved his wife, he remained true to her, even when away from her. "Well," answered she, "it seems that the Russians here have different customs. They go to other girls and wives, even when they have their own wives with them."

Above: The Siberian birchbark love letter sent to Waldemar Jochelson, 1895–96

Opposite, above: Waldemar Borgoras on the Kolyma River, 1900–1901

Opposite, below: Tasseled shaman's hat of reindeer fur, beads, dyed moosehair embroidery, brass bells, and rings

*   The other case was also near the river Yassachna. . . . In this village there lived the blacksmith Shaluguin, an old Yukaghir, who had a large family, among them several daughters. The youngest was considered to be the prettiest on the river Yassachna. For a long time I intended to take her photograph in her holiday dress, and meant to do it before my departure; but, as she was then staying with her relatives in another settlement, I asked the old man to send a boat for her. In spite of the fact that I explained to the old man what I wanted his daughter for, my request was understood in another way. The girl arrived late in the evening, and I put off taking the photograph till the next morning. My canvas tent was standing near the skin tent of Shaluguin. Imagine my astonishment next morning, when, stepping out of my tent, I noticed between it and that of Shaluguin a separate small tent, which the girl was just then taking away! She was in a very angry mood, and my photographs were not successful. Afterwards my interpreter told me that the young men laughed at the girl for having uselessly put up a separate tent. When I left the river Yassachna, I received a love-letter written on bark, in ideographic characters, by both the above-mentioned girls, without any sign of jealousy; but in this letter I was also told that their unsatisfied feeling towards me was reconciled by their more happy relations with my Cossack and interpreter.*

from the ethnological point of view, information about the life and history of a tribe which is becoming extinct is particularly important; and while witnesses of their past life are still living, haste should be made to study them, and to obtain from them all possible information as to their past."[23]

Despite this sorry state of affairs, the Jochelsons completed their work and remained in the area until March 1902, when they began the laborious task of transporting their collections to Yakutsk. What they had accomplished was unprecedented. On their two-year itinerary of tribulation, the Jochelsons had traveled close to eight thousand miles and completed extensive studies of the Koryak and the Yukaghir. Their complete collections were monumental: "Three thousand ethnographical objects, forty-one plaster casts of faces, measurements of about nine hundred individuals, twelve hundred photographs, one hundred fifty tales and traditions, phonographic cylinders . . . and archaeological specimens from abandoned village sites. I also made a small zoological collection, and obtained a large mammoth tusk weighing two hundred twenty pounds. During the whole period of my absence I kept a meteorological journal."[24]

Journey Among Reindeer

At the turn of the century, Mariinsky Post, at the mouth of the Anadyr River, was the most distant Russian settlement in northeastern Asia. From here, Waldemar Borgoras would travel almost constantly from October 1900 until the following summer, never remaining more than four weeks in any location. He had

hoped to leave earlier, but all summer he and his wife were stranded in Mariinsky Post by a measles epidemic among the Chukchi, which swept along the shores of the Sea of Okhotsk and of the Bering Sea, claiming hundreds of victims. On his journey, Borgoras would overcome obstacles that rivaled those facing the Jochelsons, while Mrs. Borgoras remained in and around Mariinsky Post, where she gathered most of the collections for the Museum.

Accompanied by a Cossack and a native guide, Borgoras traveled with three dog teams. He was able to carry only scientific instruments and small objects for barter and had to rely almost entirely on the food supply of the country: dried fish, reindeer, and seal and walrus blubber. The weather that winter was extremely severe: "Blizzards were frequent, and directly after leaving Mariinsky Post we were overtaken by one which lasted several days and spoiled the track to such a degree that our dogs were

hardly able to drag themselves through the deep snow. We had to make the greater part of the journey to Markova on snowshoes and assist our teams in dragging the sledges."[25]

Borgoras made his way to the west coast of the Kamchatka Peninsula, studying the Kamchadal language, which was rapidly being replaced by Russian. Just as he began his return trip to the Anadyr River, along the Pacific Coast through country hitherto unvisited by white men, he, too, fell ill with influenza in one of the Kamchatka villages and nearly died. For more than two weeks he lost his voice completely and could only communicate with others through sign language.

After recovering sufficiently to travel, Borgoras passed through the territory of the Kerek, a branch of the Maritime Koryak. The Kerek had in the past relied primarily on walrus to survive, but the arrival of the American whalers had driven the walrus to the north. Now the Kerek were starving to death. Between the

Kerek and the first villages of the Anadyr Reindeer Chukchi lay a forlorn mountainous region that was unknown even to the Kerek. Borgoras and his men ventured into this territory, "guided solely by the course of the frozen mountain rivers up to the watershed, and then down to the tributaries of the Anadyr. The journey lasted seventeen days, and nearly exhausted the strength of both dogs and drivers."[26]

Amazingly, Borgoras arrived in Mariinsky Post only one day later than he had planned. For the next three months he traveled in the north, studying the Maritime Chukchi and the Asiatic Eskimo. At the end of June, he headed back to the mouth of the Anadyr in a native boat that he had covered with walrus hides. This journey took thirty-two days, and he arrived just in time for the annual visit of the Russian mail steamer, which would take him home.

The Borgoras collections were as extensive as those made by the Jochelsons, and together they rivaled those in the Museum of Anthropology and Ethnology in St. Petersburg. When much of this material was displayed for the first time at the American Museum of Natural History in 1980, in the newly opened Hall of Asian Peoples, visiting Soviet anthropologists were astounded by the Museum's collections.[27]

Truth Postponed

By the end of 1902, the fieldwork for the Jesup North Pacific Expedition had drawn virtually to a close. Although Boas wanted to continue in the field, Jesup decided against it. He had contributed close to $60,000 to the expedition and felt that enough groundwork had been done; it was now time to examine the ma-

terial and to draw significant conclusions about the origins of the earliest inhabitants of North America. In the 1902 annual report of the Museum, Jesup announced the successful termination of the expedition. Yet only two of twelve planned volumes on its work had been published, and Jesup was growing impatient. The following year, he threatened to cut off funds for the publications altogether. A desperate Boas, feeling that his professional reputation was at stake, managed to secure continued support for that venture. In 1902, however, Jesup had named Hermon C. Bumpus as Museum director. Boas disagreed with him over the Museum's priorities, and eventually he felt he had no choice but to resign. After he left, he continued to supervise publication of the expedition's volumes. As late as 1926, though, Henry Fairfield Osborn, then president of the Museum, was still bemoaning Boas's inability to write the summary volume.

Boas was confident at first that he could establish the fact that the tribes of northeastern Asia and the Northwest Coast were

originally of a single race and that they still had many elements of their culture in common. He soon became convinced, however, that he needed to collect more evidence before drawing conclusions. Nonetheless, both he and Jochelson did formulate theories of migration across the Bering Strait. It has since been established that humans did first come into North America from northeastern Asia, passing over a land bridge across the Bering Strait. The exact time of the first migration remains uncertain.[28]

Because of the escalating political turmoil in Russia, Boas also had great difficulty obtaining the ethnographies and linguistic studies that he expected from Jochelson and Borgoras. In the spring of 1905, Borgoras wrote to Boas to apologize for the slow progress of his work on the Chukchi, claiming that events such as those taking place in Russia occurred only once in many centuries. Boas responded, "An investigation by Mr. Borgoras of the Chukchee happens only once in eternity, and I think you owe it to science to give us the results of your studies."[29] Months later, Borgoras

Opposite: Tossing on Walrus-Hide, a Chukchi midsummer ceremony to ward off dangers from contagious diseases or to assuage violent tempests, 1900–1901. Photograph by Waldemar Borgoras

was arrested in Moscow for his political involvement with the Farmers' Congress. He sent a cablegram to Boas with the message: "Am arrested, reasons unknown."[30] He was soon released from prison and in later years became director of the Institute of the Peoples of the North, an agency that promoted education and development among the northern Siberian peoples.

Borgoras did eventually write up his scientific work, and his output was substantial: seven monographs, including five important volumes on the Chukchi. Jochelson published monographs on the Koryak, the Yukaghir, and the Yakut and the handbook *Peoples of Asiatic Russia*. These definitive ethnographies and the well-documented, comprehensive collections have proved to be the invaluable products of the expedition, rather than the conclusive summary volume that Jesup never got.

Revivals

Anthropology has changed in fundamental ways since the beginning of this century, when it was in its infancy. The idea of preserving a "pristine" culture through records of its art, mythology, religion, and everyday objects, as Boas hoped to do, without any connection to the people who make up the culture, is no longer the goal of the anthropologist. Cultures in contact are never static, and the ongoing impact of change is never simple. Indeed, the direst predictions of

the extinction of native tribes proved mistaken. Under the Soviets, other ethnic groups were moved into Siberia; native communities were destroyed and the inhabitants relocated. A great deal of cultural intermingling occurred, and children, placed in state kindergartens at the age of a few months, never learned to speak native languages. Stalin promoted forced collectivization of reindeer herders and genocide of shamans.[31]

In spite of all this, the native Siberian cultures survived, and in 1992 the American Museum of Natural History assumed a role in their revitalization. Riding a post-Soviet wave of cultural revival among the peoples of Siberia, two Yakut scholars, Vladimir Ivanov-Unarov and Zinaida Ivanova, visited the Museum and conducted a comprehensive study of the Museum collections. They returned with photographs of objects that have since become a source of knowledge and inspiration for local craftspeople. The Yukaghir people have received a grant from the MacArthur Foundation that will enable them to translate Jochelson's monograph back into Yukaghir. This information constitutes a major source of knowledge for a group that no longer has any direct links to its cultural heritage and is attempting to reconstitute itself as an ethnically distinct group.[32]

The Museum's collections have also served as a source for cultural revival among the Kwakiutl people of the Northwest Coast. In Boas's time, and for decades after, the potlatch was the target of missionaries and British Columbia Indian agents. Despite its suppression by authorities, the tradition has persisted without interruption to the present day,

somewhat changed but still very much intact, and what had been held in secret is now held openly. In 1991 the American Museum of Natural History's exhibition "Chiefly Feasts: The Enduring Kwakiutl Potlatch" celebrated the survival of the potlatch and presented both its past and its present. The artifacts that George Hunt and Franz Boas collected for the Jesup Expedition formed the core of the exhibition. They were complemented by the work of Mungo Martin and Willie Seaweed, who continued to create art during the years when it was against the law to hold a potlatch, and by the work of contemporary artists, including Martin's son-in-law, Henry Hunt, and his son, Tony Hunt, both of whom were trained by Martin. The elders of the community provided important information about objects used for the potlatch. Gloria Webster, the great-granddaughter of George Hunt, served as a consultant to the exhibition and curated the section devoted to the contemporary potlatch. Her eloquent words best sum up the situation of the Kwakiutl at the end of the twentieth century, one far different from what Franz Boas would have predicted:

If my ancestors from two hundred years ago were able to be with us today, I often wonder what they would think of a contemporary potlatch. Would they be able to recognize what we do as being related to what they did? Would they pity us for having lost so much, or be proud that we are still here? I think that after recovering from the shock of seeing so many changes, not only in the potlatch but in all aspects of our lives, they would tell us that under the circumstances, we are not doing too badly. They would also urge us to keep on strengthening what we have, if we are to survive and continue having our good times.[33]

Asiatic Expeditions, 1921–94

RUSSIA

Lake Baikal

MONGOLIA

ALTAI MOUNTAINS

Ulan Bator (Urga)

Tsagan Nor (The White Lake)

Shabarakh Usu (Flaming Cliffs)

Erhlien (Iren Dabasu)

CHINA

Khermeen Tsav

Ukhaa Tolgod

Tugrugeen Shireh

Baron Sog in Sumu

Urtyn Obo

Inner Mongolia

Wolf Camp

Kalgan

Great Wall

Beijing (Peking)

The camp and camel boxes of the Central Asiatic Expedition at Urtyn Obo, 1928. From a hand-colored lantern slide by James Shackelford

The Gobi:
Men of the Dragon Bones

THE ANCIENT CARTOGRAPHERS indicated unknown areas on their maps with the expression, "Here be dragons." By the 1920s, there remained few stretches of the globe where the words still applied. The poles had been achieved, the most inhospitable forests of South America, Africa, and New Guinea were fast becoming the laboratories of the scientist and theaters of commercial interest—even of tourism. But across a thousand-mile stretch of Central Asia, the Gobi of Mongolia (*gobi* means "desert" in Mongol), the dragons of the unknown still ruled. Into that expanse ventured the first large-scale motorized expedition and one of the boldest scientific efforts ever, the Central Asiatic Expedition of the American Museum of Natural History.

Five times from 1921 to 1930, teams of the Third Asiatic Expedition, or, as it came to be known, the Central Asiatic Expedition, ventured from their field headquarters in Peking into the vast basin of Inner and Outer Mongolia. They did indeed find dragons—or at least their remains. The Chinese called fossils "dragon bones" and dubbed the scientists who sought them "the American men of the dragon bones," a term of both wonder and respect. Front-page headlines brought international attention to the dramatic fossil discoveries of the Central Asiatic Expedition and to its leader, the intrepid Roy Chapman Andrews. It also sparked an interest in paleontology that would not be duplicated until the same Museum returned to the Gobi more than five decades later—to shed light on some long-standing evolutionary mysteries and to make new discoveries.

If the Gobi was a cipher before the Central Asiatic Expedition, it was not because people had not been there. Since the time of Genghis Khan in the thirteenth century, camel caravans had crossed Mongolia, carrying silk and spices back and forth between the Middle East and China. By

1920, the adventures of Western explorers such as Sven Hedin, who had nearly died of thirst in a courageous desert crossing, and Sir Francis Younghusband had made Mongolia synonymous with a certain harsh romance. Central Mongolia was unknown to science primarily because no one had bothered to stop there for very long.

It is not difficult to understand why. Across this vast, arid stretch of land, there was only a single town of size—Urga (now called Ulan Bator, the capital of the Mongolian Republic). Although water in quantity lies just below the surface in some areas, others were truly dry. Food had to be carried or hunted. Research and exploration were—and are still—practical only during the late spring and summer, for as soon as the brief fall is over, temperatures can drop to −40° F. Even in the summer the weather can be brutal. During one summer, Andrews ran into a dangerous blizzard as he tried to return to Urga from his base camp.

Until the twentieth century the Gobi held little interest for scientists. To the naturalist, its mam-

mal species were spectacular— vast herds of antelope and wild asses, for example—but not unusual. To the paleontologist, the plateau of undulating grasslands and sand dunes seemed to offer no direct access to fossil-bearing strata, and only one fossil tooth had ever been discovered prior to the Central Asiatic Expedition. Getting anywhere that might prove fruitful for research would require weeks of camel travel, not to mention the difficulty of getting the bulky, plaster-wrapped specimens out of the desert.

On top of all this, political events in Mongolia and China could be hazardous, to say the least. Charles Coltman, not a member of the expedition but a driver on the first leg of the 1922 expedition, was shot and killed by Chinese soldiers not far from Urga a few months after ferrying expedition members into the field.

The Home of Humankind?

The Museum had already sent two expeditions into China in

pursuit of animal specimens for its exhibition halls and scientific collections. Andrews had led both of them. He had traveled extensively in East Asia, from the northern forests of Korea, which he was perhaps the first Westerner to explore, to New Guinea. On the Second Asiatic Expedition in 1919, Andrews had entered Mongolia and traveled by automobile five hundred miles inland to Urga. His primary objective had been to hunt in the north, but on this trip he saw exposed sedimentary beds in the badlands of southeastern Mongolia, at the edge of the Gobi. In just such places are fossils found. No practiced geological eye had ever been turned on the rest of the desert. Andrews found desert driving tough but manageable, and he began to develop a plan for a more comprehensive expedition. He would defeat the distances by combining automobiles with the ancient method of the caravan: team and gear in and out by car; supplies and gasoline in, and fossils out, by camel caravan.

This was all the encouragement Museum president Henry Fairfield Osborn needed. Osborn, a biologist and paleontologist, proposed the theory that Asia was the likely home of the earliest ancestors of humankind. Inspired by Neanderthal and Paleolithic discoveries in Spain and France, whose caves he toured in 1912, he looked to Asia as the originating point of a migration of prehumans. There was reason to do so. The earliest protohuman remains, the fossils of *Pithecanthropus erectus*, had been discovered in Java in 1892. Now interest was turning to China. Indeed, while the Central Asiatic Expedition was on its second trip to the Gobi, paleontologist Gunnar Andersson, of the Chinese Geological Survey, and his assistant Otto Zdansky would discover the teeth of "Peking man," the most important evidence of human origins until Raymond Dart's discoveries in South Africa in 1924.

Osborn's greatest support derived from two of his chief scientists at the Museum, William Diller Matthew and William K. Gregory. Matthew was an expert on ancient mammals, whose study he had helped develop through his pioneering fieldwork in the American West. He had thought a great deal about what mammals appeared where and when around the globe. Comparing the climatic and geologic record with the known distribution of fossils, he posited the Northern Hemisphere, and Asia in particular, as the original source for all of mammalian life. He further reasoned that, if a once climatically friendly central Asia had nurtured early mammals, it also likely would have supported early primates and perhaps early members of the human family as well. Gregory had studied the fossils of extinct apes found in the Siwalik Hills along the Himalayan border. He regarded these apes as relatives of primates close to the human line, but such evidence was circumstantial. In effect, Osborn said to Andrews, "Get me the fossils of ancient man."[1] Dinosaurs never entered the conversation.

The first hurdle for the expedition was money. Andrews esti-

Raising Money the Old-Fashioned Way

"It grips the imagination," said President Henry Fairfield Osborn of the plan for an expedition to the Gobi of Mongolia. "The Museum will do all it can but that won't be much in the way of cash. Getting the money will be up to you." The Central Asiatic Expedition was among the most financially ambitious scientific undertakings of its kind. Andrews's original estimate of $250,000 proved inadequate to finance the harvest of paleontological treasures unearthed in the Gobi and the zoological collecting in China, not to mention maintaining a fully staffed headquarters in Peking, where wives and dignitaries came and went. After three seasons in the Far East and two trips into the field, Andrews returned to New York seeking an additional $250,000.

In 1920, the government was not yet the primary engine of scientific discovery. Instead, Henry Fairfield Osborn took advantage of social position, proximity, and patron self-esteem to tap the extraordinary concentration of private wealth in New York City. Railroad magnate Morris Jesup, sponsor of the historic North Pacific Expedition, was dead, but J. P. Morgan, Childs Frick, Cleveland Dodge, and others looked on the Museum as their institution and on Osborn as a distinguished man of science. Osborn opened the doors, and, maps in hand, Andrews marched in:

At the end of fifteen minutes, I stopped breathless. Mr. Morgan swung about with his eyes aglow.

"It's a great plan; a great plan. I'll gamble with you. How much money do you need?"

"A quarter of a million dollars and five years at the least, Mr. Morgan."

"All right, I'll give you fifty thousand. Now you go out and get the rest of it."

In the end, all of the Central Asiatic money (about $5 million in current dollars) came from private donors. Andrews, who remained at heart an out-of-doors kid from Wisconsin with a rifle in his hand, was both awed by and exasperated with his patrons. Although he liked to think of tycoons as "adventurers at heart," he clearly had had enough of fund-raising cocktail parties after 1924. Moreover, his idea of auctioning one of the dinosaur eggs, although successful, ultimately backfired. Both the Mongolians and Chinese suspected the expedition was a for-profit venture from which they were being financially excluded. The list of contributors to the expedition reveals how adept Andrews was. It grew to some two hundred names, including John D. Rockefeller, Jr., who, unlike Morgan, listened with only polite interest—but also gave $50,000. It did not include a prominent oil company and a major mining concern, however. When time was running out for funding, each of them offered the Museum gifts in excess of $50,000 for the privilege of sending along a prospector. The Museum turned them down.

mated the venture would cost $250,000, of which the Museum could fund only a small amount. That left a significant balance to be solicited from private sources, including individual trustees. But Andrews was by all accounts a terrific fundraiser. He also had a compelling pitch—the search for human ancestors—and it made the front pages of America's major newspapers. In truth, this was virgin territory, and the expedition was on the lookout for significant fossils of any kind. Andrews can be forgiven for overstating the case. Raising money is partly a rhetorical exercise. You must tell your audience some of what it wants to hear even if you are not sure what you are going to find—especially if you are not sure what you are going to find. Would J. P. Morgan's eyes have lit up if Andrews had told him he was going after fossil mammals, however large?

It took only a year to raise the amount needed. The staff for the expedition had long since been chosen, but the public announcement brought Andrews more candidates. His public relations apparatus had worked to perfection, and more than ten thousand letters poured in from people who wanted to find the "missing link between monkeys and humans," including a dissatisfied waiter who offered to bring his own dinner jacket and a woman whose spirit communicants had divulged to her the whereabouts of a city in the Gobi containing a record of human evolution. In 1921, Andrews headed for China with reptile specialist Clifford Pope and paleontologist Walter Granger to arrange the transport of some 38 tons of supplies and to secure the cooperation of the Chinese government.

Under an Unlucky Star

The expedition was to travel through both Outer Mongolia and the Chinese province of Inner Mongolia, which lay beyond the Great Wall. The Chinese Geological Survey and the Chinese Minister of Foreign Affairs were enthusiastic. The team would include the Mongolian Minister of Justice, T. Badmajapoff, who would act as interpreter, guide, and negotiator. But what did "government cooperation" actually mean? In 1912, the three-hundred-year-old Manchu dynasty had fallen, plunging China into a period of political instability that would last until the victory of Mao Ze Dong's Communists in the 1940s. Andrews was in China during 1912, when executions—"head-lopping parties," he called them—were a daily spectacle outside the Forbidden City. By 1921, Peking was quiet, but warlord "governors" wielded power in the provinces. They laughed at letters of transit and other official documents. Bubbling just below the surface was antiforeign sentiment. When civil war broke out in 1926, attacks against foreign-

ers began in earnest, and Americans had to be evacuated from the interior or protected. In 1927, the expedition, preparing for its fourth trip into the Gobi, was forced to mount machine guns and to defend its headquarters in Peking.

The political situation in Mongolia was also volatile. Outer Mongolia became an independent state in 1921. Bolsheviks and Czarists from revolutionary Russia were battling each other for influence there, and sometimes those two groups turned on the Mongols. At the same time, the Mongols were attempting to defend themselves against the territorial ambitions of the Chinese. And everywhere, it seemed, there were bandits.

From detentions of expedition personnel at local outposts to the murder of armed guards protecting Pope's supply parties, danger pursued the Central Asiatic Expedition until the day it left the field. In 1921, while the expedition was still negotiating with Chinese officials, Walter Granger spent time prospecting along the

Yangtze gorges and discussing with Gunnar Andersson and Otto Zdansky the field techniques that would help them discover the fossils of "Peking man." The steam launches they traveled in posed a constant nuisance to junks transporting Chinese soldiers, who expressed their annoyance by firing on the scientists. With characteristic laconism, Granger called his first trip on the river "interesting and exciting," as bullets whizzed overhead.

Andrews had enormous respect for the Mongols. He expected word would eventually cross the desert that the expedition should be left alone and that it carried nothing worth stealing. Nonetheless, at various times Andrews, Granger, head of motor transport J. McKenzie Young, and photographer James Barnes Shackelford all had to use weapons in self-defense, in Mongolia as well as China. In one dramatic instance, Andrews was driving near the spot where two Russians had been robbed just weeks earlier:

The thought came to me, "I wonder if brigands would attempt to hold me up on the same ground." Almost at the same moment, I saw the flash of a gun-barrel on the summit of a hill three hundred yards away. . . .

A moment later, as the car topped the rim of the valley, I saw three mounted bandits at the bottom of the slope. It would have been impossible to turn the car and retreat without exposing myself to close range shots and knowing that a Mongol pony never would stand against the charge of a motor I decided to attack. The cut-out was open and with a smooth stretch in front of me, I roared down the slope at forty miles an hour. The expected happened! While the brigands were endeavoring to unship their rifles, which were on their backs, their horses began a series of leaps and bounds, madly bucking and rearing, so that the men could hardly stay in their saddles. I opened up with one of my six-shooters, firing close to their heads, and in a

second the situation had changed! The only thing that the brigands wanted to do was to get away.[2]

McKenzie Young managed to get the last load of fossils to Kalgan, at the Great Wall, just two days before the border with Outer Mongolia was closed in 1930, and only after fighting off an attack by thirty bandits.

The Accelerator and the Brake

In 1922, when the five automobiles and two trucks of the Central Asiatic Expedition finally did set off from Kalgan (a caravan of seventy-five camels, each carrying four hundred pounds of supplies, had set out five weeks before), the road to Urga was deserted and the telegraph offices lay in ruins. A vast plain of hard gravel and a world of uncertainty stretched out before them. The plan was to make a five-month reconnaissance loop through the Gobi: northwest to Urga, southwest

and south toward the little-explored Altai Mountains and Tsagan Nor (the White Lake), then south toward Inner Mongolia, and finally east-northeast toward the Urga Road. This loop would serve to orient all subsequent trips, as well as the first forays of the Mongolian Academy of Sciences–American Museum of Natural History Gobi Expedition of 1991. There would not be much time for digression, and they could not linger if sites held little immediate promise. As Andrews remarked, "a paleontologist rarely digs for fossils unless he sees them."[3]

Fortunately, it did not take them long to see fossils. Walter Granger found the first ones. The story of how, at a site called Iren Dabasu, just a few days out of Kalgan, he and the geologist Charles Berkey took a drive and came back with pockets packed with tiny dinosaur fossils has become a paleontological legend. "Well Roy, we've done it. The stuff is here," Granger remarked.[4]

Indeed, it quickly became clear that bringing only one paleontologist on the expedition had been a mistake. Nearly every stop on this first tour through the Gobi yielded results. And every subsequent trip back would be characterized by major finds at new locations. At Iren Dabasu, Granger found the first dinosaur unearthed north of the Himalayas—a representative of the Cretaceous period, the final age of these creatures. Dinosaurs were something no one expected to find. Suddenly 80 million years of history were added to the Gobi's barren record.

A peculiarity of fossil hunting is that one can make momentous discoveries and not know it for months or even years, until the bones are "worked up" in the laboratory. A tiny toothy fragment may turn out to be evidence of the earliest mammals or of an unknown birdlike dinosaur. At the very end of the 1922 field trip, as the group made its final dash for Kalgan, Shackelford—

"a photographer by profession but a fossil hunter by instinct," according to Granger—unearthed, quite casually, what the scientists at the Museum would reveal months later to be the first dinosaur eggs ever seen. Until then, it had not been known for certain that dinosaurs even laid eggs.

The 1922 reconnaissance revealed the Gobi to be rich in fossils beyond expectation. Indeed, Edwin Colbert, paleontologist emeritus of the Museum, has called the expedition the beginning of the "great Asiatic dinosaur rush."[5] Andrews, however, was constantly getting scooped. While he prepared for a hunting trip, the group found its first dinosaur. While Andrews watched a sunset with his wife, who accompanied him for part of the trip, Granger found bones of a titanothere, a 50-million-year-old mammal then known only in North America. Berkey found the first birdlike dinosaur fossil, *Saurornithoides*. Shackelford found chipped flints of a Stone Age culture the scientists called the Dune Dwellers. Even Wang, one of the Chinese drivers, got into the act, discovering a humerus of the gigantic extinct rhinoceros *Baluchitherium* (now called *Indricotherium*), one of the largest terrestrial mammals that ever existed.

The fearless Andrews was the first to admit that, in spite of his Ph.D., he did not have the requisite patience to inspect terrain for hours and spend hours more excavating with awl and camel-hair brush. He was more likely to be out hunting dinner, reconnoitering the route, or chasing herds of antelope in one of the Dodge cars, to see how fast they could run. His favorite tool was the pickax, and every mangled fossil specimen was said to have "gotten the RCA." By the end of the 1922 trip, Granger, who, unlike Andrews, never earned even a high-school diploma (but did become president of the Explorer's Club), was threatening to shoot his boss if he came too near his dig. "I was the accelerator, Walter was the brake,"[6] Andrews once remarked about their teamwork.

Competitiveness is legendary among paleontologists, but Andrews's accounts reveal an almost comical preoccupation. When Wang, Granger, and Shackelford found an outstanding jaw of an *Indricotherium*, Andrews dreamed of finding the missing skull. The next day, after Andrews had been searching only a short time, there it was, poking up at him from just under the surface. During the expedition's second trip in 1923, Osborn himself, on a circuit of various Museum field sites in Asia, arrived in camp, having just missed the earthquake that had wrecked Yokohama. "Have you prospected that knoll?" Osborn admonished Andrews. In moments, Osborn uncovered the tooth of the extinct mammal *Coryphodon,* a type unknown outside of Europe.

Quite apart from the defense of campsite and caravan from bandits, packs of wild dogs, and poisonous snakes, what lends the tale of the Gobi true excitement is the urgency of its purpose. The expedition was on to something larger than any of the members had imagined, and they pursued it single-mindedly in the face of trying conditions. The camps

were regularly buffeted by dust devils—whirlwinds that could blow off and on for days and were capable of flattening an entire encampment. On one occasion during the 1923 trip, a fierce gust struck with savage force and filled the tents with sand before ripping them away altogether. Precious gramophone records and *Saturday Evening Post*s were scattered across the desert. Granger had just unearthed what would turn out to be some of the most important fossils in the history of mammalian life—the skulls of early, shrewlike mammals that had shared the earth with late dinosaurs. He protected his delicately wrapped prizes with his body while the storm howled around him. By the end of that same trip, the team had unearthed so many fossils that they ran out of material in which to pack them. Packing a fossil for transit involved wrapping it in burlap and a jacket made of a plasterlike paste of wheat flour, much like the cast used to set a broken limb. The group tore up their shirts, socks, pants, underwear, and even Andrews's pajamas for wrapping and used their bread flour to make paste for the jacket.

Unsung Heroes

As much as the Gobi expedition has been romanticized, there remain many unsung heroes. The Chinese and Mongolian assistants, admired by Andrews and Granger, have never been given their due (see opposite). It is also unlikely that the group would have been able to negotiate several sticky situations without the Mongolian representative Badmajapoff. McKenzie Young nearly lost both his hands to frostbite and gangrene after a heroic effort to recover the camel herd from bandits. Herpetologist Clifford Pope, barely into his twenties, amassed the first major collection of Chinese reptiles, which became the basis for his monumental book, *Reptiles of China*. The fish specimens he collected also made possible J. T. Nichols's book *Freshwater Fishes of China*. Working in several provinces of China because there were few reptile species in the Gobi, Pope and his assistants faced often harrowing conditions. His story, too, has never been fully told. One

Above left: Roy Chapman Andrews (top) and Walter Granger examining the skull of an Embolotherium, "a battering-ram-nosed beast," 1928. From a hand-colored lantern slide by James Shackelford

Above right: Hill mapping of the badlands, Urtyn Obo, 1928. From a hand-colored lantern slide by Roy Chapman Andrews

candidate for the most ignored hero, however, must be the expedition's chief geologist, Charles Berkey.

In order to determine the age and significance of a hitherto unknown fossil species, a scientist must understand the geology of its setting. Ages are determined in part by which layers of rock and sediment lie on top of which, and the sequence of events that has produced the layers must be sorted out, a procedure that had never been done for any of the Gobi sites. Berkey and his assistant, Frederick Morris, faced a truly Herculean task. The geologic story, covering tens of thousands of square miles and tens of millions of years, had to be "built up from the ground itself," as Berkey remarked.

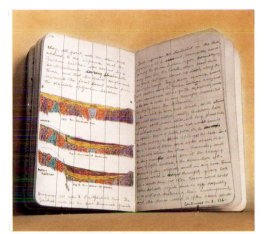

Above: "It is not unusual to make a thousand examinations of rock outcrops in a day," wrote expedition geologist Charles Berkey in 1924, "and record their meaning in whatever way is practicable, considering the speed of travel." These pages from Frederick Morris's notebook show the development of the Djadokhta Formation of Mongolia. From a hand-colored lantern slide by Julius Kirschner

Below: Kan Chuen Pao (Buckshot) excavating a dinosaur fossil with George Olsen near Iren Dabasu, where the first dinosaur fossils were found, 1923. Photograph by Walter Granger

The complex geology of the Gobi is as fascinating as the discovery of any dinosaur egg. In some areas the sediments are thousands of feet deep, having been shuffled and reshuffled by the Earth's deeper warping. Mountains arose and were whittled down and redeposited to form new features. While the rest of the crew had time to smoke a pipe, take in the scenery, and listen to a jazz record on the gramophone or a symphony on the radio from Vladivostok, Berkey and Morris were working. At every stop they were out of the car to check the barometer, check sediments, edit route maps, and take bearings. By their count they took a thousand readings a day, for three thousand miles of travel. We can sympathize with Berkey when he laments:

"No Better Group of Men"

"No better group of men has ever been brought together in China," wrote Walter Granger in 1931. He was acknowledging the extensive contributions of Chinese and Mongolian assistants to the Central Asiatic Expedition.

All field expeditions rely to some degree on local residents who know the lay of the land, but the Central Asiatic was blessed with members who were courageous and resourceful. Andrews's panegyric on his caravan leader Merin gives some idea: "All things are uncertain in Mongolia, yet I believed that when the spring had come, I would sit beside the argul fire in Merin's tent. . . . Cold and snow meant nothing to him—they had been part of his life since childhood. Brigands, too, he had always known. Time after time he had piloted our caravans safely to some desert rendezvous, circling robber bands, sleeping by day in secluded hollows and travelling by night. Time after time he had appeared smiling with his camels when we had well-nigh despaired."

By the end of the expedition, the Gobi team employed three Mongols and twelve Chinese, six of whom served as technical assistants. Among them they collected nearly three-quarters of all the fossil specimens in 1928 and 1930. Herpetologist Clifford Pope's chief assistant, Ah Sen, directed the collection of 1,150 specimens. The most accomplished were Kan Chuen Pao, nicknamed Buckshot, and Liu Hsi Ku. In addition to shouldering the menial camp duties, they were adept collectors. In 1924–25, they were brought to the Museum and trained for eight months in the techniques of fossil identification and excavation. There they were able to see the magnificent fossil displays. "One important thing," wrote Granger, "is that they understand what it is all about—why we go halfway round the earth to dig up 'Dragon Bones.'"

It is one thing to bowl along for a hundred miles over rolling plain, musing on the fortunes of the day or the fame of the morrow, and quite another to be responsible for the geologic . . . meaning of the ground over every mile of the journey. . . . It is physically impossible to record all the observations and assemble them in presentable form during the day's operations, and as soon as camp is pitched, one must therefore retire to his tent and continue on the day's notes far into the night. . . .

There are few better places to sleep than the Desert of Gobi, but it does not fall to the lot of the geologist to take full advantage even of that. After the other members of the expedition have all turned in, the geologist must wait for the proper time, set up the instruments, and "shoot Polaris," so that by means of the stars he may determine where this place is. After all these things are done, little enough time is left for rest.[7]

By the third field trip in 1925, the Central Asiatic Expedition had swelled to fifty members all told, eight automobiles, and a caravan of one hundred twenty-five camels. Although its work had barely begun, political turmoil forced it from the field in 1926 and 1927 and reduced both its size and agenda when it returned to the field for a fourth time, in 1928. The xenophobic climate also made negotiating of-

ficial permission from the Chinese increasingly difficult. In 1928, for example, all the fossil specimens gathered that season were seized by the government, and only strenuous negotiations won them back. While it is almost certain that the declining financial fortunes of the expedition's patrons after the Wall Street crash would have suspended or cut back the project—just as Andrews was envisioning the creation of an international Asiatic research center in China—the straw that actually broke the camel's back was the Chinese government's demand that the expedition turn over half of the 1930 season's collections. Today such arrangements are the norm, for the countries involved have common scientific interests. With the current joint Gobi expeditions, *all* recovered fossils are the property of the Mongolian Academy of Sciences. They are on long-term loan to the Museum for study.

Where the Dinosaur Laid Its Eggs

What, in the final summation, did the American "men of the dragon

Above left: Tea in the Gobi: Henry Fairfield Osborn, president of the Museum, taking tea with Roy Chapman Andrews while on a site visit to the Central Asiatic Expedition, near Kalgan Pass, 1923. Photograph by James Shackelford

Above right: Enjoying a concert by electric Victrola, Urtyn Obo, 1928. Walter Granger wrote of "those calm Gobi evenings in midsummer, when . . . we light our pipes and draw our camp chairs in a semicircle in front of the mess tent, and either listen to a symphony or just sit and enjoy the solitude of the place." Photograph by James Shackelford

bones" find in their five trips to the Gobi? Most important, they found sites at which to dig. Just at the end of the 1922 trip, near a well called Shabarakh Usu (now Bayn-Dzak; *usu* means "well" in Mongol), they came upon a breathtaking series of sandstone buttes that Andrews named the Flaming Cliffs, and what they found there made them hasten back the next year. This was the site of the mother lode of fossils of the parrot-beaked *Protoceratops*, the small relative of a familiar horned dinosaur giant, *Triceratops*. Fossils were everywhere, including that rarity, a

complete skull, uncovered in 1925. The finds at Shabarakh Usu made it clear that the Gobi had been as populous with late dinosaurs as the western United States. There were so many *Pro-toceratops* fossils in the field that the team was able to gather a complete life-cycle sequence of the beast, from cradle to grave. Paleontologists have since dubbed these creatures "Mesozoic sheep": they seem to have been the favorite food of every carnivorous dinosaur and larger carnivorous lizard.

Also at Shabarakh Usu, the di-nosaurs laid their eggs—dozens of them—in organized nests preserved by the dry desert sands. The eggs were a wholly unexpected treasure, and members of the expedition risked their safety to unearth them high up on an overhanging cliff. These finds have opened a window on dinosaur social behavior: did they, for example, return to their nests

to nurture their young, as birds do? Their precise nest-building indicates that they might have. Further, where there were eggs, there were also stealers of eggs—the small dinosaur predator *Oviraptor*. The team also unearthed evidence of a far fiercer predator, *Velociraptor*, which has since gained gruesome notoriety through the film *Jurassic Park*. The Flaming Cliffs contained so much material for study that the site was at the top of the 1991 Gobi expedition's agenda.

In the eyes of chief scientist William Diller Matthew, the most important fossil find at the Flaming Cliffs was one of the tiniest, and it was not a dinosaur. It was the skull of a placental (live-bearing, as opposed to egg-laying) mammal, and it occupied the same strata of rock as the dinosaur eggs. Prior to the Gobi expedition, only one such ancient skull had ever been found. Evidence of such early mammals had been limited to mere fragments of jaws or teeth. Here was an opportunity really to learn something about the origin of mammals. "Do your utmost to get some other skulls," wrote Matthew to Granger and the 1925 expedition. They did.

Andrews called Ulu Usu, which lies south of the Flaming Cliffs, the "junction of hell with the Sair Usu trail," but it had not always been so inhospitable. Once, 40 to 50 million years before, it had been verdant, and home to titanotheres, relatives of tapirs and horses. These hoofed herbivores probably migrated across the Bering land bridge from North America to Asia, exactly opposite from the direction speculated by Osborn and Matthew. Ulu Usu was a titanothere mine. The expedition found some fourteen skulls in two weeks, so many, in fact,

"The Wild Places of the World as a Playground"

Roy Chapman Andrews (1884–1960) regarded it as inevitable that "I should live the life that gave me the wild places of the world as a playground." Andrews, the Indiana Jones of his day, found the institution that would give him the opportunities and a mentor—Henry Fairfield Osborn—who would urge him toward the horizon.

Born in Beloit, Wisconsin, Andrews grew up studying nature by living close to it. While still in his teens he, like Osborn, was involved in an accident that resulted in tragic death. Osborn lost an older brother, and Andrews saw his best friend drown. He carried with him regret for the life he was unable to save. Although it has never been acknowledged, this may have contributed to the strong bond between the two men. At Beloit College, Andrews began to develop the skill in taxidermy that would bring him to the Museum, as it did African explorers Carl Akeley and James Chapin, among others. Andrews came to New York with no introduction; he simply forced his way into the Museum, asking for any job he could get. He started by scrubbing floors at forty dollars a month. Director Hermon Bumpus moved him to the preparation department and encouraged him to work on his thesis on whales for a doctorate at Columbia University. In 1908 Bumpus sent him on a whaling expedition to British Columbia. Andrews would not spend twelve months in one place for the next twenty-five years.

He made his scientific contributions early on, for exploration itself soon became his raison d'être. He even married the sister of polar explorer George Borup. Yvette Borup accompanied him into Mongolia in 1919. He traveled the world for the Museum, and, by his own count, he cheated death "only" nine times. Nothing seems to have fazed him except Walter Granger's "odious pipe." As vividly as any adventure, a brief moment shared with Granger in China reveals the essence of Andrews. The two had just returned from the Gobi in the fall of 1922 and been feted at Kalgan by the British-American Tobacco Company. That first night back they could not sleep:

Finally Walter said: "Hell, Roy, it's this damned bed. Let's get our sleeping bags and bunk outside."
   We stole out like thieves, unrolled our fur bags on the earth of a defunct flower bed, looked up at the stars for a few minutes while the soft wind caressed our faces, and dropped into a dreamless sleep.

"There is a more subtle tragedy that waits for adventurers than ruin, penurious old age, rags, contempt," William Bolitho once wrote in Twelve Against the Gods. *"It is that he is doomed to cease to be an adventurer." By his own admission, Andrews was wholly unsuited for administrative work, and his appointment as director of the Museum in 1935 after Dr. William Sherwood suffered a serious heart attack was an unfortunate conclusion to a distinguished career. Osborn had just retired as president, and an era was ending. After the Wall Street crash, the Museum's trustees could not support the ambitious program of exploration, research, and exhibition-hall construction. Tough choices were called for, of a kind Andrews had never had to make. Curators and some trustees were openly critical. "Often," he wrote, "I have presented a budget with a fifty-thousand-dollar deficit and have had the Board regard me as some evil smelling object." By 1941, Andrews had had enough and resigned—a "square peg in a round hole." He retired to Connecticut and spent much of his time writing books on natural history, evolution, and his own travels.*

that Granger suggested publishing an expedition newspaper titled *The Daily Skull.* Here, again, Granger had to use his body to shield his specimens from whirlwinds.

In 1922, when the expedition first reached Tsagan Nor, the White Lake, which lies at the southeastern end of the Altai Mountains, the sight was like a beautiful dream at the edge of the desert. Three years later, though, drought had shrunk it so much that the eminent archaeologist Nels C. Nelson, who had been brought along to search systematically for "ancient man," dismissed it with the words "little, and it stinks." Nevertheless, it in-

Opposite: "The camel is a thing of spare parts," wrote Charles Berkey, chief geologist. The camel caravan crosses the desolate dunes near Tsagan Nor in search of water, 1925. Photograph by James Shackelford

Above: Roy Chapman Andrews in camp, 1928. Photograph by James Shackelford

Left: The expedition named this badlands camp Wolf Camp, because of the animals that preyed upon the sheep and goats of the Mongols. Nearby, in 1930, they discovered a trove of fossils of the shovel-tusked mastodon Platybelodon. Photograph by Albert Thomson

spired artist Francis L. Jaques to create one of the Museum's most evocative backdrops for a habitat group, depicting the bird life of the Gobi on display in the Hall of Birds of the World. Nor did the White Lake disappoint the paleontologists, for its environs yielded further substantial evidence of the ancient rhinoceros *Indricotherium*, which may have grown to a height of nearly fifteen feet.

The Chinese government's decision to restrict access to Outer Mongolia in 1928 was the beginning of a series of frustrations that would eventually end the Central Asiatic Expedition. But the cloud of a reduced itinerary had a silver lining; it led to the discovery of a final important site.

The frontier of Inner Mongolia became the boundary of exploration, and, unable to travel farther, the expedition worked to the west of its original areas. The scientists had heard rumors of bones as large as a man's body somewhere in the east near a mysterious lake. After a number of unsuccessful tries, Andrews and his party camped at the edge of what had once been an inland sea but was now rugged badlands, populated mostly by wolves. In the autumn of 1928, at "Wolf Camp," the team had just enough time to unearth the jaw of something spectacular—a much more recent mammal, a tusked, shovel-jawed mastodon, *Platybelodon*.

Returning to the area in 1930, the expedition was aided by the sleuthing presence of Père Teilhard de Chardin. The Jesuit paleontologist had been searching for fossil remains of early humans in the Ordos desert of Inner Mongolia during the 1920s. Just six miles from Wolf Camp, Teilhard de Chardin discovered a mastodon dying ground so rich in

fossils that, once again, the expedition was able to reconstruct an extinct creature's entire life history. A skeleton was even found within the skeletal womb of its mother. Judging by their huge size, these were indeed the bones of legend.

The Central Asiatic Expedition closed its headquarters for good in 1932. It had not found fossils of early humans, although both Nels Nelson and Teilhard de Chardin had found extensive evidence of a Stone Age civilization. Despite widespread unrest in China, the Museum fully expected to resume the search. Western scientists never imagined they would have to content themselves with rumor and secondhand information for nearly sixty years.

Politics turned Mongolia into a no-man's land, a vast buffer zone between China and the Soviet Union. Off limits to non-Communists after it came under Soviet influence, it was explored extensively by Russian paleontologists, who kept one eye on the ground and another eye on the border. Intelligence-gathering responsibilities did not prevent them from

making further dramatic finds. Revisiting many of the Central Asiatic sites and pushing into the Nemegt Basin, southwest of the Flaming Cliffs, Soviet teams unearthed the remains of gigantic dinosaurs from the Cretaceous period, including *Tryannosaurus*-like predators, creatures the Museum scientists never discovered.

The Soviets prospected in the 1940s and early 1950s. In the 1960s, as Mongolia developed its own scientific establishment, combined Polish-Mongolian teams took the field. Led by the outstanding woman scientist, Zofia Kielan-Jaworowska, they unearthed the remains of more late Cretaceous dinosaurs and mammals and fully confirmed the richness of the Mongolian fossil record. They also set the stage for the return of the American Museum of Natural History.

Fossil Dreams

All paleontologists dream of the unknown fossils they hope to find. For Walter Granger, it was the dinosaur egg—or, better yet, an entire nest of eggs. This, his "futile daydream," came true in the Gobi. The Gobi has become a place where dreams are fulfilled and theories inspired. The dream of Mark Norell, paleontologist on the combined Mongolian Academy of Sciences–American Museum of Natural History Gobi Expedition, is to find a complete skeleton of the earliest modern bird, a fossil that might illuminate the relationship between modern birds and dinosaurs. Museum paleontologists Malcolm McKenna and Michael Novacek dream of finding the earliest placental mammal. But their greatest wish was realized when they were offered the chance to walk the Gobi.

McKenna and paleontologist Edwin Colbert, now retired from the Museum, kept up contacts with Russian, Polish, and Mongolian scientists for decades. McKenna himself briefly visited Mongolia in 1964. In 1988, the president of the Mongolian Academy of Sciences visited the Museum and discussed the possibility of a joint expedition. A few months later, a telegram arrived from Mongolia asking, in effect, "Where are you?" Then in 1990 Mongolia's Soviet-backed regime fell. Within weeks, Mongolian representatives returned to the Museum and invited its scientists back to the Gobi. A small team was quickly assembled and traveled to Mongolia for a few weeks to reconnoiter. Even in that short time it managed to secure interesting and important specimens. Then, with backing from the National Science Foundation, the International Research Exchange

Foundation, private foundations, and the Museum's Childs Frick Endowment, the Mongolians and Americans assembled a team and an itinerary. They were in the field just over a year after a formal agreement for a series of expeditions was signed.

With only ten people, modern equipment, three four-by-four vehicles, and a gasoline truck instead of camels, the modern team could travel light and much faster than the Central Asiatic Expedition. There were other obvious changes. Food was carried freeze-dried, not hunted; the vast antelope herds had dwindled, and caravans of two hundred or more camels were a thing of the past. Gone too were the remarkable religious compounds called lamasaries, where as many as several thousand monks lived and practiced a Mongolian version of Tibetan Buddhism. With the fall of Communism, some of these were just beginning to be rebuilt. Towns existed where none had before, including one of the largest in the Gobi, Dalan Dzadgad. There was no need to "shoot Polaris" on these trips; positions were fixed and routes plotted using an electronic direction finder linked to a satellite system. And although water was still at a premium and whirlwinds could make setting up camp an adventure, the desert had become a safer place. The worst thing to fear, according to Mark Norell, was being injured in an accident—falling down a cliff, for example, or scalding oneself with boiling tea.

Retracing parts of the Central Asiatic route, the group was able to assess the old sites and begin prospecting for new ones. On the first extended trip in 1991, the team was aided by Mongolia's most experienced paleontologist,

Demberelyin Dashzeveg. They traveled a clockwise circle from Ulan Bator, in the opposite direction from Andrews and his party, ending up at the Flaming Cliffs.

After the thrill of arrival, the Flaming Cliffs, still glowing as red as ever, proved something of a disappointment, precisely because they offered what decades of accounts said they would. Although there were, and still are, fossils to be found—the armored dinosaur *Ankylosaurus*, for example—the site is "played out," its data largely digested. Berkey and Morris had wandered widely in the 1920s, however, and one of the spots they passed through, now called Tugrugeen Shireh, forty-five miles from the cliffs, has turned out to be a treasure trove of fossils of early mammals and a small dinosaur called *Mononykus*. The discoveries are shaking some family trees.

Mononykus ("single claw") is a theropod dinosaur—a meateater with hips like a lizard that moved about on two legs. In essence, it was a flightless bird, a small, swift creature with single claws instead of arms, whose age is estimated at 70 to 80 million years. From the middle down, it looked a bit like a prehistoric turkey. In 1987 a Mongolian scientist, Perle Altangerel, found a nearly complete skeleton and named it. (Perle, who collaborates on the current Gobi expeditions, also discovered the fossils of two dinosaurs, *Velociraptor* and *Protoceratops*, entwined in battle.) Malcolm McKenna found his own specimen of *Mononykus* at Tugrug on the 1992 Gobi trip.

It is generally accepted that birds evolved from dinosaurs, but the path of that evolution remains obscure. *Archaeopteryx*, the oldest bird, was feathered and probably airborne 70 million

years before *Mononykus* appeared, but its anatomical relation to modern birds is uncertain, perhaps even misleading. It may have been an evolutionary dead end, and the true bird precursor may have come later, with *Mononykus* as its closest relative. This hypothetical latecomer in the aviary is the fossil bird Norell dreams of finding. It would confirm that the ability to fly actually evolved twice, in two different lineages, at two widely separate times.

Ironically, *Mononykus* had been nesting in the Museum collec-

Above: Paleontologist James Clark prospecting for fossils in the badlands of Mongolia, 1991. The head-down pose is characteristic of experienced fossil hunters.

Left: Perle Atangerel (left) of the Mongolian Academy of Sciences and Mark Norell excavating the bones of an Ankylosaurus, *an armored dinosaur from the late Cretaceous period, 1991*

Opposite, below: James Clark excavating fossils near the Flaming Cliffs, Mongolian Academy of Sciences–American Museum of Natural History Gobi Expedition, 1991

tions since 1923, when Granger found a "birdlike dinosaur" fossil in the Gobi. It lay thus in nomenclatural limbo for seventy years until the modern Gobi expeditions renewed interest in the Central Asiatic fossils, and paleontologist Bryn Mader recognized in the dust-covered red lump something truly extraordinary.

The Age of Mammals

Many of the creatures trying to avoid becoming the prey of *Mononykus* and its dinosaur kin at Tugrug and elsewhere would be surprisingly at home in our world, for they were rodentlike and shrewlike mammals, which appeared nearly 200 million years ago. By the time the large dinosaurs became extinct, mammals had already diverged into their modern groups—into egg-layers,

the pouched marsupials, and livebearers. How far along the evolutionary path had they traveled? To McKenna and Novacek, finds at Tugrug and another Gobi site,

Naran Bulak, suggest a long way.

These Cretaceous mammals had to stay small to survive among the predatory giants. Their tiny, fragile fossils represent

the paleontological needle in the haystack. Jaws can measure less than an inch, teeth a mere speck. No wonder Granger defended his specimens so zealously. One of the most interesting is *Zalambdalestes*—Granger's fossil prize. McKenna believes it to be the earliest relative of modern rabbits. Seeking evidence, he and his colleagues have used a CAT scan to examine a skull found by James Clark. Their laboratory work reveals the anatomical diversity of mammalian life in a world mammals did not yet rule.

This diversity was dramatically demonstrated in the summer of 1993 with the expedition's accidental discovery of rich new fossil beds in the Gobi. En route west to the Nemegt Basin—the region prospected by Mongolian-Polish teams—the gas truck got stuck. Just a few steps beyond lay the skulls and skeletons of thirteen therapod dinosaurs, including four specimens of *Mononykus* and a more-or-less complete skeleton of *Oviraptor,* one hundred seventy-five lizards, and one hundred forty-seven mammals, not to mention nests of dinosaur eggs and hundreds of other dinosaur skeletons, which the team had time only to note but not to excavate.

The new site, Ukhaa Tolgod, has introduced some previously unfamiliar names into the fossil pantheon, including the small dinosaur *Troodon*—another link in Norell's chain leading from the Cretaceous dinosaurs to the robins in our backyard. Most spectacular was the first discovery of the fossil embryo of a carnivorous dinosaur. Probably an *Oviraptor,* it was tucked inside its potato-sized egg.

Common among the Tolgod mammals are a group called multituberculates, a presumably egg-laying family that survived the

The American Museum of Natural History in the Field:

Asia

Barnum Brown India-Burma Expedition—1922–23 *Fossil mammal remains from southern Asia had been known since the earliest days of British colonialism. Their significance was so great that the American Museum of Natural History decided to launch a southern Asiatic expedition. Mrs. Henry Clay Frick promised to support the Museum's indefatigable collector-scientist Barnum Brown in a wide-ranging field program in India (today's India and Pakistan) in 1922 and Burma in 1923. Employing only local assistants, Brown made a large and important collection that included early primates from the Siwalik Hills of India west to the Salt Range in Pakistan. In Burma he pushed up the Irawaddy River to outcrops in jungle clearings to secure the finest collection of Eocene mammals from that area. This included the earliest known primates from Asia, the group sought in vain by the Central Asiatic Expedition.*

Morden-Clark Expedition—1926 *From the vale of Kashmir to the Trans-Siberian Railroad is a distance as great as that from Corpus Christi, Texas, to Winnipeg, Canada. Mammalogist William Morden and preparator James Clark traversed that arduous route by troika, yak, ox cart, camel, and foot in quest of species little studied or collected in the West. These included the rare mountain sheep Ovis poli, first written about by Marco Polo, and the illik, a roe deer of Central Asia, which Clark was seeking for an exhibit in the Hall of Asiatic Mammals at the Museum. Crossing the Himalayas and into Chinese Turkestan, the expedition swelled to some sixty porters, several of whom had to drop out because of the grueling conditions. Once Morden and Clark had their specimens, the dangerous part of the journey began. They were supposed to meet the Central Asiatic Expedition in the field, but war in China forced Andrews and company back to Peking. Morden and Clark were captured by Mongol soldiers, mistaken for spies, and tortured. They expected to be shot, but the soldiers had a change of heart. Later, in Siberia, they battled subzero temperatures, deep snow, and mountains to reach the railroad. They eventually brought themselves and their specimens to safety in Peking.*

Cutting-Vernay Tibetan Expedition—1935 *When Museum trustees Suydam Cutting and Arthur Vernay were invited to Tibet, it marked the culmination of a five-year negotiation, much of it with the Dalai Lama himself. Foreigners had to obtain special permission to cross Tibetan territory, and entry to the capital of Lhasa—Cutting's goal—was virtually forbidden. After a 1928 expedition in the region with*

Theodore Roosevelt's son Kermit, Cutting began to correspond with the Dalai Lama. An elaborate ritual of gift-giving ensued, which included among other items a pair of dachshunds (the Dalai Lama had wanted an ostrich). The subject of a visit to Lhasa had not yet been broached when suddenly, in 1933, the Dalai Lama died. But a reservoir of goodwill sustained the negotiations and the gift-giving, and Cutting was invited to Shigatse, Tibet's second most important city.

Cutting believed that once the Tibetans observed the expedition, it would be granted passage to Lhasa. He was right. Attended with elaborate formality, Cutting and Vernay were allowed to visit such sites as the magnificent Potala, winter palace of the late Dalai Lama, where they noted such anomalies as Dodge automobiles (unused) and antique French furniture. Under the Buddhist injunction against hunting, the expedition secured no zoological specimens but did manage to bring back many objects of Tibetan material culture.

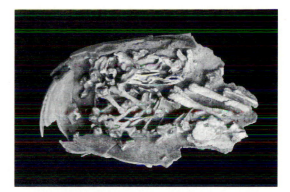

Oviraptor *egg, containing a fossil embryo, discovered in the Gobi in 1993*

giant dinosaurs only to fall before the increasingly prevalent placentals. In six decades of excavations in the Gobi prior to the discovery of Ukhaa Tolgod, the Central Asiatic, Polish-Mongolian, and Russian-Mongolian expeditions discovered close to one hundred mammal skulls and skeletons. In the space of two weeks, the Mongolian-American team unearthed more than twice that amount—in an area of only one square mile.

With the modern Gobi discoveries, we can begin to see just how complex the animal ecology of the Cretaceous period really was and how ready mammals were for a great and diverse leap forward 65 million years ago. Their diet was broad, from seeds, nuts, and dinosaur eggs to fishes and large lizards. They moved in a variety of ways and lived in a range of habitats, brought young into the world and reared them in diverse ways. To be sure, the late Cretaceous was the Age of Dinosaurs, but to a nearly equal degree it was also the beginning of the Age of Mammals. The little creatures were just waiting for the big creatures to get out of the way. How that happened is still a mystery, still controversial. But when it happened, the living world we know today truly began to take shape.

Crossing the mountains of Kashmir at the foot of the Burzil Pass, Morden-Clark Expedition, 1926. Photograph by James Clark

The Poles:
"For Whom East and West Shall Have Vanished"

Midnight sun behind an iceberg, near Etah, Greenland, Crocker Land Expedition, 1913–17. From a hand-colored lantern slide by Donald MacMillan

And now there came both mist and snow,
And it grew wondrous cold;
And ice, mast-high, came floating by,
As green as emerald

And through the drifts the snowy clifts
Did send a dismal sheen:
Nor shapes of men nor beasts we ken—
The ice was all between.

—Samuel Coleridge, "The Rime of the
Ancient Mariner"

Arctic Dreams

LEARNED MEN LONG SPECULATED that the North Pole was the site of the Garden of Hesperides, the Garden of Eden, even the lost continent of Atlantis. Whatever might lie at the Pole, Christopher Columbus thought it would be quite easy to reach it; one would pass by it on the most direct route to the Indies. In February 1477, Columbus sailed three hundred miles north from Iceland without encountering any ice. From this, he sanguinely concluded that conditions at the North Pole would not be too extreme for men to withstand.

The intervening five hundred years have banished geographers' dreams and explorers' optimism. The polar regions, north and south, have proven the most inhospitable of El Dorados. They have taken the lives of

the unprepared and the experienced alike. These realms have provoked superhuman feats of courage and endurance over the centuries, but they have yielded their secrets stingily. Indeed, well into the past century—hundreds of years after the globe had first been circled—geographers and explorers could only speculate on what they might find at both poles. As late as 1866, Isaac Hayes, echoing Columbus, proposed that the North Pole was situated in the middle of an iceless ocean. One had simply to get past the drift ice that lay to the north of the land masses of Europe, Asia, and North America, and the way to the pole would be free sailing. Hayes claimed to have seen the open Arctic Ocean from his "farthest" north, along the channel between Greenland and Ellesmere Island. In 1886, when Robert E. Peary first em-

barked on what was to be twenty-three years of polar exploration, the thick ice cap of the interior of Greenland had not yet been crossed, and Greenland's insularity had not been proved.

Scientists and explorers associated with the American Museum of Natural History changed all this. They transformed the polar regions from imaginary territories to actual places, with contours, climates, ecologies, and cultures. Beginning with Robert E. Peary's dog-sledge dash to the North Pole, through joint NASA–American Museum of Natural History studies of Antarctic meteorites, the Museum's expeditions span the history of modern polar exploration. Although Peary and other intrepid voyagers replaced mystery with knowledge, their exploits have only added to the mythic stature of the Earth's antipodes.

"I Shall Find a Way or Make One"

In 1880, the twenty-eight-year-old Peary, a naval engineer, was sent to Nicaragua to conduct surveys for a Nicaraguan canal. At that time, he had never traveled farther north than his home state of Maine, but, imagining himself an explorer in the tradition of Columbus, he looked to the poles to find terra incognita. As he sailed past San Salvador, the island that had welcomed Columbus to the New World, he had a premonition of his destiny: "Purple against the yellow sunset as it was nearly four hundred years ago when it smiled a welcome to the man whose fame can be equalled only by him who shall one day stand with 360 degrees of longitude beneath his motionless foot, and for whom East and

West shall have vanished; the discoverer of the North Pole."[1]

The idea of discovering the North Pole seems to have been planted in Peary's mind fairly early on. He had a long list of cautionary examples from which to learn. For the past four centuries, the goal of most polar explorations had not been the North Pole at all, but rather the Northwest Passage from Europe to Asia. As early as the sixth century A.D., Irish monks had crossed the icy seas to Greenland. Brendan was one who made the crossing to those glacial shores, where he is supposed to have commented to his helmsman: "Run the boat now through an opening that we may get a closer view of the wonderful works of God."[2] Indeed, the wondrous formations of this island of ice must have seemed otherworldly to these first explorers. The Irish monks were followed by a group of colonists from Iceland, who in 986 arrived at Greenland, where, records indicate, they remained until the fourteenth century. The search for the Northwest Passage did not get under way in earnest until 1576, when Captain Martin Frobisher set off from England, convinced that there were sea routes across the poles, both north and south, and that his enterprise was "the only thing of the world that was left yet undone whereby a notable mind might be made famous and fortunate."[3] He made three unsuccessful voyages; on his last, he lost forty men from his fleet of fifteen ships.

Expeditions to discover the Northwest Passage followed one after another, often with great loss of life and property, but the first man to attempt the North Pole with a large-scale, organized expedition was the Englishman Lieutenant Edward Parry. In 1819, Parry had sailed a ship into Lancaster Sound as far as Melville Island. He was halfway to Alaska before his way was blocked by ice. Even so, he had the distinction of being the first man to pass directly north of the magnetic North Pole and to witness the strange phenomenon of the compass needle pointing due south. In 1827, Parry proposed to reach the North Pole on foot from his base at Spitzbergen, a large island lying halfway between the northern coast of Norway and the Pole. The British plan had a fundamental weakness. The example of the Eskimos proved that the only reliable form of transportation in the Arctic was light sledges drawn by dogs. Parry had brought reindeer to pull his sledges, but when this plan proved impracticable, he had his men pull the sledges, which were really boats fitted up with runners that could be removed to ferry them across open water. The sledges were heavy and unwieldy, and the expedition got no farther than 150 miles north of their base, with 435 miles still to go to the Pole. Nonetheless, Parry set a record of "farthest north" that remained untouched for the next forty-eight years.

The most disastrous expedition, in terms of loss of life, was the one the British Admiralty sent out in 1845 under the leadership of Sir John Franklin. The expedition's ships, the *Erebus* and the *Terror*, with a combined crew of 129 men, were last seen in July of that year by a whaling vessel in Baffin Bay. An 1859 search party did not return with any survivors, although it did come across skeletons and relics from the ships and a record, discovered on King William Island, west of Baffin Island, of Franklin's death and the crews' abandonment of the ships, imprisoned in the ice.

As a child, Robert Peary had been inspired by the writings of Dr. Elisha Kent Kane, who launched an expedition in 1852, ostensibly to search for Franklin and his party. In fact, Kane was attempting to reach the North Pole across what he believed was an open polar sea. His party suffered scurvy, death, and the loss of their ship, but Kane survived to write the first account of life among the Eskimos of northwest Greenland.

It was not until 1906, after a three-year voyage in a seventy-foot fishing boat, the *Gjoa*, that Roald Amundsen and his five crewmates finally made their way through from the Atlantic Ocean to the Pacific Ocean. The Northwest Passage was a reality. Only one member of that expedition died, of pneumonia, even though the party was forced to spend two years on King William Island, where most of the members of the Franklin expedition had starved to death. Amundsen had learned the ultimate secret of polar exploration, one that was to prove vital to the success of both Peary and Museum explorer Donald MacMillan: in the far north it is essential to live like the native polar Eskimos, to wear their clothing, to eat their food, to live in their shelters, and to travel as they do.

The man who made the greatest impression on Peary was Lieutenant Adolphus W. Greely of the U.S. Army. The impression, however, was thoroughly negative. For Peary, Greely's disastrous adventure represented everything that an expedition should not be. In 1881, Greely established a base at Fort Conger in Grinnell Land, on the northwest coast of Ellesmere Island, where he spent two years collecting meteorological and magnetic data. When his ship, the *Proteus*, did not return to pick him up as expected in 1883, Greely headed south, expecting to find supplies cached along the route, but there were none. At Cape Sabine, the party set up camp, but they could find nothing more than sea birds and tiny brine shrimp on which to subsist. Before long, their diet consisted of lichen soup, tea, old clothing, and shoes. When help finally arrived at their camp on Cape Sabine (since referred to as Starvation Camp), in June of 1884, only Greely and six crew members remained from an original party of twenty-five. There were strong indications that the survivors had been reduced to cannibalism.

Peary was certain that the deaths of Greely's men could easily have been prevented, and over a period of twenty-three years in the Arctic, he would prove it, losing only two men, neither one to starvation. Peary actually spent the winter of 1898–99 at Fort Conger. He tore down Greely's large station and replaced it with three efficient Eskimo-style structures. As he lay on his bunk that winter, he scratched on the wall a quotation from Seneca that proved to be a polar prophecy: *Inveniam viam aut faciam* (I shall find a way or make one). Although he was confined to his bed in excruciating pain for six weeks because his feet had frozen, he did not starve, because the Eskimos with his party had found plentiful game to support them. The explorer/anthropolo-

Vilhjalmur Stefansson and the Copper Eskimos

In the fall of 1907, Vilhjalmur Stefansson visited Henry Fairfield Osborn at the American Museum of Natural History to ask for support for an expedition to a region of the Arctic that was still unknown to the white man. Stefansson had studied anthropology at Harvard with the former head of the Museum's Department of Anthropology, Frederic Ward Putnam, and had already spent several years in the Arctic with the Anglo-American Polar Expedition. On Herschel Island, a whaling station in the Northwest Territories, he had heard an intriguing report from a renegade whaling captain of a strange people who lived and dressed like Eskimos but looked more like Europeans. When the Eskimos who had been on board the ship confirmed this account, Stefansson decided to look for the tribe. At their meeting, Stefansson asked Osborn for $2,000 to buy supplies for himself and his partner, zoologist Rudolph Martin Anderson. Impressed by Stefansson, Osborn agreed to support the expedition. As he later wrote in a foreword to Stefansson's My Life with the Eskimos, *"Here, I thought, might be another Nansen or Peary or Shackleton, only awaiting a fair opportunity to put his potentiality into actual service."*

Unfortunately, the supplies never reached Stefansson, who was unable to communicate with the outside world. For four years, the two men lived off the land. In the meantime, the Museum spent close to $14,000 searching for them.

Two years into the expedition, at Point Wise, across the Dolphin and Union Straits from Victoria Island, Stefansson discovered a pile of driftwood on a beach that had been hacked with a primitive adzlike tool. Following the sled tracks and footprints that led away from the beach, his party went from deserted village to deserted village, finally turning north across the ice. The Eskimos accompanying him were nervous about following the tracks, which they were certain belonged to the "People of the Caribou Antler," who were said to kill all strangers. After several days, about halfway across the straits, they came upon a group of Eskimos sitting at seal holes. When they approached one of the sealers, he jumped to his feet, holding a large knife. "The frightened sealer began a monotonous, staccato intonation that seemed to be merely sound without words," Stefansson wrote in his autobiography, Discovery. *"I later learned that this was a defense against being struck dumb, since a man confronted by a spirit will never speak again if he fails to make a sound with every breath he draws."*

One of the Eskimos with Stefansson, Tannaumirk, was able to convince the sealer that they were not spirits, and the entire party was welcomed into the village, which was built on the six-foot-thick ice of the straits. Stefansson likened these Eskimos to "the hunting tribes of Britain and Gaul during the Ice Age." They gathered their food with weapons made of copper, and so came to be known as the Copper

"Blond Eskimos," men and one woman, Prince Albert Sound, Northwest Territories, Canada, 1911. Photograph by Vilhjalmur Stefansson

Eskimos. Their dialect was very close to that of the Mackenzie River Eskimos to the west, among whom Stefansson had lived for three years, so Stefansson had no trouble communicating with them. Although they had never set eyes on white men before, they knew of them, as Stefansson described in his autobiography: "The white man, they told me, live farthest to the east of all people. They were said to have various physical deformities and to be of a strangely eccentric disposition. Sometimes when they gave valuable things to an Eskimo they would take no pay from them. At other times they wanted exorbitant prices for useless articles or mere curiosities. White people would not eat good, ordinary food, but subsisted on various things that a normal person would not think of forcing himself to swallow except in case of starvation. The strange thing was that the white man would have had better things to eat if they wanted to. Seals, whales, fish, and even caribou abound in their country." The Copper Eskimos did not think that Stefansson was a white man. His speech was like that of Tannaumirk, who had told them he was a Kupagmiut. They did not find Stefansson's blue-gray eyes or light-brown hair strange because he resembled their neighbors to the north on Victoria Island, the Haneragmiut, the People-of-the-Shore.

Several days later, Stefansson and his party came across a tribe of the Haneragmiut people—the "Blond Eskimos." Although they had been told about them, they were not prepared for what they saw. Three of the men resembled typical Scandinavians. In fact, one of the Eskimos with the party exclaimed: "Three of them look like white foremast hands on a whaler, and aren't they huge!" Stefansson spent the next year living with the Victoria Island Eskimos and their neighbors of Coronation Gulf. Of the thousand or so persons that he saw, ten had blue eyes. A number of others had light brown beards, reddish hair, or

gist Vilhjalmur Stefansson, who also journeyed to the Arctic for the American Museum of Natural History, summed up what set Peary apart from those who preceded him: "Those before Peary pursued explorations with a heroic frame of mind. They did not set out to adapt themselves to difficulties; their whole purpose was to do or die in their attempt. Peary quickly discovered the fallacy of this attitude. He discovered the arctic is a perfectly friendly place when difficulties of existence are taken into consideration and measures are taken to meet these conditions."[4]

Peary's first trip to the Arctic was basically a reconnaissance mission, financed by a five-hundred-dollar loan from his mother. His immediate aim was to learn about arctic navigation, experiment with equipment, and explore the conditions of the ice cap. His larger goal was to cross Greenland from one side to the other, for by 1886, few explorers had penetrated Greenland's ice cap, a region of deep crevasses, icy slopes, and sudden blizzards. On his first attempt, Peary climbed to a greater elevation and went farther inland than any previous explorer. This first taste of arctic exploration whetted his appetite. He was recalled to Nicaragua to work as sub-chief engineer for the Maritime Canal Company, but he continued formulating plans for further work in the north.

In the fall of 1888, the news came that Norwegian explorer Fridtjof Nansen had completed the first crossing of Greenland. With this news, Peary had to revise his plans: he would attempt the far more demanding crossing from northwest to northeast Greenland, a route that would allow him to map unknown terri-

curly hair. The facial features of a large number of them resembled those of persons of mixed Eskimo and white descent.

On September 8, 1912, Stefansson and Anderson steamed into Seattle. The next morning, the Seattle Daily Times *printed an article with the headline: "American Explorer Discovers Lost Tribe of Whites, Descendants of Leif Ericson." The sensational story was fabricated by the reporter. It was picked up by news services around the world, however, and in the uproar that followed, the Museum was inundated with letters and telegrams branding Stefansson a charlatan and demanding that he be fired. The Museum stood behind him, but the damage to his reputation was substantial. Initially, Fridtjof Nansen compared him unfavorably to Dr. Cook but later withdrew his criticism. Roald Amundsen, who had seen no trace of these Eskimos during his Northwest Passage, continued his attacks for years. Stefansson would defend his conclusions for the next five decades. He remained convinced of his discovery, pointing to many historical references to strange Eskimos, beginning with John Davis, who visited Greenland in 1586. To Stefansson, there was only one possible explanation for the Blond Eskimos: since Greenland can be reached without difficulty from Victoria Island, they must have been descendants of Scandinavians who had mixed with the Eskimos of Labrador and Greenland from the eleventh to the fourteenth century.*

tory and to determine the insularity of Greenland.

After raising $10,000 in subscriptions, on June 6, 1891, Peary set sail in the sealer *Kite* from Brooklyn, New York. The boat was under the command of Richard Pike, who ten years earlier had taken Lieutenant Greely and his party north on their fateful journey. Peary's party included Dr. Frederick Cook, with whom Peary was later to be embroiled in the bitter controversy over the discovery of the North Pole; Peary's wife, Josephine, the first white woman to spend the winter in the Arctic; and Peary's black manservant, Matthew Henson, who would accompany Peary on all his expeditions during the following two decades and who was with him at the North Pole.

The expedition ran into difficulties almost at once. In Melville Bay in northeastern Greenland, a large ice cake hit the ship's rudder and the spoke of the wheel caught one of Peary's legs, breaking both bones above the ankle. Dr. Cook set the fracture, and Peary refused to turn back. He was carried ashore when they landed at Inglefield Gulf. Peary's leg healed well, and he was able to supervise the construction of their camp, Red Cliff House, and to ensure that, with the help of the Eskimos, they were able to set in a good supply of meat for the winter. He was proving the truth of Stefannson's vision of a "friendly" Arctic. Of his wife's first winter in the north, Peary wrote: "Within sixty miles of where Kane and his little party endured such untold sufferings, within eighty miles of where Greely's men one by one starved to death, and within less than fifty miles of where Hayes and his party and one portion of the Po-

laris party underwent their Arctic trials and tribulations, this tenderly nurtured woman lived for a year in safety and comfort. . . . Perhaps no greater or more convincing proof of this could be desired of what great improvements have been made in Arctic methods."[5]

In early May 1892, Peary set out with his Norwegian ski expert, Eivind Astrup, to cross Greenland. They carried no more than the minimum amount of food necessary to survive an excruciating twelve-hundred-mile journey, and if they had not found musk oxen at the end of their outward journey, it is doubtful they would have survived. But the sight that lay before the two men at the end of an exhausting six-week struggle across crevasses and through driving snow was more than worth it: "A few steps more, and the rocky plateau on which we stood dropped in a giant iron wall, that would grace the Inferno, 3800 feet to the level of the bay below us. We stood upon the northeast coast of Greenland; and looking far off over the surface of a mighty glacier on our right and through the broad mouth of the bay, we saw stretching away to the horizon the great ice-fields of the Arctic Ocean. . . . From the edge of the towering cliff on which we stood, and in the clear light of the brilliant summer day, the view that spread away before us was magnificent beyond description."[6]

It was July 4, and in honor of the day Peary named the fjord "Independence."

Among the Iron Mountains

In 1818, while searching for the Northwest Passage, the explorer John Ross had become the first

white man to come in contact with a small tribe of previously unknown Eskimos near Cape York in northwest Greenland. Although these Eskimos lived in total isolation, Ross was surprised to discover that they had fragments of flattened metal, which they attached to bone and ivory handles and used as knives and harpoons. The Eskimos zealously guarded the secret of the source of their metal, saying only that it came from a large mass. When the metal was subsequently analyzed, it was found to contain nickel. Ross deduced that the metal's source was meteoric, and he and subsequent generations of explorers searched in vain for its location.

Next to the discovery of the North Pole, Peary's most dramatic exploit was the discovery and retrieval of the three giant meteorites of Cape York, which now reside at the American Museum of Natural History. The search for the meteorites had been only a secondary objective when Peary departed for Greenland in 1893. He had hoped to cross Greenland again, with a larger party, and to continue mapping unknown sections of the coast to the north and the south of Independence Bay, but problems developed—illness and discontent among his crew, most of whom chose to return home after

the first year. As a result, he shifted the focus of his expedition.

By the 1890s, the Eskimos had acquired sufficient knives, guns, spears, and needles from white men to make this meteoric source of iron no longer necessary. The small tribe of Smith Sound Eskimos trusted Peary, and, in exchange for a gun, one of the men agreed to take the explorer to the northern shore of Melville Bay, where there were three *saviksue*, the Eskimos' "iron mountains."

In the spring of 1894, Peary set out by dog sledge with Hugh Lee and an Eskimo guide, Tallakoteah, who was familiar with the Cape York area and knew the location of the meteorites. May is a terrible month for arctic travel: the sea ice is breaking up and floating out to sea, and unexpected blizzards make traveling dangerous, if not impossible. The journey out was difficult; they made their way across Granville Bay by leaping from one ice cake to another. Peary finally arrived at the site of the first meteorite on May 27, 1894. It was buried

under three feet of snow, but its position was marked by pieces of blue traprock, which the Eskimos used to chip off fragments of the meteorite. With his saw knife, Tallakoteah dug a pit three feet deep in the snow, and "the brown mass, rudely awakened from its winter sleep, found for the first time in its cycles of existence the eyes of a white man gazing upon it."[7]

The first meteorite uncovered by Peary was called "the woman." Nearby lay a smaller meteorite, "the dog," and, seven miles away, on an island, was the largest of the three, called "the tent." Legend had it that a woman, her dog, and her tent were hurled from the sky by Tornasuk, the Evil Spirit. Originally, the woman had looked as if she were sitting and sewing, but by the time Peary discovered the meteorite, it was much reduced in size. Eskimos from another part of Greenland had removed the head to take home, so that they would always have a supply of metal on hand. They had lashed the chunk of metal onto their sledge and set out on their return trip, but the sea ice broke under the great weight, and the sledge and dogs were pulled under. The men survived to tell their tale, but since that time no one had dared take away anything but small fragments.

Peary scratched a "P" on the surface of the meteorite and built a small cairn nearby in which he placed a written record of his discovery. Then he set off to look for the largest meteorite. He reached the island on which it was located but was unable to dig it out of its deep blanket of snow. That August, he tried to bring his ship back to the meteorites but was unable to make his way through the ice of Melville Bay.

The three meteorites were located on the north shore of Melville Bay, some thirty-five miles from Cape York. The tent meteorite was situated on an inner island of the bay. Nearly buried in rocks and soil, it lay eighty feet above the high-water mark and one hundred yards from shore. Retrieving the meteorites would prove to be no mean feat of engineering. The area around Melville Bay is utterly desolate, and, during the winter, high winds throw up snowdrifts that rise to several hundred feet. In the summer, the southern-facing slopes are free of snow for only a few weeks, while the valleys and northern-facing slopes lie under a perpetual layer of snow. The shore remains ice-bound for eleven months, and sometimes throughout the entire year.

Eighteen ninety-five was a relatively mild year, and in August Peary managed to ram his steamer, the *Kite,* through the ice to within a mile of the shore where the two smaller meteorites were located. The crew trans-

ported these unwieldy masses over several hundred feet of boulders and down a slope of snow and ice to the shore. From the shore, the meteorites were ferried across the open water on huge ice cakes and then dragged across the ice to the ship. Before the woman meteorite could be hoisted onto the ship, the ice under it began to give way. Fortunately, the lines and chains held, and it was pulled safely on board.

While this work was under way, the tent meteorite was partially excavated so that Peary could get some idea of its size and weight. He estimated it at a whopping one hundred tons, although its actual weight was closer to one-third of his estimate. His two ten-ton jacks crumpled when he attempted to lift the meteorite. Realizing that his equipment and the ship were inadequate to the task, and that time was running out for the *Kite,* they left with plans to return the following year. The *Kite* made the journey to Saint John's, New-

foundland, safely, "though the presence of these unusual masses of iron affected our compasses to such an extent that, whenever thick or stormy weather compelled us for any length of time to

Above: The Ahnighito meteorite almost entirely buried in the ground, Melville Bay, Greenland, August 1895. Photograph by Robert E. Peary

Opposite: Marie Ahnighito Peary in native costume. Marie Peary was born on September 12, 1893, in North Greenland, the first white child to be born so far north. She received her middle name from the Eskimo woman who sewed her first fox-skin coat.

Peary wrote of his daughter: "The first six months of her life were spent in continuous lamplight. When the earliest ray of the returning sun pierced through the window of our tiny room, she reached for the golden bar as other children reach for a beautiful toy.... Entire families journeyed from far-away Cape York to the south, and from distant Etah to the north, to satisfy themselves by actual touch that she was really a creature of warm flesh and blood, and not of snow, as they at first believed."

depend on our dead reckoning, it was impossible to keep on course."[8]

The following August, Peary returned on a larger ship, the *Hope,* with more powerful equipment to tackle the remaining meteorite. Steaming into Melville Bay, he found a natural harbor for the ship just below the meteorite. He and his crew commenced to work day and night for ten days. The weight proved too much for Peary's sixty-ton jack, but he was able to pull the meteorite out of the ground and to place it on steel rails, laid upon timbers. The crew slid it to the crest of the hill and then rolled it down the slope with great difficulty.

Before they could maneuver the meteorite to the edge of the rock pier, however, a fierce southeaster sprang up and "the pack ice of Melville Bay driving in upon the shore forced us to pull

the ship out with haste to avoid having her crushed like an eggshell against the rocks."[9] Peary had no choice but to abandon the meteorite upon the pier and to make his way back to Cape York in a driving snowstorm.

Characteristically, Peary was disappointed but not discouraged. He returned in the *Hope* the following year, 1897, with even more powerful equipment. Perhaps sensing he would succeed this time, on his fourth attempt, he was accompanied by his wife; his daughter, Marie; his daughter's nurse; and various friends and colleagues.

This year he was able to enter Melville Bay earlier, by the end of the second week of August. Still, the lane of water alongside the rock pier was scarcely wider than the ship's length. Under these circumstances, they would have to work quickly. Forty-eight hours of severe cold would entrap the ship in the ice until the following summer. Peary proposed to construct a bridge, eighteen feet long, of steel rails, from the ship to the shore. They would place the meteorite in a timber car and slide the car over the rails, made slick with a thick mixture of tallow and soap. Everybody worked day and night for five days, through a blinding storm and fog that had continued since the ship was brought alongside the island.

"At last the tide was right, and while Mrs. Peary and Captain Bartlett, at the levers of the jacks, started the monster, draped in 'Old Glory,' toward the ship, the baby dashed a little bottle of wine against it and named it 'Ahnighito.'"[10] Every man set to his task, and the meteorite inched out to the edge of the pier and onto the steel bridge. An hour later, with the meteorite poised over the main hatch, Peary mo-

tioned the winch to stop; by the next afternoon, the meteorite had been braced in the hold.

Even though the *Hope* was carrying a dangerously heavy load, they were forced to ram a passage through the icebergs that blocked the exit from Melville Bay. The bergs drew back together behind the ship, sealing up the bay for the coming winter. Once they reached open water, however, their troubles were far from over. On the trip back to New York, in the worst of the weather, off Wolstenholm Island, "for thirty-six hours she dodged back and forth, a phantom ship, her decks deep with snow, her spars, sails, and rigging crusted with frozen crystals."[11] Meanwhile, Peary and four of his Eskimos worked belowdecks, lowering the meteorite inch by inch with the jacks to get it low enough to stabilize the ship.

On Saturday, October 2, 1897, the *Hope* steamed into the New York Navy Yard, and the Ahnighito meteorite was lifted from the hatch by a hundred-ton floating crane. In 1909, after years of negotiation, Josephine Peary, saying she needed money to pay for her children's education, sold the three meteorites to the American Museum of Natural History for the sum of $40,000. Five years earlier, a barge had carried the Ahnighito up the East River to the pier at Fiftieth Street. There the meteorite was placed on a cart, and twenty-eight horses pulled the load to the Museum. An analysis of the metal of the meteorites showed that all three were fragments of an original mass. At the time, the Ahnighito was the largest known meteorite in the world, although since then the Hoba, estimated at fifty to sixty tons, has been discovered in the desert of southwest Africa.

Farthest North

The northern-reaching fingers of all the rest of the great world lay far behind us below the ice-bound southern horizon. We were in that gaunt frozen border land which lies between God's countries and interstellar space.

—Robert E. Peary[12]

With the Cape York meteorites safely in New York, Peary's sights turned to what had originally attracted him—the North Pole. He would never have attained his goal without the financial and moral support of Morris K. Jesup, the president of the American Museum of Natural History and of the American Geographic Society. Jesup's first contact with Peary had been through Mrs. Peary, who had appealed to the Museum in 1894 for money to send a relief ship for her husband, then stranded in northern Greenland. The Museum contributed a thousand dollars to the Peary Relief Expedition, with the bulk of the expenses borne by an anonymous Museum trustee. Although not yet able to move the meteorites, the Peary Relief Expedition had returned with specimen collections for the departments of birds and mammals and Eskimo artifacts. In 1898, Jesup, in conjunction with several other prominent men, raised sufficient funds to send Peary back to the Arctic. The following year, Jesup organized the Peary Arctic Club, whose motto read: "To Reach the Farthest Northern Point of the Western Hemisphere; to Promote and Maintain Exploration of the Polar Regions." It was this club, financed substantially by Jesup himself, that provided money for Peary's expensive polar explorations in the following decade.

Peary returned from a fruitless four-year quest for the North

Pole in the autumn of 1902, but he was not ready to admit defeat. His ship had not been strong enough to get farther north than Cape D'Urville on Ellesmere Island. In the intense cold and perpetual dark of the arctic winter, with temperatures hovering around −60° F, Peary had transported his supplies across the sea ice to Greely's old base at Fort Conger, two hundred fifty miles to the north. He was, as usual, stoical. Stumbling into the officers' quarters, his team managed to light a stove with their scant supply of oil. "When this was accomplished, a suspicious 'wooden' feeling in the right foot led me to have my kamiks pulled off, and I found, to my annoyance, that both feet were frosted."[13]

When he was strong enough to stand, he was strapped into his sledge and carried back to the ship. Once there, all but the little toes on each foot were amputated. His feet healed, Peary had again attempted the Pole in early

April 1902, but his way was blocked by the "Big Lead." Leads, lanes of open water that can stretch for dozens of miles, are caused by high tides that result from the full moon. Every explorer in the Arctic fears them, for the only way to get across is

Above: Construction of Peary's ship, the Roosevelt, *in Bucksport, Maine, 1904. Robert and Josephine Peary are standing at the left.*

Opposite: Dogs aboard the Roosevelt, *1908–9. Captain Bob Bartlett recalled this voyage: "Mixed up with the coal were 70 tons of whale meat and 246 dogs, all fighting and screaming; the dogs I mean. In addition we had 49 Eskimos and the blubber of 50 walruses. . . . To my dying day I shall never forget the frightful noise, the choking stench and the terrible confusion that reigned aboard her as we steamed slowly down Foulke Fjord and swung into the pack of Kane Basin. We had some canned peaches that night for supper; but the odor about us was so powerful that the peaches simply felt wet and cold on one's tongue, having no fruit flavor whatsoever." Photograph by Matthew Henson*

to wait until the water freezes over or the lead closes up—a long and nerve-wracking process. Peary had reached latitude 84° 17′27″ north, a new farthest north but still a disappointment for him.

Based on what he had learned, Peary decided that the only feasible plan was to set out for the North Pole from a base on the northernmost point of land. He needed a ship that could force a passage through to the ice of the Arctic Ocean. Such a ship would cost $100,000, and Peary turned to Jesup and the Peary Arctic Club for support. Jesup raised the money, and Peary designed the ship, named the *Roosevelt,* in honor of the president of the United States. The sides were thirty inches thick, made of wood, braced by struts, and sheathed in steel.

On July 16, 1905, the *Roosevelt* set sail from New York, with veteran seaman Bob Bartlett as captain. The ship did its job, navigating the narrow icy channels, and was able to berth at Cape Sheridan, in the north of

Ellesmere Island, in a somewhat precarious position. The following year, Peary made another attempt on the Pole. Hampered by weather, he was able to push to latitude 87° 6′ north, a new record, but still well short of his goal. Peary and Henson struggled back to the boat with only forty-one of the one hundred twenty-one dogs with which they had left.

Before turning the ship for home, Peary decided to explore three hundred miles of unknown Grant Land coast. On this trip, while standing on a peak of Axel Heiberg Island, he looked to the north through his binoculars and thought he saw land. "My heart leaped the intervening miles of ice as I looked longingly at this land," said Peary. "In fancy I trod its shores and climbed its summits, even though I knew that that pleasure could only be for another in another season."[14] These shores, named Crocker Land, in honor of Peary's benefactor, George Crocker, would become the focus of a four-year Museum expedition from 1913 to 1917 (see pages 86–90).

Back at the ship, Peary received the bad news that the *Roosevelt* had broken out of its berth and been smashed against the ice foot. They managed to limp back to New York. Again, Peary was undaunted; he was already discussing plans for the next year. "I should have thought he wouldn't have wanted ever to see that place again," commented Captain Bartlett. "But it was like him when he was lowest to be still planning for the future."[15]

Peary set to work to raise money to repair the ship and to equip the expedition, but the unexpected death of Morris Jesup the following year was a severe setback. Jesup's widow continued to provide vital support, however, and on July 6, 1908, the *Roosevelt* set sail from New York. It stopped briefly at Oyster Bay, Long Island, where President Roosevelt came on board to inspect the ship and to offer encouragement to the crew. On what was to be Peary's last voyage north, he was accompanied, as always, by Matthew Henson, and by Captain Bartlett; Ross Marvin, a Cornell University engineer; Dr. John Goodsell; Donald MacMillan, who was to lead the Crocker Land Expedition; and George Borup, who studied geology at the Museum after he returned from the Arctic and who would have accompanied MacMillan on the next expedition had he not drowned in Long Island Sound in 1912.

The ship went into winter quarters at Cape Sheridan, and supplies were carried to Cape Columbia, Peary's last land base. Peary kept his men busy in the long arctic winter, sledging and hunting for meat. The "tenderfeet," MacMillan, Borup, and Goodsell, were sent ashore to learn the skills of ice camping.

MacMillan, in particular, became adept at building igloos.

Peary's plan was to send out five parties—four supporting parties and his own—that would get him within one hundred fifty miles of the Pole. With his pick of the best dogs and sledges, he would dash to the Pole and return by forced marches to land. For the entire return journey, he planned to complete a march, make tea and eat, make another march, rest for a few hours, then continue. With very little sleep, they would be on the move most of the time. They would stay in existing igloos and rely on supplies cached along the trail. Daily rations for each man consisted of one pound of pemmican, one pound of biscuits, four ounces of condensed milk, one-half ounce of compressed tea, and six ounces of alcohol for fuel; each dog was fed one pound of pemmican per day. Pemmican, whose origin is Cree Indian, consists of dried meat and suet, to which can be added oatmeal, dried fruits, even dried fish. Although it is neither easily digested nor entirely palatable, it is extremely nutritious and concentrated, which makes it ideal for polar expeditions.

Everything depended on the weather and the shifting sea ice, which could open big leads and destroy the trail. The night before they departed, Peary gave his men a pep talk, which George Borup recorded in his diary: "Said the next six weeks would be undiluted hell, the only variation in the monotony being that occasionally it would get worse."[16]

The first teams set out on February 28, 1909, with Peary following on the first of March. Three days later, they sighted a thick band of black to the north—the sign of open water. The lane was a quarter of a mile wide and extended to the east and west as far as they could see. Here they had to wait out seven anxious days, and with each passing day the lead widened, diminishing their chances of making it to the Pole. The Eskimos began to lose nerve, and Peary sent two of the older men back. Peary did not want to take the chance of crossing until the ice could support them. He was undoubtedly thinking back to his experience crossing the "Big Lead" on his return journey in 1906, when he and his starving men just barely made it back to land: "Once started, we could not stop, we could not lift our snowshoes. It was a matter of constantly and smoothly gliding one past the other with utmost care and evenness of pressure, and from every man as he slid a snowshoe forward, undulations went out in every direction through the thin film incrusting the black water. . . . It was the first and only time in all my Arctic work that I felt doubtful as to the outcome."[17]

This time, they were able to cross the lead without any trouble and the same day crossed seven more leads, each covered with rippling young ice. Except for the usual mishaps of frozen heels and Bartlett and his sledges floating away on a broken ice floe in the middle of the night, everything went according to plan. A supporting party turned back every five marches, up to the 88th parallel. Peary, Henson, and the four Eskimo drivers, Ootah, Ooqueah, Seegloo, and Egingwah, were in good shape to make the final dash. With five marches, they reached a point that Peary determined was within three miles of the Pole. There they set up Camp Morris K. Jesup on April 6, 1909. "Yet with the Pole actually in sight I was too weary to

take the last few steps. The accumulated weariness of all those days and nights of forced marches and insufficient sleep, constant peril and anxiety, seemed to roll across me at once. I was actually too exhausted to realize at the moment that my life's purpose had been achieved."[18]

Nonetheless, he was up within a few hours to raise the American flag and other flags he had brought, to take photographs, and to execute a series of sextant readings that would cause burning in his eyes and make it difficult for him to see for the next few days. This was the inevitable result of making latitude observations across the bright snow with the sun several degrees above the horizon. In the thirty hours he spent at the Pole, he also sledged about ten miles in various directions, to ensure that he passed directly over the Pole. The next day, five miles from the Pole, he lowered a sounding line through a crack in the ice; he reached fifteen hundred fathoms, without touching bottom before the line broke.

Peary had made it to the Pole, but he could not afford to relax. He faced a difficult return journey, with a window of about three weeks before the spring tides opened leads that could cut them off from land. Peary double-rationed the dogs, jettisoned everything but the bare essentials, and started on double marches. He had good weather and was able to follow his trail back, reaching Grant Land before midnight of April 22. The Eskimos, fully aware of their precarious situation, were ecstatic when they touched land, and Ootah remarked, "The devil is asleep or having trouble with his wife, or we should never have come back so easily."[19]

Back at the *Roosevelt,* an exhausted Peary was stunned to learn that on the return trip Ross Marvin had fallen through the ice of a lead and drowned. His Eskimo companions had dumped all his belongings into the water, except for a canvas packet with his last note. In 1925, when the two Eskimos who accompanied Marvin were baptized, they confessed to having killed Marvin because he had gone mad.

When Peary arrived in Indian Harbor, Labrador, on September 6, he was greeted with the shocking news that Frederick Cook, the doctor who had accompanied him on his first Greenland expedition, had announced just five days earlier that he had discovered the North Pole on April 21, 1908. Rumors of Cook's claims to have traveled far north had already reached Peary; in Etah he had questioned Cook's two Eskimo drivers, Aapilaq and Itukusuk, who insisted that Cook had

only made two marches out from land north of Cape Hubbard. In response, Peary sent out a number of telegrams from Indian Harbor. One, to *The New York Times,* was openly hostile; it read, Cook "has simply handed the public a gold brick."[20] His telegram to Hermon Bumpus, the director of the Museum, was more upbeat: "The Pole is ours. Am bringing large amount material for Museum."

Controversy was soon raging over whether Cook or Peary had reached the North Pole first. Until now, an unspoken honor system had existed among explorers; this dispute ended that. Insults were hurled and sides were taken. General Greely, who was offended by Peary's scathing criticisms of his expedition, and Rear Admiral Winfield Schley, who had led the Greely Relief Expedition, were among Cook's strongest supporters. (In reaching the South Pole, Roald Amundsen faced no such predicament, even though he, too, was in competition. The South Pole is located on land, and records left there can be verified. Records left on the North Pole, however, in the midst of shifting ice, drift away and sink to the ocean floor.)

Cook was welcomed enthusiastically in Copenhagen, where the crown prince gave him a hero's banquet. Back in America he rode through New York City in a two-hundred-car motorcade. But when the Royal Geographic Society of Denmark and the University of Copenhagen examined a copy of his notebook later that year (Cook claimed to have left his diary and his original polar observations of the sun in Greenland), the response was less than enthusiastic. Dr. Stromgen, the chairman of the examining committee, said: "Cook's action is shameless. It was an offense to submit such papers to scientific men."[21] Peary's records and observations at the North Pole were examined by a group appointed by the National Geographic Society and accepted as adequate proof of his claims.

In 1911, Peary was made a rear admiral in the Civil Engineering Corps of the Navy and given the thanks of Congress for his attainment of the North Pole. Nonetheless, Cook had managed to foment substantial opposition to

Peary among the public and members of Congress, and the controversy was not put to rest in Peary's lifetime. Today, it is generally accepted that Peary discovered, or was very close to, the North Pole in April 1909, while Cook fabricated his story.

The Land of Mist

In June 1913, the members of the American Museum of Natural History's Crocker Land Expedition gathered in New York, with Donald MacMillan at their head, eager to embark on what would prove to be the last extensive dogsledge expedition in the polar regions. Their purpose was to solve the geographical question, Is there a large body of uncharted land lying in the Polar Sea? Beyond Axel Heiberg Island and Grant Land lay five hundred thousand square miles of unexplored territory. At its boundary lay the new land that Peary had glimpsed one hundred twenty miles to the northwest of Cape Columbia in 1906. The team intended to sledge across the ice of the Polar Sea to where they supposed Crocker Land lay; if they discovered land, they would map it. Evidence for its existence was sketchy at best, and scientific opinion was divided.

After settling the question of Crocker Land's existence, the expedition planned to pursue an ambitious research agenda: to explore the region between Flagler Bay (eighty miles northwest of Etah) and Cape Thomas Hubbard; to explore the interior of Ellesmere Island; to climb to the summit of the ice cap of Greenland east of Cape York to study meteorological and glaciological conditions there; to collect scientific and ethnological data and specimens throughout.

The expedition was plagued

Life in a Lifeless Land

Explorers in Antarctica discovered a land as barren of life as they had surmised. With 99 percent of the continent permanently encased in ice, and its inland peaks swept by constant and violent storms, the edge of land in Antarctica effectively marks the end of plant and animal life. There are no land mammals there, and the seals and penguins never venture farther inland than several hundred yards from the water. Only two flowering plants and a number of nonflowering lichens and mosses have been discovered.

How different it is from the Arctic, which, as W. Elmer Ekblaw discovered, is truly a botanist's paradise. Ekblaw wrote in Natural History *in 1919, "When the explorer from the southland approaches the rock-bound, glacier-ribboned coasts of Greenland, his first impression is one of bleakness and barrenness. The frowning cliffs, stern and unchangeable, the gleaming glaciers, cold and immobile, suggest no possible refuge for flowers, no likely niche for ferns or grasses. But in summer when he enters some little bay, or goes up one of the deep fjords and sets foot upon the land, he finds that Greenland is not so cold, nor so bleak, nor so barren as he imagined."*

During a summer spent at North Star Bay, Greenland, Ekblaw, geologist and botanist of the Crocker Land Expedition, found more than eighty species of plants within a radius of a half-mile. The recorded species of flowering arctic plants number in the hundreds, as do the mosses and lichens, in addition to at least twenty types of ferns. The abundance of plant life attracts insects, birds, and mammals. Caribou and musk oxen are found on the northernmost arctic islands. During the darkness of the winter, the musk oxen survive on the frozen grass, swept clean of snow by the fierce winds. Peary found a bumblebee one half-mile north of the last land in the Arctic, and, two hundred forty miles from the Pole, he saw the snow tracks of the arctic fox.

Ekblaw spent years studying the unique environmental factors that allow for such rich and diverse plant life in northwest Greenland, a thousand miles within the Arctic Circle. His work focused on Smith Sound, the region stretching from Cape York to Humboldt Glacier. There he discovered a narrow strip of land between the ice cap and the sound that is free of ice in the short summer, which lasts from mid-June, when the snows begin to melt, to mid-August, when killing frosts recommence. The leaves of the willow trees start to turn yellow in mid-July. The weather is never balmy: the warmest summer noonday temperature does not exceed 60° F, and snowstorms in July are not uncommon. Nonetheless, on these rocky slopes grow flowers, ferns, and low grasses.

The strong tide and currents in Smith Sound keep open water along the shore for most of the year, circulating warmer, moister air over land and encouraging plant growth. This, combined with twenty-four hours

Borup Lodge, the headquarters of the Crocker Land Expedition at Etah, Greenland. Their base, which MacMillan described as "one of the warmest buildings ever constructed in the North," had a living room, four sleeping rooms, a workroom, an electrical room, and a darkroom. Lighted by electricity, the lodge had telephone communication with the surrounding dwellings, which housed the Eskimo members of the expedition. From a hand-colored lantern slide

of light each day during the summer months, enables the plants to grow quickly during their short growing season. If the summer snows do not last too long, the plants can withstand them. Most of the plants found in the Arctic are perennials. When fruiting does not occur because the weather is unusually harsh, the plants will still survive until the next year. They are adapted to the long period of bitter cold—most are low, creeping varieties with tough outer tissues. Ekblaw was also surprised to find edible mushrooms near the base camp in Etah, often growing as large as a dinner plate.

Perhaps the most unusual plants in the Arctic are trees. The tallest are no more than three inches high. The most common tree, the arctic willow, Salix arctica, often spreads over a square yard, with its fuzzy catkins rising above the height of the tree itself. The tiny trunk grows no thicker than a person's thumb, although the tree can live for more than fifty years, as Ekblaw discovered by counting the growth rings. The smallest known tree, Salix herbacea, another species of willow, reaches only one inch high, producing two small leaves and a catkin each summer.

with problems from the start. Its ship ran aground off the coast of Labrador, and supplies and crew had to be transferred to another ship, which brought them safely to the Eskimo settlement of Etah. They had hoped to land on the far side of Smith Sound at Flagler Bay but were stopped by drifting ice. They would have to ferry 1,738 pounds of biscuits and pemmican across the thin ice of the treacherous sound in December. From Etah to their goal and back was twelve hundred miles, three hundred of which were over the rough ice of the Polar Sea—a considerable undertaking.

MacMillan had mapped out a demanding route: across Smith

Field of arctic poppies at Sunrise Point, Greenland. The arctic poppy is one of the first flowers to bloom in the north, opening around June 20 and continuing to bloom until the last week of August. An especially hardy plant, the poppy can be found at the edge of the Polar Sea, only 370 miles from the North Pole. Arctic poppies are usually mandarin yellow in color, although a white variety does exist. From a hand-colored lantern slide

Sound to Ellesmere Island, climbing the sheer wall of the Beistadt Glacier, which rose almost a mile high, down to Eureka Sound on the far side of Ellesmere Island, and from there northwest to Cape Thomas Hubbard, where Peary had had his Crocker Land vision. On March 11, 1914, in their second attempt of the season to reach Crocker Land, MacMillan set out with a scaled-down party consisting of himself, Fitzhugh Green, W. Elmer Ekblaw, seven Eskimos, and one hundred dogs. Before they reached Cape Thomas Hubbard, Ekblaw, whose feet had been frostbitten during the crossing, dropped out to return to Etah. In the end, only Green, MacMillan, and two Eskimos, E-took-a-shoo and Pee-a-wah-to, set out across the frozen Polar Sea in search of the land mass. After a week on the ice, they thought they had their first glimpse of it:

Green was no sooner out of the igloo than he came running back, calling in through the door, "We have it!" Following Green, we ran to the top of the highest mound. There could be no doubt about it. Great heavens! what a land! Hills, valleys, snow-capped peaks extending through at least one hundred and twenty degrees of the horizon. I turned to Pee-a-wah-to anxiously and asked him toward which point we had better lay our course. After critically examining the supposed landfall for a few minutes, he astounded me by replying that he thought it was *poo-jok* (mist). E-took-a-shoo offered no encouragement, saying, "Perhaps it is." Green was still convinced that it must be land. At any rate, it was worth watching. As we proceeded the landscape gradually changed its appearance and varied in extent with the swinging around of the sun; finally at night it disappeared altogether.[22]

With serious misgivings, the men checked their position the next morning and discovered they were thirty miles past their goal. If Peary had actually seen anything from Cape Thomas Hubbard, it would have had to lie a minimum of two hundred miles to the northwest. At that distance, he would have been able to make out land only if it were at least thirty thousand feet high. Since the highest peaks of the Arctic do not rise above six thousand feet, the only conclusion that Green and MacMillan could come to was that Crocker Land did not exist. It was already late in the year. They had crossed more than thirty leads to reach their present position and a full moon was due soon; they could expect more leads to open. The expedition could not risk even another day's journey north over the ice. The disappointed explorers turned around and headed back.

When they were within a mile of land, they spotted Peary's cairn on the summit of a low point lying to the south. At its base was a cocoa tin with a piece of the American flag and the record: "Peary, June 28, 1906." They replaced this piece with a small silk flag and a duplicate of the Peary record. Then they turned to look out over the Polar Sea, from Peary's vantage point. "The day was exceptionally clear, not a cloud or trace of mist; if land could be seen, now was our time. Yes, there it was! It could be seen without a glass, extending from southwest true to north-northeast. Our powerful glasses, however, brought out more clearly the dark background in contrast with the white, the whole resembling hills, valleys, and snow-capped peaks to such a degree that, had we not been out on the frozen sea for 150 miles, we would have staked our lives upon its reality."[23]

From the start, MacMillan had been unable to get his radio to work, so for four years the expedition was essentially cut off from the outside world. After the first year, they received letters from home, brought to Etah by the Danish trader Peter Freuchen. By

Right: Christmas dinner, 1914, Borup Lodge, Etah, Greenland. Left to right: Dr. Harrison Hunt, Fitzhugh Green, W. Elmer Ekblaw, Maurice Cole Tanquary, Jerome Allen, Mene, Jonathan Small. "On Christmas Day," wrote MacMillan, "we . . . sat down to a glorious dinner especially prepared and packed in New York by President Osborn of the American Museum of Natural History." On the menu were cocktails; mock-turtle soup; roast turkey with cranberry sauce; green corn on the cob; plum pudding with brandy sauce; pineapple and ginger; nuts and raisins; coffee and cigars.

"Enrico Caruso, Melba, Schumann-Heink, Gorgoza, Evan Williams, and other operatic stars were each introduced for our pleasure through the kindness of the Victrola Company.

"In the evening, each one of our sixty-one Eskimo visitors received a portion of one of three large, delicious fruit cakes presented to me by my good friend, M. J. Look, of Kingston, New York, and each one exclaimed, 'Ma-much-to-suah!' (My, but that tastes good!)" Photograph by Donald MacMillan

the following year, however, they had resorted to placing letters in bottles in the sea as their only hope of communication.

The Museum had to assume the worst. If it received no word for two years, it was to send a relief ship. Unfortunately, the first two relief ships, the *George B. Cluett* and the *Danmark*, sent in 1915 and 1916, were both unsuited for arctic travel. The *Cluett* was crushed in the ice and frozen in for the winter ninety miles to the south, at Parker Snow Bay, where members of the expedition had traveled to meet the ship. The *Cluett* had only enough food for three months, so the men returned to Etah to obtain relief supplies for the relief ship. Finally, on July 29, 1917, the Newfoundland sealer *Neptune*, under the command of the redoubtable Bob Bartlett, steamed into Etah Bay to rescue MacMillan and the

mechanic Jonathan Small. All the other members of the original expedition had already gone south by sledge. MacMillan ran out to the point, where he was directly under the bow of the old gray ship:

A ringing command from her bridge sounded very familiar.

"Is that you, Bob?" I yelled.

"Of course! Who in hell do you think it is?" was the characteristic reply. . . .

"How's the war?" was my first question.

"The war is still on. America has joined the Allies."

"Who is President of the United States?"

"Wilson."[24]

The initial costs of the expedition had been projected at $6,000, but the length of the expedition, combined with the costs of chartering so many ships, had raised the cost to nearly $100,000. In addition, the other backers of the expedition, the American Geographical Society and the University of Illinois, had reneged on their financial commitments, leaving the Museum to foot the staggering bill at a time when it was experiencing financial difficulties.

Despite the great expenses incurred by the Crocker Land Expedition and the discovery that Peary's sighting was only a mirage, the expedition's many accomplishments were substantial. During the four years at Borup Lodge, MacMillan took fifty-five hundred photographs and ten thousand feet of motion-picture film. Members of the expedition undertook work in geology, botany, and ornithology, including the discovery of two sets of the rare eggs of the sandpiper *Tringa canutus*, which breeds in the Arctic. Meteorological studies continued without break for nearly the entire time. The expedition's ethnographic work included the compilation of a three-thousand-word Eskimo dictionary and records of the tales, traditions, music, and religious practices of the Smith Sound Eskimos. In the numerous surveys and explorations of the coasts of northwest Greenland, Ellesmere Island, Grant Land, and Axel Heiberg Island, the expedition was the first to reach the shores of King Christian Island to the west.

There is something especially fitting about the Crocker Land Expedition's final achievement. It

Shoo-e-ging-wa and her dog, Crocker Land Expedition, 1913–17. From a hand-colored lantern slide by Donald MacMillan

Opposite, above: Eskimo men in kayaks, 1917. The boats, made of paper-thin skin, were perfectly adapted for harpooning walrus, narwhal, and seal, the main staples of the Eskimo diet. From a hand-colored lantern slide by Robert Bartlett

Opposite, below: Building an igloo on Eureka Sound off Ellesmere Island, 1914. Photograph by Donald MacMillan

discovered the records of a number of previous expeditions—Dr. Elisha Kent Kane's 1853–55 Second Grinnell Expedition, Peary's 1906 Expedition, and Sir George Nares's 1875–76 British North Pole Expedition. Having sought an illusion and found instead a history of its precursors, the expedition had brought the saga of dog-sledge exploration full circle—and written its final chapter.

Above the White Horizon

In the library . . . [they] were on a low shelf, easily reached by a boy of twelve,

Learning from the Eskimo

Before setting out across the Greenland ice cap in 1892, Peary took a trial run with Dr. Cook and the Norwegian Eivind Astrup. After climbing two thousand feet to a camp where two of his men had built the base of an igloo the previous day, they laid a flat roof of snow blocks on top, using skis and snowshoes as supports. Then Peary and his companions removed their furs and lay down in their underclothes in their sleeping bags. At dawn they awoke to discover that snow was pouring in through the end of the igloo where the wall met the roof and was covering them. Peary and Cook extricated themselves, but Astrup lay buried in the snow. Leaving Cook with Astrup, to keep a breathing hole clear, Peary rolled out of the igloo in his bag, reached the shovel, rolled back to the side where Astrup lay, and managed to dig through the side wall. Peary and Cook were able to drag him out. With no shelter from the raging storm and all their clothes buried deep under drifts of snow, the three men had to wait out another day and night of the blizzard. Eventually they managed to dig their clothing out, warm themselves with exercise, and make their way back. Peary had learned why the Eskimos always build round igloos. It was one of the many survival lessons he, Stefansson, and Donald MacMillan learned from the denizens of the ice and snow. As MacMillan wrote in his book, Four Years in the White North:

It is a pleasure to see an Eskimo cut and handle snow. One cannot but admire the skill and dexterity with which he cuts it on the surface, breaks it out with his toe, lays it up on the wall, bevels the edges, and thumps it into place with his hand. I wonder if there are any other people in the world who attempt to build an arch or dome without support. Starting from the ground in a spiral from right to left, the blocks mount higher and higher, ever assuming a more horizontal position, until the last two or three appear to hang in the air, the last block locking the whole structure. This work can be done by two good men in about an hour.

Entering a newly constructed igloo seems like a vision of fairy-land, the light filtering through the snow a beautiful ethereal blue; everything—the bed, the two side platforms, the wall—absolutely spotless.

Before Peary left for his dash to the North Pole, the Eskimo women with his party busily sewed the explorers' clothes: bearskin trousers, deerskin coats with hoods, hareskin stockings, bearskin boots lined with arctic grass, and bearskin mittens. Although a man's clothing weighed only twelve pounds, it enabled him to survive a blizzard at –50° F.

MacMillan also used native clothing, and he credited Peary with figuring out how to adapt the Eskimo's clothing to his own purposes. In his account of the Crocker Land Expedition, MacMillan wrote:

I believe Peary was the first Arctic explorer to attempt work during the extremely low temperatures of February and March without a sleeping bag. We adopted the Peary method on many of our journeys. We contracted slightly the fur-bordered

opening of the hood; bound the bottom of our caribou-skin coats tightly between our legs; withdrew our arms and placed them upon the warm body; tucked the ever-to-be-desired mittens into the empty sleeves; and then, with a hunch of the shoulder, placed the sleeve over the face to protect it from freezing.

Sleeping in this manner, one is ever ready for an emergency call, such as the inevitable rush of one's dogs, which frequently break the fastenings; the visit of a polar bear; or the remote possibility of the cracking of the sea ice, resulting in a slowly widening fissure beneath the bed.

and with their drawings and charts I could entertain myself for hours. Atlases. Too heavy to hold up like an ordinary volume, I opened them on the floor and lay on my stomach to pore over them.

In those colored maps were white patches marked *Unknown* or *Unexplored*—many more white areas than there are today.

"Why don't people go there?" I wondered. "What can be in those white places?"

—Lincoln Ellsworth[25]

Lincoln Ellsworth grew up wanting to explore, to name the last white spaces on the map. His wealthy father had hoped he would eventually go into the family coal mining and railroad business. Instead he had set out to do all the things he had dreamed of as a sickly boy: "I have hunted buffalo, lived among the Indians, prospected for gold, and dragged the surveyor's chain across the unmarked western prairies."[26] By the time Ellsworth began to make plans for his first polar expedi-

tion, his peripatetic life had included exploratory surveys for the Grand Trunk Pacific Railway; working as a engineer in his father's coal mines in Pennsylvania; a stint as field assistant in the deserts of lower California and Mexico for the United States Biological Survey; and several years as an observer in the Aviation Service in France during World War I, when he learned to fly. He was already well into his forties.

His dream of polar exploration began in the Museum. Ellsworth, who became a trustee of the Museum in 1927, had visited it regularly in the years from 1908 to 1912. Murals depicting the Polar Sea seized his imagination: "A gaunt land. A waste of cold and storm. What was the attraction, wherein the fascination? Just how or why would be difficult to explain. . . . There, too, were the sledges that had reached the North and South poles. How it thrilled me to trace their journeys on the relief maps on the walls above them."[27]

Those dreams crystallized into something more substantial when Ellsworth met George Borup in 1912. Borup had chosen Ellsworth for the Crocker Land Expedition, but after Borup's untimely death, Ellsworth decided not to go. From that day on, however, he never abandoned his ambition to be a polar explorer. In 1914, he had lunch with Peary and his daughter, Marie, in Washington. During the meeting they discussed the feasibility of using airplanes to explore the Arctic. Peary, who had become an active promoter of aviation development, encouraged Ellsworth. A new age of polar exploration was dawning.

Roald Amundsen had long been one of Ellsworth's heroes, but Ellsworth scarcely imagined the discoverer of the South Pole would become his partner in exploration. In 1923, Ellsworth avidly followed Amundsen's unsuccessful attempt to fly across the Pole from Alaska to Spitzbergen. A year later, on a stopover in New York, he saw a small announcement in the *New York Herald Tribune* that Roald Amundsen had just arrived in New York. Ellsworth had a ticket to Peru; instead he wound up going to the North Pole. He called Amundsen's hotel. An hour's interview grew into dinner; by the end of the evening they were planning an expedition by air to the North Pole. Over the next two years, they would make history.

Amundsen, beset by financial worries, had planned to retire from exploring, but the prospect of Ellsworth's financial support led him to reconsider. Although MacMillan had all but disproved the existence of Crocker Land, the myth of the arctic continent died hard. As Ellsworth remarked, "Every explorer in 1924 believed in its existence, and its discovery was the great objective of all polar adventuring."[28]

For years, Ellsworth had tried to secure his father's financial support for a polar expedition. Now, with someone of Amundsen's stature and experience as his partner, he would make one final attempt. The two men convinced a reluctant James Ellsworth to contribute $85,000 to pay for the bulk of the expenses, with the rest of the money coming from the Aero Club of Norway. Fearful of his only son's safety, James Ellsworth immediately reversed himself. While he kept his financial promise, he began an unsuccessful campaign to prevent his son from accompanying the expedition. He must have had a premonition, for this was to prove to be one of the most harrowing adventures in the history of polar exploration.

Polar explorers need luck, and Amundsen's was proverbial. "It was luck that saved him from the uncharted reef during his northwest passage," wrote Ellsworth, "luck that gave him good weather at the South Pole in December, whereas in January, ordinarily a better month, the blizzards overwhelmed Scott and his party."[29] But it was not luck that saved the Amundsen-Ellsworth party near the North Pole; it was incredible fortitude and perseverance in the face of overwhelming odds.

In 1924, Charles Lindbergh had not yet flown the Atlantic, and nonstop flights across the United States did not exist. With aviation still in its infancy, the range and dependability of airplanes was limited, to say the least. The Aero Club of Norway would agree to sponsor only a reconnaissance flight to the North Pole and back from Spitzbergen Island, which, five hundred miles south of the North Pole, was the northernmost site of human habitation in the world. Amundsen and Ellsworth had greater ambitions. They hoped to fly in two planes from Spitzbergen across the Pole to Alaska. They would land at the Pole, leave one plane there after taking its remaining fuel, then continue on together.

Early in the morning of May 21, 1925, Amundsen and Ellsworth took off in the two Dornier-Wal airplanes, N 24 and N 25, from the ice of King's Bay, Spitzbergen. After traveling most of the day through heavy fog, Amundsen's plane lost power in one engine and was forced down. Ellsworth went after him. They were one hundred thirty-six miles short of the North Pole:

The two planes of the 1925 Amundsen-Ellsworth Expedition forced down on the ice, 136 miles from the North Pole

As we corkscrewed lower we saw that even our glasses had failed to reveal the roughness of the polar pack. I have never looked down upon a more terrifying place in which to land an airplane. It was like trying to set down a ship on the bottom of the Grand Canyon. . . . The leads that looked so innocent from aloft proved to be gulches and miniature canyons.

Nevertheless . . . we had no choice but to follow, since our strictest law of the expedition was that the two planes must at all cost stay together. The N 25 finally dropped into a narrow chasm surrounded by hummocks and ridges of such height that she disappeared from our sight instantly.[30]

Hjalmar Riiser-Larsen, Amundsen's pilot, had somehow managed to find a long shallow lead and had landed relatively safely, while Ellsworth, in the N 24, had come down in a lagoon and run up on the ice at the end, damaging the forward engine beyond repair. Three miles apart on the ice, the two crews were unable to see one another.

Of the six men now stranded on the polar ice, only Amundsen had spent any time in the north.

It was a rude introduction for the rest of them. The first order of business for Ellsworth's party was to pull the N 24 out of the water so that it would not sink with its load of fuel. When they finally located the other plane, the sight was not encouraging. "She was upended at an angle of forty-five degrees, her nose against a wall of ice that looked forty feet high."[31]

Ellsworth and his men were not able to reach Amundsen for another four days, but in the intervening time something happened that probably saved their lives. Instead of separating them farther, the movement of the ice brought the two planes to within half a mile of each other, while the huge pressure ridges and heavy block ice floated out. This stroke of luck eventually allowed the Ellsworth party to salvage fuel and food supplies from the N 24. Once the two groups were in sight of each other and Amundsen had sent a signal to come over, Ellsworth and his crew members, Leif Dietrichson and

Oscar Omdal, set out for the other plane. Carrying eighty-pound packs, and wearing skis to distribute their weight on the thin ice, they moved ahead cautiously. But the young ice was not strong enough to support them, and Dietrichson and Omdal fell through at the same time. "At the same instant I felt the ice sag under my skis," wrote Ellsworth. "I slid sideways. The fact that there was a frozen-in block of thick ice right there enables me to tell this story now."[32] Crawling on his stomach onto firm ice, he reached out his skis and was able to pull both men from the icy water. Half frozen, they struggled through waist-deep snow the rest of the way. Unfortunately, Omdal and Dietrichson had both lost their skis, which would have spelled disaster if they had tried to return to land on foot.

Ellsworth saved the lives of the entire expedition when he pulled his companions out of the icy waters. The N 25 had been repaired, and all six men were needed to

push the plane up onto the ice and to prepare a runway. Using an ice anchor, a pocket safety ax, and three wooden shovels, the men shoveled more than three hundred tons of ice in the following two weeks. Their first attempt at takeoff, on June 2, was a failure: the plane broke through the ice crust and nosed down into the slush. At five o'clock in the afternoon of the same day, in his villa in Italy, James Ellsworth died of pneumonia, unaware that his dire predictions were coming true.

Other attempts to get airborne ended in failure. The discouraged crew had to pull the plane out of the water repeatedly when ice closed in and threatened to crush it. Finally, when they had almost given up hope, Riiser-Larsen and Dietrichson found a large ice floe a half mile away that might provide a suitable runway. It took two days just to ferry the plane over the ice—to cut passages through fifteen-foot-thick pressure ridges and to build bridges across wide crevasses. Once there, they faced the monumental task of building yet another runway, this one more than four hundred meters long. They packed down the snow with their feet, and it froze hard during the night.

The N 25 finally managed to get into the air on June 15, the deadline they had set themselves before attempting to cross the ice on foot. Their magnetic compasses useless, the two pilots flew blind through the fog. Their fuel lasted just to the shore of Spitzbergen, where they landed in rough seas and managed to taxi to North Cape, one hundred miles east of King's Bay. There, fortuitously, they were picked up at once by a sealer and arrived in King's Bay exactly four weeks to the day after their departure.

Despite their ordeal, Ellsworth declared the flight a scientific success. He had charted more than one hundred twenty thousand square miles, and he could say, definitively, that there was no land on the European side of the North Polar Sea. He had also proved the usefulness of airplanes for exploration in the polar re-

Opposite: The Daisy at anchor in King
Edward Cove, Cumberland Bay. From a
hand-colored lantern slide by Robert
Cushman Murphy

The American Museum of Natural History in the Field:

The Polar Regions

gions. In just one hour of flying at a cruising speed of seventy-five miles per hour, he could cover the same distance that a man traveling by sledge covered in one week. He and Amundsen parted with plans to cross the Pole from Spitzbergen to Alaska the following year, this time on a dirigible, which had the advantage of a longer flying range and the ability to hover at low altitudes for observation.

Because of the huge costs involved, Ellsworth and Amundsen chose a small Italian airship, which Colonel Umberto Nobile was building for the Italian government. When Nobile himself agreed to pilot the craft, called the *Norge*, the venture became the Amundsen-Ellsworth-Nobile Expedition and received financial support from both the Italian and Norwegian governments.

The weather would play the greatest role in the outcome of this voyage. The plan was to have Finn Malmgren, the chief meteorologist, fly aboard the *Norge,* while his assistants at King's Bay relayed the latest weather reports from a ring of stations around the Arctic. By the time the craft arrived in King's Bay, it had already flown five thousand miles up from Rome through inclement weather without any serious mishaps. Fully loaded, it carried nearly seven tons of fuel and had a flying range of forty-four hundred miles, nearly twice their projected flight.

While the sixteen-man crew, composed entirely of Italians and Norwegians, excluding Ellsworth, waited for the weather to clear in

South Georgia Expedition—1912   The New Bedford whaling brig Daisy *departed in May 1912 for South Georgia Island, near Antarctica, with scientists from the American Museum of Natural History and the Brooklyn Institute of Arts and Sciences. In 1912, South Georgia was the base of one of the largest whaling operations in the world, site of one hundred years of indiscriminate destruction of sea animals. The sea elephant, which had managed to reestablish itself there after near extinction in the previous century, was now at the mercy of the whaling companies, which took seal oil as a sideline. The expedition studied the life history of the sea elephant, in addition to twenty-three species of birds that breed on South Georgia. Writing of his work for* The American Museum Journal, *Robert Cushman Murphy, then curator at the Brooklyn Museum and later curator of birds at the American Museum of Natural History, decried these practices, at the same time assuming, mistakenly, that the whales would escape the same fate: "The difficulties and expenses of the fishery make it almost impossible for any species of whale to become completely extirpated, however persistently it may be chased, but the unfortunate sea elephants have no such hope of preservation. Slow, unsuspicious, gregarious, they can be hunted profitably until the last one has gone to his ancestors and the calamity of the Antarctic fur seal is repeated."*

(continued on page 98)

Alaska, Commander Richard E. Byrd and Floyd Bennett flew in an airplane from King's Bay to the North Pole and back. When they returned to land, Ellsworth and Amundsen were waiting on the ice to welcome them. At Byrd's celebration dinner several days later, Ellsworth and Amundsen announced that they were ready to leave on their voyage. At 8:55 the following morning, May 11, 1926, the ropes holding the airship were released and it floated into the sky. "Then came a phenomenon for which we were not prepared. Swarms of gulls and other polar birds flew out from their rookeries in the cliffs to inspect this huge new cousin of theirs. The air vibrated

with thousands of flashing wings and shrill, excited cries. In the stillness of our cabin we could hear the roaring of the *Josephine Ford* far below, as Byrd and Bennett took off to bear us company during the first stage of our journey."[33]

Amazingly, the voyage across the Pole proceeded without incident. At the spot where the planes had gone down the previous year, Nobile descended low over the ice. "We called to Omdal, and he clambered down from the rigging to stare with us at the ferocious scene below— exactly as it had been: tumbled ice, pressure ridges, inadequate leads."[34] When they reached the North Pole, Riiser-Larsen shouted,

"Here we are," and Nobile shut down the motor, bringing the huge ship to a dead stop. While they hovered over the Pole, Amundsen dropped the flag of Norway, Ellsworth the flag of the United States, and Nobile the flag of Italy. The staffs of the flags were fitted with vanes that made them drop straight down and stick in the hard ice.

After this brief ceremony, the *Norge* headed full speed for Alaska, and, for Ellsworth, the interesting part of the voyage began. Flying at twelve hundred feet, with fifty miles of visibility in each direction, he was now entering the largest unexplored territory left on Earth. They had perfect visibility until latitude 86° north, when heavy fog began to roll in. After an hour of blind flying, an iced aerial knocked out their radio reception. Forty-seven hours after their flight began, they sighted land, and just in

time, for ice on the craft was causing serious trouble. In their flight, they had looked down at one hundred thousand square miles of new territory and ascertained that no land lay between Alaska and the North Pole. "We had established the fact that the North Polar Region is a vast, deep, ice-covered sea. The white patch at the top of the globe could now be tinted blue."[35]

The *Norge* still had to be brought down. The airship wandered throughout the night and following day, facing treacherous mountains inland, gale winds at sea; they never knew precisely where they were. As they went up and down the coasts of Alaska and Siberia, the crew gnawed on frozen chocolate and pemmican. Finally, exhausted and hungry, after a thirty-four-hundred-mile journey, they were able to bring the airship down safely on the ice of Seward Peninsula, without a

trained ground crew to receive them.

Amundsen retired after his flight across the Pole, claiming that aircraft had effectively replaced ships and dog sledges, and that he was too old to learn to fly. He had one last journey left to make, however. In the spring of 1928, he and Leif Dietrichson set out in search of Nobile, who had crashed his airship *Italia* in the Arctic. Although Nobile was eventually rescued by the Norwegian pilot Lundborg, Amundsen and Dietrichson were lost on their flight.

Seven years passed before Ellsworth embarked on another polar expedition. This time, he was the expedition leader, and his destination was the other end of the globe—Antarctica. In the intervening years, the Arctic had been thoroughly covered, but the Antarctic was essentially unexplored except for the areas

crossed by Ernest Shackleton, Amundsen, and Robert Falcon Scott. Only Byrd had flown to the South Pole and back from his base station, Little America, and had mapped Marie Byrd Land to the east.

This was the kind of challenge that Ellsworth loved. In 1932, he bought a herring boat, fitted it for ice-breaking, and christened it the *Wyatt Earp*. In his cabin, Ellsworth hung Earp's own cartridge belt. His airplane, the *Polar Star*, a low-wing monoplane custom-built by the Northrup Corporation, had a cruising range of seven thousand miles, the longest of any plane at the time, and a top speed of two hundred thirty miles per hour. Yet it took Ellsworth three years to get his expedition in the air. The first year, 1933, his plane was crushed in the ice. The second year, during a test run, the engine failed. Ellsworth had brought along crates full of spare parts, all except the one needed to fix the engine. He had to sail a thousand miles to the north to Chile to fetch a spare rod. This setback, in conjunction with bad weather, dashed their hopes for that year.

Ellsworth planned to fly across Antarctica from Dundee Island

near the Weddell Sea to Little America in the Bay of Whales, landing as needed to weather storms. There he would wait to be picked up by his ship when it would be able to break through the ice in January.

On November 22, 1935, Ellsworth and his pilot, Herbert Hollick-Kenyon, took to the air. This time, he sensed that they would succeed in their flight and would not be stopped by the mechanical problems and bad weather that had plagued them in the preceding days. Flying at an altitude of thirteen thousand feet, they passed over a magnificent mountain range that rose to twelve thousand feet, which Ellsworth named the Eternity Range. Eight hours into the flight, the *Polar Star*'s radio transmitter malfunctioned. The crew of the *Wyatt Earp* feared that Ellsworth was lost in Antarctica, and rescue efforts were set in motion.

Meanwhile, they made four landings during the crossing. At the first landing, after nearly fourteen hours in the air, Ellsworth raised the American flag. He named the area extending from 80 to 120 degrees west longitude James W. Ellsworth Land after his father, a tribute he had been waiting many years to pay. After two more short flights, he and his pilot reached their third camp, where they were delayed for seven days by a blizzard featuring forty-five-mile-per-hour winds. When they finally managed to lift off from the new snow, Ellsworth wrote in his diary: "I suppose our snow wall will stand for a long time. I thought it would be our mausoleum."[36]

They came down again on the ice on the other side of Antarctica, fourteen days after they started their journey, their fuel tanks empty. In that white waste-

Stoll-McCracken Arctic Expedition—1928 *Led by Museum mammalogist H. E. Anthony and Harold McCracken, a scientific party sailed aboard the schooner* Effie Morrissey, *along the coast of Alaska, through the Bering Strait and into Arctic waters in search of mammals, sea birds, and archaeological material. Their most important scientific contribution was the collection of a full representation of the Pacific walrus for the Pacific walrus group in the Hall of Ocean Life. On the voyage north, the schooner stopped at inhospitable Little Diomede Island, where auklets, puffins, murres, kittiwakes, cormorants, and other seabirds flocked in huge numbers. The scientists made extensive collections and studies for an exhibit of arctic birdlife.*

Alaska Expedition—1939 *In the spring of 1939, Helge Larson, anthropologist at the Danish National Museum, joined Louis Giddings and Froelich G. Rainey, of the University of Alaska, and scientists from the American Museum of Natural History on an expedition to excavate Eskimo ruins in Alaska. What they found, instead, was a huge ancient "Arctic metropolis" with the ruins of a culture older than that of the Aztecs and the Maya. The settlement lay on the north shore of Point Hope, two hundred miles north of the Bering Sea, at a place the Eskimos called "Ipiutak." In 1939, the expedition excavated several houses, but it was not until the following summer that they began to realize the extent of the ruins: six hundred to eight hundred houses arranged along five "avenues." The town was nearly a mile long and probably supported upwards of four thousand inhabitants. Today Point Hope is inhabited by a small Eskimo population. On this sandbar, twenty miles from the mainland, with no trees and little vegetation, it is difficult for settlements of two hundred fifty Eskimos to survive the grueling winters. The discovery of the ancient ruins immediately raised a number of intriguing questions: How could a large settlement support itself on a site with such limited resources? Were these ancient people related to present-day Eskimos? If not, where did they come from and where did they go? Many of the hundreds of objects found, including elaborate ivory carvings in a unique spiral form, could not be identified, and the Eskimos were as puzzled as the scientists by the findings. The fine workmanship of the Ipiutak suggested a connection to the Neolithic people of eastern Asia, a more sophisticated center of primitive culture*

land with no markers to be seen, Byrd's station could be anywhere. It turned out to be only sixteen miles away, but it took them six days, traveling one hundred miles over the ice, to find Little America. All that distance the two men pulled a two-hundred-pound sledge, packed with fifteen days'

rations, a stove and fuel, and their sleeping bags. Ellsworth, however, had neglected to bring one essential item—his eyeglasses. In the bunk room of the radio shack, waiting to be rescued by the *Wyatt Earp*, he was reduced to lying on his bunk, for hour upon monotonous hour,

than America. This mysterious tribe could well have migrated across the Bering Sea to the northern coast of Alaska some time before the birth of Christ.

Coalsack Bluff Antarctic Expedition—1969   *The theory that the continents we see today actually represent the fragmentation of a single original land mass was almost as revolutionary when it was first proposed in 1910 as Darwin's theory of evolution had been in the mid-nineteenth century. For decades, scientists lacked the hard evidence to prove the validity of "continental drift." In 1969, paleontologist Edwin Colbert of the Museum joined with scientists from a number of universities to search for fossils in Antarctica, in an attempt to determine the distribution of life at the time such an Ur-continent existed. The team landed at Coalsack Bluff near the Beardmore Glacier, four hundred miles from the South Pole. In the Transantarctic Mountains are many cliff exposures above the glacier, and the very first day the expedition struck gold—some thirty fossils. A week later they found the jaw of a 200-million-year-old mammal-like reptile, Lystrosaurus. This fossil and others found later established a faunal link between Antarctica and southern Africa, demonstrating that the two land masses had once been joined.*

Antarctic Meteorite Field Research—1990s   *Supported by NASA and led by curator Martin Prinz, scientists associated with the Museum's Department of Mineral Sciences have been studying meteorites in the Antarctic for evidence of early events in the history of the solar system. Unusual combinations of elements in the meteorites can provide clues to the precise steps in the evolution of the planets, and Museum scientists have sought these combinations of elements by excavating meteorites in the Antarctic ice, often under the most challenging conditions. The most recent fieldwork involves the recovery of meteorites no larger than dust grains, a seemingly impossible task. These micrometeorites, as they are called, must be recovered by melting and filtering tons of snow. Analysis by Prinz and his team has revealed a composition different from that seen in micrometeorites found elsewhere, suggesting that perhaps a more complicated process than had been suspected took place in the time before the Earth was born.*

while Hollick-Kenyon, a taciturn man, read piles of detective stories he had discovered in the cabins. In addition, Ellsworth was developing gangrene in his left foot, which had been frostbitten during the search for the camp. When the men were finally rescued after one month by a ship sent by the Australian government, it was not a moment too soon.

With this successful flight, Lincoln Ellsworth became the first man to fly across both poles. He had claimed a huge area, three hundred thousand to five hundred thousand miles, for the United States, had contributed to the mapping of the continent, and had collected important geological data. With that great achievement, he effectively ended his career as a polar explorer. Ellsworth ventured out only once more, on a 1939 expedition to Antarctica, when, hampered by bad weather, he flew two hundred forty miles inland before turning back.

Ellsworth's successful transpolar flights ushered in a new age of exploration. Despite the dangers faced by explorers in the early days of aviation, their experience was radically different from that of the generation that preceded them. Of his voyage in the *Norge*, Ellsworth commented wistfully, "[It] was a far cry from my youthful vision of polar exploration—the painfully established bases, the bitter journeys with sledges and dogs, the heroic battle against the elements. . . . The *Norge* and its crew were but a machine in which the explorer could sit at ease and watch unroll the panorama of the unknown."[37] Nonetheless, what impelled these intrepid explorers to risk their lives time and again remained the same—a desire to make known the unknown. Donald MacMillan did not regard the Crocker Land Expedition as a failure even though it found only a bank of clouds; he felt he had made important discoveries. In justification, he wrote, "Man has been content to leave home, to live in savage places, to plod along through deep snows, to land upon primeval shores, to suffer privations and discomforts, and all this in order to add his mite to the sum of the world knowledge. And man will continue to do these foolish things and to undergo these useless hardships until the sum of human knowledge is complete."[38]

CENTRAL
AFRICAN
REPUBLIC
(FRENCH EQUATORIAL AFRICA)

SUDAN
(ANGLO-EGYPTIAN SUDAN)

ETHIOPIA

Uele R. Niangara

Mbunza
Okondo
Faradje

Mt. Morungole ▲
KIDEPO
VALLEY

Lake Turkana

Lang-Chapin Exp.,
1909–15

Aruwimi R.
Medje
ITURI
FOREST

Lake Albert

Mt. Elgon ▲

Uasin
Gishu
Plateau

Lindi R.
Avakubi

Congo R.
Kisangani
(Stanleyville)

UGANDA
(BRITISH EAST AFRICA)

KENYA

▲ Mt. Ruwenzori

Mt. Kenya ▲

Tana R.

Lomami R.

ZAIRE
(BELGIAN CONGO)

Lake Edward

Lake Victoria

Nairobi ✛

Lukenia
Hills

Lake Kivu

RWANDA
Virunga
Mts.

Serengeti
Plains

Lake Natron

BURUNDI

TANZANIA
(TANGANYIKA)

Mt. Kilimanjaro ▲

African Reflections

IN 1910, ON A COLLECTING EXPEDITION in central Africa for the American Museum of Natural History, Herbert Lang and James Chapin came to a village Lang had long desired to visit. In the northeast corner of the Belgian Congo near the Uele River, the village was home to the Mangbetu people, renowned for their ivory carving, metalwork, and physical adornment. Here resided the court of a Mangbetu chief, Okondo, one of a long line whose antecedents included the proud and fierce Mbunza. Lang had steeped himself in the most detailed account of the region and of Mbunza's court, a sometimes lurid narrative by the German explorer Georg Schweinfurth. Schweinfurth had described a teeming royal society ensconced in two magnificent halls—"One might truly be justified in calling them wonders of the world," he wrote.[1] Piles of human skulls littering village refuse heaps gave evidence that these Mangbetu were also unredeemed cannibals. Lang and Chapin, however, found the reality to be radically different:

A large deputation greeted us about a mile from the royal residence, and we soon discovered the king—poor slave to fashion—clad in an officer's old, shabby uniform. Although satisfied that, in this part of Africa, at least, the days of the kings had passed, we had no reason to complain. . . . When we expressed our regret at the lack of the great halls made famous by Schweinfurth's account, the architects were bidden to proceed at once. We had to start northward for the southern Sudan, and laughed incredulously as we handed the king, in advance, the gifts we had promised. . . . Two loads of salt and one of brass wire for anklets for his queens proved satisfactory. His promise was kept; one year as many as 500 men worked at the structure, of course with continual interruptions for dancing and drinking.[2]

The hall was ready for Lang and Chapin's return. In Africa, life could imitate art, demolish preconceptions, and challenge a powerful Western myth.

The myth portrayed a savage, changeless, and boundless Africa, against which individuals measured their fortitude and from which they

Mangbetu Queen Nenzima, Okondo's village, northeastern Congo, 1910. Her long fingernails were an indication of her elite position as a principal wife of Chief Okondo. She was the wife of four kings between 1875 and 1926 and probably a cousin to the famed Mbunza. Her wisdom was widely recognized and her powers were feared. Photograph by Herbert Lang

extracted fabulous wealth. It began to be created as early as 1482—and contradicted almost immediately—when Portuguese sailors entered the mouth of the Congo River. This contact was the first between Europeans and a civilization south of the equator. Initially welcomed, then banished, then brought back by one of the Congolese kings, the Portuguese were engaged in the most complex of relations with a non-Western civilization. One son of the Congo king Affonso even became a bishop at Rome.

The myth of Africa grew, nonetheless, reinforced by the fabrications of such popular writers as Daniel Defoe in the eighteenth century and, in the nineteenth, accounts by newspaperman-turned-explorer Henry Morton Stanley of his attempts to find Dr. David Livingstone and to rescue Emin Pasha in central Africa. By the end of the nineteenth century, not only Portugal but also England, Germany, the Netherlands, France, Italy, and Belgium had staked claims. In the process, the vast territory along the Congo River—today's Zaire—became known as "darkest Africa." This dense equatorial forest and its bordering savannas stretched

eighteen hundred miles, from the Atlantic Ocean nearly to the Nile River. Within it lived fantastic creatures: the white rhinoceros, eagles that devoured entire monkeys, full-grown human beings no taller than Western children, and cannibals with elongated heads. Here, danger and disease were the adventurer's companions. Fortunes in rubber and ivory awaited the taking—if a white man had the courage and strength to survive.

The scientists from the American Museum of Natural History found all of these things and none of them. From the experiences of Lang and Chapin to those of anthropologist Colin Turnbull, fifty years later, the Museum's encounters with the people and wildlife of Africa have measured not some unchanging "heart of darkness," in Joseph Conrad's phrase, but the inexorable reality of change itself. In diaries, films, and photographs, the Museum scientists have recorded cultures confronting and altering each other, a lush landscape yielding to human exploitation, and the relentless

reduction of what once seemed an inexhaustible wealth of wildlife. An elegiac note sounds constantly through their African reflections, a sadness at animals no longer seen and cultures lost to "civilization."

An equally profound change, however, took place among the explorers and scientists themselves. They were altered by Africa, and nothing was the same for them once they had known the continent. Herbert Lang returned to Africa in 1925 and never left. James Chapin kept returning throughout his life, like the birds he studied that migrate back and forth along the equator but never leave the Congo. Carl Akeley, who planned the Hall of African Mammals that bears his name, lies buried on the slope of an African volcano, in the wildlife preserve he helped create. Of all of the Museum's venturers to the interior, Colin Turnbull traveled farthest, in spirit. He found in Africa evidence of the human capacity for creating both heaven and hell on earth. In the face of overwhelming experiences, he abandoned the only refuge of the anthropologist in the field—his objectivity.

The Lang-Chapin Expedition

In 1901, Sir Harry Johnston, an explorer and linguist, brought from the Congo to England the first hide and head of a rare animal, the okapi. Slightly larger than a zebra, whose relative it was thought to be, the delicate, strikingly patterned creature proved to be the only extant species kin to the giraffe. Few Westerners had ever seen it, for its home was the dense forest near the Ituri tributary of the upper Congo River, a remote region of jungle inhabited by the Mbuti Pygmies. Almost at once, the okapi became one of the most sought-after safari prizes. The American Museum of Natural History was beginning to gather specimens for a new hall of African wildlife, and it put the okapi high on its list. Competition also provided an impetus: President Theodore Roosevelt, Jr., was planning an elaborate collecting expedition for the United States National Museum. New York would not be outdone. The American Museum of Natural History was determined to have the finest okapi display in the world.

The Museum had an inside track. King Leopold of Belgium, who ruled his own private tract in the region, the so-called Congo Free State, was a friend of trustee J. P. Morgan, Jr. Just before international objections to his inhumane policies of coerced native labor forced Leopold to turn over control of the area to the Belgian parliamentary government, his agents made a collection of some

thirty-five hundred ethnographic objects and presented it to his friends in New York. The Museum suddenly possessed the material for a major African exhibit, showing animal trophies alongside cultural treasures. With support from trustees and the controversial King Leopold himself, the Museum decided to mount an expedition not only to search for the okapi and other specimens but also to gather a complete repertoire of artifacts from the cultures of the Congo. The expedition was planned to last two years; instead, it lasted nearly six. It was led by a pair of unproven naturalists, who, together, accomplished an almost superhuman feat of collecting.

Herbert Lang, a native of Germany, had joined the Museum in 1903 after learning the craft of taxidermy in Europe. In 1906, he accompanied Richard Tjader on a Museum expedition to collect large mammal specimens in British East Africa (now Kenya). In the eyes of Museum president Henry Fairfield Osborn, that qualified the twenty-eight-year-old mammalogist to lead his own expedition. Compared to James Chapin, however, whom he selected as his partner, Lang was a seasoned veteran. Chapin, a junior at Columbia University, was barely nineteen. The precocious naturalist had been working part-time at the Museum since age sixteen. He, too, had learned taxidermy; he was especially interested in birds. Neither man liked hunting, but, as Chapin remarked, "No sportsman offered to lead the party into what was reported to be anything but a healthful region."[3]

Their task was simple: sail to the west coast of Africa, travel northeast up the Congo River some seven hundred miles, disem-

bark at the tiny outpost of Stanleyville (now Kisangani), then proceed northeast five hundred more miles on foot, eventually reaching the border of Sudan in the north and Uganda in the west. All Lang and Chapin had to do on the way was collect specimens of the entire fauna of the Belgian Congo. Luckily, neither of the two men was averse to doing a day's work for a day's pay: "Lang was a human dynamo," Chapin recalled later. "He could work from daybreak to midnight, and always doing something useful. Often he was still developing his films after midnight, because all that had to be done at night when the air was cool. . . . I admire even myself in my younger years, because I know I couldn't do it anymore. Now it sounds simple to go out and shoot a few birds, but that was only one very small part of my job. I was there to do anything I could to aid Lang."[4]

Chapin's aid included making sure the expedition porters—sometimes as many as one hundred fifty at a time—were fed and recompensed; designing and helping to build packing cases; making hundreds of delicate watercolor sketches of wildlife; soldering together tins used to "pickle" the reptile specimens in formaldehyde; and learning Kiswahili, as well as two African dialects. Chapin judged that he would not win any contest at hunting birds, but he managed to collect some six thousand bird specimens, many of them species new to science. The collection formed the foundation for a thirty-year book project, the

Opposite: The rare okapi, the original motivation of the Lang-Chapin Expedition, c. 1915. Photograph by Herbert Lang

monumental four-volume *Birds of the Congo*. In spite of Chapin's industry, Lang was always two steps ahead of him, collecting everything from ants to elephants and teaching both Chapin and his Congolese assistants. In a short time, Chapin came to regard Lang as a foster father and was known by the natives as *mtoto na Langi*—Lang's son.

"Anything but a healthful region," Chapin called the Congo. The understatement is characteristic of the man. Anyone who went to the Congo in 1909 risked dying of malaria, amebic dysentery, and sleeping sickness, which was endemic to the region. Admonishments to avoid tsetse flies and take quinine adorned every Congo River outpost. Lang and Chapin consumed eight grams of quinine each day. When Chapin skipped a few days, he immediately found himself in the grip of a raging fever. Yet, throughout five and a half years, neither man ever lost a day to illness, and only

one of the thousands of porters and dozens of native assistants who traveled with them was ever injured.

In 1909, the former Congo Free State was anything but free. Its natives had been the subjects of King Leopold and were just then under the rule of the Belgian state. Those in the forests were forced to pay a regular tax in rubber to Belgium. Periodically some would resist, with bloody results. Moreover, although the Belgians had systematically attempted to stamp out cannibalism in the Congo for two decades, they had not fully succeeded. The expedition's route would take it through several areas where the threat might still be real. One was near their main base, located some two hundred miles overland from Stanleyville, at an outpost called Avakubi, on the edge of the Ituri Forest.

They arrived there in 1909. With its eighty-foot-high trees and hanging vines as thick as a

man's arm, the Ituri Forest was so dense that, at noon on a cloudy day, it seemed like twilight. This great forest was home to the seldom-seen Mbuti Pygmies (later studied by Museum anthropologist Colin Turnbull). They were reputed cannibals, but Lang and Chapin saw no evidence of the practice. To the west, where the two traveled next, dwelt the Meje, whom the Belgians had not subdued until 1903. At one point Lang, who already had more plantains than he could use to feed his crew, was asked to buy more by the women of a Meje village. He refused, and as he left, one remarked, "Never mind, we'll eat the white man with his own salt."[5]

As it happened, the Meje were enormously helpful, and Lang and Chapin remained in the area for nearly a year. From there they commenced their collecting in earnest, fanning out with their assistants into the jungle. They tried not to kill large mammals themselves but rather to take the skins and heads from animals already hunted by the natives. These collections they sent back to a warehouse in Avakubi. The Meje even offered to find Lang his precious okapi, and they delivered on their promise. Their worship of the animal, however, permitted them to kill it only with a club, disfiguring the specimens and making them useless for exhibition. Lang was determined to secure an intact specimen even if he had to stay on in the Congo. That, ultimately, is what he did.

Meanwhile, Chapin was gradually falling under the spell of the Congo's astonishing bird life. High above his head, he first heard the call of the "invisible" bird he would pursue for nearly three years. *Nyete, nyete, nyete,* it sounded. The natives insisted it

Above: Mbuti encampment in the Ituri Forest, northeastern Congo, 1913. When Colin Turnbull first came to Africa (see page 121), he found the Pygmies living much as they had when Lang and Chapin entered their territory, more than forty years before. From a hand-colored lantern slide by Herbert Lang

Left: Two men at Banda Sundi(?), mourning a chief, c. 1909–15. From a hand-colored lantern slide by Herbert Lang

Right: This Mangbetu pot, with elongated head, is a stylized representation of the way fashionable Mangbetu women adorned themselves early in this century.

could not be seen, but still Chapin sought it. Not until he returned to Avakubi in 1913 to begin packing his specimens did he manage to bring down the starling-sized bird whose tail feathers formed an inverted fleur-de-lis. It was a honey guide, a species venerated in the Congo for its ability to find beehives. In a complicated behavioral evolution, it had "learned" to lead human beings and other mammals to hives, in order to feast on the spoils. Chapin heard the familiar sound above his head and deduced what would not be proven for thirty-four years: it is the honey guide's tail feathers, whirring through the air, that announce to mammals to follow the bird to honey. "By the Azande tribe of northeastern Congo the bird is called *turubwa*," Chapin later wrote, "and I was told that before the arrival of Europeans an Azande chief would have cut off the ear of any man so stupid as to have killed a honey guide."[6]

The Meje village of Medje was located at a place where the Mangbetu people mingled with the Azande—tribes rich in traditions of music and art. The songs sung by the native porters spurred Lang and Chapin on the trail toward Niangara and sent them to sleep each night. Forty-five years after he first heard them, Chapin could still sing the songs. While Chapin fell under the spell of the music, Lang fell under the spell of Mangbetu art and the Mangbetu themselves.

At the last moment, the Museum had asked Lang to make ethnographic collections even though he was not a trained ethnographer. There was no Franz Boas to instruct him, as members of the Jesup North Pacific Expedition had been tutored a decade earlier. What Lang accomplished was a labor of love. Like Schweinfurth before him, he recognized artistic expression of the highest order. Everything from ivory hair combs to musical instruments to iron spear points displayed superb workmanship. Not only did Lang barter for all he could get—thirty-eight hundred objects—he asked questions about the origin and use of each one. How was it made? For what purpose or ceremony was it intended? What story did its images depict? He took more than a thousand photographs of people, artifacts, and artists at work. His collections were valuable for the same reason that Chapin's collection of reptiles were, although Chapin was not a herpetologist: he took good notes. In 1990, the Museum mounted a landmark

exhibition of Lang's collections, "African Reflections: Art from Northeastern Zaire." Enid Schildkrout, the American Museum of Natural History's curator of African ethnology, recently remarked, "We might wish that Lang had been more thorough and less gullible, but because of what he did, these objects can provide not only esthetic pleasure but meaningful evidence about a culture."

Unlike others who collected artifacts, Lang did not assume that "authentic" meant old (or untainted by Western contact). He was happy that the Mangbetu artists of Okondo's great village were mobilized to create works expressly for the Museum. As a result, his collection documents both the varied artistic styles of a vital culture and the rise of new approaches, especially in the carving of human figures. Lang's appreciation of the Mangbetu also enabled him to form unusual personal relationships. Okondo was reputed to have 180 wives; the eldest was Queen Nenzima. Nearing age sixty, she had survived the ritual destruction of property (and sometimes wives) that attended the death of Mangbetu kings. When Lang asked about the fate of artworks, she replied: "'There is nothing left, not a single object, except myself. I am the only thing, such a very old thing. Do you want to take me home?' As a result of this interview, I was presented with a necklace of extremely long finger and toe nails, an emblem of dignity and especially cut to show her high regard. . . . She shrewdly added that were I to give her all the loads the expedition owned, I had but badly repaid her trust. I quickly offered part of my thumbnail, regretting its comparative shortness."[7] She accepted it, kept it in a small vial, and grew a new set of nails, which she also presented to him when he returned two years later.

Lang and Chapin pushed on to the northeast, to the outpost of Faradje, near the Sudan border. The jungle ended, the forested savannas began, and the Azande predominated. Large mammals

The Quest for the Congo Peacock

When James Chapin was collecting birds in the Congo, he was often put on the track of species from feathers he saw in native headdresses. The most tantalizing specimen led him on a quest that would last for twenty-four years and carry him more than seven thousand miles.

In 1913, when Chapin plucked the blue-black feather from the headdress of a man in Avakubi, in the Ituri Forest, he could not believe it was what it seemed—evidence of a pheasant species, distinct from a quail, partridge, or cuckoo. No such birds had been noted in the Congo, and Chapin did not see any on the expedition. He brought the feather home in a bundle with others he could not identify. Over the years, it was the only one that remained a mystery. Unknown to Chapin, however, someone else was also intrigued by the plumage, and he had the entire bird to study. Henri Schouteden, of the Musée Royal du Congo Belge in Brussels, acquired a full specimen from a mining company in 1914. It sat in his museum puzzling him for twenty-two years, until Chapin, by now a friend and colleague, visited. He saw the bird on a shelf and, amazingly, made the connection. The two scientists deduced that it was a native Congo peacock, a genus of pheasant, and dubbed it Afropavo congensis. *It was like no other peacock ever seen. But where had it come from? Did the species still exist somewhere in the Congo? Chapin had to find out.*

Just days later, he happened to lunch with another Congo acquaintance, who, knowing of Chapin's interest in such things, told him about an unusual bird he had eaten in 1930—a Congo peacock. More important, he told Chapin where the native hunter had killed it, in the

replaced art on Lang's collecting agenda, while Chapin cast fond glances southwest to the mountains of Uganda and the birds of upper elevations. Although they collected for more than a year near Faradje, their written records convey a sense of dust, frontiers, and transitoriness. The outpost attracted a collection of big-game poachers and various Conradian characters. Pickering, an ivory hunter from England who drank too much, can stand for all of them and for an aspect of the colonial experience in Africa. One day, inebriated, he pulled out his elephant gun and began shooting at the Belgian flag. Then he seized a .45 auto-

Opposite: Ornithologist James P. Chapin painting a watercolor at the expedition's camp at Avakubi, on the edge of the Ituri Forest in the eastern Congo, 1910. Photograph by Herbert Lang

Left: Man of the Logo tribe, at a dance, wearing a hat with feathers inserted into a basketry base. Faradje, northeastern Congo, 1911. James Chapin collected many feathers from such headdresses in order to help him track and identify bird species in the Congo. Photograph by Herbert Lang

forest a hundred miles from Avakubi. Gradually, Chapin began to form a plan to return to the Congo to search for the bird. He contacted one of the native assistants whom he had trained in 1926, and they were reunited in the Congo in June of 1937. Driving the same roads along which he and Herbert Lang had trudged in 1909, Chapin pursued his quest for nearly a month before he finally encountered the living bird that for decades he had known only as a single feather.

matic, headed for town, and rode down the main street taking potshots at whatever appealed to him. Finally Lang confronted the man: "Come Pickering, let's have the pistol," he said, and simply took it away. No wonder Chapin was in awe of Lang. Years later Chapin heard of Pickering's demise: he had been trampled so thoroughly by an elephant that there was little left to identify.

In 1913, Lang headed southwest in a final attempt to secure okapi specimens. Chapin returned to Avakubi to prepare the collections stored there for transport to Stanleyville. At Stanleyville, these and additional material would have to be prepared for the river trip to the coast. Of all the tasks so far, this was perhaps the most daunting. Two hundred loads were stored in Medje, two hundred at Niangara, and six hundred at Faradje. It took a year to pack all the material and a thousand porters to carry it to Stanleyville. All the while, Chapin and his assistant Nekuma, whose knowledge of birdcalls was encyclopedic, continued to observe and collect. At one point Chapin camped for three days under an enormous tree to obtain a specimen of the crowned eagle, which feasted on monkeys. He dropped it with a single shot, but it fell back into the nest. His assistants retrieved it only after a dangerous

forty-five-foot climb. Lang and Chapin had collected so many specimens that Chapin ran out of nails to build packing cases and was reduced to forging his own from defunct shotguns.

Lang arrived in Avakubi crowned with success. He had secured the finest examples of the okapi possessed by any museum. He and Chapin did not have long to celebrate, however. The postmaster, Louis Kraft, called all the Europeans and Americans together to announce that war had been declared between England and Germany. Lang held only a German passport. Kraft looked at his guest and remarked, "Look here, you didn't start this war. We'll go on being friends as before."[8]

Lang and Chapin finished packing the collections in Stanleyville, and Chapin took charge of ferrying more than fifty tons of material downriver. The two would not see each other again for another year. As a German, Lang could not obtain passage on most of the ships leaving the Congo. He traveled down the coast to Angola and finally managed to find a Portuguese freighter to take him to New York. Meanwhile, Chapin's ship had to run a German U-boat blockade outside Liverpool in

Opposite, above: Grinding flour, Okondo's village, 1910. Mangbetu agriculture centered around grain, which was hand-ground, stored in granaries, and used to make porridge or beer. From a hand-colored lantern slide by Herbert Lang

Opposite, below: Barambo mu *dancers, Poko, 1913. The dance is part of a ritual to bestow the blessings of the forest on the community. An intoxicating drink made from a local root called* naando *energizes the dancers. Lang wrote in his field notes, "As soon as he feels the action of the beverage, he starts a very irregular and wild dance, which he accompanies with a series of yells, the gongs accompany the dance, which causes general merriment among the onlooking crowd." From a hand-colored lantern slide by Herbert Lang*

Above: Zande woman in a headdress of cowrie shells and human hair, northeastern Congo, c. 1909–15. From a hand-colored lantern slide by Herbert Lang

Above right: A Barambo chief in costume before a dance, possibly the mu *dance, near Poko, northeastern Congo, 1913. His costume includes a wide variety of natural materials. It is part of the Museum's Lang-Chapin collection. From a hand-colored lantern slide by Herbert Lang*

order to bring the specimens to port. Collections and collectors made it to New York intact late in 1915. Chapin arrived just in time to resume the second semester of his junior year.

For both men, however, their African experience was just beginning. Lang was a dynamo not only on the trail but also at the Museum, encouraging scientists in many departments to "write up" the expedition results—some ten volumes' worth. The volume on Congo fishes proved as essential as Chapin's bird series. Lang also used his photographs and writing to call attention to the accelerating slaughter of Africa's wildlife. A decade later, during a 1925 expedition to Angola led by Museum trustee Arthur Vernay, Lang left the group. He reappeared in South Africa, where he lived the rest of his life as one of that nation's most distinguished nature photographers. In 1930, he rejoined Vernay for another

expedition, to the Kalahari desert of southwestern Africa.

Chapin became so immersed in the study of the birds of the Congo that, in a very real sense, he never left. He went back four more times and on each visit accomplished remarkable feats. In 1926–27, he fulfilled his wish to visit the Kivu volcano region on the border of the Congo and Rwanda and study its mountain birds. Chapin never considered himself an adventurer, and yet on the same trip he became only the second Westerner to ascend the glaciers of Mount Stanley, at 15,400 feet. He climbed the last part alone, for his African guides thought him mad to continue into snowy regions, where, they were convinced, contact with the "white powder" meant certain death. He climbed several of the peaks of Uganda's Ruwenzori mountain range years in advance of the Duke of Abruzzi's famous mountaineering expedition. During these years, Chapin also found time to collect more than two thousand bird specimens. Seven species were named after him. His dissertation was published in 1932 as the first of four volumes on Congo birds (the last was published in 1954) and won the Daniel Giraud Elliot Medal of the National Academy of Sciences. By that time Chapin had earned many honors, including the *Ordre de la Couronne* from the Belgian government.

Chapin's last visit to Africa, in 1955, was his most poignant. He had not seen his friend and mentor Herbert Lang since Lang's departure for Angola thirty years before. At Lang's farm in Pretoria, South Africa, Chapin found his old colleague recovering from a recent stroke but still passionate about the land he could not leave. "Lang seemed in good health and spirit, full of plans for developing the farm. . . . I was pleased to find him in such good shape with a surprising amount of his old enthusiasm," Chapin wrote the Explorers' Club, which Lang had joined just before the Congo expedition. When Chapin returned to Pretoria a month later, Lang was seriously ill. He died in 1957, and Chapin provided an epitaph in that same letter: "With so many of his friends in America and Africa, I mourn the passing of a great naturalist, a tireless worker, and a faithful companion and leader."[9]

In Brightest Africa

Three monuments commemorate the Museum's other great African explorer, Carl Akeley. One, a small concrete marker, identifies the place of his tragic death and burial in the mountain gorilla country at the eastern edge of the Congo forest. The other two em-

body his life and work: the Akeley Memorial Hall in the Museum and the group of parks in Zaire, Uganda, and Rwanda that preserve the wildlife he cherished. Akeley was that paradox of Africa's colonial period, the "white hunter" who became a defender of the species he himself had hunted. Although Akeley spent only five of his sixty-two years in Africa, Africa dominated his life. His three expeditions for the Museum trace his progress toward a vision of Africa not as the "dark continent" of Stanley's myth but as a bright one of beauty and wonder.

The place to begin with the contradictory Carl Akeley is the exhibition hall that bears his name, for this was the culmination of Akeley's labor, courage, and thought from his first Museum expedition in 1909 until his death in 1926. "When I returned to America in 1911, my mind saturated with the beauty and the wonder of the continent I had left," he wrote, "I was dreaming of African Hall."[10] He conceived and planned it, collected, politicked, and raised money for it, created many of its exhibits, and, ultimately, gave up his life for it.

The mounted group of African elephants, entitled *The Alarm*, and the twenty-eight surrounding dioramas, designed in the Art Deco style by Akeley himself, occupy an enormous amount of Museum space. An addition to the Museum had to be built in order to house it. From the first, the size of the proposed hall was controversial, as was its estimated cost and the decision to commit a scientific institution to a static vision of African wildlife, however dramatically portrayed. Yet for Akeley two truths outweighed any criticism: many African species, from gorillas to wild

dogs, were dwindling in number and might soon be extinct, and most people who visited the Museum would never experience the natural splendor of Africa firsthand. He intended the hall to be both an accurate historical record and a transporting experience. Nothing like it had ever been attempted, and only a driven person could have seen the project through. Akeley was nothing if not driven.

In 1908, the Museum had sought to lure Akeley away from Chicago's Field Museum, where the animal displays he created were provoking admiration and controversy. Akeley was pioneering revolutionary techniques for mounting large mammals. His innovation of constructing a superstructure of papier-mâché, rather that simply stuffing skins with straw, bestowed an unprecedented realism—not to mention accuracy—on his displays. The method was time-consuming and expensive, and Akeley, never one to compromise, was labeled an unrealistic dreamer by his colleagues at the Field. The American Museum of Natural History, however, wanted his realism for the displays it was organizing in its African hall. While still working for the Field, Akeley volunteered to collect elephant specimens for a display, and the Museum accepted. Although Akeley would never become a salaried employee, preferring instead to work independently in his own studio and then in the Museum itself, he would become one of the Museum's best-known figures over the next two decades.

Akeley came to museum work through an interest in creating animal mounts. He had grown up on a farm in Clarendon, New York, and learned the trade through an apprenticeship at the nation's leading taxidermy atelier, Ward's Natural Science Establishment, in nearby Rochester. Many eminent naturalists associated with the American Museum of Natural History passed through Ward's in the 1880s, including the entomologist William Morton Wheeler, explorer George Cherrie (see pages 163–71), and future Museum director Frederic Lucas. One of Akeley's first tasks was to mount the skeleton of the world-famous circus elephant Jumbo. At Ward's, Akeley realized that mounted exhibits could be works of art. He spent several years in Milwaukee perfecting his methods and moved to Chicago in 1895, where work was more plentiful; there he gained a reputation for his lifelike taxidermy. He had been in Chicago less than a year when Field Museum director Daniel G. Elliot offered him a place on the first American zoological expedition to Africa.

From the first, the expedition was beset by difficulties, not the least of which was an uncertainty about its destination. Eventually Elliot settled on Berbera, on the Gulf of Aden. The desert climate was grueling, even for one as hearty as Akeley. The camels were recalcitrant, and Elliot was felled with a near-fatal case of malaria. At the same time, Akeley, who was not yet an experienced hunter, learned a terrible lesson.

Toward the end of one long day, as he was searching for the carcass of a warthog he had shot, he heard what he thought was a hyena. He fired without looking carefully and soon realized he had wounded a leopard. The angered cat began stalking him. When Akeley ran out of bullets, the cat attacked. Probably because it was wounded, the leopard seized Akeley's arm instead of

his throat, or he would certainly have been killed. Somehow he managed to hold it away and grab its throat while he called for his gun bearer to bring a knife. No one came. Akeley forced the animal to the ground and eventually strangled it. The struggle became a kind of baptism of fire:

When I came inside [the compound], my companions were at dinner before one of the tents. They had heard the shots and speculated on the probabilities. They had decided that I was in a mix-up with a lion or with natives, but that I would either have the enemy or the enemy would have me before they could get to me; so they continued their dinner. The fatalistic spirit of the country had prevailed. When I came within range of vision, however, my appearance was quite sufficient to arrest attention, for my clothes were all ripped, my arm was chewed into an unpleasant sight, and there was blood and dirt all over me.[11]

Fatalistic or not, the spirit of Africa prevailed on Akeley. He seized the first chance he could to return.

That chance came in 1905, when he convinced the Field Museum to launch another African collecting expedition, this one to the heart of central Africa—Mount Kenya, in what was then British East Africa. Akeley hoped to create the first realistic elephant exhibit in any museum. Under the tutelage of one of Africa's most famous "white hunters," R. J. Cunninghame, he and his wife Delia learned how to hunt what Akeley called "the first of animals." He regarded the African elephant as the most intelligent, powerful, and dangerous of foes, and in photographs from the time, Akeley, still a young man, had begun to assume the haggard look of a war veteran. Africa was many things, but it was not a place to relax, and

his expeditions would take an increasing toll, both physical and mental.

On the trail, Akeley was an unforgiving taskmaster, and Delia Akeley had to overcome her fear and learn to face down a charging elephant in order to shoot without giving ground. The Field Museum had expected that she would only collect butterflies and "native curios." Her courage later saved Akeley's life, although it could not save their marriage.

Bibi and Bwana, as Delia and Carl Akeley were often called, traveled along the Great Rift Valley, which runs from Ethiopia down to Mozambique. On Mount Kenya, they hunted their first elephants. Akeley prepared all the specimens himself, a grueling task. When Akeley eventually finished mounting two of his elephants, in a display called *Fighting Bulls*, museums took note, for the vividness of the figures was astonishing. By then Akeley had been to the White House to advise Theodore Roosevelt on his upcoming safari and had agreed to return to Africa to collect an entire family of elephants for a far more ambitious exhibit proposed by the American Museum of Natural History. He had little inkling that he would become a landlocked Ahab, "heaped and tasked" by his own Moby Dick.

By 1909, when the American Museum of Natural History's British East Africa Expedition departed, much had changed in Africa, and Akeley himself was beginning to change. He was no longer interested simply in hunting specimens. He had begun to study the elephants in an attempt to understand what seemed to him astonishing animal behavior. He had heard about their protective instincts, and, on this expedition, he witnessed a group at-

trees, the squeals and screams and roars of hundreds of elephants. . . . The forest is as dry as tinder, the ground covered with dead leaves and even the leaves on the trees are dry and parched. There was some sort of general alarm sounded. All monkey chatter ceased, as the elephants apparently all moved off in one direction, and there was no sound except the scuffling of dead leaves, the swish of branches at their sides. The sound was like that of a mighty wind storm in the forest.[13]

Silent and almost invisible one moment and then, with a scent, as relentless as a freight train—and less predictable—these forest elephants were extremely dangerous. Akeley's first adversary, however, was microscopic. Laid low with malaria, dysentery, and blackwater fever, he was nursed back to health again and again by Delia. Meanwhile, the expedition fell behind schedule, and the Museum finally cabled that it could send no more money. Undaunted, Akeley traveled west to the highlands to recover, made arrangements to sell some of his property in New York State, and borrowed money from a safari outfitter. Akeley and Delia decided to try their luck with the elephant herds on nearby Mount Kenya.

Delia was alone in camp with her porters and gun bearers on a cold, rainy evening in June of

tempt to shoulder up a bull who had been shot. Akeley wanted to express these qualities in his exhibit. He wanted a perfect group of specimens and only those, for his disgust at hunters who killed indiscriminately was growing. He had seen the havoc they were wreaking across Africa.

As early as 1900, only four decades after Stanley's explorations, the encroachment of hunters on African wildlife and native farmers on the animals' habitats had begun to reduce the great herds, from the grasslands of Uganda to the Serengeti plain of Tanzania. This had spurred colonial nations to issue game licenses and limit the number of certain species a hunter could kill. Today the limits seem profligate—lions, for example, were considered vermin and could be killed at will. Although leopards still threatened the houses of Nairobi, for Akeley, the handwriting was on the wall. His sense of a vanishing Africa would shape the African hall.

Practically speaking, elephants had become harder to find, particularly large-tusked bulls. Even though Roosevelt agreed to help with the hunting while on his own expedition (the two teams met in 1909), the crowning figure for the display eluded both men. Herds of nearly a thousand elephants still existed in the lowland jungles of Uganda, and Carl and Delia Akeley traveled there in pursuit. "In the semi-darkened forest, the eerie silence and the mighty grandeur of the vine-draped trees are so appalling as to terrify the human senses and rob the invader of his courage,"[12] wrote Delia Akeley.

Carl Akeley's description captures the elephants' majesty and the danger of pursuing them.

As I stood on that rocky grass-smothered kopje, it was to receive an impression which somehow seems to make all other African experiences fade away. From my position, the view was over the top of the forest. There was scarcely a breath of wind. From all directions came the crash of breaking

1910 when a runner delivered the news in Kiswahili: *Tembo piga bwana*—"an elephant has struck the mister." Akeley had been surprised in the forest, and his gun had jammed. The elephant, a bull, caught him between its tusks, tore the skin off the side of his face, and attempted to crush Akeley into the ground. Its tusks struck something hard, a root or rock, and, distracted, it took off after the porters. This distraction saved Akeley's life, for an elephant will often return to finish a job by sitting on the victim or hurling him against a tree with its trunk. Some of the porters hauled Akeley to the edge of the clearing and wrapped him in a light blanket; they assumed he would soon be dead.

Delia did not, but she faced long odds. In pitch darkness and frigid weather, she would have to induce a group of angry Kikuyu natives, who would rather kill her than set foot in the forest at night, to climb a steep, narrow mountain path slick with rain and carry

her husband down. When the guides deserted, she searched them out and convinced them to return. Somehow, with threats, jokes, and bold action, she succeeded, nearly breaking down in despair several times. She found her husband with three broken ribs and a cheek opened to the jawbone. It took Delia three days to get him out of the forest, and it took him three months to recover physically—longer to regain his "morale," as she called it. Delia herself bore scars, too: "The horror and suffering endured that awful night have never left me. Indeed, the thought of the torment of an orthodox hell pales into insignificance by comparison."[14]

They were more than a year late when they finally brought back the elephants midway through 1911. Akeley brought back something else even more important. While recovering on a cot in the field, he had begun to plan a new African hall for the Museum. The elephants that had

Below: Carl Akeley recovering in camp after being mauled by an elephant on Mount Kenya, 1910

Opposite: Akeley filming the crater of an active volcano near Mount Mikeno, on the border between the Congo and Rwanda, with the camera he invented, 1921. After his experiences on the Akeley Gorilla Expedition, Akeley lobbied for the creation of a gorilla sanctuary among the volcanoes.

nearly cost him his life would be its grand centerpiece. He would pursue this vision for the rest of his life.

In 1912 the Museum's trustees approved Akeley's ambitious plan for a new hall, but World War I halted any work on it, and the subsequent Depression allowed little progress. Akeley continued to plan the forty dioramas. He imagined every detail of the exhibits and sought fidelity to natural habitats down to the leaves on the artificial trees. He let his imagination go, however, in positioning the animal figures, endowing them with distinctly human attributes—nobility, courage, scurrilousness, even familial loyalty. The hall would require a physical addition to the Museum that the city probably would not agree to build. It was also becoming clear that Akeley himself would have to raise most of the money to gather the material for the exhibits. Museum president Henry Fairfield Osborn thought the whole project was likely to kill Akeley and that he ought to scale it back. Akeley refused. At the deepest level, his narrow identity as a hunter was gradually being subsumed by a larger purpose that can only be called artistic.

In a profound reversal, Akeley's pursuit of the image of a

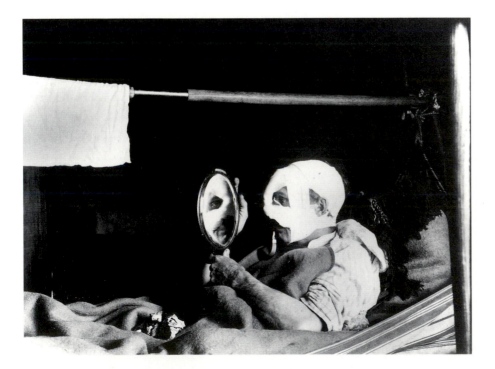

vanishing Africa revealed to him a way in which a living Africa might be preserved. The epiphany occurred in 1921 on Mount Mikeno in the Virunga Mountains, near the border of Rwanda and the Congo. Akeley had journeyed to the Kivu volcano region to hunt gorillas for one of his most important exhibits. He had also come equipped with the new, portable, lightweight camera he had perfected to take the first motion pictures of gorillas in the wild. Mountain gorillas had not even been discovered until 1902, but already they were being threatened in their nearly inaccessible highland homes. Akeley had killed many animals for specimens, but this hunt, he soon began to understand, was unlike the others. As he followed and filmed them, he began to feel a powerful sense of kinship with these animals. In contrast to everything he had read, he found

the gorillas anything but belligerent, with a complex social behavior. Akeley was initiating a field of primate study that would be inherited by such scientists as George Schaller and the late Dian Fossey. By expedition's end, Akeley, feeling more like a murderer than a naturalist, had formed a resolution that would change the fate of African wildlife.

When he returned to the Museum, he used his position there as a soapbox from which to draw worldwide attention to the destruction of the mountain gorillas. His voice was joined by Osborn's. They were eventually heard by King Albert of Belgium, who had toured several national parks with Osborn in 1919. In 1925, following a plan Akeley outlined, King Albert established an unprecedented wildlife sanctuary in a triangle of land between the Virunga volcanoes—the Parc National Albert. In 1929, he

increased its area tenfold, to 500,000 acres. Today the park is divided among three countries: in Zaire it is the Parc National de Virunga; in Rwanda, the Parc National des Volcans; in Uganda, the Kigezi Gorilla Sanctuary. As George Schaller remarked, "The mountain gorilla is Akeley's living monument, and those who follow his lead remain his most enduring legacy."[15]

Carl Akeley's final expedition was one he never should have made. By 1926, he had seen his African hall further delayed, criticized by his Museum colleagues, and reduced in scope. His own fanatical attention to detail slowed progress even more and drove costs up. He was desperate for a patron when George Eastman came on the scene. Eastman, the photographic pioneer who had founded the Eastman Kodak Company, had known Akeley since the 1890s and was inter-

Left: Carl and Mary Akeley in camp, Lukenia Hills, southeast of Nairobi, Kenya, on Akeley's final African expedition, the Eastman-Pomeroy-Akeley Expedition, 1926. Behind them is a model for a Museum habitat exhibit.

Below: Flying and filming during the Johnsons' photographic expeditions, c. 1933. Photograph by Martin Johnson

Opposite: The Meru chief Songa, himself the son of a chief, near Mount Kenya, c. 1924. Songa was to have been the subject of a Museum-sponsored film by Martin Johnson on native peoples, but it was never completed. Photograph by Martin Johnson

Wings over Africa

In a world where CNN and the nightly television news have brought the entire world into peoples' living rooms, it is difficult to imagine that, until the 1940s, people's visual experience of the world beyond their own city, not to mention beyond their country, came from weekly newsreels and occasional "documentaries" seen at local movie houses. Audiences would flock to see narratives of strange people and unusual creatures in exotic settings. Usually these films, which purported to be true accounts, were confected from footage shot at many different times, often in wildly varied locations. If their provenance was often dubious, however, their impact could be stunning. The king and queen of this tarnished screen were Martin and Osa Johnson.

The Johnsons, who photographed in Kenya for the Museum between 1924 and 1928, were adventurers with cameras. Born in Illinois, Martin Johnson grew up in Kansas, and, working in his father's jewelry store, he became intrigued with the photographic samples that came with the Eastman film the store sold. He decided to become a photographer and got a boost when he was kicked out of high school for doctoring photos of the faculty in the darkroom to make them appear to be romantically engaged. In 1907, he signed on as a cook with the novelist Jack London and sailed to the South Pacific, where he explored locales he would later depict in the popular Cannibals of the South Seas. *In a fascinating encounter, he later showed some of the film to its subjects, who were amazed to see companions since deceased suddenly brought back to life.*

Osa Leighty was a perfect traveling companion, though she had never been more than thirty miles from her Kansas home when she married Johnson in 1910. She learned how to cover him with a rifle when he photographed rhinos and lions, and she used a natural impetuosity and an ear for languages to win the trust of the people they photographed.

By 1920, the market for ethnographic documentaries had diminished, and Johnson decided to film vanishing wildlife, especially in Africa. Backed by the Museum and George Eastman, the Johnsons mounted an ambitious three-film project, which included footage of the Eastman-Pomeroy-Akeley Expedition. Only one film resulted, the jungle pastiche Simba, King of the Beasts: A Saga of the African Veldt. *By then they had a new technology and a new angle: airplanes.*

In 1933, the Johnsons acquired two Sikorsky amphibian airplanes and launched one of the most ambitious photographic expeditions of the period, flying some sixty thousand miles, from Capetown to Cairo, in eighteen months. Although Johnson was a photographic pioneer, his eye toward commercial success made his visual record less valuable than it might have been. Yet several dozen of his images have taken their place among the classics of nature photography. In 1935, he was killed and Osa Johnson injured in the crash of a commuter airplane outside Los Angeles.

ested in the movie camera Akeley had developed. At seventy-one, Eastman wanted an experienced hunter to take him on an African safari. He agreed to make a contribution to the African hall, and Akeley agreed to lead the expedition, expecting that more money would follow.

On this expedition, which Akeley himself had to help finance, he brought along William Leigh, "the sagebrush Rembrandt," to make studies for the hall's background paintings. They were accompanied by two stalwart companions, Akeley's second wife, the explorer Mary Jobe Akeley, whom he had married in 1924, a year after divorcing Delia, and Dan Pomeroy, the sponsor of Akeley's camera company. The expedition was elaborate, expensive, and doomed.

Once in Africa, Eastman soon began to dislike Akeley. He also had no interest in memorializing wildlife; he had come to hunt. Akeley resented his subservient position, and, when Eastman turned down his request of $500,000 for the African hall,

Akeley grew desperate. Increasingly tyrannical and compulsive about safari details, he drove himself mercilessly and killed animals unnecessarily. Then his health broke.

By the age of sixty-two, Akeley had suffered many bouts with tropical diseases; further exposure was foolhardy. He soon found himself in a Mombasa hospital for three weeks with dysentery and blackwater fever. Eastman, who hated any sign of weakness, left the expedition without ever visiting him. Akeley was desperate to salvage something from the trip and, as soon as he could walk, headed for the Kivu volcano country to participate in a gorilla survey of the new Parc National Albert and determine sites for possible research laboratories. Museum ornithologist James Chapin, who was searching for birds in the Ruwenzori range, planned to meet Akeley in gorilla country. The meeting never took place.

Akeley soon collapsed completely. First he could barely walk, then barely sit up. Dysentery continued to waste him, and still he ordered the group to push on. Mary Akeley later wrote that she had not known he was dying, but she could see how weak he was. At the same time, she also knew that his only desire was to see the gorilla country again. On Karisimbi, one of the peaks of Mount Mikeno, they pitched their final camp. When the mists lifted, they could see the glow of the other volcanoes. She buried him on that slope a week later, in November 1926, within sight of the spot where he had first conceived the plan to preserve the mountain gorillas of Africa.

Akeley's hall, with its majestic elephant group, was completed by others and opened in 1936. It was—

and is—much as Akeley envisioned it. Times have changed, however. Africa is closer to us, and the fate of its wildlife is well known, if not so well understood. Do these frozen images of what was, after all, only Carl Akeley's Africa, still convey a meaning, a transcendent truth about the living world? In 1991 John Heminway, chairman of the African Wildlife Foundation, wrote: "What is so remarkable about Carl Akeley's contribution is that it never fails *anyone*. Here I am today, with three-quarters of my life spent pondering Africa, and my heart still races with his gorillas. . . . It's clear to me that in the 1920s Carl Akeley was well ahead of his time, as are the dioramas today. I believe his achievement was his fidelity to nature. . . . I'm convinced that what Carl Akeley intended—a vision of Africa as if you had discovered it yourself—still works."[16]

Heaven, Hell, and Colin Turnbull

My heart is all happy,
My heart takes wing in singing,
Under the trees of the forest,
The forest our dwelling and our
*   mother.*
                    —Mbuti Pygmy song[17]

We crossed a small oror that ran into the ravine below, and edged our way up another hill to Village Number Two. Here there was indisputably someone inside, for I could hear loud, raucous singing, a rapid staccato of Icien vowels. . . . The singing went on and we walked around the outside of the stockade until we came to a spot where the spiders had woven a gigantic cobweb that almost covered the small compound inside. The singing stopped, a pair of hands gripped the stockade, and a craggy head rose into view, two uneven rows of broken teeth giving me an undeniably welcoming smile. . . .

Atum introduced me, and Lokelea encouraged me by saying how well I spoke Icietot, and at least he understood one of my questions. When I asked him what he had been singing about, he answered simply, "Because I'm hungry."
                    —Colin Turnbull[18]

The distance between the Ituri Forest of the Congo, where the Pygmies dwell, and the arid escarpment of the Kenya-Uganda border, where a tribe called the Ik reside, is not very far by the standards of a vast continent—a few hundred miles. Anthropologist Colin Turnbull traversed it numerous times during the course of his work for the American Museum of Natural History. Yet the journey took him as far as one can travel, between the antipodes of human possibility.

On some level, all anthropologists seek to contribute to a definition of "human nature," whether through the study of physical evolution, through insights into particular cultures, or through broader description, based on many cultures, of the underlying mechanisms of social organization. A few, however, make anthropology an explicit act of imagination. Facts can be contested, theories revised. Colin Turnbull's encounter with the peoples of Africa inspired him to a task beyond objectivity, nothing less than the renovation of the modern soul.

Colin Turnbull first visited the Garden of Eden on a motorcycle. In 1951, after studying at the universities of Oxford and Benares, India, Turnbull took a motorcycle tour through central Africa. In the Congo, he was introduced to the Harvard-trained anthropologist Patrick Putnam, who had established a hospital and leprosarium in the domain of the Mbuti Pygmies. This was the same

Kenge—hunter, musician, poet of the forest and, for Colin Turnbull, symbolic free spirit, Ituri Forest, northeastern Congo. Here Kenge plays his hunting bow as a mouth harp. Photograph by Colin Turnbull

Patrick Putnam whom Museum ornithologist James Chapin had visited twenty years earlier. Turnbull recognized immediately that he had encountered an environment and a culture different from any he had known, and he wound up staying almost a year. In 1954 he returned as a graduate student of the distinguished Oxford anthropologist E. Evans-Pritchard, and in 1957 returned again to complete his fieldwork.

People of short stature inhabit the equatorial forests from the Cameroon to Uganda. The Pygmies of the Ituri, in spite of their isolation, were known to the Egyptians four millennia ago and to the Greeks of Homer's time. By the time Turnbull arrived, they had been enshrined in Western myth. They were regarded as everything from freaks to a superseded stage of human evolution. When Lang and Chapin went to the Congo, they expected to meet vicious cannibals. Instead, they found a people completely at home in a forbidding environment, experienced hunters with an intimate knowledge of their forest world. For Turnbull, the product of a wartime English upbringing, the Mbuti Pygmies challenged the central values of Western industrialized society as he knew it.

The Mbuti called themselves "the children of the forest," and Turnbull came to see this not as a poetic conceit but as a realistic appraisal. Living in self-enforced isolation, they received everything they needed from the for-

est—food, shelter, clothing, and protection. They hunted with bows and arrows and spears, gathered edible plants, and practiced limited seasonal agriculture. They had few possessions and no need to store food against lean years. They went where the food was and had a vast forest in which to seek it. "If one day's hunt brings in an exceptionally large amount," Turnbull wrote, "then the following day will be spent lazing in the camp, doing a few odd chores that gradually accumulate."[19]

Mbuti social life resembled a Marxist fantasy. There were no kings, designated leaders, hierarchies, or even—bane of the ethnographer—dominating kinship relations. It was a fully cooperative society, whose decisions were made as a group, although hunters usually took the lead. Disputes were rare and were always resolved for the good of the group or, as the Pygmies saw it, for the good of the forest.

Turnbull's three sojourns with the Mbuti led him to question all the assumptions of his culture: its pursuit of individuality, its technological dependence, organized state authority, and, especially, alienation from and exploitation of the natural world. The Pygmies appeared to him to have achieved complete harmony with nature, a oneness that made possible what Turnbull regarded as the greatest virtue of Pygmy life—aesthetic joy. This joy was embodied in a young boy named Kenge, whom Turnbull studied closely:

One night . . . I heard a noise from a clearing just behind the BaMbuti hunting camp where I was living. I went to see who it was because usually, at night, the Pygmies do not leave their huts. The sound was being made by a young friend of mine, a youth called Kenge: he was dancing in the moonlight all by himself, with a flower stuck in his hair, singing his heart out. Kenge was one of the most incorrigible flirts I knew, so I asked him why he was dancing alone. He looked at me in surprise: to him this must have seemed an exceptionally stupid question. He answered: "But I'm not dancing alone. . . . I'm dancing with the Forest. I'm dancing with the Moon."[20]

For Turnbull, the 1960s had already arrived in 1957. *The Forest People*, the popular account of his fieldwork published in 1961, today seems to presage the social revolution that followed during the next decade. At least since the time of the sixteenth-century philosopher Montaigne, Western thinkers had found in so-called primitive societies lenses through which to take a critical view of their own culture, but never had the criticism been so sweeping and attractive as Turnbull's Ituri Eden. The notion of human progress, long ago overturned as a logical and evolutionary fallacy,

he showed to be an emotional and aesthetic fallacy as well. Who wouldn't want to be a Pygmy?

A subsequent generation of anthropologists has drawn a more equivocal picture of this Eden, challenging many of Turnbull's conclusions, including those regarding the quality of the Pygmies' relations with their neighbors. A similar fate has befallen some of the work of another Museum anthropologist, Margaret Mead, who found her utopia in Samoa. In both instances, specific qualifications or even refutations are to some degree beside the point. Turnbull felt he was in touch with a central truth about human society. He believed its particular forms were intimately linked to and—until modern times—expressed an accord with the natural world. This conviction shaped his approach to the design of the Museum's Hall of Man in Africa, which opened in 1969. This series of exhibits celebrates the range of human responses to different environments, from Cairo to the Cape of Good Hope.

Turnbull was hired by the Museum in 1959, after his fieldwork with the Mbuti was completed. In the mid-1950s, he had corresponded with the Museum about Patrick Putnam's papers, which were in the anthropology department. At that time, the Museum desperately needed an African ethnologist to put in order its collection of artifacts, much of it Herbert Lang's Congo legacy. It was clear to department chairman Harry Shapiro that Turnbull was both gifted and energetic. The Museum hired him, and he arrived with plans for a new hall already taking shape in his mind.

He was eager, too, to begin new research that might answer a compelling question: Was Pygmy society anomalous, or might other hunting-and-gathering cultures confirm aspects of human social life that he had glimpsed there? He first sought to study people living in the Andaman Islands, off the coast of India, but after months of negotiating with the Indian government, he was denied permission to visit. In 1964, Turnbull headed for eastern Africa to canvas the cultures of northern Kenya and Uganda

and to collect examples of metal-working. Finally, with time and money running out, he decided to study a little-known group of about two thousand people scattered along the escarpment overlooking Kenya and into northern Uganda near Mount Morungole. They were the Ik—the mountain people.

Turnbull knew nothing about them because virtually nothing had been written. The anthropologist Elizabeth Marshall Thomas had told him they were delightful and full of fun. Their language was extremely difficult to learn, closer to Middle Kingdom Egyptian than to any modern African tongue. Indeed, Turnbull did not even know the group's proper name. Nevertheless, he eagerly anticipated gaining intimacy with a new culture, the great pleasure of anthropological fieldwork. That was his first mistake. His second mistake was to assume that the Ik were hunters and gatherers. His third and greatest mistake "was to assume that these gentle, smiling friendly looking people who extended such a warm welcome were as gentle and as amicable as they appeared."[21]

In fact, the Ik were less hunters than subsistence farmers, barely subsisting. After World War II, national boundaries had rigidified and, later, the Ugandan government had set aside part of their hunting grounds near Mount Morungole as Kidepo National Park. These developments may have disrupted the Ik's move-

Above: Deserted Ik village. Photograph by Colin Turnbull

Opposite: Lolim, a ritual priest of the Ik, staggers off to die of starvation. Photograph by Colin Turnbull

ments in search of game and forced them to depend more heavily on the cultivation of an arid land, statistically certain to be barren from drought one year in four. From this land they managed to coax harvests of millet, tomatoes, squash, and a few other crops.

One might say euphemistically that, when Turnbull arrived, the Ik were in transition. In reality, they were starving. In the bare pursuit of survival, to which the Ik had been reduced, elements of communal social life were being jettisoned: ritual, intergenerational ties, bonds of family. In an incredibly short time, the people seemed to Turnbull to have fallen into what the philosopher Thomas Hobbes called "the war of each against all."

When Turnbull saw the Ik villages, he noticed something peculiar: the enclosed groups of thatched conical huts had no true common space. Every hut, even those at the center, was surrounded by its own fence, with an entrance that communicated directly to the outside. No Ik need see another in coming and going. The interior fences were as tall as the encircling one. It was as if the Ik were seeking protection as much from each other as from the outside.

The catalogue of harrowing scenes Turnbull witnessed over the next two years seemed to confirm his intuition. The Ik's struggle for food rendered superfluous everything that might jeopardize the next meal. When Turnbull first saw Ik villagers perched silently, like sentinels, gazing out from the escarpment, he thought they were taking in the spectacular scenery. They were looking for vultures who could lead them to food—decaying and possibly diseased, but food nonetheless.

Behind Mud Walls

For the Muslim women of northern Nigeria, purdah, or seclusion, does not necessarily mean isolation. Although once they are married, they rarely venture beyond the walls of their houses to conduct daily business, they nevertheless earn money by trading. As Museum anthropologist Enid Schildkrout discovered, they make economic contact with the outside world through their children. In her fieldwork among the Muslim Hausa, she overturned conventional notions of childhood dependence and assumptions about the restricted economic domain of women in Muslim families.

Schildkrout, the Museum's curator of African ethnology, went to the northern city of Kano, Nigeria, in 1975 and, over the next six years, investigated a complex, symbiotic relation between mothers and children, especially daughters. Most Hausa women engaged in some form of enterprise, anything from making bean cakes to dyeing cloth. The female children were their salespeople, go-betweens, negotiators, and traders. They also went to school. Because some men had as many as four wives, the children were communally "on call" to all the adults in the family. It was a disciplined yet not inhumane childhood, as the compelling first-person accounts Schildkrout collected make clear. One young girl, Binta, went to work directly after morning prayers, selling her mother's bean cakes, collecting customers' empty bowls, and going to market for a neighbor on a small commission, using the earned money to buy guinea corn and other necessities.

Children barely out from under their mother's skirts learned to make sharp judgments, for their parents depended on them. Yet the girls, too, depended on this trade, for they were able to make a small profit along the way. This and the money their mothers earned went toward their dowries, which enabled them to buy the most precious commodity of all, a measure of security and independence.

Goodness and virtue were defined as having a full stomach.

From this premise, everything followed with frightening consistency. Anyone who shared anything was considered a fool. As far as Turnbull could tell, if an Ik managed to kill game, he did his best to eat it all and not to carry any back to the village, to his wife or his family. In return, they did the same. Thus it was that the stout and the starving lived side by side. The starving did not complain; they knew the rules. Concepts such as "family" had become almost meaningless. Children were a nuisance and an impediment; they formed their own bands, with their own savage pecking orders. Likewise the "aged," who were often no older than forty, represented an insupportable burden. In a particularly cruel game, children would compete to see who could snatch food from the mouth of an elderly person before it could be swallowed.

As with the beatings regularly administered to Adupa, a ten-year-old retarded girl, no one interfered or seemed even to notice.

The Ik had an economy, of sorts. In times of drought, the Turkana of northern Kenya would drive their cattle up the escarpment into the territory of the Dodos, another cattle-herding tribe, to search for pastureland. Fierce battles would often ensue, which the government did its best to check. The Ik benefited by supplying spears to both sides and tending the stolen cattle. The Ik later insisted that they never engaged in such sharp dealing.

The depth of Icien nihilism appeared so great that for Turnbull the tribe acquired a blasted grandeur. When Turnbull suggested that sex with a partner was more economical than masturbation because effort gave pleasure to two, not just one, he received the philosophical reply, "Who knows what the other is

Free from the rules of purdah, children move in and out of their houses. Women depend on them to sell food or other goods prepared at home. The girl on the left is helping with child care. Photograph by Enid Schildkrout

feeling? In each you only know your own feeling."[22]

As for Turnbull himself, the Ik made him the butt of their jokes. He was grateful when they built him a thatched hut like their own so he would not have to sleep in his Land Rover. After the hut was broken into, he realized that the builders had deliberately neglected to tie down the roof, so it could be removed easily. When he gave away food to the starving, the healthy became furious. Why waste grain on a dying person? As Turnbull later remarked, "The villages were villages of the dead and the dying, and there was little difference between the two."[23]

In this dystopia, Turnbull met a distorted mirror image of his Pygmies—a people without possessions, fixed abodes, hierarchies, or cares for the morrow, but also without a connection to the land, a social life, or fellow feeling. The oppositions are almost too pat, but one is particularly resonant. For the Mbuti, fire was not only a necessity, it was a source of cultural and social continuity. They kept a fire burning continuously. When they traveled to a new location, they wrapped glowing embers in thick leaves and rekindled a flame when they made camp. The Ik made fires clandestinely and extinguished them quickly, for smoke would give away the location of food and draw unwelcome company.

Hell, wrote Sartre in a famous phrase, is other people. But was this hell? The few anthropologists who have since studied the Ik have disagreed with Turnbull. Language appears to have been a greater barrier than he was willing to acknowledge, cutting him off from more detailed knowledge of Ik history, belief systems, and agricultural practice. He had difficulty confirming what he was told and may even have confused Ik informants with those of neighboring tribes, a common pitfall of the anthropologist in unfamiliar territory. Although Turnbull returned a year later for more study, he did not spend enough time to witness the re-

The American Museum of Natural History in the Field:

Africa

Sanford–LeGendre Abyssinia Expedition—1929   *"In Abyssinia, no one knows the meaning of hurry. Tomorrow is as good as today," wrote Gertrude Sanford, voicing the most common lament of the Western traveler in unfamiliar lands. She had come with Sidney and Howard LeGendre and T. Donald Carter to seek a specimen of the "Queen of Sheba's antelope," the Abyssinian nyala, for a Museum exhibit. Arriving in what is now Ethiopia, Sanford's knowledge of French stood her in good stead at a dinner at the palace of King Negus Tafari Makonen, who was so impressed with her conversation that he made the expedition a present of his best pack mule. It was one of the few things that went right, as the explorers soon learned. They could not trust their guides and ran out of food. Once they managed to secure their nyala, the true trek began. The expedition made a twelve-day march across the fierce desert south of Addis Ababa, where it was feted by the chieftain Desjasmatch Beru. The group had hoped to travel all the way to the Nile, but disease and torrential rains eventually defeated them, and they turned back.*

American Museum of Natural History–Columbia University Gorilla Expedition—1929   *After Carl Akeley's pioneering study of the mountain gorillas of Central Africa, the Museum and Columbia University organized a wide-ranging expedition to investigate the gorilla's behavior and bring back specimens for anatomical studies. The expedition included two of the Museum's foremost scientists, Harry*

silience of Ik society. For the Ik did not disappear, as seemed inevitable; they came back stronger than ever.

Turnbull could not bear to spend more time with the Ik. They were starving, and starvation pushed them to extremes of callousness. Turnbull was unprepared to respond to what he saw. They challenged him as the Pygmies never had. Perhaps ironically, the Ik called Turnbull *Iciebam*—"friend of the Ik"—and in the end, that became his greatest obstacle to objective knowledge. At one time or an-

other in their careers, nearly all anthropologists have a bad experience in the field. Turnbull began to adopt what he saw as their attitudes. He stopped asking so many nagging—but necessary—academic questions; he went for days without speaking; he engaged in psychological warfare with the Ik. The one thing he could not do was change anything. His letters from the field poignantly express the essence of his frustration. In one instance, during a raid by the Turkana, he witnessed the death of one of the Ik he cared for:

Raven, an expert on primates, and William K. Gregory, an evolutionary theorist. The expedition ranged from Akeley's gorilla preserve in the Kivu volcano country to the forests of Cameroon in western Africa. In the Kivu region, they were assisted by the Batwa Pygmies, who knew the habitat of the gorillas intimately. The greatest challenge was transporting their largest specimen, which weighed nearly five hundred pounds, over the treacherous mountain terrain. The gorilla was so large that they had to widen the entire trail from two to ten feet to get it through.

Vernay-Lang Zoological Expedition—1930 Herbert Lang left the Museum staff while on an expedition with Arthur Vernay in Angola, but in 1930 the two again joined forces to mount an expedition into the Kalahari "desert" of Bechuanaland (now Namibia and Botswana). The team, which included fourteen scientists from the Museum and the Transvaal Museum of Pretoria, surveyed the mammals, insects, and plants across the very heart of the desert—a task never before attempted. The Kalahari was an arid grassy plain with a rich diversity of wildlife, including burrowing snakes, unusual short-legged toads, and an abundance of weaverbirds, all adapted to the dry environment. They also found the first evidence that Paleolithic humans had resided in the western Kalahari. Most impressive to Vernay, however, were the !Kung, a group of nomadic hunters. Vernay marveled at their amazing faculty for tracking game and their ability to conserve water, which they stored in blown ostrich eggs. "Almost everywhere," wrote Vernay in Natural History, *"our scientists found themselves on new paths of discovery, surprise, or admiration."*

I was up before dawn, and seeing the light, old Nagole, the witch-doctor's daughter, came over and told me that my friend Lomeja had been shot and needed help. I thought at first he had been shot while on the hunt. . . . But no, damn it, he had been shot in the menyatta [village], and nobody had said a darned thing, but just left him lying there all night . . . and when I arrived I found his old sister propping him up in a real pool of blood. (I've always read about pools of blood but never seen one.) . . . They laid him down with his arms and legs drawn up in the burial position and threw a dirty rag over him. It was plain that he was far from dead, and cursing myself for not knowing exactly how it feels to be shot in the stomach, I looked him over.

. . . He badly wanted some tea, and knowing how both the Ik and the Didinga like it strong and sweet that was how I made it, and it was good to see him enjoy a little and swallow some Anacin, which was all I had to help relieve the pain. For headaches and nervous disorders, it said. I have never felt so futile and utterly worthless in all my life. . . . The doctor never came. I hope he enjoyed his breakfast, because while he was eating his bacon and eggs, I was holding Lomeja and telling him everything was going to be just fine, feeling him get colder and colder and hearing his voice get weaker and weaker until I was just holding a corpse. . . . I felt all alone. Nobody even wanted to take the body from my hands or show it any care. And all the

time I was thinking that if instead of playing at being an anthropologist and taking notes in a comfortable Land Rover I had gone out to see if the shots had done any harm, I might have been able to do something. . . .

Excuse all the gory details, Harry, but one of the worst things about it all is that everyone here just takes it all as a matter of course, and I find it impossible to find any release for my feelings since I am the only person that seems to have any.[24]

The necessity to feel and the struggle to resist feeling overwhelmed the responsibility to question everything, including himself. Turnbull would attempt to reconcile his experience of the Ik and the Mbuti until the end of his life (he died in 1994). In doing so, he traveled far beyond the domain of anthropology per se, offering a record of the uncertain process of gaining knowledge. Africa is neither heaven nor hell, but it gave him the form of a prayer for humanity, and that is, perhaps, what he always sought. The writer Laurens van der Post once told Turnbull a story common among the Bushmen of southern Africa. In it, a young boy glimpses a rare bird, the most beautiful thing he has ever seen. He abandons his role as a hunter and determines to seek it out. Everywhere he goes, he is urged on by his people, as though he were pursuing beauty not just for himself but for them, too. Finally, at the end of his life, he thinks he may have found the bird amid the ice and snow of a mountaintop, but it eludes him again. At the moment of his death, he calls out to his mother, who gave him his life, and with that cry, a single feather drops from the sky into his hand. "That, the Bushmen say, is a life well lived, and the story is a lasting joy to all."[25]

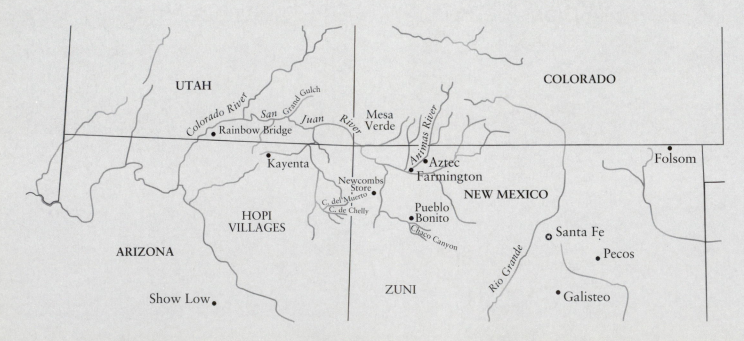

Early Americans

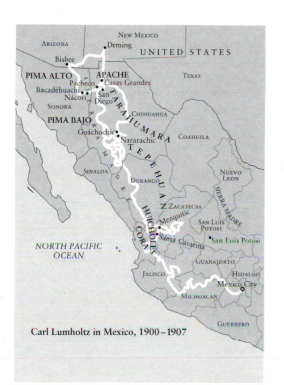

Carl Lumholtz in Mexico, 1900–1907

IN 1874, A PARTY OF white men, guided by a local prospector and accompanied by the photographer William Henry Jackson, ventured into a series of canyons in southern Colorado called Mesa Verde. There, where sheer cliffs drop a thousand feet to the canyon floor, Jackson discovered the ruins of a two-story house set high in the rock face. He named the edifice Cliff House and took a remarkable series of photographs the following day, for he recognized at once the significance of what he had seen—an unusually well-preserved prehistoric ruin that could open a window on the lives of the earliest inhabitants of the region.

During the nineteenth century, Americans in search of a past traveled to Europe, Greece, and Egypt to explore the monuments of great cultures. Cathedrals, temples, amphitheaters, and pyramids were the evidence of antiquity, which, it was thought, could only be contemplated elsewhere. Jackson's photographs gave Americans their first glimpse of an ancient world within their own country, a history written in stone, older than Europe's cathedrals and more mysterious. The monuments of that world were the ancient cliff dwellings and pueblos of the American Southwest.

In 1888, Richard Wetherill, the oldest son of a Quaker ranching family, and his cousin accidentally stumbled onto an even more remarkable set of ruins while looking for stray cattle in the northern plateau of Mesa Verde. These ruins, which Wetherill called Cliff Palace, looked like a medieval fortress. Set seven hundred feet above the ground and accessible by ropes and ladders, the ruins contained more than two hundred rooms and twenty-three kivas (round underground chambers used for ceremonial purposes). The next day, Wetherill discovered another set of ruins, Spruce House, in an even better state of preservation.

Explorers soon realized that the magnificent cliff dwellings at Mesa Verde were only the first of many discoveries to be made in the

Pueblo Bonito, Chaco Canyon, New Mexico, from the mesa during the Hyde Exploring Expedition, 1896

backcountry of the Four Corners, the region where Colorado, Arizona, New Mexico, and Utah meet. Mesa Verde alone contained as many as five hundred cliff ruins. As the list of prehistoric sites grew, inevitable questions arose: Who were the people who had once occupied these unusual dwellings? What had become of them?

Richard Wetherill borrowed the Navajo term *Anasazi*, meaning "enemy ancestors," to describe the people whose traces he had discovered high on the cliffs of Mesa Verde. In the coming decade, he would play a key role in the American Museum of Natural History excavations at Chaco Canyon in New Mexico, the site at which Anasazi culture reached its highest expression.

The Living Cave Dwellers of the American Continent

The mystery of the cliff dwellers inspired the leader of the Museum's first anthropological expedition, Carl Lumholtz. His search for answers took him into the land of what he referred to as the living "cave dwellers," in northern Mexico, far from his native Norway.

At the turn of the century, little attention was devoted to the natural sciences in Norwegian schools, and, to please his father, Carl Lumholtz abandoned his first love and turned to theology. The result of studying for up to sixteen hours a day for months on end was a nervous breakdown. While recuperating in the country, he collected birds and animals. "Love of nature took stronger and stronger hold of me," he later wrote, "and one

day it occurred to me what a misfortune it would be to die without having seen the whole earth. I could hardly endure the thought which haunted me."[1] Salvation came in the person of Professor Robert Collett at the zoological museum of the University of Christiania. He proposed that Lumholtz travel to Australia to collect zoological specimens for his museum. After a year with the natives deep in the bush of Northeast Queensland, however, Lumholtz decided to dedicate himself to the study of human beings.

When Lumholtz came to the United States in 1890 to lecture on his experiences in the Australian bush, he was also looking for support for his next project, a detailed study of the people of the Sierra Madre, a remote mountainous region of northern Mexico. The American Museum of Natural History was then in the process of reorganizing its ethnography collections and was ready to sponsor an expedition. By the fall of 1890, with the

backing of the Museum and the American Geographical Society, Lumholtz was in the field.

Lumholtz's interest in northern Mexico sprang from the fact that it was rarely visited by white men. The Apache, who, until recently, had made travel in the Sierra Madre between Sonora and Chihuahua extremely dangerous, were by this time confined to reservations; the territory was open to exploration. The tribes who lived to the south of the Apache had had little contact with outsiders; Lumholtz believed that their ancient customs remained as they had been before the Spanish conquest. Here was an opportunity to record ways of life that had vanished almost everywhere else.

As early as the 1870s, William Henry Jackson had dismissed the notion that the Anasazi had connections to either the Aztecs or the Toltecs of Mexico. There was simply no evidence for it. Jackson and others, however, saw a connection between the Anasazi and the present-day Pueblo Indians of the Southwest, whom Lumholtz visited before heading to Mexico. Lumholtz sought the origins of the Anasazi and thought clues might lie with the inhabitants of the Sierra Madre. There was an additional intriguing clue. Both the Hopi and the Zuñi Indians preserved in legends the story of their origins in the south. "I have reason to believe," he wrote, "that in the rugged fastnesses of these almost unknown regions there may dwell tribes who are in the most primitive state of culture, even to the extent of dwelling in cliffs and caves. What light might one not hope to throw on the early development of the American race by a close study of the culture, manners and mode of life of such a primitive people."[2]

In December 1890, after a two-month journey from the plains of Bisbee, Arizona, Carl Lumholtz, accompanied by a party of thirty men, including eight scientists, and seventy pack animals, set off from Nácori, Mexico, a small town at the foot of the Sierra Madre range. It soon became obvious why the Indians were isolated. "There are barrancas [valleys] into which tradition says that not even the enterprising missionary fathers found it possible to descend, but they can at a few places be crossed, even with animals, if these are lightly loaded. It is a hard task upon flesh and blood."[3] They crossed four towering sierras, rising to nine thousand feet. On Christmas Day, the temperature ranged from 150°F in the sun to 22°F at night. The expedition made its own trails, at times following old Apache tracks. "In some places our pack animals had to be led one by one alongside of yawning abysses. Many a time the beasts lost their balance and rolled down the mountain sides."[4]

They passed through a landscape of virgin forests, with pine trees rising a hundred feet above their heads. The slopes were slick with pine needles a foot long, and "on exposed places we met with trees split like matches, telling us what terrific winds sometimes may blow over these solitary regions."[5] The flora and fauna were magnificent, almost surreal; Lumholtz once encountered a flower stalk of an agave plant fifteen feet tall. This stalk was seventy inches in circumference at its widest point and covered with twenty thousand bright yellow flowers, each one half as big as a man's fist. Two men were needed to carry the stalk, and they were followed by swarms of feeding hummingbirds.

In January of 1891, Lumholtz reached the first settlement on the eastern side of the Sierra Madre, the Mormon colony of Pacheco. From here, with a smaller group, he set out to explore the upper reaches of the Piedras Verdes River valley. At the head of the Piedras Verdes, seven thousand feet above sea level, they discovered old cave dwellings, on ledges in the cliff walls, consisting of groups of houses made of porphyry pulp. Over the space of twenty miles, Lumholtz discovered fifty such dwellings, usually several hundred feet up from the canyon floor. Up to three stories high, with stone stairs and small windows and doors in the shape of a cross, they were clearly the dwellings of highly sophisticated builders. In recent times, the Apache had inhabited the caves, leaving pictures on the walls, but the houses themselves were far older. One wall was covered with thirteen coats of whitewash.

Ten miles south of Casas Grandes, Lumholtz spent six weeks excavating several large mounds, uncovering the ruins of houses similar to those found in the caves. They were communal dwellings, probably of two stories, with several rooms. There were no artifacts in the rooms, but beneath the concrete floors, he discovered beautiful earthenware bowls and jars. Their decoration resembled that of pottery found in the excavations of pueblos of the American Southwest.

In the middle of 1891, Lumholtz returned to the United States with thirty cases of collections, leaving a small party in the field to continue the excavations. Several months later, however, he was back in Mexico, eager "to investigate accurately the language, habits and customs of the primitive people of the Sierra Madre by living with them as I did with the natives of Australia."[6]

In January 1892, Lumholtz arrived at his camp in San Diego to begin his second expedition. With a much reduced force, he climbed the Sierra Madre range and followed it south to the State of Chihuahua. The old church books in the Sonoran town of Bacadéhauchi recorded the Jesuits giving the sacrament to the Tarahumara Indians, who lived in caves in the mountains. Lumholtz sought evidence that this tribe still inhabited caves. After traveling for a few months, he sent his three remaining assistants back to the United States and continued on alone with native guides and several Mexican interpreters into the increasingly wild canyons where the tribe lived. Running short of money, Lumholtz sold his animals and most of his supplies, and with the "untiring efforts of two American ladies whose friendship [he] highly esteemed,"[7] he was able to raise enough to remain among the Tarahumara for the following year and a half. This gave him the necessary time to make a detailed study of the tribe and to compile vocabularies of the Tarahumara and Tepehuan and of the Tubares, who were by that time almost extinct.

As Lumholtz saw it, he was stepping back into the Stone Age, or nearly so. Although the Mexicans had encroached on their territory, taking the best land for their ranches, the Tarahumara appeared largely untouched by Western civilization. They kept domesticated animals introduced by the Spanish and used iron axes and knives, but many of them did not speak any Spanish. Although the Tarahumara were nominally Christian, they mixed Catholicism with their old customs and, "on feast-days," he wrote, "they mingle their heathen dances and sacrifices with semi-Christian ritual."[8] In the most remote barrancas, Lumholtz found several thousand Tarahumara called "Gentiles" by the Mexicans, who would not associate with the Christian Tarahumara and spoke no language but their own. In his desire to study a group untouched by any outside cultural and historical influences, however, Lumholtz may have exaggerated the tribe's isolation.

Lumholtz established his base at the small Mexican ranch of Guachochic, and from there he went out for up to five months at a time. He traveled on foot through the barrancas, accompanied by his Indian carriers. He slept on the ground, with nothing more than a rock ledge as a shelter, and depended on the Indians for his food—primarily corn and native herbs and roots.

The Tarahumara were extremely suspicious of strangers. When approached, they would go so far as to abandon their homes and belongings. Lumholtz always

Opposite: Tarahumara women dancing hikuli at Guájochic Station, c. 1892–93. "The Tarahumaris [sic] . . . descended originally from heaven with corn and potatoes in their ears. Their god was with them at the beginning, but the devil molested him, and to such purpose that he had to retreat. Once when their god was intoxicated, the devil robbed him of his wife. 'I cannot remain here any longer,' said he, 'because the devil took my wife; but I will leave two crosses in the world.' He placed one cross where the sun sets and one where it rises. The cross in the east their god uses when he comes down to visit the Tarahumaris; that in the west is for the Tarahumari when he dies and goes to heaven. Between these two crosses lives the Tarahumari tribe." Photograph by Carl Lumholtz

Right: Inhabited cave of Tarahumara near Nararachic, c. 1892–93. Photograph by Carl Lumholtz

sent an Indian ahead to prepare the Tarahumara for his arrival, and he depended on the services of a *lenguaraz* (Mexican interpreter) to communicate. "The lenguaraz upon whom I depend," he wrote, "is a man who enters almost as one of the tribe into the Tarahumari ceremonies. He dances with them and mourns with them. A good one will weep with the weepers and rejoice with the joyful."[9]

Despite Lumholtz's careful preparations, the Indians turned a cold shoulder to him. In fact, they feared that he was a cannibal, feasting "entirely upon women, children and green corn. They used to disappear wherever I travelled," he wrote, "so that at one time my task appeared almost hopeless." Fortunately, the weather intervened. "I had the good luck to start out with rain. The Indians had for months and months been praying and dancing for rain, which now, for some weeks, seemed to follow me. They soon associated my pres-

ence with the rain, and from that time on I was of good omen to them. They were now pleased to pose before the terrible camera, which, in their eyes, had become so powerful a rain-maker."[10]

Lumholtz found what he was searching for. As he progressed south through the State of Chihuahua, he encountered a number of tribes who dwelt in caves and rock shelters, including the southern Pima, the Tarahumara, the Guarijío, and the Tepehuan. Of all these related tribes, the Tarahumara most often lived this way, generally in the winter months. To provide new pasture for their animals, the Tarahumara moved frequently, from caves to wooden huts to the shelter of rocks or trees, planting corn crops in different locations. Neither the missionaries nor the encroaching Mexicans were able to force the Tarahumara into the pueblos. Living year round in fixed dwellings made of stone and adobe was incompatible with their mode of subsistence.

Lumholtz could not fully recognize the complexity of this response to a rugged land; he had his primitive society. He soon discovered, however, that the "cave dwellers" of northern Mexico had little in common with the ancient cliff dwellers of the Southwest. The Anasazi built huge pueblos and inaccessible cliff houses; both were communal dwellings, some of which had been inhabited continuously for hundreds of years. By comparison, the Tarahumara were merely subsisting. They lived in small family groups at considerable distance from one another. Their cave dwellings were easily accessible, with at most the aid of a ladder or a notched tree trunk. They tended not to improve the rock shelters and never excavated them. Sometimes they constructed a stone wall in the front as a screen from the elements. The Tarahumara usually pulled down a house or abandoned a cave dwelling after the death of an inhabitant. They needed little and left little behind.

In the Magic Land of Peyote

Once upon a time the all-important thing for the Huichols to eat—the deer—became god, and he is to them the symbol of life and of fertility. With his blood the grains of corn are sprinkled before being sown. The great god of hikuli, *when he appeared the first time out in the country of the* hikuli, *showed himself as a deer, and every one of his tracks became a* hikuli-*plant—the plant of life; and the life is that of the deer.*

—Carl Lumholtz[11]

Lumholtz had resolved a great question to his satisfaction, but his most fascinating journey lay ahead. He had heard from the governor of the State of Jalisco of a tribe of "absolute savages, who wear their hair long, and refuse to pay taxes to the government."[12]

Little was known of this tribe, which made Lumholtz eager to make their acquaintance. In March 1894, the Museum sent him into the field for his third expedition, which would last for three years.

Mexicans referred to these people as "los Huicholes," a corruption of the tribal name Virárika, which means "healers." The first village Lumholtz came to, San Andrés, was four days' journey from the nearest large town, Mezquitic. The Huicholes, like the Tarahumara, were wary of strangers. Even though he had discharged his Mexicans and was accompanied only by Indians, Lumholtz was met first with indifference and then, at the main village, Santa Catarina, with threats against his life. Only by

singing the songs the shamans sang at the feast for rain was he able to gain their acceptance. Once over that hurdle, Lumholtz came face to face with what the writer Fernando Benítez has described as "the best-preserved body of archaic myth and ritual in Middle America"[13]—the hikuli ritual.

The hikuli, a small cactus (*Lophophora williamsii*, var. Lewinii), the Spanish peyote, was found in the central mesa of Mexico, near San Luis Potosi. Tradition had it that the Huicholes originated in the south, became lost under the Earth, and surfaced in the east, in the country of the hikuli. It was to this country that they made pilgrimages each September to gather the cacti. The journey there and back

Opposite: Teakata, Santa Catarina, Mexico, birthplace of the Huichol god of fire, Tatewarí, c. 1895. The custodian of the god of fire agreed to take Lumholtz, in the company of several of the hikuli seekers, to this sacred spot, "a large, shallow cavern, called Hainotega, which means 'the place of haino,' a small bird from the coast, which Grandfather Fire used to keep while residing here. In the middle of the cave lies a huge block of tuff, supposed to be the god himself when he was an infant. Near the wall of the cave, at a little distance from the block, I was shown his actual birthplace, where he sprang forth as a spark." Photograph by Carl Lumholtz

Right: The painting of faces of the hikuli seekers and their wives with a root and water brought from the land of hikuli plays a significant part in the preparations for the feast and the feast itself. The various designs are always yellow, the color of the Tatewarí, the Huichol god of fire.

took forty-three days, with visits to the sacred places along the route. The Huicholes believed that the cactus was the votive bowl of the god of fire, Tatewarí, and if they failed to procure it, rain would cease. In a land where large amounts of water were necessary to cultivate corn on the steep slopes of the barrancas and where droughts caused severe hardship, much of the tribe's ceremonial life revolved around rainmaking.

During the months prior to the feast for eating toasted corn, which usually took place by January, the Huicholes ate slices of the fresh hikuli plants, usually four or five slices and sometimes as many as twenty a day. When taken in excess, the plant caused hallucinations and worse. Lumholtz observed men trying to kill others or tearing off their clothes in a mad frenzy. He himself tried the plant and found its effects to be quite pleasant: "The plant . . . exhilarates the human system, and allays all feelings of hunger and thirst. It also produces color-visions. When fresh, it has a nauseating, slightly sour taste, but it is wonderfully refreshing when one has been exposed to great fatigue. Not only does it do away with all exhaustion, but one feels actually pushed on, as I can testify from personal experience."[14]

Lumholtz never actually made the pilgrimage, but he did receive reliable details of the journey from his informants. No outsider was permitted to accompany the pilgrims until Benítez did so in the 1960s. Yet Lumholtz felt his observations on the hikuli ritual were his most important contribution to the understanding of another culture.

Lumholtz could not help romanticizing the people he encountered. Their lives were harsh, and they were by no means as "untouched" as he believed, but he was pursuing a myth of the primitive, and it colored what he saw. In the end, however, Lumholtz experienced more than a myth. He recognized a way of life utterly different from his but suited to its world. This experience transformed him. He had been raised to regard primitive peoples as representative of all that was "crude, evil, and vicious." The Huicholes and Tarahumara dispelled those misconceptions. He concluded *Unknown Mexico*, his classic study of the Indians of the Sierra Madre, with this thought: "Primitive people as they are, they taught me a new philosophy of life, for their ignorance is nearer to truth than our prejudice."[15]

The Ancient Ones

That they don't crumble is the mystery. That these little squarish mud-heaps endure for centuries after centuries, while Greek marble tumbles asunder, and cathedrals totter, is the wonder. But then, the naked human hand with a bit of new soft mud is quicker than time, and defies the centuries.

—D. H. Lawrence

In 1893, Talbot and Frederick Hyde, brothers from New York

who had inherited a fortune from their grandfather's Babbit Soap Company, funded an expedition to explore archaeological sites in the Southwest. The Hydes' interest in Southwestern archaeology had been sparked by a visit to the Chicago World's Columbian Exposition earlier that year, and they enlisted the services of Richard Wetherill as their guide.

After his discovery of Cliff Palace, Wetherill and his brothers had continued to explore the canyons of Mesa Verde and served as guides to the many visitors who came to view the ruins. In 1891, when Richard Wetherill led the Swedish geologist Gustav Nordenskiöld into Mesa Verde, he little suspected that he was embarking on a new career, as a self-taught archaeologist. Nordenskiöld hired him to supervise excavations at Mesa Verde and taught Wetherill the most up-to-date European methods of excavation, along with proper documentation in field notes and photographs. After his visit, Nordenskiöld wrote the first account of Southwestern archaeology, *The Cliff Dwellers of Mesa Verde.* Wetherill went on to excavate hundreds of sites over the next fourteen years, a number in conjunction with the American Museum of Natural History, where much of his collection of magnificent Anasazi artifacts now resides.

In 1893, the Hyde Exploring Expedition began work in the Grand Gulch of southeastern Utah, some of the wildest canyon country in the region. The Hydes intended to donate the artifacts they found to the American Museum of Natural History. In Whiskers Draw, digging under the floor of a cave in which he had found Anasazi artifacts, Wetherill came upon burial cists containing spears and fine baskets made of yucca and willow. At other Anasazi sites, such as Mesa Verde, he had found pottery and bows and arrows. This was something completely different. Wetherill also unearthed skeletons with long, narrow skulls; they did not have the round and flattened craniums characteristically found in ruins all over the San Juan Basin. (Later archaeologists deduced that the flattening of the craniums was caused by the hard cradleboards into which cliff-dweller infants were strapped.)

Wetherill coined the term Basket People to describe the culture he had uncovered; the term Basketmakers is still used today. Because the remains were buried underneath the Anasazi artifacts, Wetherill concluded they belonged to a racially distinct people older than the Anasazi cliff dwellers. In his dramatic scenario, the Anasazi invaded and massacred the Basketmakers. By making the connection between the location of the remains and their relative age, he anticipated the seminal work of Museum archaeologist Nels C. Nelson in the Galisteo Basin of New Mexico two decades later. Further investigations in the region, in particular those by Earl Morris, eventually proved that these two groups were expressions of a single continuous culture.

After the close of the Hyde Expedition to Grand Gulch, Wetherill returned to work on his family's ranch. Then, in the fall of 1895, he took the Palmers, a family of traveling musicians from Kansas, on a trek to the desolate Chaco Canyon in New Mexico. This was Wetherill's first visit, and he was impressed by the ruins there. That winter Wetherill wrote the following lines to Talbot Hyde: "[The ruins] of Chaco Canyon being the greatest in New Mexico and almost unknown . . . for that reason more than any other I wished to examine them."[16]

White men had known about the ruins in Chaco Canyon as early as the middle of the seventeenth century, when the Spaniards mounted military expeditions against the Navajo, who had settled in the canyons to raise sheep and goats. No one took particular notice of these ruins until 1849, when Lieutenant James Simpson of the Army Topographical Engineers rode through Chaco Canyon. He immediately appreciated the fine masonry of the remaining walls, which rose above centuries of accumulated debris and dirt: "Indeed, so beautifully diminutive and true are the details of the structures as to cause it, at a little distance, to have all the appearance of a magnificent piece of mosaic work."[17] Simpson carefully documented seven major ruins and a number of smaller ones, giving them names supplied by Indian and Mexican guides accompanying his party.

The result of Wetherill's letter was the four-year Hyde Exploring Expedition to Chaco Canyon, which commenced excavations of one of the largest ruins, Pueblo Bonito, in 1896. The expedition was under the scientific direction of Frederic Putnam, of the American Museum of Natural History. George Pepper, who had studied with Putnam and was an assistant in the department of anthropology, was named field supervisor and Richard Wetherill foreman.

Situated in the middle of an arid basin, Chaco Canyon is a strip of land ten miles long and a mile wide, running between sand-

Right: Rear wall of Pueblo Bonito, showing joint in masonry, Chaco Canyon, New Mexico. From a hand-colored lantern slide by N. C. Nelson

Below: Room 73, Pueblo Bonito, Chaco Canyon, excavated by the Hyde Exploring Expedition, 1897

stone walls that rise to one hundred fifty feet. It is an inhospitable place; the stream that cuts through the canyon runs only during the rainy season. The once-fertile canyon floor, where the Anasazi farmed, is now overrun by saltbush, snakeweed, prickly-pear cactus and a few scrubby juniper and piñon. At the height of Chacoan occupation, the canyon and mesa top were crisscrossed by a complex system of roads, irrigation canals, and huge ceremonial kivas, with access to the mesa top by stairways cut into the sandstone walls.

Chaco Canyon became the center of a regional network of

towns that spread for hundreds of miles. Pueblo Bonito, built in the shape of a D, housed up to a thousand people in more than six hundred rooms. As many as fifty rooms were still intact when the Hyde Expedition began excavations. This huge town contained at least thirty-two kivas; two of striking size were referred to as great kivas. The settlement's most remarkable feature was its curved rear wall, which continued unbroken for eight hundred feet, rising as high as five stories.

The expedition began dismally. The team spent the initial month excavating two huge refuse mounds in front of Pueblo Bonito, but their search yielded only rubbish and debris. Frustrated, they turned their attention to the ruins themselves, excavating thirty-seven rooms. By the fall, they had accumulated a freight car full of artifacts—

pottery, arrows, wooden staffs, wooden flutes, stone effigies, turquoise beads and pendants—which they shipped back to the Museum in New York. By the end of another three seasons, they had excavated close to two hundred rooms.

A spectacular "lost city" emerged from the rubble. In spite of a vast range of artifacts, however, the Anasazi remained shrouded in mystery. Edgar Hewett, who spearheaded the drive to protect ruins on public lands and to have them named national monuments (Chaco Canyon was so named in 1907), later wrote eloquently of the inhabitants of Chaco Canyon: "No written word of history exists concerning them. No convincing tradition of them has ever been found among the living peoples. . . . The name by which they knew themselves and were known

and varied styles of doors and windows at Pueblo Bonito led Pepper to conclude that the structure had been occupied continuously for many years. He had found evidence of earlier ruins underneath the present structure, and he was certain the site was prehistoric.

In spite of these tantalizing insights, Pepper could not solve the puzzle of what had become of the inhabitants of Chaco Canyon. After seven hundred years of occupation, it appears that the Chaco people simply walked away from the huge complex. Paleoecological research has since identified a prolonged drought in the San Juan Basin during much of the twelfth century as the primary cause of the abandonment of Chaco Canyon and the beginning of the demise of Anasazi culture, but certainly there were other factors, from deforestation and erosion to disease and social unrest.

After the Hyde Expedition closed down its operations, Richard Wetherill and his family remained behind in Chaco Canyon, running the successful Chaco Canyon Trading Post, set up along the north wall of Pueblo Bonito by the Hyde brothers, and ranching the surrounding lands. Then, in June 1910, Wetherill was dragged into a dispute with the local Navajos concerning one of his horses. Tensions escalated. On June 22, Richard Wetherill was shot off his horse while driv-

among their contemporaries is lost utterly. If the language they spoke still exists, we do not know of it. Of all the peoples of the ancient world whose achievements have survived the ages, none has more completely attained oblivion."[18]

The Hyde Expedition began the long process of understanding the world of Chaco Canyon. Pepper noted the relationship between the domestic and ceremonial architecture of the Chacoans and that of the present-day Pueblo Indians. He also remarked on the similarities between the artifacts discovered at Chaco Canyon and those at other sites in the San Juan Basin, such as Mesa Verde. The use of different construction methods in the masonry walls

Right: Reconnaissance expedition passing Cabezon, New Mexico, 1917. From a hand-colored lantern slide by N. C. Nelson

Below: Three-color glazed Tano pottery. From a hand-colored lantern slide by N. C. Nelson

ing a herd of cattle down the canyon. His wife buried him in the shadow of Pueblo Bonito.

Marking Time

"It is the universality of change in the ways of human living," wrote Clark Wissler, curator of anthropology at the American Museum of Natural History from 1905 to 1942, "which makes archaeology possible; these changes register the march of time."[19] For much of the nineteenth century, European archaeologists had used a technique embodying Wissler's maxim to establish a chronology for archaeological remains. As early as 1830, C. J. Thomsen, a Danish scientist, determined the relative age of objects of iron, bronze, and stone that had been discovered by laborers in local peat bogs. Thomsen came up with a straightforward and logical idea—stratigraphy. Since peat is a sediment deposited on the bottom of swamps and ponds, it made sense that the oldest artifacts would be found at the deepest level, while the ones at the top would be of more recent age. Thomsen and subsequent scientists could ascribe no actual dates to these objects. Their chronologies were strictly relational. This remained the case until the advent of radiocarbon dating in the 1950s.

Thomsen was able to classify the Stone, Bronze, and Iron ages as stages in the technological de-velopment of human society. The insight began to transform archaeology from the amateurish collecting of old artifacts into a systematic field of study.

Archaeologists had never used the method in the United States. It was generally thought that New World sites were occupied too briefly for this method to be effective. In addition, although pot hunters had unearthed a wealth of artifacts of wood, bone, shell, stone, and pottery in the Southwest, no metal implements were found that could be used as time markers.

Nels C. Nelson changed that. Curator of prehistoric archaeology at the Museum, he learned his craft in Europe, where President Henry Fairfield Osborn, who had a passionate interest in the continent's archaeology, sent him in 1912. While working on excavations at Castillo Cave in Spain, Nelson observed thirteen distinct strata, a complete history book, from the Paleolithic period through the Bronze Age. When

he returned to the United States, he turned to stratigraphic methods to solve the temporal riddle of the ruins of the Southwest.

Castillo Cave was old and had not been disturbed; the layers were not jumbled. In his early experiences in the Southwest, however, Nelson often found a chaos below the surface. Then, in 1914, at Pueblo San Cristobal in the Galisteo Basin south of Santa Fe, New Mexico, Nelson located a large ash heap that was relatively untouched. In the middle of this mound, he excavated a section ten feet deep and three by six feet wide. Since this section did not exhibit the discrete geological strata observed at Castillo Cave, Nelson divided it arbitrarily into twelve-inch sections, cataloguing what he discovered in each section. Using pottery sherds as time markers (he found more than two thousand sherds there), he was able to prove that distinct types of pottery are characteristically located at different levels in the trash mounds, much as fossils are associated with specific geologic strata, with the oldest at the bottom. Once he had established the progression of pottery types at San Cristobal, he could date other archaeological deposits by the presence of certain kinds of pottery. As Museum anthropologist David Hurst Thomas puts it, "Nelson created his own stratigraphy."

Nelson proposed a sequence for three types of prehistoric pottery found at large ruins of the Tano Indians in New Mexico, based on their relative position in the refuse heap. Two- and three-color painted ware, most commonly black on white, was the oldest. Two-color glazed ware came next, then three-color glazed ware, which dated from prehistoric times to sometime after the Spanish occupation, around 1540. In addition, he identified two categories of more recent pottery: two-color glazed ware, from the occupation of the Tano pueblos in the years 1540 to 1680, when the Pueblo Indians came under Spanish domination; and modern painted pottery, dating from 1680 to 1850, rarely found in most of the Tano pueblos. He was thus able to distinguish five styles of pottery that corresponded to five successive periods. The method spurred others to look more carefully at the history under their feet.

The eminent archaeologist A.V. Kidder, of Harvard's Peabody Museum, visited Nelson at San Cristobal to observe his methods. In 1915–16, using stratification at Pecos Pueblo, twenty-five miles to the east of San Cristobal, Kidder was able to trace the evolution of habitation at the pueblo over the course of several centuries. With Nelson's groundbreaking work in stratigraphy and Kidder's practical application of the method at Pecos, the early history of the Southwest could be written.

The person who was to add the next chapter to this history had skipped his commencement exercises at the University of Colorado to work with Nelson in the Galisteo Basin. His name was Earl Morris. In many respects, his career in the first half of this century closely parallels the evolution of Southwest archaeology itself.

Among Ancient Ruins

In 1916 Morris was ready to embark on his journey to uncover each "element of the mosaic picture of the life and customs of the prehistoric Pueblo people."[20] With the enthusiastic recommendation of Nelson, Morris was named head of the Museum's excavations at Aztec Ruins, near Farmington, a small town in northern New Mexico. Patents had been issued covering the ruins as early as 1889 and, thus, had largely protected the site from rampant vandalism.

The Museum had arranged with H. D. Abrams, the owner, to undertake a complete excavation.

This project was the culmination of a lifelong dream for Morris, who had spent much of his life near Aztec, the most spectacular and well preserved of a large group of ruins located in the valley of the Animas River, named Río de las Animas Perditas—"River of Lost Souls"—by the Spanish. Morris had dug there with his father in the 1890s. Scott

Opposite: The Great Kiva at Aztec Ruins, New Mexico, from above. Photograph by Earl Morris

Above: Excavations at Canyon del Muerto, Arizona, 1923. A. V. Kidder recalled, "The digging was as difficult as such work can possibly be. . . . Dust rose so chokingly and blindingly at every touch of the shovel that respirators and goggles had constantly to be worn." Photograph by Earl Morris

Morris, a construction worker and sometime pot hunter, had been the first person to dig into the mound of debris that lay outside Pueblo Bonito at Chaco Canyon, and, puzzled by the lack of burials, to ask the question of what had happened to the dead.

Scott Morris was a good teacher: "One morning in March of 1893," his son reminisced:

Father handed me a worn-out pick, the handle of which he had shortened to my length, and said, "Go dig in that hole where I worked yesterday, and you will be out of my way." At the first stroke of the pick into the wall of the pit, there rolled down a roundish, gray object that looked like a cobblestone, but when I turned it over, it proved to be the bowl of a black-and-white dipper. . . . Thus, at three and a half years of age there had happened the clinching event that was to make of me an ardent pot hunter, who later on was to acquire the more creditable, and I hope earned, classification as an archaeologist.[21]

The excavation at Aztec Ruins was the largest project of its kind ever undertaken in the United States. The first season of fieldwork was funded by J. P. Morgan. The following year, Archer M. Huntington agreed to fund the project as part of the ongoing Archer M. Huntington Survey, an ambitious attempt, initiated in 1909 by Museum anthropologist Clark Wissler, to investigate both the prehistoric ruins and current inhabitants of the American Southwest. In 1920, with funds provided by Huntington, the Museum purchased a twenty-five-acre tract that included Aztec Ruins and parts of six complexes in the area. The Museum planned to hold onto the land until excavations were completed, then deed the property to the National Park Service. In 1923, President Warren G. Harding declared Aztec Ruins a national monu-

ment. The Museum was given a three-year excavation permit, and Morris was named first custodian, with an annual salary of twelve dollars.

Like Richard Wetherill, Morris had the rare privilege of living next to the ruins that dominated his life. In 1920 he built a small house in Anasazi style behind the pueblo, where he lived until 1933.

During a decade of excavations at Aztec Ruins, Morris excavated nearly three-fourths of the ruins. He also stabilized the ruins and later restored the Great Kiva to what he believed it might have looked like when the complex was inhabited. Containing about five hundred rooms, Aztec consisted of three adjoining structures built around a rectangular courtyard. On the fourth side, the courtyard was bounded by a curved wall, with a small door leading to the outside. The outer walls of the buildings rose to the height of three or four stories, with no openings large enough for a person to gain entry into the complex. Even if an enemy managed to scale the wall, there was no direct access from the courtyard to the tiers of rooms, which could only be reached by outside ladders that were easily drawn up. Aztec was a sophisticated fortress.

Morris and his crew had to sort through tons of rubble and dirt. The dry dust, full of gypsum and ashes, penetrated their masks of wet cloths and sponges, inflaming their lungs. The most demanding aspect of the work, however, was gathering and grouping the pottery fragments, which required the attention of a detective and the patience of a saint. One of the most unusual finds of the first season was a large red bowl. The bowl had

broken in a second-story room, and, as the floor timbers decayed over time, many of the fragments had fallen into the room below, where they were covered over by centuries of earth. A workman first noticed a red potsherd as he shoveled earth from the lower room. In order to retrieve the pieces of this single artifact, the crew had to run six wagon loads of dirt through the sieve, a task that consumed more than a day.

In 1920, Morris accompanied Kidder, the pioneer Mayan archaeologist Sylvanus Morley, and Neil Judd on a reconnaissance trip to Chaco Canyon. Judd was looking for a site that would be appropriate for further excavation by a National Geographic Society expedition. There Morris was awed by the great kivas in the courtyards of Pueblo Bonito and Pueblo Chetro Ketl. The massive structures, far larger than any of the other kiva pits, have been described by the archaeologists Robert and Florence Lister as "a super-sanctuary for the village, a kind of primitive cathedral in which the most important religious ceremonies could have been held."[22]

Because archaeologists lack any written records of the Anasazi, they have had to speculate on the purpose of these structures. *Kiva* is a Hopi Indian word for an underground circular chamber, entered through an opening in the roof, where various activities take place, from meetings on secular matters to the performance of sacred rituals. Smaller kivas, common at prehistoric ruins, were most likely used for the performance of clan ceremonies, and present-day Indians have also proposed that they were used as sweat houses.

Morris resolved to commence work immediately on Aztec's Great Kiva. He knew Judd was about to begin work on the Great Kiva at Pueblo Bonito, and Morris wanted to be the first archaeologist to excavate such a structure and to establish a standard. By March 1921, he had completed his project. The huge ceremonial chamber, set seven feet below the level of the plaza and with a diameter of forty-one feet, was surrounded by a concentric ring of rooms, with stairs at the north and south ends. The structure was a marvel of architectural ingenuity. Four pillars of cedar and masonry had once supported a roof of nineteen hundred square feet. Upon a timber framework lay earth to the depth of one foot—an estimated 90 tons' worth. The entire construction was accomplished without a single peg, nail, or mortise-and-tenon joint.

Morris saw Aztec's Great Kiva as evidence of a cultural tie to Chaco Canyon, where there were at least ten such structures. Indeed, excavations were increasingly linking Aztec, which was located halfway between Mesa Verde and Chaco Canyon, to both sites. Archaeologists had been able to discern differences in the form and design of pottery from Chaco Canyon, Mesa Verde, and Kayenta, in northeastern Arizona, and they had found evidence of the different styles at Aztec. They also uncovered evidence of ceramic trade among these groups.

By 1920, Morris was certain that Aztec Ruins had been occupied by two distinct groups: an earlier people related to the inhabitants of Chaco Canyon, then later Mesa Verdeans from the north. Excavation in the southwest section of the Aztec plaza, where Morris had earlier decided there was no more need to continue digging, revealed the most important finds thus far: two kivas, built one on top of the other, filled with pottery of the Chaco type. He recovered two small effigies, one of which, a hunchbacked figure, resembled an effigy discovered by Pepper at Pueblo Bonito. This was not simply trade pottery; it was evidence of prolonged Chacoan occupation. Further digging in the plaza and underneath the house itself uncovered traces of an ancient town almost as extensive as that of Pueblo Bonito. The Chacoans of Aztec had worshiped in the same fashion as their relatives to the south; they had also traded with other groups as far away as central Mexico and disposed of their dead in an unknown fashion. Proof of Chacoan occupation, so crucial to an understanding of the long-term development of Aztec, and to that of the entire San Juan Basin, could easily have eluded Morris: "It seems rather curious that we should have begun at just the wrong end of this ruin," he wrote to Clark Wissler, "but perhaps it is best as it is because we shall have worked over the whole in anticipation of the solution."[23]

Morris speculated that perhaps a hundred years after the Chacoans suddenly abandoned Aztec, just as abruptly as they had left Pueblo Bonito, people from Mesa Verde, perhaps driven south by overpopulation, took over what remained of the town. They used parts of the old building, adding on, reusing the materials, introducing their distinctive T-shaped doors and kiva styles. The Mesa Verdeans remained at Aztec for a number of years, their culture flourished, and then, like the Chacoans before them, they disappeared. Morris wrote with intense feeling of this final decline, inspired by the details he had uncovered in a decade of sifting and sorting:

But there came a time when they had become a dwindling remnant, huddled into filthy quarters, their women and children dying off rapidly, and being laid away in rooms beneath and beside those in which they dwelt, with few or no accompaniments. Architecture had become a dead art. Their last buildings were tawdry makeshifts, weak and flimsy to the limit of belief. The same condition held in the field of ceramics. There is recognizable at the close a distinct variant of the Mesa Verde pottery complex in which the paste is frail and friable, the pigment impermanent and poorly handled, the decoration not only crude but decadent, and grace of form almost entirely lost. Upon this condition of cultural senility or disease came the fire of intentional origin which for an interval transformed all but the western side of the pueblo into a veritable furnace. Whether the remainder of the Mesa Verde people evacuated the place and then fired it, or whether an enemy was the incendiary, may never be known, but the burning thereof marked the close of human habitation of the Aztec Ruin. During the centuries which followed, there labored within the great house only the effacing hand of time.[24]

The Basketmakers

Excitement about new discoveries in the American Southwest spread from scientists to amateurs, some of whom were wealthy enough to become patrons and to fund their own expeditions. The Hyde brothers, J. P. Morgan, Archer M. Huntington, and New York legislator Ogden Mills, among others, provided the necessary funds for large-scale excavations. In 1921, Earl Morris met the man who was to become his patron—Charles L. Bernheimer, a wealthy cotton broker who had already taken one trip to Rainbow Bridge, an immense natural stone arch deep in the remote canyon country of the Four Corners. Intrigued by what he had seen, Bernheimer asked Clark Wissler to recommend a scientist who could accompany him and provide information on the ruins they passed. The obvious choice was Earl Morris, who, in June 1921, joined Bernheimer's party, which included John Wetherill, brother of Richard Wetherill. Morris would make eight exploratory trips, known as the Bernheimer Expeditions, under the auspices of the Museum.

By 1923, after three trips to Rainbow Bridge, Bernheimer was looking for a new focus for his explorations. Morris, impatient with Bernheimer's geological interests and eager to win his support for archaeology projects, suggested that he visit a dig at Cemetery Ridge near Newcomb's Trading Post in New Mexico. This strategy was a success; Bernheimer wanted to see more, and the party headed for Canyon de Chelly, just across the border in Arizona. Morris was skeptical about what he might find there, for the former owners of the nearby trading post were reputed to have ransacked all the important sites in this large forked canyon. John Wetherill knew otherwise. He guided the party into the narrow confines of Canyon del Muerto, a cut that ran between sheer red sandstone cliffs six hundred feet high. Immediately, the Canyon of the Dead, named for the massacre of the

Who Were the Earliest Americans?

While Earl Morris was seeking to clarify the relationship between the Basketmakers and the later Pueblos, archaeologists working in the Southwest were looking in the opposite direction for clues to the ancestors of the Basketmakers, the earliest known inhabitants of the Southwest. There was no scientific evidence to support claims that Homo sapiens *had evolved independently in the Americas, or that the species had been here for anywhere near as long as it had been in Asia, Europe, and Africa. Modern humans were clearly relative newcomers in the New World, but when did they arrive?*

In 1925, a chance discovery by a cowboy riding through northeastern New Mexico was to change forever thinking about the antiquity of humankind in the New World. The cowboy spotted old bones along the banks of the Cimarron River, near Folsom, New Mexico. He gave the bones to a rancher known to be interested in such things, who called in a local collector to look at the site. The two men collected samples of the bones, which they sent to J. D. Figgins, director of the Colorado Museum of Natural History. These samples, which turned out to be bones of an extinct species of bison and a large deerlike animal, intrigued Figgins. The following summer, the Colorado Museum sent a team to excavate the site. In the first season, they found two finely chipped projectile points, lying in the dirt under the bones, and a triangular piece of flint, fashioned of the same material, sunk deep in the clay surrounding a bone. Although this was not the first discovery in the region of projectile points in contact with bones of an extinct bison, this was the first time evidence of the physical link between an artifact and an extinct animal had been preserved intact for future study.

Figgins immediately recognized the significance of his discovery, but other scientists reacted with disbelief. The American Museum of Natural History, however, reviewed Figgins's finds and encouraged him to search for more evidence. In the May–June 1927 issue of Natural History, *there appeared two articles discussing the Folsom points, one written by Figgins and the other by Harold Clark, a geologist at the Colorado Museum. Clark, the first geologist to visit the site, was convinced the deposits dated back to the Pleistocene period. Both men were certain that their finds would result in a reevaluation of current thinking.*

There were yet more significant discoveries during the 1927 season; the most important was a projectile point embedded between two bison ribs. Paleontologist Barnum Brown, visiting the site as the representative of the American Museum of Natural History, felt that with this discovery the evidence of true association was proved beyond doubt. In addition, he helped establish that these points were different from those previously discovered in the region.

By 1928, *the Museum had joined forces with the Colorado Museum at the Folsom site, and the entire project was placed under the leadership of Barnum Brown, who uncovered the remains of forty bison and seventeen points. Almost all the bison lacked tail bones, evidence that they had been skinned after they had been slain. A steady stream of archaeologists, geologists, and paleontologists visited the site. With the indisputable evidence laid out before them, even the most skeptical scientists could no longer deny that they were witnessing one of the most important discoveries in American archaeology—incontrovertible proof of early human presence in the American Southwest.*

Rainbow Natural Bridge, Utah, 1920. Earl Morris wrote: "So true are the proportions, so perfect the symmetry of the gigantic bow of stone that when gazing upward at it, one unconsciously bares one's head in reverence to the Master Architect whose handiwork it is. The fact that the aborigines shared this sentiment is evidenced by the ruins of two ancient altars in the shadow of the eastern base."

Navajos by the Spanish in the winter of 1804–5, began to yield its secrets. In a single day of digging, Morris uncovered twenty sandals, a cradle, matting, fragments of cloth, buckskin, a flute, and four pipes.

At a site called Mummy Cave, Morris found material evidence of Richard Wetherill's Basketmakers as well as the slab structures and remains of the pre-Pueblo people, who were just beginning to make crude pottery. Morris was trying to determine the relationship between the late Basketmakers and the pre-Pueblos. In order to so, he had to find a site where the artifacts of the Basketmakers were found alongside the earliest forms of pottery. Here was evidence Morris had dreamed of finding, clues that might help him solve the riddle of the Basketmakers, and he was "literally wild over the wealth of specimens and of information that lay snugly tucked away in the dry ledge shelter."[25]

In 1882, Colonel James Stevenson of the U.S. Bureau of Ethnology had uncovered two natural mummies in the talus slope below

the cave, which he dubbed Mummy Cave. Set six hundred feet above the canyon floor and its seasonal stream, the "cave" was really a massive cleft in the rock face, containing two buildings with upward of fifty rooms. The structures were connected by a retaining-wall causeway with an elegant three-story tower.

Mummy Cave presented Morris with an ideal opportunity to map the entire Basketmaker-Pueblo sequence. All the necessary layers seemed to be there, from evidence of the Basketmakers near the bottom of the extensive refuse talus (the natural slope of rock debris); to the traces of pre-Pueblo slab houses farther up the slope, accompanied by pre-Pueblo potsherds; to the enormous cliff house, the largest of the canyon system, probably dating from early Chaco times, which showed evidence of two culture periods in its masonry. The first four, perhaps even five, culture periods of the San Juan Basin were outlined with stunning clarity. Morris and others had already established the chronological sequence of these periods; now they might have the perishable artifacts—baskets, sandals, even foodstuff—to fill in the picture.

Hours after Morris started digging in the slope of ash and trash below the cave, he found objects in an astounding state of preservation. There were baskets of various sizes and shapes, some as large as the span of a man's outstretched arms, and an endless stream of woven sandals, essential in the desert terrain, which gave evidence of extremely sophisticated craftsmanship. The Basketmakers had clearly inhabited Mummy Cave for a long time and had developed a complex culture.

By the end of his first season, Morris had no doubt that both the Basketmakers and what he referred to as the early and late pre-Pueblos had inhabited the slab houses at Mummy Cave, but the proof of this would continue to elude him for years. It depended on fixing absolute dates to ruins, but Morris's "chronology" was entirely relative. The solution to his puzzle came from an unlikely source, a professor of physics and astronomy at the University of Arizona named Andrew Douglass.

In 1901, Douglass began a study of sunspots and their effects on the Earth's climate. Having observed that annual tree rings are of varying widths, depending on the amount of moisture a tree receives during each growing season, Douglass was able to make a clear connection between sunspot cycles and rates of rainfall. The pattern of thick and thin rings provided a chronological fingerprint.

From here, he took the next logical step—comparing the ring patterns of living and dead trees

Opposite, above: Central tower of Mummy Cave, Canyon del Muerto, Arizona, 1925. Photograph by Earl Morris and A.V. Kidder

Opposite, below: Earl Morris digging at Canyon del Muerto, Arizona, 1929. Photograph by E. M. Meyer

Right: Stenciled handprints left by the Anasazi on the wall of Canyon de Chelly near Sliding Rock Ruin, Arizona, 1925. Photograph by Earl Morris and A. V. Kidder

to form a continuous sequence of tree rings, each one corresponding to a specific year. Douglass hoped the process, known as tree-ring dating, or dendrochronology, would ultimately enable him to date building timbers at ancient sites. He was able already to match sequences of overlapping tree rings that went back over five hundred years, but there his dating stopped. He could find no sample that overlapped with the tree-ring sequence that he had established for beams used in prehistoric ruins. As a result of the gap between the two series of tree rings, Douglass could establish only relative dates among the ruins he studied, not specific years for each one.

In 1914, Clark Wissler wrote to Douglass to express interest in his efforts and to offer samples from beams in the ruins of New Mexico. Douglass's work in dendrochronology was soon included in the Huntington Survey of the Southwest. In 1919, Morris sent to Douglass samples that he had obtained from Aztec Ruins, and the following year the Museum sent sections from logs obtained by the Hyde Expedition at Pueblo Bonito. Comparing the samples from these two locations, Douglass concluded that construction at Aztec had begun forty to fifty years after that of Pueblo Bonito. He was also able

to determine that all the logs from the Aztec Ruins were cut during a time span of little more than nine years. This meant that the entire structure, containing as many as five hundred rooms, had been planned in advance and built with amazing speed, with nothing more than crude stone, bone, and wood implements. This accomplishment was even more impressive considering that, without any animals of burden, the builders transported sandstone from hills five miles away and huge timbers from up the valley.

Douglass initiated a search for samples that would span the gap between the absolute and the relative tree-ring sequences. He enlisted the help of the National Geographic Society and the Carnegie Institution of Washington, D.C. Morris and other archaeologists searched for years until finally, in 1929, a team of the National Geographic Society came across a charred log at Hopi ruins near Showlow, in eastern Arizona, which provided the missing link. At last, Douglass had a continuous tree-ring chronology that went back as far as A.D. 700. Within a month, forty ruins of

the Southwest were assigned exact dates: Mesa Verde was built between A.D. 1073 and 1262, Pueblo Bonito in Chaco Canyon between A.D. 919 and 1130, and Aztec Ruins between A.D. 1110 and 1121.

Of all his contributions to our knowledge of the early peoples of the Southwest, Morris felt that providing samples for the tree-ring chronology was his greatest. No one understood better than he the importance of this technique as a tool for tracing the development of culture in the Southwest. By the early 1930s, Douglass was able to trace the sequence back to A.D. 10. Once he had dated various Basketmaker and early Pueblo sites, Morris was able to determine that there was no break between the Basketmakers and the Pueblos, that they were part of a continuous Anasazi culture. The Basketmaker people had already developed agriculture, crafts, weapons, and houses before they evolved into the pottery-making Pueblos, who simply built upon and developed the culture that their ancestors had created. It was for the Basketmakers, who had so mystified him, that Morris reserved a special respect: "It is easy to take that which is found existent and to carry it to further development. But to invent, to innovate, is another matter, demanding creative ability, that rarest of mental qualities, which put upon its possessor the true stamp of genius."[26]

There was a footnote to Morris's work at Canyon del Muerto. In 1931, with the consent of the Navajo Tribal Council, the entire canyon system, including Canyon de Chelly and Canyon del Muerto, was named a national monument by President Herbert Hoover. As a final gesture, Morris offered to help the National Park Service in rebuilding a missing corner of the tower at Mummy Cave and replacing several ceiling poles to stabilize the ruin.

The Cheyenne sun-dance pledgers. Photograph by Edward S. Curtis

The Sun Dance of the Plains Indians

In 1907, Clark Wissler, curator of anthropology at the Museum, organized a systematic ethnographic survey of the Plains Indian area. For most of the following decade, he sent anthropologists into the field to study the Arapaho, Assiniboin, Blackfeet, Crow, Dakota, Hidatsa-Manda, Iowa, Kansa, Kiowa, Paiute, Plains-Cree, Plains-Ojibway, Sarsi, Shoshoni, and Ute tribes. The most important work of the survey was published in two companion volumes of the Anthropological Papers of the American Museum of Natural History; *one volume covered the societies of the Plains Indians, the other the sun-dance ceremony as practiced by the various tribes. Like the societies, the sun dance is typical of the Plains Indians and is essential to an understanding of their culture. The sun dance, which Museum anthropologist Leslie Spier described as both "spectacular and sacred," is the only ceremony in which the entire tribe participates, and the only ceremony performed by all tribes of the Plains Indians, with the exception of the Comanche. By the early decades of this century, a number of tribes no longer practiced this ritual, and among other tribes its occurrence was becoming less frequent. Nonetheless, older tribe members could still provide reliable information about it.*

While each tribe had its own version, certain essential elements were consistent throughout. The ceremony always took place during the summer buffalo hunt, when the tribe came together from its scattered winter quarters. The sun dance was initiated by a man or woman pledger to fulfill a vow made to the gods or in response to a dream. While the pledger and the associates were instructed by a shaman, rehearsed songs, and assembled their regalia, other members of the tribe collected wood to build the dance lodge at the center of the huge circle of tents that formed the encampment. They also searched for a forked tree, cut it, and carried it to the lodge, accompanying these actions with ceremonies. In the fork of the tree they tied a bundle of brush, often referred to as an eagle's nest or a thunderbird's nest, a buffalo bull hide, and offerings of food and cloth. Once the pole was raised in the center of the dance lodge, the dancers, who abstained from food and drink during the ceremony, began to dance, all the while gazing fixedly at the offerings on the pole or at the sun. The dance did not vary among the tribes—a line of dancers remained in one spot, rising on their toes with a springing motion and blowing on whistles they held in their mouths. The dance continued for up to four days and nights and sometimes included acts of self-torture in which skewers placed in the skin of the breast and the back and fastened to the pole were pulled through the skin. Spier considered the entire ceremony to be an elaborate process of

Dakota Sun Dance painted by Short Bull, Chief of the Oglala Dakota, Pine Ridge Reservation, 1893

self-mortification, including fasting, continuous staring, dancing without resting, scarification, and severing of flesh and fingers.

Among the Eastern Dakota, the sun-dance ceremony had become primarily a vision-seeking experience. Anthropologist W. D. Wallis provided a number of fascinating personal narratives of the ceremony among this tribe:

A man said he was going to perform the sun dance, having been directed in a dream to do so. He invited all of the men. They procured the pole, put up the tipi, and made all preparations. When about to begin he passed the pipe around, asking if some wished to participate. One of the young men said he wished to join him, took the pipe, smoked it, and passed it on. Another said he would participate, and then a third volunteered. They began preparations, all of them painting their legs gray and their bodies red. The leader walked out of the tipi, announcing that he would dance two days.

They danced all night and the following morning. At noon he announced that there would be great excitement among them in the camp. There would be no Cree but the trouble would originate among themselves. He could not understand clearly but said he might see it more clearly next time, before the dance was over, as the event was to take place before the completion of the dance. He then finished his smoke. They danced all that night and until noon on the following day, when he stopped for a smoke. He said the excitement would occur in a short while and before they stopped dancing. He saw the spirits of dead buffalo, and, in their midst, a man. They resumed the dance and continued it throughout the afternoon. A little while before they stopped a large herd of buffalo came. All of the young men mounted the horses and started in pursuit of the herd. One man was riding a wild horse. As he mounted, it reared and ran with him, throwing the man. As he fell to the ground his gun was discharged into his left side, killing him. When the dance was finished the leader announced that he was very sorry this sad accident had occurred before the dance was finished, but it could not be avoided. He had been anxious to finish the performance and said he was glad it was completed. He thanked the men who had sung for him, saying this was all he would do, and stepped from his place. All that he said would happen did happen.

Today Clark Wissler is largely ignored as an anthropologist and his theories have been criticized. Yet as the force behind the Archer M. Huntington Survey of the Southwest, he fostered the study of the Indian heritage of America, and not just prehistoric Indians. The other goal of the Huntington Survey was to conduct extensive ethnological studies of the Southwest that would draw comparisons between the historic and prehistoric cultures of the area.

In his studies of the modern people of the Southwest, Wissler attempted to break new ground. Because the Rio Grande Valley was an important center for the development of Pueblo culture, it became the Museum's base of operations. From there, Wissler sent Pliny Goddard to study the White Mountain and San Carlos Apache, Mary Lois Kissell to study the textiles of the Papago and the Pima, and Herbert Spinden to study the art and material culture of the contemporary Pueblo villages. Other anthropologists involved with the Huntington Survey, which continued from 1909 to 1921, included Elsie Clews Parsons, who established Laguna genealogies; Leslie Spier, who established a chronology for Zuñi ruins and studied the Havasupai of the Grand Canyon; and Alfred Kroeber, of the University of California, whose work at Zuñi Pueblo and its environs encompassed both living people and ruined villages. For the survey, Wissler gathered together perhaps the most important group of anthropologists ever to work on a single project. That we have so extensive a record of Indian life in the early

Plains Indians on horseback. Photograph by James Dixon, in the Wanamaker Collection

years of this century is due largely to him.

Wissler hoped these anthropologists would bring back evidence to support his contention that the Indians of North America belonged to distinct "culture areas," which were determined primarily by environmental factors. In 1917, Wissler published *The American Indian*, the first comprehensive synthesis of Indian culture, in which he outlined the main culture areas of North and South America.

Perhaps Wissler's most enduring contributions, however, were his detailed descriptions of the myths, art, social organization, and material culture of the Plains Indians. Like Franz Boas, one of Wissler's teachers at Columbia University, Wissler believed that Indian culture was on the wane and the only way to preserve it was to record every aspect of pre-reservation culture.

"We realized early in our career," wrote Wissler, "that the aboriginal Indian, who has so

onto reservations in Montana in the 1880s and 1890s.

Wissler got "backstage" with the help of his interpreter, the blacksmith David Duvall, who made it possible for Wissler to record the recollections of tribesmen who were old enough to remember the days when the Plains Indians hunted the land from the Mississippi to the Rockies for buffalo, antelope, and deer to provide food and clothing. Wissler's clear sympathy for the people he studied and his refined powers of observation are evident in his extensive writings about the Blackfeet. The numerous anecdotes that he related in articles for *Natural History* and his popular account *Indian Cavalcade* provide ample material for reflection.

In one story, a medicine man, Bull Shield, asked if Wissler would agree to receive an Indian name. Since it was impossible to translate white names into their language, most Indians did not know how to speak of their white friends. Wissler gladly consented and also agreed to provide a steer and crackers for a feast to accompany the name-giving.

Upon the appointed day everyone was so radiant with happy expectation and so enjoyed the aroma of boiling beef which filled the outdoor air, that I felt amply repaid for the expense involved. The leading men sat in a great circle passing a big pipe back and forth amid dignified silence broken only occasionally by subdued conversation. I remarked the contrast here, for if one brought an equal number of white men together there would have been such a chatter that even the magpies would have retired discouraged. After the feast, Bull Shield made a speech explaining why the Indians had been called together, as if they had not already known it for a long time. Several other old men made long speeches, the tenor of which I dimly understood to be that they approved of the idea. In

gripped the imagination of the world, was rapidly being transformed from his old ways by reservation life. The stage was being set for a new order of things in which what went before would be forgotten. If we were to know the American Indian and understand his place in the drama of civilization, we should have to get back-stage during this period

'between the acts.' And so some forty years ago we heeded Horace Greeley's famous exhortation and went west."[27]

In 1902 he began his study of Indian culture with a visit to the Sioux. The following year, he made the first of several trips over three years to the Blackfoot people, who were reduced to near starvation after they were forced

due time, Bull Shield announced that he was ready to give out my name, that of a distinguished chief long dead, meaning in English, "He-who-gets-what-he-goes-after." So far as I could see that was a good enough name, though just how it applied to me, I could not understand.

As soon as the name was announced, the crier mounted his horse and rode about shouting out my new name. The women cheered and that was the end of it. Many times I visited that reserve always to be greeted by that name. Even the children knew it. Some people fancy that when a name is conferred upon a white man he thereby becomes a member of the tribe, but that is nonsense. I asked old Bull Shield how one became a tribe member; at first he said a white man could not do it, but afterward qualified the pronouncement somewhat by saying that if one would take an Indian woman, settle down there, learn the language, etc., he might finally be tolerated; yet even after all this, he would still be a white man.[28]

Wissler would have many other occasions on which to ponder the fundamental differences between the Indian and the white man. Take the phonograph, for instance, which he used to record songs and tales. While white men considered Edison to be a genius for having invented the phonograph, the Indians simply considered him a lucky man. "Day Star said that Edison was undoubtedly sleeping one time when some of the powers appeared to him, telling him to put wood and iron together, thus and so, and the voice could be reproduced. He did nothing himself, but he was very lucky in being chosen as the person to introduce this machine into the world. So, he said, it is with everything, man himself creates nothing."[29]

Even the Indian who made money in the white man's world, and lived as they did, held in his heart a different way of seeing things. Wissler told the story of a

The American Museum of Natural History in the Field:
Native Cultures of North America

Skinner Seminole Indian Expedition—1910   *In 1910, Alanson Skinner, an assistant in the Museum's Department of Anthropology who had worked with Clark Wissler on the Plains Indian research program, went to the Florida Everglades to study the Seminole Indians. The culture of the Seminole Indians was disappearing at the same time that their environment was being compromised by the beginnings of development in South Florida. Skinner, who collected artifacts, was accompanied on his expedition by the photographer Julian Dimock, whose haunting photographs of the Seminole Indians reflect lost traditions.*

Vaillant Expeditions to Mexico—1927–41   *In 1927, Clarence Hay, a trustee of the American Museum of Natural History, hired a brilliant young archaeologist, George Vaillant, as assistant curator of Mexican archaeology. Hay sent Vaillant on ten trips to Mexico to study the prehistoric cultures of the Valley of Mexico, the area surrounding the great ruins of Teotihuacán. Vaillant was in search of the origins of the Aztecs, the sophisticated civilization destroyed by the Spanish conquistadors, and he pioneered the use of stratigraphy at Mexican sites. Excavation of pottery at different levels in rubbish heaps enabled him to survey centuries of human activity and to begin to assign relative dates to the pre-Columbian cultures of Mexico. At the time he began his work, it was generally believed that a state as elaborate as that founded by the Aztecs could not have developed on its own. Archaeologists sought elsewhere for its origins. Vaillant's stratigraphy, however, presented the picture of a civilization that had evolved over a long period of time from a village culture into a complex state.*

In 1932, Vaillant led a Museum expedition to Gualupita, in the central highlands of Mexico near Cuernavaca, where he found important evidence of one of Mexico's earliest complex societies, the Olmecs. Olmec is an Aztec word meaning "People of the Rubber Country" and is applied to both the prehistoric peoples who lived in the Mexican Gulf coastal region and to an artistic style that became popular over a large part of ancient Mesoamerica between 1200 and 500 B.C. Vaillant found artifacts of an early non-Olmec people in the central highlands that clearly showed the artistic influence of the dominant culture. The discovery, along with finds from other sources, including the Kunz ax and the Necaxa tiger (both of which are in the Museum collections), enabled Vaillant and other archaeologists to begin to describe an intriguing period that before had been a virtual cipher.

Poverty Point Expedition—1955   *In 1955, James Ford, associate curator of North American archaeology at the Museum, led an*

expedition to excavate the remarkable earthworks at Poverty Point, Louisiana. Ford had done preliminary work at the site a few years earlier, and the artifacts he found there did not conform to any of the known periods of human prehistory of the lower Mississippi Valley. It was not until he examined aerial photographs of the area in 1953, however, that he recognized the magnitude of what its inhabitants had built. Poverty Point consists of six concentric ridges, arranged in a semicircle, and four large mounds. The settlement, constructed between 1800 and 500 B.C., housed as many as several thousand inhabitants. Ford estimated that it had taken 3 million hours to move the millions of cubic feet of earth necessary to construct the earthworks. Later archaeologists discovered that Poverty Point was not an isolated phenomenon; it was the largest and most unusual of a group of at least one hundred settlements spread widely across the lower Mississippi River Valley.

Excavation of Mission Santa Catalina de Guale—1978–present
Museum anthropologist David Hurst Thomas had read about the Spanish Franciscan Mission Santa Catalina de Guale in historical records. In 1978, when he began searching for its remains, he knew only that the Mission was located on St. Catherines Island, a fourteen-thousand-acre island off the coast of Georgia, overrun by live oak, scrub palmetto, and briar patches. Finding the thirty-acre Mission site would be literally like looking for a needle in a haystack. The Mission, founded by the Spanish among the Guale Indians in the late 1500s, was the northernmost outpost of colonial Spanish Florida. When Thomas embarked on his search, not one of the twelve Spanish missions in Georgia had been discovered. Santa Catalina de Guale held the most promise for discovery because St. Catherines Island had been spared from development by the St. Catherines Island Foundation.

Thomas was determined to locate the site of the mission in the most efficient and nondestructive manner. It took him three years of work, narrowing down the area in which he searched by means of controlled survey sampling, vertical sampling with a posthole digger, and remote sensing with a magnetometer to detect microscopic iron particles in the marsh mud (one of the ingredients used in the wall plaster). Although there was no surface evidence of the Mission's buildings, Thomas was successful, ultimately excavating the kitchen, church, and convent. During six seasons in the field, Thomas recovered thousands of potsherds and numerous other artifacts, which comprised a detailed record of sixteenth- and seventeenth-century life in the Southeast. It is the story, as Thomas puts it, of "the head-on collision of Native American and Old World culture."

Seminole girls and Charley Tommy in canoe, Everglades, Florida, 1907. Photograph by Julian Dimock

medicine man who had made money from the rental of his lands and lived in a well-appointed modern house, while in his attic he had built a replica of a primitive dwelling with dirt floor, altar, sacred bundles, blankets, drums, and rattles. "At least once a day the family climbed those narrow stairs and, shut in from the white man's world, gave whole-hearted devotion to the gods of their fathers."[30]

The Blackfeet recognized in Wissler a kindred soul, who understood them and valued their differences at a time when the white man was trying to erase all traces of their culture, and with frightening speed. Smoking-star, the Blackfoot shaman, concluded the tale of his life with these words to Wissler:

In the year of the Camp-at-bad-waters-winter the Bull society sold out as I have said. That was the end of that society; there were but three of us left when we sold to the Catchers and those to whom we sold soon died. The ways of the white man were coming among us and many things were passing away. I was now an old man, fit only for sitting in council. I could no longer run buffalo, no longer go to war. So we have come to the last fork in the trail. I have smoked many pipes, I have sat in many councils, I have made many speeches to restrain our young men from rash and unjust actions. We are near the end. The Smoking-star will soon pass down in the west. Soon it will lead me to the sand hills where my spirit will wander about among the ghosts of buffalo, horses, and men. Your way is not our way, but you have loved us. Perhaps your spirit also may return to wander with us among the sand hills of our fathers. I pray that it may be so. Now, it is finished.[31]

South America:
Discoverers of Lost Worlds

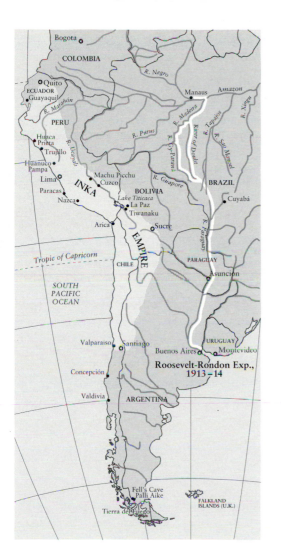

On the plain of Nazca, Peru, a pre-Inka civilization inscribed a vast system of lines and figures whose purpose remains obscure. This photograph was taken on a survey trip with Museum archaeologist Craig Morris, 1985.

"SOUTH AMERICA IS a place I love, and I think, if you take it right through from Darien to Fuego, it's the grandest, richest, most wonderful bit of earth upon this planet. . . . Why shouldn't somethin' new and wonderful lie in such a country, and why shouldn't we be the men to find it out?"[1] So spoke Lord John Roxton, one of the fictional heroes of Sir Arthur Conan Doyle's novel *The Lost World*. In the novel, an expedition sets out to explore an unknown area of South America and discovers, among other anomalies, living dinosaurs.

The true "lost worlds" of South America are more compelling than fiction and have drawn explorers since Sir Walter Raleigh visited Guyana in 1595. These lost worlds have been found among the ruins of civilizations that rose and fell long before the arrival of Columbus; they have been found buried with the fossil bones of extinct mammals in Patagonia and atop the mountains that rise above Venezuelan savannas. The discoverers have brought to light what once was lost and shed light on what is always present—the unfolding spectacle of life's diverse forms.

Before the Inka Empire

Reports of the Spanish who accompanied conquistador Francisco Pizarro and the subsequent chronicles of Garcilaso de la Vega and Pedro Cieza de Leon revealed to Europe the true magnitude of the South American civilization destroyed by the Spanish conquerors. At its height, the Inka empire reached the length of the Andes, twenty-four hundred miles along the coast of South America from Ecuador to Chile. It was the largest empire in the New World and one of the largest the world had seen since the time of Genghis Khan. Its architecture and gold work have never been surpassed, and its textiles were perhaps the most technically

Above: Machu Picchu, view through the window of the Temple of Three Windows. Wendell Bennett investigated the most famous Inka site for the Museum in 1933, and members of the American Museum of Natural History–Grace Peruvian Eclipse Expedition visited in 1937, when this picture was taken.

Above right: Llama made of sheet silver joined by soldering. The Inka state, families, and local leaders controlled large flocks of llama and alpaca. The figure is from the collection of Miguel Garces, who once owned the island of Titicaca. Adolph Bandelier acquired the entire collection for the Museum in 1896.

Opposite: The central ceremonial platform at Huánuco pampa. Photograph by Craig Morris

Machu Picchu's Rival

In a remote area of the Peruvian central highlands, about one hundred twenty miles northeast of Lima, lies the largest well-preserved city of the Inka. Built just a few decades before the Spanish conquest, Huánuco Pampa was about ten times the size of the well-known Inka site of Machu Picchu and rivaled it in isolation and spectacular environment. But while Machu Picchu was impressive because of its cloud-forest setting, Huánuco Pampa, like Tiwanaku before it, was impressive because of its altitude—nearly thirteen thousand feet above sea level. When archaeologist Craig Morris joined the staff of the Museum in 1975, he had already begun piecing together a picture of life in this unusual city.

Morris embraced the opportunity to pursue science in an out-of-the-way place and under difficult conditions. Huánuco Pampa could be reached only by Land Rover. After an initial expedition, the Museum team built a primitive but semipermanent camp near the ruins. A field laboratory was set up in a town six hours away, which could provide electricity, running water, and a source for supplies. During the ten-year project, Morris and his team spent a total of more than two years in the camp at Huánuco Pampa and more than three years in the field laboratory. Computers helped them to cope with the avalanche of artifacts and other information, and modern archaeological sampling procedures enabled them to form a representative picture of the city.

Morris eventually identified more than three thousand buildings. He excavated some three hundred, recovering twelve tons of ceramics and other artifacts. Morris documented an enormous Inka warehousing system with a sophisticated insulation and ventilation system; the city kept stored food cool by taking advantage of the high altitude. His work has also suggested that the number of people living in this ancient city varied greatly by season, a result of the ceremonial calendar and the Inka labor tax system. Some of the population lived in quarters segregated by gender, and Morris uncovered evidence of the enormous economic importance of a large group of permanent women residents of the city who wove cloth and brewed chicha (maize beer) for the Inka state.

sophisticated of any civilization.

Yet the Inka empire was only the last and greatest of many kingdoms and cultures that arose along the west coast and in the highlands of South America—cultures such as the Nazca, who inscribed in the ground a vast and still mysterious system of lines and animal figures, and the Moche of northern Peru, whose splendor continues to be unearthed. South American civilizations erected monumental buildings contemporaneous with the pyramids of ancient Egypt and achieved a consummate artistry in textiles and pottery. Indeed, the Andes are being recognized as one of the birthplaces of civilization.

This should come as no surprise. Human beings have inhabited South America for at least twelve thousand years, perhaps longer. Reconstructing the record of this evolution, from arrival to empire, is one of modern archaeology's greatest achievements, on a par with the uncovering of the civilizations of Egypt and Mesopotamia. In the cradle of the Andes, archaeologists from the American Museum of Natural History began to piece together the history of the Andean past, from the first peoples through the Inka. Pioneers such as Junius Bird, Wendell Bennett, and Adolph Bandelier made mute stones speak and gave life to some very old bones.

Junius Bird first came to the Museum's attention in 1928 as a Columbia University undergraduate in the extended process of giving up school for a life of exploration and discovery. He had participated in two Arctic expeditions with the publisher George Palmer Putnam, himself an enthusiastic supporter of Museum ventures. On these trips the young Bird displayed a prescient ability to detect archaeological sites. He also learned a few things about sailing from the redoubtable Captain Robert A. Bartlett, veteran of Robert Peary's polar expeditions. In 1931, for example, on an abortive Museum expedition to Central America, Bird was at the helm when a hurricane struck the port of Belize. Only two ships were left afloat; one was his.

"Bird luck," his Museum colleagues called it, but it was surely more than luck. As archaeologist Grahame Clark remarked, "This man Junius Bird seems always to be digging at just the right time in just the right place to provide the answers to some of the most important questions."[2]

Not many people can change history while on honeymoon, but Junius Bird did. In fact, he wrote the history of the earliest human beings in South America, where before there had been only a gap as empty as the Patagonian landscape he explored. Admittedly, it was a long honeymoon—two and a half years, from 1934 to 1937. During that time Bird, who was still an assistant in the anthropology department, and his wife, Peggy, sailed thirteen hundred miles in a nineteen-foot boat among the islands of Tierra del Fuego in southern Chile and along the Straits of Magellan, ex-

amining shell mounds and other refuse heaps for traces of early humans. It seemed a bleak place to search, and even Charles Darwin had asked himself why human beings would ever have come there. Bird reasoned that if people had migrated south long ago, they would eventually have come to Tierra del Fuego and Patagonia as the end of the line.

The "most important question" Bird helped answer in Patagonia was, How long had human beings been in South America? Just a few years earlier, in 1927, J. D. Figgins had stood the world on its ear by announcing in *Natural History* that he had discovered a spear point in close conjunction with the skeleton of an extinct bison. Knowing the approximate age of the animal enabled Figgins

to set a "horizon" for man's habitation of North America of at least 15,000 years. No such conjunction and very few early artifacts had been found in South America when Bird began to excavate a cave called Palli Aike, on the north side of the Straits of Magellan. A rock shelter far from water, it had been at most a camping place in the barren, volcanic landscape. As the Birds began to dig, however, it became obvious from the flaked points buried at various levels that human beings had been there, off and on, for a very long time. Digging still deeper, they found bone tools, then the burnt bones of an extinct sloth, the *Mylodon*, and finally human bones, partially cremated. Based on the sloth and the position of the various strata,

Bird estimated a maximum age for the human bones of 11,585 years. When radiocarbon dating methods were perfected years later, the date turned out to be around 11,000 years.

Another shelter twenty miles away, Fell's Cave, was close to a river and had been occupied almost continuously in prehistoric times. Choked with dirt, the cave "promised little more than pure exercise," as Bird noted in his journal. Quickly, however, the strata yielded to the spade until Bird had unearthed a record as extensive as Palli Aike's. Archaeologists always want to dig below the bottom, and the true bottom of Fell's Cave lay deeper—a single, isolated refuse layer clearly associating human remains, implements, and extinct animals. One find—the bones of a horse—puzzled the Birds. Horses had not come to South America until the Spanish invasion, thousands of years later. These were, indeed, horse bones, but of a long-extinct native species. Bird's field notes show him peeling away the layers of time, noting the simplified shapes of the projectile points and scrapers, some apparently mere lumps of stone, almost unrecognizable as tools. Bird seems to have possessed an almost occult ability to identify the telltale signs of human industry.

Bird had placed human beings on South America's geological calendar, but many of the dates were still blank, including the mysterious period when civilization began to take shape. That, too, he discovered in characteristic fashion. In 1946, he undertook a Museum field project on the north coast of Peru to look for evidence of culture older than the ceramics that were exciting other archaeologists. They were pursuing predecessors of a coastal civilization called the Chavín culture, which flourished between 800 and 500 B.C. Objects such as textiles are highly perishable, and, in any case, there was no reason to think that ceramics should not come first. His colleagues, however, were working downward from a fully flowered civilization—the Inka; Bird was working from the bottom up, and that gave him a different perspective.

He chose to excavate a black, featureless coastal refuse mound called Huaca Prieta. Where others had found an unpromising hodgepodge, Bird found a missing history book: sherds of pottery older than any known in South America, and, predating them, evidence of extensive plant domestication, South America's earliest permanent architecture, and, preserved by the dry, nitrate-laden soil of the coastal desert, fragments of textiles.

It is now known that people around the world have been creating textiles for at least seven thousand years, longer than they have been making pots and bowls. Textiles represent the oldest continuous artistic tradition in the Andes, and Bird dedicated himself to interpreting it until his death in 1982. He fostered (single-handedly, at first) the study of Andean textiles. He was able to trace the common motifs and rectilinearity of almost all Andean art back to the patterns in the tiny fragments he had discovered at Huaca Prieta. He described the earliest weaving techniques and recognized the explosive impact of the introduction of the loom on textile production. In a piece of cloth such as a burial mantle from the Paracas peninsula, he found clues to everything from the society's agricultural methods to its knowledge of chemistry and architecture to the personalities of the weavers themselves. By following the skein of this single technology, Bird unraveled nearly five thousand years of cultural activity in the Andes.

Birthplace of the Sun and Moon

Before his Fuegean honeymoon, Bird had learned the rudiments of South American archaeology from the dean of the discipline, Museum curator Wendell Bennett. In 1934, the two traveled to the highlands of southern Peru to investigate a great civilization that preceded the Inka by several hundred years, but about which almost nothing was known—Tiwanaku. At 12,600 feet in the Andes, an altitude higher than Tibet's Lhasa and Nepal's Katmandu, the Tiwanaku people built an enormous city and, between A.D. 400 and 900, spread their influence up and down the coast a thousand miles. On this expedition, Bennett and Bird were looking for evidence of Tiwanaku culture near the legendary lake called Titicaca.

Travel posters and television specials have enshrined a picturesque image of Titicaca—brightly clad Indians in knit caps poling reed boats across a lake of steel-blue water, surrounded by a treeless shore and snow-capped mountains. In spite of its beauty, it is an isolated place, the highest navigable lake in the world, straddling the border of Peru and Bolivia, and its environs now yield only a meager subsistence.

Yet in pre-Columbian times, the shores of the lake were home to thousands of domesticated llamas and alpacas, making it a region of great wealth. It was a sacred site for the Inka and almost certainly for the people who preceded them. "The Indians," wrote the Jesuit Joseph de Acosta, "relate that from the great lagune of Titicaca there came out one Viracocha, who made his abode at Tiaguanaco, where today are seen ruins and parts of ancient and very strange edifices, and that from there they came to Cuzco, and so the human family began to multiply."[3]

In Inka mythology, the lake's two large islands, Titicaca and Coati, were the birthplace of the sun and the moon, respectively, thus important places of ceremony and, apparently, human sacrifice. Its surroundings also hold clues to how a civilization as important as Tiwanaku was able to sustain itself in a harsh land.

In exploring Titicaca, Bennett and Bird were consciously following in the footsteps of the Museum's first Andean archaeologist and one of the seminal figures in the field, the Swiss-born Adolph Bandelier. Before coming to Peru in 1892 with the support of New York millionaire Henry Villard, Bandelier had already established himself as the leading archaeologist of the American Southwest. He did it the hard way, by walking thousands of miles, crisscrossing New Mexico and parts of Mexico and Central America, living with many native groups, and excavating sites from Pecos Pueblo in New Mexico to the gigantic Mexican pyramid of Cholula. His companion, the writer and photographer Charles Lummis, admired his extraordinary facility with languages and his equally extraordinary sta-

Opposite: Some two thousand years ago, on the Paracas peninsula of the south coast of Peru, there flowered an art of textile weaving that would never be surpassed. The most elaborate pieces were mantles used to wrap funerary bundles. This example depicts shaman figures

Right: Archaeologist Adolph Bandelier near the peninsula of Copacavana, Lake Titicaca, 1895. Photograph by Fanny Bandelier

Below: Lake Titicaca and the Island of Koati, 1895. "When the Indians go to the village [on the mainland], a balsa or two will cross and recross," wrote Adolph Bandelier, "but if they have no reason for making the trip, a visitor on Koati may remain cut off from all the world for several weeks." Photograph by Adolph Bandelier

mina. "When he first visited me, in Isleta, he knew just three words of Tigua," Lummis wrote. "In ten days he could make himself understood by the hour with the Principales in their own unwritten tongue."[4] Bandelier survived a bout with smallpox and a blizzard that killed two of his traveling companions. Once, when he was attacked by Apache Indians, he managed to elude death by pretending to be insane.

In 1894 Villard donated Bandelier's collections to the American Museum of Natural History, and the Museum began to spon-

sor his work, which was just concluding at Tiwanaku itself. His work at Lake Titicaca showed that he was an athlete not only of the trail but of the library as well. Bandelier's method is fascinating. He read everything that existed about the lake, its people, and the Andes, including all the original Spanish documents available. He studied and lived with the people around the lake, weighing what they told him and comparing their words and ways with the ancient descriptions. In his mind, archaeology and anthropology were inextricably linked. Finally, for a year he surveyed and excavated. He revealed above all the variety of human activities that focused on the lake, from agriculture to building to burial to elaborate ceremony. He also clearly delineated artifacts, buildings, and even whole cities, of a culture that he called *chullpa*, after the local Indian word for a type of stone burial structure.

The term is a capacious grab bag, indicating everything not Inka. Bennett and Bird carefully searched through the bag and found striking evidence of Tiwanaku culture. After exploring various island sites, they were directed by one of the residents to some hewn stones on the south shore of the lake. They soon deduced that this hitherto unstudied ruin was in all likelihood a temple, and that it had occupied the entire hilltop. It had fallen into decay and perhaps even been rebuilt before the Inka held sway. Its purpose was mysterious.

It remains a mystery, like much else of this remarkable civilization. We do not know how a small regional kingdom in an isolated location could have been transformed into a major state whose religion exerted its influence in the Andes for a millen-

nium. Like its architecture, the city of Tiwanaku was monumental, with palaces, temples, marketplaces, and massive gateways. The famous Gateway of the Sun is hewn from a single piece of basalt and engraved with a rich glyphic iconography of pumas, condors, fishes, and kings that the Inka and other Andean cultures almost certainly inherited. Indeed, our only key to this wordless world is through the interpretation of Inka images, with the often dubious assistance of early Spanish chroniclers.

Most spectacular of all were sculptures. The Spaniard Pedro de Cieza de Leon described them in 1553: "Near the main dwellings is a man-made hill, built on great stone foundations. Beyond this hill there are two stone idols of human size and shape, with the features beautifully carved, so much so that they seem the work of great artists or masters. They are so large that they seem small giants."[5] There was also a large giant, which Cieza did not see but which Wendell Bennett found in 1932. While taking a survey of many Andean sites, he came to a temple location where archaeologist Arthur Posnansky had been excavating primitive stone heads. Bennett obtained permission to dig some test pits. "The depth of the pit had reached little more than half a meter when a large stone was struck, which soon was identified as the head of an enormous monolithic statue."[6]

Dubbed the Bennett Monolith, this stone sculpture, carved from huge sandstone blocks and standing twenty-four feet tall, is the largest ever found in the Andes. Bennett had time only to begin the excavation, which was itself a substantial challenge. Exposed to the air, the sandstone crumbled at the touch, a process exacerbated

by the boots of tourists and residents alike, who freely trod on the immense figure. Attempts to clean the surface only wiped away a priceless archaeological record.

But a record of what? Certainly the monolith's probable original orientation toward the east was significant, but what could be the meaning of the figures decorating both gate and monolith, and how were they organized? The answers are still elusive, but to give some idea of the speculation the figures have inspired, Posnansky began to identify the elaborate calendrical significance of the iconography and offered a provocative suggestion about the possible cataclysmic fate of the Tiwanaku.

Although Posnansky's work has subsequently spawned some farfetched theories, one thing is clear: Tiwanakans could not have sustained their empire in the mountains without a detailed knowledge of the astronomical periods and environmental conditions, for their survival almost certainly depended on seasonal agriculture around Lake Titicaca. When Bandelier, and later Bennett, noted the dominance of terraces on the landscape of the lake islands, they may have been seeing an Inka clue to Tiwanakan survival. Archaeologists working near the lake have recently unearthed a large-scale system of terraces, some nearly seven hundred feet long. Built up from layers of cobblestone, clay, gravel, and imported topsoil, they alter-

nate with channels into which lake water probably flowed. It could well be that the "temple" Bennett excavated was really an administrative center, allowing Tiwanaku to control these lakeside farming estates.

Only by paying close attention to the material realities of life in such a setting will scientists solve the riddle of Tiwanaku's mysterious symbols. The same patient study may one day unlock the final riddle—why a city so magnificent and influential was abandoned and allowed to fall into ruins.

Doubtful Rivers

Don't become an ornithologist if you can help it.

—Frank Chapman[7]

The ornithologist practices a discipline of delight. To seek birds—to study their diverse and often astonishing habits, explore their habitats, trace their patterns of migration, note their songs, and obtain rare and beautiful specimens—is in some limited way to partake of their lightness and freedom. For American ornithologists before World War I, South America held a wealth of such delight. It was a continental paradise at their geographic doorstep, "an enormous, unworked field," as Museum ornithologist Frank Chapman called it, largely unspoiled by human beings, rich in unusual species such as the Hoatzin, which climbs by the spurs on its wings before it can fly, and home, during part of the year, to many of the songbirds North Americans know so well. Under Chapman's leadership, the American Museum of Natural History's bird department made all of South America its special province.

Chapman himself traveled the Andes mountain range of Colombia, Ecuador, Peru, and Chile, the jungles of Panama, and the plains of Argentina to understand the evolution and distribution of a vast number of bird species. In one small zone of the Colombian Andes he identified more than three hundred thirty species. Colleagues Robert Cushman Murphy and Rollo Beck sailed thousands of miles along the continent's seacoast to collect and compile the definitive catalogue of its oceanic birds. Decades later, in the 1960s, evolutionary theorist Ernst Mayr found in the bird life of Venezuela's high plateaus revealing evidence of the mechanisms of evolution.

Yet paradise had its dark corners, places of "subdued light," where "little known animals spend their lives in stealth and vigilance, all oblivious of the existence of an outer world."[8] So wrote Leo Miller, a collector for the bird department. Pursuing birds in Brazil brought him and fellow collector George Cherrie face to face with conditions that tested the limits of endurance and nearly took the life of the most famous expedition leader in the Museum's history—former president Theodore Roosevelt. The Roosevelt-Rondon Expedition of 1913–14 would find itself on a river called Doubt, in an unexplored region of the Amazon Basin, facing the greatest uncertainty of all—whether its members, not to mention their zoological specimens, would ever see civilization again.

Through the Amazon and its tributaries flows one-tenth of the world's moving water. The river itself is four thousand miles long, beginning in the eastern foothills of the Andes and crossing Brazil to the Atlantic Ocean. Only the Nile is longer. Its major tributaries enter from higher land to the north and south. These watercourses cut through an area that contains one-third of the Earth's remaining rain forests and is home to many of the estimated fifty thousand species of rainforest trees. Even with the inroads made by commercial interests, much of the Amazon Basin is untraveled, if not unexplored.

Roosevelt had long wished to visit the interior of South America and indulge his proclivities as a naturalist. The opportunity arose in 1913 with invitations to lecture in Brazil and Argentina.

He sought, as well, to make his trip a collecting opportunity for the museum he loved best. His father had been a trustee of the American Museum of Natural History, and he had walked its halls as a boy. While president, he had summoned Carl Akeley from the Museum to the White House for advice on his Africa expedition of 1909. Now, Roosevelt asked Frank Chapman to recommend staff to accompany him and to conduct scientific study.

The original itinerary was just the thing to appeal to seasoned naturalists: from Brazil, the expedition would proceed to Paraguay, then by boat up the Paraguay River to the edge of the vast plain in the Brazilian province of Mato Grosso. It would travel overland nearly five hundred miles to the Tapajóz River and descend it to the Amazon and the town of Manaus, that wilderness Xanadu, with its grand plazas and enormous opera house, built for the ladies and gentlemen of the jungle rubber trade. The journey would take them through highlands and swamps, across mountains and fertile plains—every kind of sub-equatorial habitat.

Chapman recommended two of his most experienced field collectors, Miller and Cherrie, the latter called by Chapman "the prince of tropical American bird collectors." Both men had traveled extensively in tropical and highland South America and knew what to expect. They were to collect specimens not only of birds but also of mammals, reptiles, and insects. Although neither was a trained ornithologist, the two had other virtues, which would be displayed in sharp relief on the River of Doubt.

A lynch mob in a South American town once called Cherrie a *macho*, meaning a "mule," a derogatory name applied to white travelers in the jungle. When Cherrie got going, he was hard to stop. The mob could not do it; he escaped them. The river crocodiles could not do it. He once searched out and shot one that had seized a small child from the arms of its mother in the village where he was staying. Nor could the flesh-eating river fish called piranhas. He once fell into a school of them while fishing and lived to tell about it. Above all, Cherrie proved himself suited for the trip in his ability to deal with the most unpredictable of natural elements—human beings.

Like most naturalists in the field, Cherrie employed local assistants, as collectors, guides, paddlers, and porters. On one bird-collecting expedition to the western foothills of the Andes, a hundred miles from the Pacific coast, Cherrie was ambushed by a former employee whom he had discharged a few days before. He survived the fight (his assailant did not), but a shotgun blast nearly tore off his arm. Tying up

the wounded limb with a make-shift tourniquet and tucking his gun and bag of specimens under the other arm, he set off for the nearest coastal village. If he arrived in time, he might be able to catch the weekly boat to Guayaquil, where the doctor might be able to save his life, if not what remained of his arm.

Everywhere he stopped, the response of the Indians was the same: "You have been shot, Señor? That is too bad. It looks fatal. You will surely die." He replied, *Tal ves* (perhaps). Amazingly, his arm was not yet infected, but it hurt so much he could not sit in a saddle and had to walk to the coast. When he arrived, the boat had just left. He pursued it down the coast in a canoe, although he did confess to feeling, for an instant, like giving up. He and his paddler caught the boat, but Cherrie soon had further reason to wonder, in the words of the Antarctic explorer Douglas Mawson, "if ever there was to be a day without some special disappointment." In Guayaquil he was arrested for murder. By now his wound was infected, and the police took him to the doctor, a former New York City health commissioner. The doctor echoed the Indians: "Amputate? Mr. Cherrie will be dead in the morning."[9]

He was not dead the next morning, but for five and a half months he lay in the hospital. The doctor salvaged his arm, and by the time he was ready to return to the United States, the police had decided he was not worth waiting for and had dropped their inquiry.

The anthropologist Claude Lévi-Strauss once warned about enjoying such tales. He called adventure "an unavoidable drawback" and travelers' tales "pabulum," distracting readers from the intellectual substance of genuine discovery. "Nowadays," he grumbled, "being an explorer is trade."[10] Yet none of the expedition members, except perhaps Cherrie, who confessed to flirting with life on the edge, embraced adventure as a goal. Their heroism was incidental, which makes it all the more inspiring. Miller represented the matter-of-fact explorer, the sort of person Roosevelt would later admonish for being too self-effacing. Still, he loved the jungle. He and Cherrie were a perfect combination.

Two additional passengers proved essential: Roosevelt's son Kermit was just twenty-three years old but thoroughly schooled in rugged travel in Africa. Colonel Cândido Mariano da Silva Rondon was Brazil's most celebrated explorer. Leader of the Brazilian Telegraphic Commission, Rondon had traveled more than fourteen thousand miles in Brazil's interior. Today, one of its provinces is named after him—Rondônia. His previous explorations near the headwaters of the Gy-Paraná (now Jiparaná) River had very nearly cost the lives of him and his crew, and by the time they managed to reach a rubber-tapping station, three of them were completely naked.

The Roosevelt-Rondon Expedition began in October of 1913 as an affair of state, with champagne receptions and fanfare. At one of the first celebrations in Río de Janeiro, however, a fateful decision was taken. Roosevelt remarked that he wanted to travel off the beaten track. The Brazilian foreign minister asked him to change his plans, turn his zoological expedition into a geographical one, and map the route of an uncharted river discovered by Rondon, the *Río da Dúvida*—"the River of Doubt." Roosevelt was fifty-six years old and weighed a portly two hundred twenty pounds. He did not hesitate to accept.

While Roosevelt discharged his diplomatic obligations, Cherrie and Miller headed for Paraguay and the Paraguay River, where they began collecting in earnest. They explored several tributaries and nearby rivers and found precisely what they had hoped for—a bird collector's paradise: "We had entered the great pantanal country and the vast marshes teemed with bird life. As the *Asunción* fought the strong current and moved slowly onward countless thousands of cormorants and anhingas took wing; lining the pools and dotting the marshes were hordes of wood storks and scarlet ibises, together with a sprinkling of herons and spoonbills; egrets covered the small clumps of trees as with a mantle of snowy white, and long rows of jabiru storks patrolled both shores."[11]

Such visions compensated for what Miller laconically labeled the "troublesome" aspects of the voyage: mosquito swarms so thick it was impossible to raise a rifle; riverbanks harboring caymans, the South American cousin of the alligator; shallows teeming with piranha (one took a nasty bite out of Miller's hand); and maribundi wasps, whose poison, Miller remarked, "was as rapid as it was remarkable." On a later expedition to Bolivia he was stung four times and almost completely paralyzed within five minutes.

In December of 1913, the expedition members, including Roosevelt, rendezvoused at the village of Corumba, then sailed by steamer farther up the Paraguay to the Sepotuba River, where they transferred to large dugout ca-

Collecting Artifacts in the 1990s

When anthropologist Napoleon Chagnon came to the headwaters of the Orinoco River in southern Venezuela to study the Yanomami Indians and collect artifacts for the Museum in the 1960s, he found a society he called "the fierce People." Despite a more complicated reality, the term stuck. It might better have been applied to the Shavante people of Brazil's Mato Grosso.

For decades, the Shavante have fiercely and often successfully resisted the encroachments of Amazon gold miners and ranchers. They are the only tribe that has succeeded in regaining lost land from the government. Yet change has come here, too. The Shavante use political pressure and the media to protect their land, and now they are reaching out to the world—as always, however, on their terms. When two Shavante visited the Museum's Hall of South American Peoples in 1990, they were disappointed not to see more of their own culture on display, and they later negotiated an unusual agreement with the Museum. In 1992, the Shavante invited scientific assistant Laila Williamson to their Mato Grosso village to collect some three hundred implements of daily life, from feathered bows and arrows to headdresses. In return, the Museum would contribute funds to a preventive-medicine program. The Shavante made the transaction into a test for their visitors, and Williamson passed just by getting there, enduring a breakneck ride across the savanna in a rattling Toyota, while the driver watched her closely for signs of panic.

The Shavante made every object according to the highest standards and provided Williamson with extensive information about the use of each one. As a woman, however, she was not allowed to receive one ritual object, a small whistle—at least, not in broad daylight and not in the village. Williamson, however, was also an outsider, and that, in part, mitigated her status as a female. The night she was leaving, one of the Shavante, under cover of darkness, overtook her outside the village and placed the whistle in her hand, in order to make sure that the collection, and the world's view of Shavante artistry, would be complete.

noes and headed for the Mato Grosso, a plain that stretches north and west for hundreds of miles. At Tapirapoan, the expedition gathered itself for a long overland journey by mule. It took forty-four days, arduous but relatively uneventful, save for one other "troublesome" aspect. Their route took them through the territories of many different groups of native people, some of whom were openly hostile to whites. Rondon never permitted his soldiers or telegraph workers to retaliate when attacked by Indians, and Cherrie likewise deeply respected their ways of life. Yet such sentiment might avail them very little among, for example, the Nambikwara. In one deserted village, the expedition discovered the graves of several soldiers ambushed by the Indians. Their heads and shoulders had been left protruding from the ground.

There were ten Americans and Brazilian military officers and more than thirty-five *camaradas*, Brazilian porters and paddlers. Rondon insisted it would be impossible for the entire group to descend the River of Doubt, so the expedition agreed to split in two. Miller would lead a team down the Gy-Paraná River, where Rondon's telegraphic survey had ended. The Roosevelts, Rondon, and Cherrie would venture into the complete unknown. If all went well, the two teams would meet again in Manaus, some five hundred miles away. In his gear, Theodore Roosevelt carried a copy of Thomas More's *Utopia*.

The two teams parted company on February 27, 1914, on the bank of the River of Doubt. The expedition was already five months out, with the hardest leg yet to come, and Miller felt a palpable sense of foreboding: "Then, with a parting 'Good luck!' their dugouts swung into the current and were whisked away. For several minutes we stood upon the fragile structure that bridged the unexplored river and stared at the dark forest that shut out our erst-while leader and his Brazilian companions from view; and then, filled with misgivings as to whether or not we should ever see them again, we turned our thoughts to the task before us."[12]

The task before Miller was an overland journey of several more days to the Gy-Paraná. There the group discovered the boat that was supposed to meet them had not arrived. They commenced hewing a huge dugout canoe, which they had nearly finished when the large, wooden rowboat finally arrived. The group headed downstream on a smooth, swift-flowing path of water. Several times the expedition had to portage around rapids, and all the members suffered from fever, some seriously, but there was leisure to make an occasional collection. When they reached Calama, on the Madiera River, where the steamer for Manaus would meet them, they encountered their first and only Indian attack. One day, lunch was interrupted by a rain of arrows, wrapped with hair and skin from victims of previous raids. Arriving in Manaus, Miller settled in to wait for Cherrie, Roosevelt, and the others. He would have some time on his hands.

Opposite: Shavante/Wai'a male initiation ceremony, village of Pimentel Barbosa, 1992

Right: Jabiru stork, common to the Orinoco and the Amazon. To George Cherrie, its majestic flight was without rival: "The great bird soars, in wide circles round and round, mounting higher and higher, until it is only a distant speck in the blue sky." From a hand-colored lantern slide by George H. H. Tate

Below: Río Téodoro Roosevelt, the River of Doubt. "Like an arrow of light through the walls of green," George Cherrie captioned this picture. Roosevelt wrote, "It was a view well worth seeing; but . . . its character was such as to promise further hardships, difficulty, and exhausting labor." From a hand-colored lantern slide by George Cherrie

At the point where Miller had watched the seven canoes depart, the River of Doubt was a hundred yards wide and swollen by rain. It promised a fast trip. Just miles later, however, and almost without warning, it narrowed to a few feet and began to drop through a steep canyon. The expedition had to pull the boats out, cut a swath through almost impenetrable jungle, lay down logs for rollers, and drag the boats and supplies. It was a portent of things to come.

In reality, the River of Doubt could not be navigated. Winding back and forth to the Aripuaña River, which joins the Amazon, it plunged from one set of rapids to another, flattening out just long enough to raise hopes, then dashing them in a caldron of white water. The oldest canoes were lashed together for stability and loaded with food and gear. Kermit Roosevelt and Lieutenant João Lyra took the lead and carried out the geographic survey. Cherrie, Rondon, and Roosevelt brought up the rear. A contingent of *camaradas* cut a trail along the shore and carried extra provisions. Every afternoon a campsite had to be carved from the jungle. The dense vegetation made hunting for food, not to mention specimens, very difficult. For Cherrie, the possibility of doing any serious zoological work soon began to evaporate.

After fifteen days on the river, the expedition had traveled fewer than forty miles north. At this rate their ultimate goal might lie one hundred fifty days away; they had food for only thirty-five. Then the first disaster struck. Rising rapidly from continuous rain, the river tore the double canoe from its mooring and dashed it to pieces on the rocks. The Brazilians set to work carving a large

replacement, but like Robinson Crusoe, they failed to consider the density of the wood. The boat was ponderously heavy and barely seaworthy. Misfortune quickly turned to tragedy. In the lead as always, Kermit's boat was caught in a whirlpool and hurled over a waterfall. One of the paddlers, Simplicio, was lost, and Kermit survived only by grabbing onto a tree branch. "On an expedition such as ours," wrote Theodore Roosevelt, "death is one of the accidents that may at any time occur, and narrow escapes from death are too common to be felt as they would be felt otherwise. One mourns, but mourning cannot interfere with labor."[13] Gone, too, were valuable tools and ten days' worth of food.

A few days later, the expedition lost its new boat when a rope broke during a tricky attempt to lower it down yet another waterfall. Roosevelt began to experience the fever and dysentery that would soon immobilize him, and eerily, without warning, one of the hunting dogs was pierced by two arrows as long as spears. No one ever saw Indians, who left a trail of abandoned campsites al-

ways just ahead of the agitated explorers.

It was imperative to move faster. Down to four canoes, the group took inventory and jettisoned everything not absolutely necessary. They cut their rations in half, and Cherrie wrote in his journal, "It is doubtful if all our party ever reaches Manaus."[14] Almost incidentally, Cherrie noted the most intriguing discovery of the entire journey—rock carvings of a kind Rondon had never seen, almost certainly predating the civilization around them and possibly very old. There was no leisure to explore them, however, for a looming mountain range portended more rapids. Roosevelt's demoralization was evident later when he wrote: "Beautiful although the country ahead of us was, its character was such as to promise further hardships, difficulty, exhausting labor, and especially further delay."[15]

Roosevelt also notes modestly that Rondon insisted on conducting a ceremony to rename the river the *Río Téodoro Roosevelt* in his honor, but he glosses over just how seriously ill he was. When he tried to walk, infected wounds on his legs caused such pain that "three or four times he threw himself on the ground and begged me to go on," wrote Cherrie. The explorers talked constantly of food, of Kermit's strawberries and cream and Cherrie's griddle cakes with maple syrup. At the end of March, the countryside became even more rugged, forcing them to work the canoes downriver by ropes and the *camaradas* to make a dangerous trek across a sheer cliff face. Colonel Rondon finally stood before them and said, "We shall have to abandon our canoes and every man fight for himself through the forest." Roosevelt asked Cherrie and Kermit to leave him, saying, "Boys, I realize some of us are not going to finish this journey."[16] Roosevelt never mentions these incidents in his account.

Had the expedition split up, it is unlikely anyone would have survived, although Rondon clearly stood the best chance. Instead, they forged on, hunting what game they could, buoyed by occasional discoveries of honey and Brazil nuts, from which they made a stew. Cherrie finally succumbed to fever, and some of the crew were near mutiny. One of them, Julio, mulling over his grievances, ambushed the expedition's most dependable hand, Paixão, shooting him dead with a stolen rifle. He fled and Roosevelt, galvanized by the outrage, gave chase, but the forest swallowed Julio—as it threatened to swallow them all. As they paddled away, they caught a sudden glimpse of his forlorn figure on the riverbank.

Survival in such situations rarely turns on a single dramatic act. It is most often incremental. Tiny opportunities, not decisive leaps, enabled the expedition to turn the corner. With starvation looming, a troop of monkeys provided fresh meat. The countryside began to level out, and the rapids diminished. The fever Kermit had contracted suddenly rose to 104 degrees, but by then he could afford to be ill, as could his father, who lay in his canoe delirious, under a burning sun. Finally, a signpost on the riverbank marked with the letters "J. A." assured them that rubber tappers

Splendid Isolation:

George Gaylord Simpson in Patagonia

In its climate and seasons, South America seems an upside-down version of North America. Its plants and animals, however, reveal a world unto itself. North America does not have Surinam toads, for example, which carry their young on their backs, although there appears no physical reason why it should not. After all, the continents are connected. The geological past makes the picture even more puzzling, as George Gaylord Simpson found when he explored Patagonia in 1930–31 and 1933–34 for the Scarritt Patagonia Expeditions.

One of the foremost evolutionary theorists of his time, Simpson had been studying the fossil remains of early mammals from South America. He saw evolutionary paths distinct from those of any other continent. He managed to interest a drinking companion, Horace Scarritt, in these issues, and Scarritt funded two expeditions. The first trip began inauspiciously: revolution broke out the day Simpson arrived in Argentina. Later, working along the forlorn east coast of Patagonia, he unearthed a pivotal collection of fossils that helped him reconstruct a "curious history." It appeared that at the beginning of the Cenozoic era—the Age of Mammals—South America had had an on-again, off-again relationship with North America. At times, primitive mammals had migrated from the north and established themselves in the south. This traffic ended almost as soon as it began. But South America was part of a larger continent, which included Australia and Antarctica, and it also shared some primitive species with them. That began to change when the southern continents drifted apart, 45 million years ago. The species in South America began their own development, in "splendid isolation," as Simpson put it.

Simpson spent five decades thinking and writing about what he collected. He was able to identify reflections of the ancient continental neighbors in the living and fossil fauna of South America. He also described what happened when a bridge between North and South America reappeared three million years ago and new migrations began. The southern natives fared poorly in the north and most become extinct, but northern migrants such as otters felt at home in the south. One fact perplexed him: the sudden appearance in South America of primates and certain types of rodents. Their nearest relatives were so far distant geographically that their presence was inexplicable. It will remain so until scientists fill in a 10- to 20-million-year gap in the continent's fossil history. About his profession Simpson once remarked, "The fossil hunter does not kill; he resurrects. And the result of his sport is to add to the sum of human pleasure and to the treasures of human knowledge."

were ahead. When the expedition reached a rubber outpost and saw their first human faces in forty-eight days, they knew that even with weeks of travel ahead to Manaus, their survival, like the river they had charted, was no longer in doubt.

The expedition members presented a shocking sight when they arrived in Manaus. Roosevelt was "a shadow of his former self," in Cherrie's words, and all bore the marks of malaria. Nevertheless, a year later Miller was back in the field in Bolivia, and Cherrie returned to the Mato Grosso in 1916, after a journey across the Andes, to fill the gaps in his earlier collections. There were significant ones, even though the two had managed to gather several thousand specimens. Both expeditions were supported with funds contributed by Theodore Roosevelt. In 1925, nearly six years after the elder Roosevelt's death, Cherrie joined Kermit and his brother Theodore in a rugged expedition across the Himalayas.

Roosevelt's career and reputation have undergone intense and unflattering scrutiny in recent years, yet it is appropriate that the American Museum of Natural History should have dedicated a hall and a rotunda to this particular president. His interests as a naturalist and conservationist were kindled at the Museum, and his adventures in the field

feathery vegetation, which sloped upwards and ended in a line of cliffs dark red in color and curiously ribbed like some basaltic formations which I have seen. They extended in an unbroken wall right across the background. At one point was an isolated pyramidal rock, crowned by a great tree, which appeared to be separated by a cleft from the main crag. Behind it all, a blue tropical sky. . . .

"Well?" he asked.

"It is no doubt a curious formation," said I, "but I am not geologist enough to say that it is wonderful."

"Wonderful!" he repeated. "It is unique. It is incredible. No one on earth has ever dreamed of such a possibility!"

—Sir Arthur Conan Doyle, The Lost World[18]

The legend that helped launch a Museum expedition unfolded this way: In the 1920s, an airplane pilot working in Venezuela, Jimmy Angel, was commissioned by a mysterious passenger, a prospector named Williamson, to fly his plane to a location not on any map—an eight-thousand-foot, flat-topped peak rising out of the Venezuelan jungle called the Devil Mountain by the Arekuna Indians and Auyantepui by others. Angel insisted he had landed on the rugged, mist-shrouded summit, a vast plateau of nearly three hundred square miles, cut with a deep chasm. Down this chute plunged the tallest waterfall in the world, twenty times the height of Niagara Falls. His passenger found a stream, and together they sifted out seventy-five pounds of gold nuggets. Angel vowed he would return if he could raise the money to mount an expedition.

His name notwithstanding, Angel almost certainly did not land on Auyantepui—at least, not then. But he did return a decade later, and although he lost his plane on the mountaintop, he did

concluded with a Museum expedition. His fate was bound up with the Museum, and in the Brazilian wilderness he came to respect Leo Miller and to depend on George Cherrie for his life. As Kermit Roosevelt wrote: "Father, as soon as we were alone, told me that he had, at the outset, reached the conclusion that no better companion could be found for an arduous voyage. . . . There were many dark days when sickness and lack of food, and the uncertainty of the outcome caused tension to run high. Through it all Cherrie stood forth like a tower of support."[17]

Devil Mountains and Lost Worlds

It was a full-page sketch of a landscape roughly tinted in color. . . . There was a pale green foreground of

manage to bring back photographs of the mountain. One of the people who saw them was William H. Phelps, Sr., a Caracas businessman with an extensive private bird collection, who was also a trustee of the American Museum of Natural History. Phelps recognized that Angel had discovered an isolated habitat potentially rich in biological interest, if not in precious metals. He wrote to the Museum with an offer to finance a joint expedition, the first scientific exploration of Auyantepui. (*Tepui* is a Pemón Indian word for mountain; it is used to refer to these unique flat-topped formations.) In Frank Chapman's words, "It was a letter such as curators may dream of but few ever receive."[19] At the end of 1937, a Museum expedition assembled in Ciudad Bolívar, on the Orinoco River, joined the Venezuelan team, boarded a Lockheed airplane, and headed for a jungle landing strip near the base of the tepui.

Museum staff had been studying the lost worlds of southern Venezuela since 1911, when zoologists Henry Crampton and Frank Lutz ventured through the wilderness of British Guiana (now Guyana) to the foot of Mount Roraima, the probable model for Conan Doyle's "lost world." The next year the indefatigable Leo Miller attempted to explore another large tepui far to the southwest, Mount Duida. At that time, the source of the Orinoco River, which flows north and east across Venezuela to empty into the ocean near Trinidad, was still unknown. Miller traveled fifteen hundred miles up the river, nearly as far as its headwaters, and established a camp at the base of the tepui, but when his partner, F. X. Igsleder, was felled by complications from beriberi and malaria and their

Makiritare assistants deserted as the season of thunderstorms and flash floods began, Miller had to retreat.

In 1927, a Museum team led by mammalogist George H. H. Tate worked its way to the top of Mount Roraima. A year later, with Tate again at the head, an expedition fulfilled Miller's goal and became the first scientific team—and perhaps the first human beings—to reach the moss-covered summit of Duida, with its strange and highly specialized forests. Roraima had been small and barren, with comparatively few although intriguing species. Mount Duida was ten times as large and rich in plants as well as birds, small mammals, and insects—a true lost world.

The initial catalogues of species from these isolated habitats, three hundred miles distant from each other, showed unexpected similarities. Scientists speculated that the tepuis were once part of a single vast plateau and might contain close relatives of the animal and plant species that thrived eons ago. In 1931 the Museum decided to mount a large-scale expedition to look for other tepuis, the first ever by air into the region. The destination was a promising but unknown area. At that time, however, plane travel was still difficult in this wilderness, and the Museum could not raise sufficient funds, so the expedition was put on hold. Chapman and Tate wondered if they would ever discover what lay where they had drawn their X on the map. The answer would turn out to be Auyantepui.

No dinosaurs or prehistoric people roam these high-altitude tablelands, but Conan Doyle was right about one thing: they are worlds unto themselves. They sit atop one of the oldest geological

Opposite: Escarpment of Auyantepui, the Devil Mountain, from just below the south wall. On the plain far below lay the base camp, barely visible through binoculars. Photograph by E. Thomas Gilliard

formations in the world, the Guyana shield. Some 1.5 billion years ago, sandstone deposits began to form on the shield. In a complicated geological ballet of erosion and upthrust, an extensive plateau arose, with intrusions of volcanic rock. Over time water ate away much of the sandstone, leaving isolated formations that range in area from less than three square miles (Uaipantepui) to nearly four hundred square miles (Auyantepui). At least, it may have happened this way, for scientists still are not certain how the tepuis were formed. Some one hundred of them dot the jungle and savanna south of the Orinoco River, and only half have been explored.

Scientists are drawn to the tepuis for the light they cast on the distribution and evolution of species. Where habitats have become isolated for one reason or another, species that once shared territory and ancestry diverge as they adapt to different conditions. Darwin discovered the consequences of physical isolation on the Galápagos Islands. Frank Chapman discovered it in the mountains of Colombia, where changes in elevation divide climates, habitats, and, thus, bird species themselves. The tepuis partake of both kinds of isolation. A mesa such as Auyantepui encompasses a range of habitats, from lowland rain forest to cold, damp, high elevations. There is a high degree of what scientists call endemism—unique native

Above left: Ladder trail, Mount Duida, on the 1928 Sidney F. Tyler, Jr., Expedition, the most influential of all the early tepui *expeditions. Duida's size and the wealth of life supported at the summit provided extensive collections and spurred further Museum expeditions. From a hand-colored lantern slide by George H. H. Tate*

Above right: Camp on Mount Roraima, Venezuela, at sixty-nine hundred feet. From a hand-colored lantern slide by George H. H. Tate

Left: The Arekuna Indians, who lived near Mount Roraima, were essential to the zoological success of the Lee Garnett Day Roraima Expedition of 1927. "The Indians can imitate the calls of birds and animals almost exactly," wrote George H. H. Tate. "With no difficulty whatever, they reproduced the clicking of my typewriter and the swishing sounds of photographic solutions being shaken." From a hand-colored lantern slide by George H. H. Tate

Right: An expedition member looking over the Camarata valley of Venezuela from Auyantepui's eight-thousand-foot height. Photograph by George H. H. Tate

Below: Base camp at Auyantepui, 1937, constructed by the Arekuna Indians. Photograph by George H. H. Tate

species. Botanists estimate that half the plant species are native to the region and many to the particular tepui.

The picture of life offered by the tepuis is complex, for the lowlands and the summits do share some species, as do the different tepuis. On Auyantepui, Tate and his colleagues, including two W. H. Phelpses, senior and junior, found that, in places with higher altitudes, the lack of topsoil precluded the growth of all but the smallest plants—low forest, shrubs and bromeliads, which can withstand both intense sunlight and cool, humid conditions. Lower elevations were another matter. Bird life was profuse and

little-known species of flowering plants grew in abundance, including, as was later discovered, more than sixty species of orchids. Many of these stand only inches tall, with blossoms no bigger than a pinhead.

The Museum continues to mount major expeditions to the tepuis to search for new species, study their evolution and distribution, and track the patterns of similarity and difference. In 1978, a small Museum expedition to Mount Yapacana turned into a significant collaboration with Venezuelan scientists. In 1984, with support from W. H. Phelps, Jr., the most ambitious such expedition ever mounted explored

Cerro de la Neblina, "the Mountain of the Mist," the tallest mountain in South America outside the Andes. In 1990, a smaller group went to the summit of Mount Guaiquinima, and in 1994, in a reprise of Tate's journey, a combined Museum-Venezuelan team returned to Auyantepui.

The Mountain of the Mist

"We want to know what's there," states Museum herpetologist Charles Myers, "for this vast area is still poorly understood." Since 1838, when explorers first began to study the tepuis, birds and plants have been the focus. Many species have been identified and questions about distribution and evolution have become highly specific. In the late 1960s, for example, William Phelps, Jr., and Ernst Mayr made a heroic attempt to describe and explain the distribution of tepui birds. For other types of creatures, such as insects and reptiles, scientists are still taking a census.

To understand fully "what's there" will take generations, and the tepui region is certain to change dramatically over the next few decades as it is visited and developed. A huge national park has been created in the lowland area called the Gran Sabana, and tourism is on the rise. Partly in response to this growing urgency,

the Museum collaborated on a truly epic expedition to the Mountain of the Mist in 1984. Sponsored by Venezuela's Foundation for the Development of the Physical, Natural and Mathematical Sciences (FUDECI), it eventually included, at one time or another, more than eighty scientists. As soon as the team began to plan the expedition, it became clear why the Mountain of the Mist had been left alone.

First explored in 1953 by a joint expedition from the New York Botanical Garden and the Phelps Collection, this tepui stands on the Brazil-Venezuela border close to the equator. It is difficult to reach by foot because most of the surrounding lowlands are flooded from the rainwater that pours off its slopes. The so-called tabletop is difficult to reach and hard to traverse. A canyon eighteen miles long cuts through it, and mountain peaks rise higher into the mist. With the help of the Venezuelan military, however, the 1984 team developed several routes.

Part of the expedition traveled south down the Río Negro, whose name comes from its dark water, caused by tannic acid that leaches from vegetation. At a pickup spot, helicopters ferried scientists and supplies to a camp on dry land at the base of the tepui. Another group went by canoe, first along the Casiquiare canal, which links the Río Negro to the north-flowing Orinoco, and then into a labyrinthine, unmapped waterway stretching almost to the mountain itself. Boats had to be poled through the shallows in the gloomy light of dense vegetation. At the mountain, the team built an elaborate base camp with living quarters and room for scientific study. Indian hunters supplemented the food

The American Museum of Natural History in the Field:
South America

Brewster-Sanford Expedition—1912–17   *At the end of 1912, ornithologist Rollo Beck set sail on a bird-collecting expedition financed by Museum trustees Dr. Leonard C. Sanford and Frederick F. Brewster. Its route took him along virtually the entire coast of South America, from Peru around Cape Horn and back to Cuba. For five years, he and his wife contended with fierce weather, dangerous seas, and inhospitable conditions, in a variety of boats large and small, to collect specimens representing more than a hundred species of water birds. Beck also collected inland and in the mountains. He possessed a preternatural ability to discover the feeding grounds of rare sea birds. On one occasion, far from shore, he called for a dinghy when no birds were in sight. The captain scoffed, but in no time Beck's bait of grease and scraps had attracted a long line of sea sprites. This important collection of oceanic birds formed the foundation for curator Robert Cushman Murphy's classic book* Oceanic Birds of South America.

Bassler Expeditions to Brazil—1921–31   *Headquartered at the Amazon River outpost of Iquitos, Peru, petroleum geologist Harvey Bassler spent a decade prospecting the mountains and jungles of South America for Standard Oil. All the while, he made extensive zoological and ethnographic collections, including the only known specimen of a type of spotted poison frog. Bassler was an amazingly energetic collector. In one memorable trek, he and a few assistants covered four hundred four miles of rugged country on foot in just thirty-nine days, all the while collecting, mapping the trail, and making geological observations—this, immediately after six hundred miles of river travel. When Bassler wrote to the Museum for advice on how to dispose of his collections, it recognized a rare opportunity and offered to take them. Bassler later joined the Museum as a research associate, and he spent the rest of his life cataloguing and studying the wealth of data he had collected.*

American Museum of Natural History–Grace Peruvian Eclipse Expedition—1937   *"The most beautiful phenomenon in nature," was how Museum scientist Clyde Fisher described a total eclipse of the sun. Fisher led a team that included Japanese and Peruvian astronomers and photographers to the southern hemisphere to make a record of a little understood aspect of the eclipse—the bright corona around the sun, which is visible only during the eclipse. Even today, the Andes are among the best spots on Earth to record astronomical events because there is little static interference, ambient light from cities, moisture, and dust. Major Albert Stevens came along to take the first pictures of an*

On the 1984 expedition to the Mountain of the Mist, helicopters enabled scientists to reach parts of the summit that had never before been visited.

eclipse from the upper atmosphere—at twenty-five thousand feet. The eclipse began in the South Seas and moved in a great curve across the Pacific Ocean and up through Peru. Stevens flew over the middle of the path of the total eclipse. Not only was the weather splendid, but he also had time to shoot: the length of the totality at midpoint in the Pacific was estimated to be the longest in twelve hundred years.

Vertebrate Paleontology Expeditions to Chile—1986, 1988   *George Gaylord Simpson's work is known throughout Patagonia, so when fossils were found on a ranch in southern Chile, the ranch's owner decided to bring them to the Museum. The vertebrae of an ancient whale spurred the Museum in 1986 to mount a joint expedition with Chile's National Museum of Natural History. In Patagonia, the team found additional whale fossils; more important, they prospected intriguing new localities. The promise of still other unexplored sites encouraged Museum scientists to return in 1988, through a joint expedition with the University of Chile. This time, scientists visited the central highlands of Chile in search of dinosaur fossils from the Cretaceous period. They found something potentially more important— a new fossil-rich locality called the Tuiguirica, containing evidence of South America's earliest rodents, approximately 31 million years old. The discovery begins to fill in a 20-million year gap in the South American fossil record, a gap that has frustrated scientists' attempts to understand the origins and evolution of the continent's unique fauna.*

brought from Caracas. From the camp, scientists branched out to study lowland fauna and to ascend the mountain.

Helicopters made the trip to the top, which the earlier expedition had reached by climbing, a relatively easy task, albeit a damp one, for the clouds around the summit rarely lifted. More important, helicopters allowed the scientists to study previously unreachable sites on the three-thousand-foot peaks that rise from the mesa. The natural setting was complex and strange, rich in species unique to the tepuis and in many cases new to science: the gnarled, branching tea plant *Bonnetia maguireorum*, known nowhere else; the prolific insect-trapping pitcher plant *Heliamphora tatei*, named after Tate, who first discovered it on Mount Roraima; vampire bats; and, although reptiles are rare at the tepui elevations, several new species of frogs and lizards. For the first time, ichthyologists explored the river of the great canyon, whose acidic, nutrient-poor water was completely devoid of fish. Lowland waters, however, supported many species, from freshwater stingrays and electric eels to a new species of catfish.

The western tepuis, near the border of Venezuela and Colombia, represent a final frontier for naturalists. Their proximity to the Andes and its environment will certainly add more dimensions to a complicated history of life in the region. Says curator Charles Myers, "We are looking at a palimpsest of life. We don't know how much has been erased in the past and how much continuity remains. Although these are some of the oldest parts of South America, they are still a new world to us."

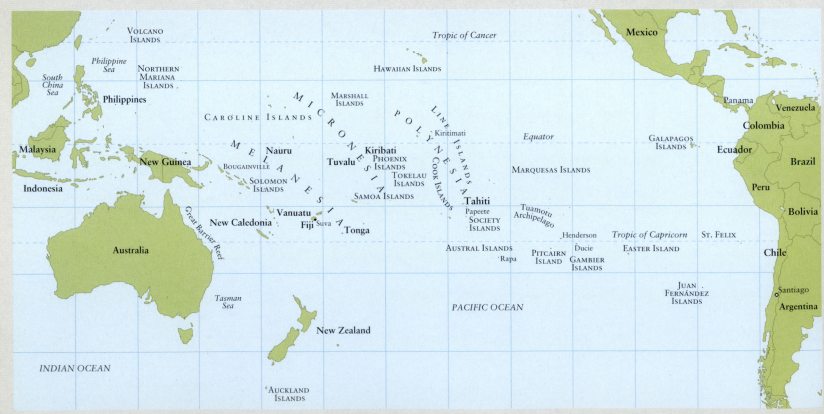

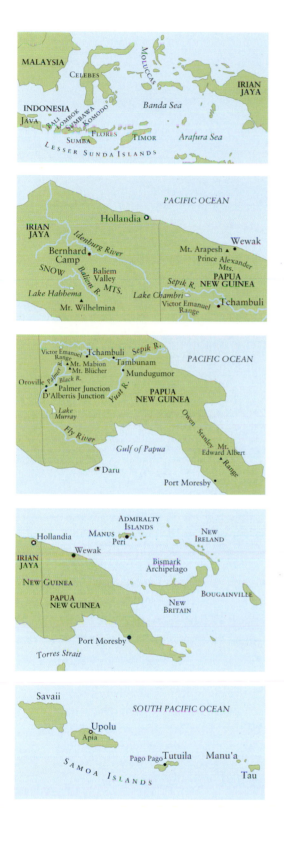

Ahurei Bay, Rapa Island, from the vantage point of an old hill fort, with taro beds along the shores, 1921. Photograph by Rollo Beck

The South Pacific: Errands In Eden

Mysterious Islands

Few men who come to the islands leave them, they grow grey where they alighted. The palm shade and the trade-wind fans them till they die, perhaps cherishing to the last the fancy of a visit home, which is rarely made, more rarely enjoyed, and yet more rarely repeated. No part of the world exerts the same attractive power upon the visitor.

—Robert Louis Stevenson

Stevenson never left the South Seas; Rollo Beck, the first leader of the Museum's Whitney South Sea Expedition, did return home, although not until he had spent nearly a decade collecting birds. Even then it took him two tries to escape. Beck first went into the field in 1920, and, in June 1928, on the way home from the Solomon Islands, headed for retirement in California, he received a wireless message from the Museum, requesting him to go to New Guinea. Beck and his wife, Irma, headed straight for Australia, refitted the expedition, and put in another eight months.

In its scope and duration, the Whitney South Sea Expedition was unprecedented in the study of birds. For two decades, Museum scientists systematically explored the islands of Polynesia, Melanesia, and Micronesia. The expedition covered a wide range of habitats. "Some, like certain of the Marquesas and Austral islands, are little more than bold rocks rising from profound depths," wrote Museum curator Robert Cushman Murphy. "Others, such as Tahiti, are lofty, heavily forested, volcanic peaks, rimmed successively by narrow coastal shelves, sandy beaches, coral fringes, moatlike lagoons, and barrier reefs. Still others, like the majority of the Tuamotus, are low-lying bars and atolls, upon which mangroves and coconut palms make up the conspicuous vegetation."[1] The islands support both marine and land birds; some are indigenous and some seasonal migrants that make the long journey down from Alaska and Siberia or up from the Antarctic region. Bird populations differ significantly from island to island, and distinct species inhabit separate islands, often within sight of one another. Through the Whitney Expedition's collections, scientists could begin to study the often puzzling geographic distribution of species in the islands of the South Pacific.

The idea for the Whitney Expedition did not originate with its patron, Harry Payne Whitney, but rather with his close friend, the surgeon and bird collector Leonard C. Sanford, a Museum trustee and honorary fellow. Sanford had already contributed money, and raised more from fellow trustee Frederick Brewster, to support the Brewster-Sanford Expedition, which in 1912 had sent collector Rollo Beck on a five-year journey along the coast of South America and through the Caribbean (see page 176). The success of that expedition only whetted Sanford's appetite. He envisioned an enterprise whose expense and scope would have overwhelmed others—a voyage by boat through the thousands of little-known, inaccessible islands of the South Pacific. This was one of the few remaining fields of inquiry left to ornithologists, for in this huge area only the larger island groups had been explored, and even these only haphazardly.

Changes in the region made it imperative that the work commence at once. Many of the islands, previously without mammals, had witnessed the introduction of rats, dogs, pigs, cats, and the mongoose. These were proving disastrous to native bird populations. Habitat

destruction and divers seeking pearls were completing the ecological devastation.

Sanford convinced Whitney to fund the enterprise, initially for four years, but after that time there was so much work still to be done that Whitney agreed to continue his support. He remarked to a friend, "Len's got me hogtied." In truth, Whitney himself was an enthusiastic supporter of the project. In 1929, when Sanford approached him about a new addition to the Museum, to be devoted entirely to the Department of Birds, Whitney agreed to help finance the building. Harry Payne Whitney died the following year, but his widow, Gertrude Vanderbilt Whitney, carried on his work. In 1931, construction began on an eight-story wing that provided storage for the huge collections arriving from the South Pacific and showcased the work of the expedition in a series of habitat groups in the Whitney Memorial Hall of Oceanic Birds.

The Museum launched the Whitney South Sea Expedition in

1920 by sending Rollo Beck to Tahiti, which served as his base for the first four years. For the first year, the expedition traveled on local trading vessels that called at many of the small Polynesian islands to pick up cargoes of copra (dried coconut kernel used for soap), but Beck also wanted to visit islands that were far from the traditional trade routes. In December 1921, the expedition acquired its own vessel —the seventy-five-ton schooner *France*. By the end of 1923, the expedition had traveled twenty thousand miles and visited one hundred islands, including the Society Islands; the Marquesas, where they discovered fourteen new species; the Austral Islands; the Tuamotu Archipelago, which had never before seen naturalists; and Rapa Island.

Already Beck had made many intriguing discoveries. At Tureia Island, he observed a species of warbler that he had seen on Henderson Island, six hundred miles to the east. It was absent from the islands in between, although they appeared to provide equally suitable habitats. Such inexplicable distribution of species was to occur over and over again. On Ducie Island, Beck was struck by the odd nesting habit of the Fairy Tern, which laid a single egg precariously upon a tree branch, without any supporting nest. "That this bird really survives the perils of infancy," commented Beck, "is evidenced in nearly every island by the abundance of the species."[2]

In 1924, the expedition transferred its base to the Fiji group, and from there it explored the Samoan Islands, Solomon Islands, New Hebrides Islands (now Vanuatu), and Tonga Archipelago. Upon his arrival in both Suva and Papeete, the first thing that Beck noticed was the prevalence of recently introduced species—the Common Mynah, the Red-vented Bulbul, and the Spotted Turtle-Dove—in the more populated areas. As he moved farther afield, he began to encounter native Fijian birds, especially on small islands and at higher altitudes where the ecology had not been modified. The region exhibited extremely varied bird populations, including brightly colored parrots, orange and yellow pigeons, hawks, thrushes, oldworld warblers and flycatchers, and finches. Once again, Beck remarked on the unusual distribution of species. In this instance, birds that were perfectly well equipped to fly from island to island remained in a very limited range. On Matuku Island, Beck observed the barking pigeon, Peale's Pigeon, which emitted the sound of "an aged, well-fed, medium-sized dog." This pigeon did not occur on islands that were within sight of Matuku. The nearby islands of Totoya and Kambara were separated by only forty-five miles, but each was home to a different species of pigeon. Each small island was able to support only one species of pigeon, but then, sixty miles to the north, on Nayau Island, Beck was surprised to find all three species.

Spending so many years in the South Pacific, Beck could scarcely have avoided running into trouble. On Oeno Island, a small boat carrying sailors overturned, and the men had to spend three hours in the shark-infested waters before they were rescued. In the Solomon Islands, Beck and his wife were taken hostage by a group of natives but were released unharmed. For Beck, such incidents, and years of isolation and rough living conditions, were a small price to pay for the thrill of discovering new species. Perhaps his greatest reward was the rediscovery of a population of the rare Little Shearwater, long thought to be extinct. On February 15, 1769, during Captain James Cook's first voyage around the globe, a specimen of a seabird was obtained, then thrown away, and only a manuscript description by Carl Solander and a pencil drawing testified to the bird's existence. Kuhl named the bird *Procellaria munda*, and over the years, as other ornithologists consulted the manuscript, the bird attained a near-mythic stature. No one had ever obtained another specimen. On February 16, 1926, Rollo Beck collected six specimens of *Procellaria munda*, all on the same parallel of south latitude as the 1769 discovery, but 815 miles to the west.

Darwinian Delights

Like Rollo Beck, Ernst Mayr also had a hard time escaping the South Seas. In 1928, Sanford sent the twenty-four-year-old Mayr to New

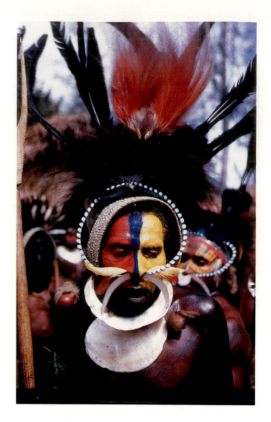

Above: Dancer with bird-of-paradise-plume headdress, East Highland Province, New Guinea, 1952. Photograph by E. Thomas Gilliard

Left: Birds of the Pacific, collected by Ernst Mayr, drawing by Francis Lee Jaques

Below: E. Thomas Gilliard observing the bower of the Amblyornis inornatus, Tamrau Mountains, West Irian Jaya (formerly Netherlands New Guinea), 1964

Opposite: Adult male Lesser Bird of Paradise, Paradisaea minor, New Guinea, 1953. This bird was a favorite of the plume hunters at the turn of the century, and thousands were killed each year to provide adornments for women's hats. Photograph by E. Thomas Gilliard

Guinea to collect birds for the American Museum of Natural History and Lord Rothschild's zoological museum in Tring, England. He had gone into the field a tenderfoot and emerged an explorer. While climbing the Arfak Mountains of Netherlands New Guinea, accompanied only by native carriers and three Javanese assistants, Mayr en-

The Dance of the Elusive Birds of Paradise

In the eighteenth century, skins of birds of paradise brought to Europe by traders were prepared by New Guinea natives in their customary manner—the legs removed and the skin dried over a fire. This prompted the botanist Carolus Linnaeus to name one species Paradisaea apoda—*the footless one from paradise—now known as the Greater Bird of Paradise. The otherworldly creature was reputed to float through the air, unable to land on a branch, with its face always turned to the sun, subsisting on dew from heaven.*

Birds of paradise are found almost exclusively on New Guinea. For centuries, few Westerners had observed birds of paradise in the wild, and fewer still had left records of their observations. The first to do so was the great British naturalist Alfred Russel Wallace, who had recorded the "strange arboreal dances" of the Greater Bird of Paradise in the Aru Islands in 1852. Wallace wrote of his experience: "The emotions excited in the mind of the naturalist, who has long desired to see the actual thing which he has hitherto known only by description, drawings, or badly-preserved external covering—especially when that thing is of surpassing rarity and beauty—require the poetic faculty fully to express them. . . . Should civilized man ever reach these distant lands and bring moral, intellectual, and physical light into the recesses of these virgin forests, we may be sure that he will soon disturb the nicely-balanced relations of organic and inorganic nature as to cause the disappearance and finally the extinction of these very beings. . . . This consideration must tell us that all living things are not *made for man. Many of them have no relation to him."*

The hunting and exportation of birds of paradise, whose plumes adorned ladies' hats in Paris and London, was effectively halted by 1924. Milliners had paid fabulous prices for the plumes, and in the years before the international ban, as many as a hundred thousand birds were exported during peak years from New Guinea. When Ernst Mayr arrived in Hollandia in 1928, he found Lesser Birds of Paradise common on the outskirts of the town, once a center for the plume trade. Their populations had already made a strong recovery. Mayr, too, was enchanted by these creatures of extraordinary plumage: "The many shapes into which Nature has been able to mold their feathers are a constant source of amazement. There are the true plumes of the genus Paradisaea, *which surpass the feathers of the egrets in soft daintiness. Others have the prismatic sparkle of highly polished metal, their reflections changing with the angle of light to pass through the whole spectrum of the rainbow. The Superb Bird of Paradise has a velvet cape of softness and dignity to make every well-dressed lady envious."*

In 1948, the Museum sent E. Thomas Gilliard, then assistant curator in the bird department, to the Philippines and New Guinea to collect material for two habitat groups. Gilliard was captivated, just as Mayr

countered serious difficulties carrying in supplies. He managed to overcome them, but there were many others to take their place:

The rainy season was not yet quite over and on some days the fog and rainstorms prevented collecting completely. The drying of the skins was also quite a task, as the air was saturated with moisture and the sun was not seen very often. Half-starved native dogs broke into my tent during the night and managed to get away unharmed with a few skins, thoroughly poisoned with arsenic. I never saw anything so thin and shabby as these dogs, which are related to the Australian dingo and do not bark. All these things, however, were only minor difficulties. What was much worse was that most of my boys fell sick, and all at the same time. One developed arsenic poisoning on his hand, and his whole arm swelled so he could not work. The other of my mantris had malaria and alarmed me by his fantastic speeches in his delirium, while another helper fell sick with pneumonia. His life was saved only by the most careful nursing day and night. My sore foot had not healed and my plant collector was also laid up with a big tropical sore, so that my camp resembled a hospital more than a collecting station.[3]

had been. *Over the next sixteen years, he would make six more trips to New Guinea, collecting and studying birds of paradise and the bower bird. Gilliard went to many different locations, from the Eastern Highlands to the Sepik River and the Victor Emanuel Mountains, from the Huon Peninsula to the western offshore islands.*

In effect, New Guinea's high ranges break up the huge island into a series of mountain islands, each of which has its own distinct bird fauna. These "islands" must be studied separately to map the distribution of different species. In many areas, Gilliard was the first to make bird surveys, using modern methods of collecting supported by adequate data. The results of his observations were published in two important volumes: Birds of Paradise and Bower Birds *and, with Austin Rand,* Handbook of New Guinea Birds.

Equally remarkable was the behavior of male bower birds, who build any of four different types of elaborate twig bowers to attract females for mating. The males decorate the bowers with many different objects: green berries; red berries; gray and blue stones; fruits of many colors; red flowers; yellow leaves; white eggshells; and, today, objects discarded by Westerners, such as blue plastic toys and Kodak film boxes. Like the type of bower, the choice of decoration is in most cases specific to each species. The reasons for this behavior are not understood, but ornithologists do know that birds are extremely sensitive to color, which they use to recognize their own species.

In 1954, in the village of Telefomin, in a valley between the Victor Emanuel and Hindenburg mountains, Gilliard met a local man named Femsep, who had just been released from jail for his part in a bloody revolt against the local Australian officials. Femsep possessed an encyclopedic knowledge of birds of paradise that easily surpassed all the information gathered by a century of exploration. The ornithologist and the native naturalist quickly formed a strong bond. Of Femsep, Gilliard wrote: "He pantomimed with his body the dances of the Birds of Paradise. He formed the nests with his hands; he imitated their calls. On the ground he scratched the shapes of their plumes at full display. . . . When forming a map, he often stopped to gaze into the distance and to point, describing range after range surrounding the Telefomin region."

Guided over trails by local people, Gilliard and his wife, Margaret, explored the hidden dwelling places of the birds of paradise in the surrounding mountains and moss forests. They found many, including the fantastic King of Saxony Bird of Paradise, but the rare Kondimkait, *which Femsep himself had only seen on a few occasions, eluded them. So great was Gilliard's faith in his fellow naturalist, that he was certain the elusive* Kondimkait *would eventually be found just where Femsep said it lived. This still remains a possibility forty years later.*

By the following year Mayr, understandably, was ready to go home. Awaiting him in a remote village in the Herzog Mountains, however, was a cable, not unlike Beck's: "Can you join the Whitney South Sea Expedition in exploration of Solomon Islands?" The temptation to explore a group of scientifically unknown islands was irresistible. In July 1929, Mayr boarded the *France*, headed for the islands that, according to Ernst Hartert, the bird curator of Lord Rothschild's museum, constituted the most interesting group in the world.

From small coral islands and atolls to larger islands blanketed with limestone hills to the biggest islands with high mountain peaks, the Solomon Islands offered an intriguing diversity. The largest island of the group, Bougainville, was named for the French explorer Louis Antoine de Bougainville, who was fascinated by the "Isles Solomon dont l'existence et la position sont douteuses." The existence and position of the islands were indeed doubtful. The Spaniard Álvaro de Mendaña de Neyra first saw them in 1568 but was never able to find them again. This prize had eluded French, British, and Spanish explorers until Bougainville rediscovered the mysterious islands in 1768.

When members of the Whitney Expedition first visited Bougainville in late 1927, its densely forested interior had never been entered by Westerners. The largest mountain, Mount Balbi, an active volcano soaring nine thousand feet, was first climbed in 1928 by Hannibal Hamlin, who had taken over leadership of the Whitney Expedition following Beck's retirement that year. This was considered one of the greatest achievements in mountaineering in the area since the ascent of Mount Albert Edward in New Guinea in 1903.

Most of the other islands in the group remained unexplored and unsurveyed. When the expedition headed to the interior of Malaita Island, Australian government officials gave them a fifty-fifty chance of returning alive, yet they had no conflicts with the natives, and their efforts were rewarded with many rare birds. Prior to the expedition, not a single mountain bird of the Solomon Islands was known. The results surpassed their expectations: at least thirteen new species and, with the inclusion of subspecies of lowland birds, more than eighty new kinds in all.

The Solomon Islands offered Mayr striking examples of evolution. He would go on to write a groundbreaking work on the subject, *Systematics and the Origin of Species*, based largely on specimens acquired by the Whitney Expedition. In the forests, he was able to study the Golden Whistler (*Pachycephala pectoralis*), which he described as "one of the most spectacular cases of evolution, one that would have delighted Darwin." The male Golden Whistler, whose distinctive ringing song was unforgettable, generally had a yellow yoke, with a black band across the breast, while the upper parts of the body were olive colored, but on every major island in the Solomons group, the combinations of colors were different. Mayr later identified close to seventy-five subspecies of the Golden Whistler, which has the highest number of subspecies of any species and a wide range in the Pacific.

The various projects of the Whitney Expedition continued through the 1930s. In 1931, William Coultas assumed leadership, and the expedition's arena moved on to the Admiralty Islands and the Bismarck Archipelago, including New Ireland and New Britain, whose central mountains had never been scaled by Westerners before Coultas's ascent. In all, the Whitney South Sea Expedition collected an estimated thirty-two thousand specimens from five hundred islands. In addition to its bird collections, it collected other animals and plants and photographed native animal and plant life and the human inhabitants of the many islands it visited.

The Whitneys left a final legacy during this period—in 1932 Gertrude Vanderbilt Whitney purchased the Rothschild bird collection in memory of her husband, Harry Payne Whitney. Combined with the expedition results, it would give the American Museum of Natural History the finest bird collection in the world, including 99 percent of all known species. Lord Rothschild had spent forty years building up his private bird collection, paying whatever was necessary for new and unusual specimens. Its two hundred eighty thousand birds represented many rare species from the Pacific archipelagos, North Africa, Europe, and Asia. It included a Great Auk, a marvelous collection of Hawaiian honey creepers, and six thousand American hummingbirds. The greatest treasures were the birds of paradise. Beck had been sent to New Guinea, in large part, to collect these birds. He and primarily Mayr gathered the most extensive collection of birds of paradise in the United States, but it was nothing compared to Rothschild's, which included nearly all of the known species and seventeen he himself had identified, as well as several rare hybrid forms. In addition, his collection contained series of male and female birds in various stages of their life cycle. As Mayr wrote: "It seemed utterly beyond our fondest hope that the American Museum should ever come into possession of such a magnificent collection."[4]

Simply unpacking, cataloguing, and installing the Rothschild collection occupied many members of the Department of Birds in the late 1930s. The Whitney and Rothschild collections, with their careful records and series of specimens from particular locales, have since provided invaluable data—including DNA samples—to scientists seeking insights on geographical distribution of bird populations and evolution in isolated island settings.

Savage Paradise

The peaks of the Snow Mountains, on bright mornings, part the dense clouds and soar into the skies of Oceania. Beneath the clouds, like a world submerged, lie the dark rocks which form the great island of New Guinea.
—Peter Matthiessen[5]

In the early 1930s, Richard Archbold, a young and wealthy volunteer in the Department of Mammalogy at the Museum, asked curator Harold Anthony, "Where on Earth that is least represented in your mammal collections would you like to send an expedition?" Anthony did not even have to consider his response: "New Guinea."

Even before the Portuguese discovered New Guinea in 1526, Europeans had a glimpse of its exotic natural life in the stunning plumes of the birds of paradise that spice traders brought from Singapore and the Moluccas. Centuries later, when naturalists first made their way into the heart of the rugged island, they

British control); the Territory of New Guinea (under Australian control). In the postwar years, boundaries shifted, and the island was divided down the middle into the independent state of Papua New Guinea and Irian Jaya, annexed by Indonesia. New Guinea is part of Melanesia, whose name comes from the dark skin of its inhabitants.

The influence of Western civilization, apparent only in a few outposts along the coasts and in scattered missions, had not penetrated the heavily forested interior. Outsiders were just beginning to explore New Guinea by airplane—to prospect for gold and to search for oil deposits. The

discovered spectacularly varied flora and fauna, including as many as seventy species of rhododendrons, some with blossoms up to seven inches wide.

Lying south of the equator and just one hundred miles north of Australia, New Guinea is the second largest island on Earth. It contains many of Earth's climatic zones. In its forests, which blanket almost the entire island, grow evergreen oaks with acorns the size of baseballs, evergreen beeches, mosses, and subalpine conifers. Its plant and animal species display complex origins. In the not-too-distant geologic past, a land bridge connected New Guinea to Australia. Its fauna still show these roots, but its flora probably originated in Asia and Austral-Melanesia.

No aspect of this world had ever been systematically studied when Archbold asked his question. Explorers had been turned back by snow-capped mountains rising to fifteen thousand feet and impenetrable rain forests. Anthony knew that collections there would be rich in new species and genera.

Archbold had the means to make Anthony's wish a reality. His grandfather John Archbold had founded the Standard Oil Company with John D. Rockefeller, and Richard Archbold had come into a substantial inheritance. This largely self-educated explorer and amateur mammalogist had already participated, on the Museum's behalf and with his family's backing, in the Franco-Anglo-American Zoological Mission to Madagascar in 1929 and 1930, collecting birds, mammals, and fossils. As a result of his conversation with Anthony, Richard Archbold established the Archbold Expeditions. Over the next four decades, he would support a series of pioneering expeditions to study the relationship between plants, mammals, and birds of New Guinea and the Indo-Australian region.

In February 1933, the First Archbold New Guinea Expedition landed in Port Moresby, the capital of the Territory of Papua. Before World War II, the huge island was divided into three territories: Netherlands New Guinea; the Territory of Papua (under

In the Ghost Forest

Inspired by Alfred Russel Wallace's classic book, The Malay Archipelago, *mammalogist Guy Musser went to live for three years in the forests of Central Sulawesi, a large island east of Borneo. When he arrived in 1973, he found a world largely unchanged from the one Wallace had described a century earlier. It was an uncanny, mist-shrouded world: "The air is wet and cold," he wrote. "Sounds are muffled as if they were absorbed by the thick wet moss that envelops rocks and rotting tree-falls on the ground, covers trunks and gnarled limbs, and hangs from branches in wet lacy curtains. At night the chill intensifies, the wet persists, the silence continues, broken only by the soft songs of frogs and insects, a low hoot from an owl, and the muffled cry of the* hantu . . . *a call announcing the ghost of the mossy forest."*

Musser came to study the altitudinal distribution and ecology of small mammals, primarily squirrels and rats, before the area was transformed forever by economic development. Rodents have existed for tens of millions of years and comprise one-half of all living mammals. In far-flung habitats from South America to Sulawesi, small rodents have evolved independently but along parallel lines, so that unrelated species exhibit similar characteristics. They have much to tell scientists about how species radiate and evolve. In addition to identifying and describing species, Musser wanted to establish the relationship between the fauna of Sulawesi and that of New Guinea and Indochina. Mammals in profusion came across the sea to Sulawesi from Asia, but once there they stopped. He is still seeking the reasons.

Musser's approach to collecting was far different from that of the earlier Archbold Expeditions, which entered the field like an army, with much of the time consumed by complicated logistics. On his own, Musser could devote himself to a careful study of the forest. To observe the native mammals, he had to establish camps far from populated areas. With no radio and only his two young native assistants for company, Musser had to think like a native in the forest—moving carefully to avoid danger and injury in places where medical help was a week's journey away.

At each camp, Musser and his assistants set hundreds of traps, meticulously noting their locations. Slight changes in elevation or humidity could mean different species. Musser's aim was to learn everything possible about each specimen—where it lived, what it ate. The tedium was banished by the thrill of discovering new species. One new species of rodent, found only at a certain elevation along creek beds, he named Bunomys karokophilus *because it subsisted on the* karoko, *a small fungus as soft as a human earlobe.*

Getting to know the forest and its habitat niches was no simple task where a small patch of camp could contain one hundred species of canopy trees. In time, however, the chaos of the forest began to make sense and its mysteries to reveal the predictable logic of living things.

Opposite, above: Men's house, Bismarck Archipelago, 1906. Photograph by Eugene Schroeder

Opposite, below: Two basketry figures stand in front of a daima *(men's house) at Tovei, Urama Island, Territory of Papua, June 1921. Photograph by Captain Frank Hurley*

Above: Aminudi, one of Guy Musser's native assistants, checking traps in the forest of central Sulawesi, June 1975. Photograph by Guy Musser

expedition's destination was the summit of Mount Albert Edward, in the Wharton Range, about which little was known.

The most important discovery of Archbold's first expedition was not scientific but logistical—the almost insurmountable difficulties of inland transport on New Guinea. For eight days, the group, which included Archbold, two scientists, a transportation manager, sixteen native carriers, and two cookboys, followed a crude road from the coast to the Sacred Heart Mission Station, founded in 1913 in Ononge, about sixty miles inland. From this point, they cut their own trail through the dense forest for three more days. The expedition soon discovered that food could not be obtained from the natives, who had none to trade. Entirely dependent on supplies carried by pack animals and native porters, they were able to transport

enough food and equipment to sustain the field party for only five or six days of work. Yet Archbold managed to assemble the first comprehensive collection of plants and animals of New Guinea, much of which came from the lowlands just to the west of the Fly River.

Archbold was not daunted: he made plans to return to explore an even less accessible area, the mountainous region around the headwaters of the Fly River in central New Guinea. He realized, however, that he would have to devise another means of supplying his expedition. The Fly River, named by Captain Blackwood of HMS *Fly*, who sailed past the mouth of the river in 1843, was barely explored. In 1876, Luigi Maria d'Albertis, the Italian naturalist, had traveled upriver more than five hundred miles in a wood-burning steamboat, a journey that was a series of tribula-

tions: unfriendly tribes, lack of food, and rampant beriberi among the crew. As late as 1927, no white man had crossed the limestone barrier at the headwaters of the Fly River and climbed the mountains to the river's source. In that year, the Papuan governor sent out the Northwestern Patrol to find the source and to cross the mountains to the Sepik River, which emptied into the Pacific Ocean. The account of the patrol's sometimes harrowing journey was the only description of the area in which Archbold planned to collect.

Archbold felt that the airplane offered the only practical means of transporting a large party and sufficient supplies to support extensive collecting inland. As soon as he returned to the United States in 1934, he purchased a Fairchild amphibian airplane and the most sophisticated radio equipment then available. The last problem—how to resupply his inland party from the coastal base—could be solved by parachute drop.

In March 1936, the Second Archbold New Guinea Expedition arrived at Daru, a small island at the mouth of the Fly River. The government station there had a permanent population of ten, mostly officials and traders. The expedition's first order of business was to make a series of five reconnaissance flights over the southern part of the island. From the plane the crew mapped unexplored territory, traced the uncharted sources of rivers, soared over unclimbed mountain peaks. At Lake Murray, to the east of the Middle Fly, they landed "on the water near an island and after some time a canoe with two men in it put out from the island and came toward us. They were very shy. The old man in the bow stood up and waved a white dance ornament made of cockatoo feathers at us while they were still out of hailing distance. We were not sure whether this was merely a friendly greeting or whether it was made to show us that they desired to trade with us. . . . Finally they came alongside and the old man in the bow caught hold of the wing of the plane and began admiring what to him must have been an extraordinary canoe."[6] On one of the flights, Archbold was accompanied by the resident magistrate at Daru, who marveled that he was seeing more of his district during a two-hour flight than he had seen in ten years of travel by boat and on foot.

The expedition chose several sites as supply depots and planned the itinerary: part of the inland party would collect along the Upper Fly River, while an advance party went into the mountains and collected at two-thousand-foot intervals up to ten thousand feet. This would enable the expedition to acquire a representative cross section of the flora and fauna of the southeastern section of the island.

In early May, the inland party, consisting of three scientists, a transportation manager, a patrol officer and six native police, and fifty-four native carriers, set off. The Fly River was in flood, and the high water enabled them to reach the junction of the Palmer and the Fly rivers—the farthest a boat that size had ever gone. It took two weeks to travel the five hundred twenty-eight miles, a distance the airplane could cover easily in two hours. The group set up their first camp at a long straight stretch in the river where the plane would be able to land easily, and an advance party headed overland to the six hundred ten–mile mark on the Palmer River.

Travel beyond Palmer Junction was far more difficult than anyone had anticipated. The advance party had to cut a trail through tangles of lawyer cane and wade across muddy swamps; covering just twenty-five miles took fourteen days. They stopped just below the meeting of the Black and Palmer rivers, fifteen miles short of their goal. After a few days' rest, they continued on to Mount Blucher, near the upper valley of the Palmer River.

At the Palmer Junction Camp, the birds were plentiful but difficult to collect; they hid in the treetops and avoided the undergrowth. Fortunately, the local natives were especially adept at collecting birds, which they gladly traded for white beads. The natives built small huts covered with leaves high in the trees, which they climbed easily. They also constructed cleverly camouflaged shooting houses on the ground, near the fruiting bushes that drew birds. There they waited patiently for their prey with bow and arrow. If no birds alighted on the nearby bushes, they attracted them by imitating their distress calls. The collections made in the short time the expedition spent at Palmer Junction contained more than one hundred species of birds, including the Wood Shrike, obtained only once before, and the rare Streaked Fairy Lory.

By early June, Archbold was ready to transport the camp upstream to the Black River. This would offer new opportunities for collecting and would place the main camp four or five days closer to the mountain party. In two days, the airplane made eight trips, transporting the men and five tons of supplies, including an entire month's worth of emergency stores. Such a move overland would have been impossible. In the end, the extra supplies proved essential.

Meanwhile, the advance party received its first parachute drop at Mount Blucher, then headed on to Mount Mabion, near the Dap Range. The drop was accomplished with the loss of only ten pounds of rice. In later attempts to drop supplies, dense cloud cover in the valleys prevented the airplane from locating the camp. In early July the expedition decided to send the portable radio unit from the Black River Camp to the advance party in the mountains, so that they could report on weather conditions before the airplane at-

tempted to fly in. It took George Tate, the expedition mammalogist, who also served as radio operator, seven days over rough trails to reach Mount Mabion. Once he arrived, Tate set up the radio only to discover that disaster had struck: the airplane had sunk during a violent storm at Port Moresby.

Plans to collect in the mountains had to be abandoned. The immediate goal was to retreat to a point on the Fly River where the expedition could be rescued by boat. At the Black River Camp, the men began building rafts to carry the entire party, as well as several tons of collections, supplies, and equipment, downriver to meet the relief boat. A dozen rafts, built of twenty-foot logs bound together with lawyer cane, and oars made of split logs were completed by the first week of August. They set off at once into territory known only through reports from the 1927 patrol and from the reconnaissance flights. Those reports were not encouraging: dangerous rapids awaited them several miles below the camp.

In the end, the flotilla of rafts

made its way one hundred miles downstream. It survived blinding rain, rapids, floods, crashing trees, and huge whirlpools before straggling into Palmer Junction. From there it was another thirty miles to Oroville, where a gold mining camp had recently been established, but the river was now wide and slow. Four days after they arrived in Oroville, the expedition saw the lights of the relief ship gleaming downstream.

The expedition left the field in 1937 with its valuable collections from the Upper Fly intact and a confidence in their new methods of transportation. Archbold already had plans for his next expedition the following year—to collect in the Snow Mountains of Netherlands New Guinea, a range "where even the most recent maps, little more than a year old, leave big white spaces labeled 'unexplored.' "[7]

On June 2, 1938, Archbold took off from San Diego Bay on his third expedition. His new airplane was christened the Guba in memory of the guba (tropical storm) that had destroyed his first airplane. He was flying a twin-engined bomber used by the U.S.

Navy, which he had modified for his purposes. His initial destination was Hollandia, on Humboldt Bay in northern New Guinea, where the rest of his expedition was waiting for him. Archbold planned to establish one of the inland bases on the shore of Lake Habbema, at an altitude of 11,342 feet. First, however, he had to find out if the Guba could take off from water at such a high altitude, a feat no one had ever attempted.

In an early reconnaissance flight over the area to the north of the Snow Mountains, between the Idenburg River, where they planned to establish their main camp, and Lake Habbema, they made a totally unexpected discovery. In a valley of the Baliem River, forty miles long and ten miles wide, lived more than forty thousand people in stockaded villages surrounded by neat walled gardens. Because this region is so heavily forested and the terrain so rough, earlier explorers had passed near the valley without suspecting that it was home to such a large native population.

The expedition's success depended on the takeoff and landing of the Guba at Lake Habbema, because this site offered a base for exploration in the mountains. So, on July 15, after careful study of aerial photographs, Archbold and his crew left Hollandia, provisioned with two months' emergency supplies and a portable radio. After determining that the lake was at least five feet deep, the minimum landing depth, they brought the plane down: "An awesome silence settled upon us as we shut off the engines. I opened the afterhatch and looked about. Thin, firlike trees dotted the hillsides which frowned down on this strange bird of ours. We were on the top of little-known New Guinea and entirely dependent for safety upon the two motors of our ship. Were they to fail us, we should be lucky to get back to the coast alive."[8] Their two little motors proved sturdy enough, and the *Guba* rose easily from the surface of the lake.

It took forty-five days for the *Guba* to transport the entire expedition—a party of one hundred ninety-five persons, including native carriers, collectors, scientific personnel, and an escort of fifty soldiers provided by the government of the Netherlands Indies; food; materials to build their camps; and scientific equipment—to the interior. After the airplane completed the delivery of sixty thousand pounds of supplies to Lake Habbema, they celebrated the new camp with a feast and toasts to Queen Wilhelmina of the Netherlands and President Franklin D. Roosevelt of the United States.

Scientific work proceeded well, first in the vicinity of Lake Habbema, then along the slopes of Mount Wilhelmina, one of the highest peaks in the Snow Mountains. William Richardson, the expedition mammalogist, collected unusual specimens, including rats three feet long and aquatic rodents that resembled muskrats, while Austin Rand, assistant leader and ornithologist, collected high-altitude birds and assembled a collection of grass, shrubs, and tree trunks to be used for the bird habitat display at the Museum.

Most exciting for Rand was the rare opportunity to observe in the wild the elaborate courtship display of the Magnificent Bird of Paradise. The bird's complicated courtship rituals had been observed in captivity, but its behavior was little understood, and no one knew whether this was a solitary or communal activity. For days, from the shelter of a little

Right: Harry Shapiro standing next to an Easter Island statue, 1935

Opposite, above: Descendants of the Bounty mutineers weaving a hat, Pitcairn Island, 1935. Of his departure from Pitcairn Island, James Chapin wrote, "On the morning of New Year's Day a large share of the populace came out to bid us good-bye. A race was rowed between two of their large boats, and then toward noon came the last farewell, with the singing of 'God be with you.' These fine people had won our deepest respect and sympathy." Photograph by Harry Shapiro

Opposite, below: The Archbold Expedition train crossing the Baliem Valley, Netherlands New Guinea, 1938

palm-leaf hut on the top of a ridge in the lower slopes of the Snow Mountains, Rand patiently watched the brightly colored male Magnificent Bird of Paradise. He observed the bird fastidiously clearing away his "court" and leaving only vertical perches—carrying leaves and twigs in his beak, breaking twigs off saplings, tearing off pieces of bark—then driving away intruding males, attracting females with loud calls, arousing the female with his ornate display, mating, and engaging in a post-mating pecking display. From this, Rand concluded that the dance area is the property of a single male, not a communal space as earlier naturalists had thought.

The expedition's encounters with the isolated people of the Baliem Valley confirmed their guess that they had never before had any contact with outsiders. The contact provoked, above all, mutual curiosity. It might have been otherwise. In 1961, when the Harvard-Peabody Expedition came to document the culture of the Kurelu people of the Baliem Valley, the same people whom Archbold had discovered by chance in 1938, they found a

After Strange Gods and Mutineers

When Templeton Crocker's yacht Zaca traveled through the myriad tiny islands of southern Polynesia to collect material for displays at the American Museum of Natural History, it followed the route of the earliest explorers and colonizers, the Polynesians. On board for the 1934 expedition were Museum ornithologist James Chapin and anthropologist Harry Shapiro. Shapiro made the voyage halfway across the Pacific to satisfy his scientific curiosity about the inhabitants of two legendary islands—Pitcairn Island and Easter Island.

In 1789, the mate of HMS Bounty, Fletcher Christian, organized a mutiny of twenty-five crewmen against the harsh discipline of Captain Bligh. They abandoned Bligh and eighteen loyal crew members in the middle of the Pacific Ocean in a small, provisioned boat. In a marvel of navigation, Bligh led his party on a voyage of three thousand miles to the East Indies. Meanwhile, the mutineers set sail for Tahiti, where most of the men settled. A group of nine, however, along with a number of native men and women, set forth to start a new life beyond the reach of the law. They chose the tiny volcanic island of Pitcairn, unsettled because its single harbor was too dangerous for sailing ships to enter.

The founding of the Pitcairn colony was a bloody process. The British sailors fought with the native men and among themselves. In the end all the native men and most of the mutineers died violently. Their descendants, however, lived an idyllic existence. Totally self-sufficient, the islanders developed a government that granted men and women equal rights and regulated the exchange of goods. All members of the community attended school until age sixteen and received religious instruction. In 1856, due to overcrowding, part of the colony moved to Norfolk Island, north of New Zealand. When Shapiro arrived in 1935, there were a hundred seventy-five inhabitants on Pitcairn Island and six hundred on Norfolk Island. The Norfolk Islanders had kept meticulous records, from which Shapiro made detailed genealogical tables of this unusual isolated human population.

After a week's visit to Pitcairn, the Zaca sailed on to mysterious Easter Island, which lies fourteen hundred miles to the east. Pitcairn is its closest neighbor, and no one knows where the first colonists of Easter Island, the men and women who crossed the seas in narrow canoes, came from. "The mere presence of man on this detached chip of land," wrote Shapiro, "symbolizes better than anything else the nautical genius of the Polynesian." Although culturally and linguistically related to Polynesians, the precise origins of the Easter Islanders remains unknown.

The island was most likely sighted by Dutch sailors on Easter Day of 1722, hence its name. In the later part of the century, Spanish, English, and French explorers visited the grass-covered island. In the nineteenth century, Easter Island's population was decimated by the Peruvians, who enslaved the inhabitants and forced them to work in the guano fields of Peru. The few who survived the ordeal and returned to Easter Island in 1871 were further beset by new diseases. The one hundred seventy-five survivors had grown to four hundred forty inhabitants by the time of Shapiro's visit. Today the island belongs to Chile.

Just as mysterious as the origins of the earliest inhabitants were the huge statues, called moais, that they left behind. Of these, two hundred fifty remain—some upright and some prone; some completed and some just begun. Rising up to forty feet, they ring the inner and outer slopes of Rano Raraku, an extinct volcano in the island's southeast corner, and follow the curve of the island's coastline. Carved of fragile stone from the volcano's crater, the moais display considerable artistic and engineering skill. Indeed, the true magnitude of the carvers' achievement was only revealed in 1955, when some of the full figures were excavated by Thor Heyerdahl. Their brooding presences have provoked many farfetched theories but no conclusive explanation. How were the statues, each weighing up to twenty tons, transported as far as fifteen miles and then placed in rows upon large stone platforms or set in holes in the ground? Heyerdahl was able to demonstrate how it might have been accomplished using only primitive technology. What was their original significance and how old are they? Captain Cook, who landed on Easter Island in 1774, noted that, although the islanders did not worship them, they were reluctant to walk within the boundaries of the platforms.

Shapiro and the artist Toshio Aseida chose one of the representative figures, ten feet tall, as a model for a reproduction. Aseida spent four days making a mold of the figure, in sections, which he reassembled back at the Museum. There, visitors to the Hall of Pacific Peoples can confront the eerie gaze of the Easter Island figures.

fierce society whose ritual life revolved around warfare. The writer Peter Matthiessen, who accompanied that expedition, along with Michael Rockefeller, who served as photographer, felt he was afforded a last glimpse of an untouched civilization: "The Kurelu offered a unique chance, perhaps the last, to describe a lost culture in the terrible beauty of its pure estate. The armed patrols and missionaries invaded their land on the heels of the expedition, and by the time this account of them is published, the proud and warlike Kurelu will be no more than another backward people, crouched in the long shadow of the white man."[9]

World War II brought bombers over New Guinea instead of explorers. After the war, the Archbold Expeditions resumed work in the South Pacific, at Cape York, Australia, in 1948, followed by four more expeditions to New Guinea from 1953 to 1964. Although Archbold did not accompany these expeditions, his botanist, Leonard Brass, led the first three postwar expeditions, which concentrated primarily on plants and mammals.

"New Guinea would still be a cipher if it were not for the work of the Archbold Expeditions," says Guy Musser, Archbold Curator at the Museum. In attempting to make an inventory of every species of plant, mammal, and bird they encountered, and to collect in a variety of habitats, the scientists gathered a huge amount of material that would reveal the relationship of species, their distribution, and how the fauna reached the island in the first place. Yet early important studies by expedition scientists such as Leonard Brass and George Tate only scratched the surface of what the collections might reveal. Years later, Australian mammalogist Timothy Flannery, the author of *The Mammals of New Guinea*, traveled all the way to New York to study the mammals of Australia's island neighbor. Much of New Guinea still remains unsurveyed, and Flannery recently discovered a new species of large mammal—a tree kangaroo. He wants to know why many mammal species are different in the mountains of the east and the west, as if they had been separated by a great wall. "If we could experience New Guinea with an animal's senses," says Flannery, "we might get definite answers. Short of that, we depend on the clues that we uncover in these collections."

"Makelita"

Field work is, of course, very ancient, in the sense that curious travelers, explorers and naturalists have gone far afield to find and bring home accounts of strange places, unfamiliar forms of plant and animal life and the ways of exotic peoples. Ancient records refer to the unusual behavior of strangers, and for thousands of years artists have attempted to capture some living aspects of the people and creatures evoked in travelers' tales or the sacred

mythologies of some distant, little-known people.

—Margaret Mead [10]

In the summer of 1925, a twenty-three-year-old American anthropologist set sail for Polynesia to study adolescence among the young girls of Samoa. Margaret Mead was just out of adolescence herself. She had completed her doctoral thesis on cultural stability in Polynesia for Columbia University and just been hired by the American Museum of Natural History, where she would begin work the following year, but this was her first experience in the field. Mead had never spoken a foreign language or been abroad, but she had read everything about the Pacific peoples and, in her own words, "had all the courage of almost complete ignorance." Over the next fifty years, she would return numerous times to study the peoples of the Pacific region. By the time of her last trip into the field, she was studying the grandchildren and great-grandchildren of her first subjects. She was also witnessing first-hand the changes wrought by the onslaught of Western civilization—and the amazing resiliency of many native Pacific cultures. For most of that time Mead was also a curator of anthropology at the American Museum of Natural History. The Hall of Pacific Peoples, which opened in 1971, embodies her personal involvement with the inhabitants and cultures of this far-flung region.

Like those of many anthropologists who worked at the Museum, Mead's story really begins with Franz Boas, her teacher at Columbia. The choice of her first fieldwork had not been hers alone. Boas felt that anthropological investigations should proceed

Opposite: Dance masks representing spirits, made of wood and bark fibers, northern New Ireland, on display in the Museum's Margaret Mead Hall of Pacific Peoples

systematically. He had already determined to his satisfaction that no human culture evolves in isolation; exchanges between different cultures occur continuously. The next issue to be tackled was the development of individuals in the context of specific cultures. For instance, was the often painful and rebellious process of adolescence in Western society biologically inevitable, or was it the result of pressures brought to bear on young people coming of age in that society? Was "nurture" (cultural factors) more important than "nature" (biological factors)?

Mead was willing to defer to her mentor and study this problem, but she was set on going to Polynesia. The paternal Boas thought Polynesia too dangerous for a woman, but Mead remained determined, a characteristic she would display throughout her career. Boas capitulated, but he insisted that she go to an island where ships called regularly.

After making an initial survey of the life and customs of Samoan girls on the island of Tutuila, the largest island of American Samoa, and acquiring a rudimentary knowledge of the language, Mead headed for the island of Tau, in the Manua group, located one hundred miles to the east. Unlike the villages in Tutuila, which were greatly influenced by the presence of Americans, the original culture of Tau had been preserved. Boas would have been pleased to know that the government steamer called there every three weeks.

Mead found a very different way of life in Tau, and, in the be-

ginning, she could make little sense of it. When she asked the women the names and ages of their children, she would receive answers such as the following: "Names,—well, the baby's name is Pandanus Nut, that's what we call it, or just Nut for short. But its name from its father's father's family is 'The One that Does Not Move,' and only yesterday my younger brother gave it his name of 'Lighted House,' so perhaps we will call it that now. And how old is he? Well, he was born after the second Palolo Fish Feast, and before my young cousin, Hibiscus, had her baby girl."[11]

Several months passed before she understood these answers were emblematic of fluid social relations in Tau, and before she began to be accepted as part of the community. Mead was christened "Makelita," after the last queen of Manua. In January 1926, she wrote home: "Have I not three dark spots on a white dress, spots from the blood of the pig which was sacrificed for the birth feast of the tenth child of Mealeaga? Have I not woven *polas* for the great guest house of the Siufaga and argued with the members of the *Aumaga*—the young men—on the advisability of burning down what is left of Ofu, because the people of Ofu stoned the meddlesome pastor of Tau out of the village? And has not Talala, Tufele's royal mother, the only woman *matai*—chief— in all Samoa, put her arm lovingly on my shoulder."[12] Mead was doing what she set out to do—to study a society radically different from her own by gaining intimate knowledge of its culture and the individuals in it.

Mead returned to New York in 1926 and began her work at the Museum in a tower room, which, over the years, she transformed into her domain. The results of her fieldwork, the book *Coming of Age in Samoa*, brought her a notoriety that continued for the rest of her career. Indeed, she came to symbolize the anthropologist as heroine, someone able to enter into other cultures and interpret them to an often puzzled Western audience.

Mead concluded that in culturally isolated parts of Samoa, the stresses of adolescence so common in the West were absent. The rules that determined behavior for girls in Samoa came from within, from attitudes learned in infancy and childhood, in opposition to what Boas described in his foreword to Mead's book as "a reaction to the restraints put upon us by our civilization." With the exception of a few deviant persons, Mead had observed that "adolescence represented no period of crisis or stress, but was instead an orderly developing of a set of slowly maturing interests and activities. The girls' minds were perplexed by no conflicts, troubled by no philosophical queries, beset by no remote ambitions. To live as a girl with many lovers as long as possible and then marry in one's own village, near one's own relatives and to have many children, these were uniform and satisfying ambitions."[13]

For Mead, anthropology was not only a form of implicit social criticism, it was a way of leaping beyond the limitations of class, race, and her own personal circumstances. The leap was not always as easy to make as it was in Samoa, and it took some innovative forms.

"Piyap"

The ethnologist cannot march upon a native community like an invading army. . . . He must slip in quietly, lower himself or herself as gently as possible into the placid waters of native life, make the unprecedented arrival of an inquiring white person as inconspicuous as possible. For such an expedition there are no camera men, no preparators, no army of carriers.
—Margaret Mead [14]

In 1928, Margaret Mead embarked on a series of trips to Melanesia and Bali that had as their goal nothing less than a study of native peoples from birth to death. Her observations in Samoa had taught her that, in order to understand the development of adolescents, she would first have to study younger children. The question she sought to answer was very much of its time and involved the notion that the mentality of primitive people was qualitatively different from that of civilized individuals.

First Mead had to find a "primitive" society. Her work on Pacific cultures for the Museum encouraged her to look to Melanesia. This group of little-explored islands stretches three thousand miles across the southwest Pacific. Since the voyages of Captain James Cook in the eighteenth century, the peoples of the Pacific had had increasing contact with Westerners, from explorers and traders to missionaries and colonial administrators. The Admiralty Islands to the north of New Guinea remained relatively isolated from this contact.

Mead's second husband, the anthropologist Reo Fortune, would accompany her into the field. The only descriptions that Mead and Fortune could find of Manus Island, the largest of the Admiralties, were a short account by a German explorer and an old collection of texts compiled by a German missionary. Discussions with an officer of the New Guinea Service directed them to the sea-dwelling people along the southern shore of Manus, where conditions would enable them to live and work with relative ease. Their choice of a location and a village, Peri, turned out to be ideal for their purposes:

In their vaulted, thatched houses set on stilts in the olive green waters of the wide lagoon, their lives are lived very much as they have been lived for unknown centuries. No missionary has come to teach them an unknown faith, no trader has torn their lands from them and reduced them to penury. Those white men's diseases which have reached them have been few enough in number to be fitted into their own theory of disease as a punishment for evil done. . . . It is essentially a primitive society without written records, without economic dependence upon white culture, preserving its own canons, its own way of life.[15]

From the thatched house on piles that the people of Peri built for them, Fortune and Mead—whom the Manus referred to as *Piyap* (woman of the West)—spent the next six months carefully observing daily life in the lagoon village. The men went off in outrigger canoes to fish and carried their trade goods to the mainland markets, where they bartered them for vegetables and other necessities, from wood for building canoes to gum needed to caulk them. The Manus used dog's teeth and shell money to pay for the services of those with special magical knowledge, the obligations incurred at marriage by the bridegroom's family, and nonessential objects.

The focus of Mead's days, however, was the children who played in her house, in the waters of the lagoon, and on the small islet that adjoined the houses. They lived in what she described as "a paradise for children"—they were allowed to do as they pleased in an unstructured environment and assiduously spared the heavy work of the adults.

Mead watched the children interact with one another and with their parents, in both formal and informal settings. Along the way, she mastered their language and the intricacies of social, economic, and religious life that formed the foundation of the little world in which a child grows up.

Mead's detailed observations became the basis for her second book, *Growing Up in New Guinea*, in which she portrayed a culture that she "learned to know intimately enough not to offend against the hundreds of name tabus."[16] In a simple and compact social setting, Mead could see the ways in which Manus parents prepared their children for adulthood: they taught the children a respect for property, to observe taboos, and to be enterprising and industrious. The methods of passing on traditions may have seemed chaotic and even unproductive to outsiders, but in a society as homogenous as that of the

Manus, Mead concluded, "as long as every adult with whom [the child] comes in contact is saturated with the tradition, he cannot escape a similar saturation."[17] When she compared the children to the adults, she saw freedom transformed into a devotion to work and economic success. They had no leisure time in which to cultivate creative activities—art, dance, music, story telling—or even for casual conversation and friendships.

Mead returned to her work at the Museum in 1929, but by 1931 she and Fortune were back in the field for a two-year comparative study of three northeastern New Guinea tribes. She had renewed the nature versus nurture debate, this time regarding the formation of male and female social roles.

The first tribe with whom Mead and Fortune lived had no name for themselves as a group. The anthropologists named them the Mountain Arapesh, a word that simply means "human being" in their language. Their plans were to study the plains people, on the far side of the coastal mountain range, who were known for their rich artistic tradition. The native carriers, however, refused to go beyond the mountain village of Alitoa on the Prince Alexander Ridge, and they left Mead and Fortune stranded there. Making the best of the situation, Fortune "made a speech telling [the people] that he approved of all their old customs and that if we came to live here the village would always be full of matches and salt—the two great desiderata. So they said we could build a house and Reo marked out a place the right size in the spot they assigned to us."[18]

They remained in Alitoa for eight months. The Mountain Arapesh had a very simple cultural tradition, with little ritual or art. Basic to their existence was an elaborate trading system with their neighbors on the plains and along the coast. While they were able to provide the necessities of life, they depended on their trading partners for all luxuries and ritual and decorative articles. From the Beach Arapesh they acquired bows, arrows, and stone axes and songs, dance steps, musical instruments, new clothing, and hairstyles. From the Plains Arapesh, universally feared for their use of sorcery, the mountain people received carvings and sago-bark paintings, which they copied, and shell rings, spears, and net bags. Mead was surprised to discover that the social roles of men and women in this society were very similar: they both participated fully in the nurturing of their offspring. Although Arapesh men and women assumed different economic, religious, and social roles, there was no sense that men and women had innately different temperaments—that one sex tended naturally to be more aggressive, dominant, brave, or conversely more nurturing and flexible.

Mead's next experience in New Guinea with the Mundugumor would confirm her early impression that Western expectations regarding male and female behavior are a product of that society and that "the temperaments which we regard as native to one sex might instead be mere variations of human temperaments, to which members of either or both sexes may, with more or less success in the case of different individuals, be educated to approximate."[19]

The Fierce People

In September 1932, Mead wrote home, "In the mind of the most suburban Rabaulite and in the mind of the wildest bush native, the Sepik stands for mosquitoes, crocodiles, cannibals and floating corpses—and I can assure you we have seen them all."[20] When the two anthropologists discovered they were unable to reach the inland tribes north of the Sepik River, where they had planned to work, because of the difficulties of overland transportation, they chose their next destination from the map. The Mundugumor, who lived along the Yuat River, a tributary of the Sepik River, were the nearest large population beyond the "mission's clutches." All that was known of them at the district government office were the names of the villages and where their language began.

The Mundugumor had come under government control only a few years before, and they offered a complicated picture of a people who had lost their cultural identity, for their ceremonial life revolved around warfare and headhunting. Memories of their old way of life were vivid—even the young children had participated in cannibalistic ceremonies—but the loss had not been replaced with a new set of rituals. "This absolute acceptance of a break with the past, which is very characteristic of Sepik cultures, led to a kind of cultural paralysis."[21] It fell to Mead to attempt the difficult and frustrating task of recording a culture that a people felt no longer existed.

Like Colin Turnbull among the Ik (see page 122), Margaret Mead got more than she bargained for when she went to study the Mundugumor. Both the Arapesh and the Mundugumor shared social and enonomic conditions, and they lived within one hundred miles of each other, but temperamentally they were worlds apart. The Mountain Arapesh were a warm and open people who disapproved of aggressive behavior. When Mead and Fortune left, the old Arapesh men warned them: " 'You are going up the Sepik River, where the people are fierce, where they eat men. You are taking some of our boys with you. Go carefully. Do not be misled by your experience among us. We are another kind. So you will find it.' "[22] This advice scarcely prepared her for the hard and disturbing reality. It was difficult to live among a people whose life was predicated on distrust and anger, among whom brothers often fought one another, children were fearful of their relatives, and voices raised in anger were a common occurrence along the river paths. The village lacked the communal plaza and men's house customary among many tribes of the Sepik River.

Each man seeks to live unto himself within a palisade in which cluster a number of houses: one for each wife,

Sacred flute figure named for the village Kenakatem, Yuat River, New Guinea, and made for Margaret Mead and Reo Fortune by the Mundugumor. Mead wrote, "The sacred flute is a baby crocodile, its mother a water drum, and they took the water drum down to the water where it bore the sacred flute, which cried at first with a weak little newborn voice and then more full-throatedly as it emerged, was carried up the river bank and finally was lodged in state in our house, where someone came to feed it every day."

or perhaps for each two wives, a special, badly thatched hut for his adolescent sons, where they sleep miserable and mosquito-bitten, not even worthy of a mosquito-bag among them; . . . This compound, containing nine or ten wives, a few young and dependent males, sons or sons-in-law, and a few unaggressive nephews, is only attained by about one man in twenty-five. Such a household, however, is the ideal, and the man with two or three wives, sometimes with only one wife and some stray old female relative to swell his *ménage*, will clear himself a little secluded patch in the bush and take care to approach it by a circuitous path, so as to preserve the secret of its location.[23]

Far more disconcerting was the tribe's general repudiation of children. In its most extreme expression, babies of unwanted sex (men preferred females, and women preferred males) were wrapped in a bundle of bark and thrown into the river still alive. Despite Mead's uneasiness, relations between the Mundugumor and their two visitors were very cordial; they parted with "gayer words and friendlier adieus" than they had ever received. As a farewell present, the Mundugumor made Mead and Fortune a sacred flute, named Kenakatem, in honor of the village, which they presented with great ceremony.

Like the Arapesh, the Mundugumor generally did not exhibit different sexual temperaments: both male and female were equally harsh in their treatment of children. After three-and-a-half months among the Mundugumor, Mead was not any closer to finding an answer to her question of how societies shape temperamental roles for the sexes. So, in early 1933, Mead and Fortune traveled to Chambri Lake, near the Sepik River, where they encountered yet another distinct culture, the Tchambuli. This tribe was returning to its village after

having been displaced by people from the Middle Sepik River, and they were in the process of reconstructing their ceremonial life. Everything they owned, from ceremonial stools to slit gongs, had been destroyed or stolen in raids. Here Mead continued to study the many ways in which culture determines the roles of men and women and the many forms these roles can take. Among the Tchambuli, she did find temperamental differences between men and women, but, in another unexpected reversal, she discovered that the conventional roles of the sexes in Western society were reversed: the women managed the business affairs of the community, working in cooperative groups, while the men engaged in artistic activities and gossiped together. Mead also made important collections for the Museum, for the Sepik valley was one of the richest areas artistically in all of New Guinea. It was becoming increasingly clear to Mead that one cannot make generalizations about primitive societies or the "primitive mind." Instead, she needed a new way of portraying different cultures.

Inside Bali

When Mead and her third husband, the anthropologist Gregory Bateson, arrived in Bali in March 1936, the island, usually teeming with life, was quiet and empty. It was the Balinese New Year, referred to as *Njepi*, the "Silence," which comes once every four hundred days. The two anthropologists needed an official dispensation just to drive across the deserted island. They had come for what would be Mead's longest and most intricately organized period studying one group in the field. For the next two years, Bateson and Mead literally absorbed this ancient and artistically sophisticated culture. They returned home not only with voluminous notes but also with many reels of movie film, twenty-five thousand still photographs, and Balinese texts—a complete record of the human interactions that they had witnessed during their stay. They later organized this wealth of material in an innovative volume, *Balinese Character: A Photographic Analysis*, in which they sought through images to transcend the limitations of language in translating disparate aspects of another

The American Museum of Natural History in the Field:
The South Pacific

Crocker Pacific Expedition—1934–35, 1936–37; Fahnestock Expedition—1940 *In order to create the eighteen habitat groups for its Hall of Oceanic Birds, the Museum needed to supplement the extensive bird collections with additional photographs and background materials. It sent out three expeditions to the South Pacific to make studies for eleven of the habitat groups. In 1934 and 1936, Museum scientists and artists sailed the ocean on Templeton Crocker's yacht, the Zaca. The ornithologist James Chapin led the first expedition and was accompanied by the artist Francis Lee Jaques, who painted the backgrounds for the dioramas and the dome that graced the new hall. On its return from southern Polynesia in 1935, the Zaca called at the Juan Fernández Islands, the guano islands of Peru, and the Galápagos Islands to collect additional material for the bird groups. The 1936 expedition also stopped at the islets of Tongareva, two thousand miles south of Hawaii, to collect materials for the Pearl Divers group in the Hall of Ocean Life. Ichthyologist Roy Waldo Miner and his assistants made at least seventy dives to collect tons of corals and other invertebrate specimens. They took thousands of feet of underwater film, made sketches of the colorful fish and coral, and photographed the native divers to use as models for life-size figures. The centerpiece of the Museum group is a nine-hundred-pound coral five feet in diameter.*

In 1940 scientists visited Fiji and New Caledonia on board the Director II, *a yacht provided by the brothers Sheridan and Bruce*

culture. The aim of Bateson and Mead was to create a book "about the Balinese—about the way in which they, as living persons, moving, standing, eating, sleeping, dancing, and going into trance, embody that abstraction which (after we have abstracted it) we technically call culture."[24] As anthropologists, Mead and Bateson were taking on a Promethean task, to represent a culture from the inside, not merely describe it or analyze it.

Clearly, Bali offered a far different experience from that of New Guinea. There, after months

Opposite: Gregory Bateson and Margaret Mead working in the mosquito room of their house in the Iatmul village of Tambunan, Territory of New Guinea, 1938

Fahnestock. The schooner rammed into the Great Barrier Reef off the coast of Australia, but they were able to unload the collections as the boat slowly sank. Fortunately, no lives were lost in the accident.

Burden Komodo Island Expedition—1926   *The tiny volcanic island of Komodo is part of the chain of Lesser Sunda Islands, which stretches from Java to Timor. For centuries, strong tidal currents and dangerous offshore coral reefs discouraged human settlement and exploration. Because of the island's location, there were no large mammalian predators of Asian or Australian origin, and more primitive forms of life had dominated in their absence. In 1912, a Malay pearl diver brought the skin of a huge lizard from Komodo Island to P. A. Ouwens, director of the Zoological Museum in Buitenzorg, Java. Ouwens had heard many tales of dragon-like creatures that roamed the island, and he sent out collectors to obtain specimens for study. Ouwens named the lizard Varanus komodensis, known popularly as the Komodo Dragon.*

Museum trustee W. Douglas Burden learned of the Komodo Dragon in a paleontology course at the Museum taught by G. Kingsley Noble. He was inspired enough to propose an expedition to Komodo Island to collect specimens, to film the lizards in the wild, and, if possible, to bring back a live animal. Accompanied by herpetologist E. R. Dunn and the experienced hunter E. J. Defosse, Burden set out to explore Komodo Island. Once they located the animals on the volcanic slopes, they found it easy to obtain specimens. It was far more difficult to capture a live animal. They eventually managed to trap two smaller lizards, after the huge old lizard they had captured clawed its way through the steel mesh of its cage.

of grueling fieldwork, inevitably accompanied by unbearable heat, relentless insects, and recurring bouts of malaria, the anthropologist might well miss seeing the one ceremony necessary to an understanding of a particular culture. Even worse, an entire village might pack up and move away overnight. There were more than seven hundred dialects and languages in New Guinea, many spoken only by several hundred people. Bali's inhabitants all spoke the same language and had been exposed to written language for centuries.

In Bali, they were surrounded by art, music, dance—the many expressions of ceremony. Even with the help of two American collaborators and three Balinese assistants, there was too much material to record. "On feast days," wrote Mead, "the roads are crowded with processions of people in silks and brocades, walking in easily broken lines behind their orchestras and their gods; gods represented by temporary minute images seated in small sedan chairs; gods represented by images made of leaves and flowers; gods which are masks or bits of old relics. With the processions mingle groups of people grimed from work, hurrying lightly beneath their heavy loads; and theatrical troupes, their paint and fine costumes tucked away in little bundles, trudge wearily behind the two-man mask, the patron Dragon (*Barong*) who walks quietly with covered face."[25]

For Mead, the basis of anthropological work was comparison. After their experience in Bali, both she and Bateson felt they needed material from another culture that had been gathered with the same attention to detail. They chose to return to New

A young Balinese girl in an itinerant troupe of dancers from Tiga performing the role of a prince, Bajoeng Gede, May 12, 1937. "The little dancers," wrote Margaret Mead, "are put into trance by incense and singing. . . . Only after the gods have entered them and they are in trance, may the sacred headdresses and sacred bibs be placed upon them. If, in this sacred state, they go from one temple to another, they are carried on men's shoulders, and part of the dance is danced standing on a man's shoulders." Photograph by Gregory Bateson

Ancestor's Return

Anthropology is changing even as the world changes.

—Margaret Mead

In her final work, Mead confronted head-on the issue that had always presented an obstacle to her studies: cultural change. She had sought culture in some idealized "pure" state; now she confronted a people who had traveled "in the short space of twenty-five years a line of development which it took mankind many centuries to cover."[27]

In 1953, at the urging of colleagues in Australia, Mead returned to Manus Island and revisited the people of Peri village. In the postwar years, they had voluntarily cast aside their old way of life: the ornaments, the native dress, the dog's teeth and shell money, along with the arranged marriages, innumerable taboos, and customs associated with childbirth, puberty, and marriage. In 1947, at the time of the religious outbreak, which they referred to as "The Noise," the people of Peri had literally thrown all their old things into the sea. They had abandoned their water-bound village, moved onto land, and built new houses with kitchens and windows. De-

Guinea, to the Iatmul village of Tambunan on the Middle Sepik River. Bateson had previously done fieldwork among the Iatmul, and he knew the language, while Mead was familiar with the region. Despite problems with the complex language, a lack of native assistants to record material, Bateson's bout with illness, and a drought that forced the people to abandon their ceremonies to go crocodile hunting, the two did manage in six months to accumu-

late important information for comparative studies. "We could contrast the way the Balinese confined drama and action to the theater and maintained their everyday relationships placidly and evenly," wrote Mead, "never allowing children to contend even for a toy, whereas the Iatmul, who struggled and screamed and quarreled in real life, used their artistic performances to introduce moments of static beauty into their more violent lives."[26]

spite her initial shock at these extraordinary developments, Mead felt these changes did not constitute a loss. "The curious thing about what has happened here," she wrote, "is that it is not really supernaturalism at all, but rather a sort of collective assertion of the dignity of man."[28]

The abrupt changes were the results of inexorable pressures—from missionaries, from so-called "cargo cults" that exaggerated the impact of white contact, and from an expanding educational system. To the Manus, the changes seemed to come from within—from a wish to choose whom to marry, where to work, and who would govern their community. This was a bloodless revolution of the imagination.

During her half-century in the field, Mead discovered that it was possible for cultures to be very different and yet share the same world. This was the same conclusion that her mentor, Franz Boas, had come to many years earlier. The one thing a culture could not do was remain static. In the end, the tough-minded Boas proved himself a romantic: in his eyes change was loss. The dwindling of native cultures filled him with pessimism about the fate of human diversity. Margaret Mead,

ever the crusader, came to see change as a natural process, a source of surprise, not despair.

Perhaps the greatest gift that Mead left to the people of Peri was their own cultural legacy, recorded in her words and photographs and the artifacts that she collected in 1928. As the children began to go to school and learned to read and write, her books became a precious record of their past: "The names of the old men who died before they

were born can be supplied with visual images. The changes through which their parents have lived are there before their eyes."[29] Mead wrote those words in 1965, during a short visit to the village, where she was received by old friends and new children alike as an "ancestor." She made her last visit there in 1975. When she died three years later, she was ceremonially mourned for five days by the people of Peri.

Dinosaurs and Mammals:
Countrymen of Bones

*Do you wonder that the paleontologist, absorbed in
contemplation of his splendid edifice, walks a little apart
from the ways of men; that the little personal affairs and
interests of the fleeting present which make up the world
of his fellows, seem to him but geegaws and trifles of no
importance? His field of vision embraces the whole of life.
His time scale is so gigantic that it dwarfs to insignificance
the centuries of human endeavor. And the laws and principles
which he studies are those which control the whole great
stream of life, upon which the happenings of our daily
existence appear as little surface ripples.*

—William Diller Matthew[1]

Giants in the Earth

RULERS OF THE WORLD they lived in, dinosaurs rule the
world of our imagination as well. Above all the creatures that
have ever lived, dinosaurs have the power to inspire fancy and
disturb dreams. Size is one obvious reason. We never fully outgrow our
childhood fascination with anomalies of scale, as Jonathan Swift understood when he created his Gulliver, and dinosaurs are the largest animals
ever to have walked on land. A world populated by such creatures as
"Ultrasaurus," whose hundred-foot length has been inferred from some
crushed vertebrae, seems to defy credibility and reason.

Yet size cannot be the only explanation for dinosaurs' appeal. After all,
our world boasts its giants, albeit aquatic ones—whales, for example. Nor
were all dinosaurs large; some were smaller than turkeys. Their extravagant shapes have certainly added to the mystique. Think of *Stegosaurus*,
with its backbone plates. Such shapes, however, have many rivals for
strangeness. The fossil record has divulged *Platybelodon*, a mastodon with

*Opposite, above: Countrymen of bones:
paleontologists from the American
Museum of Natural History at Bone
Cabin Quarry, Wyoming, 1899. Seated,
left to right, are Walter Granger, Henry
Fairfield Osborn, William D. Matthew;
standing, an unidentified expedition
member, Richard Swann Lull, Albert
Thomson, and Peter Kaisen. Photograph
by Albert Thomson*

*Opposite, below: Paleontologist in the
Department of Vertebrate Paleontology
assembling a nodosaur, a primitive
armored dinosaur, 1936. This may be
the specimen found by Barnum Brown
at one of his favorite sites, the Crow
Indian Reservation in Montana.
Photograph by Julius Kirschner*

an immense shovel-like jaw, and the ever-popular saber-toothed cat. Among living forms, we can contemplate the rhinoceros, the giraffe, the pangolin.

Human beings were well aware of fossils long before they arranged them into dinosaurs. They had been contemplating invertebrate fossils perhaps as far back as Pythagoras. Indeed, there are cave drawings of fossils. Robert Plott, an Englishman, is the first to mention what were probably dinosaur fossils in 1677, but he had no idea of their origin or nature. American Indians almost certainly had found dinosaur bones before that but, as they later expressed it, felt that disturbing the remains of such large beings was profoundly unwise.

The delivery of dinosaurs from the earth to the modern imagination is bound up with the discovery of Western historical time, and with it the sobering recognition of human beings' narrow place on the bank of a vast ocean of the past. The discovery of the dinosaur parallels other acts of nineteenth-century intellectual exploration: The philospher G. W. F. Hegel delivered his influential lectures on the philosophy of history as a dialectical progress in 1823, just about the time Mary Anne Woodhouse Mantell found the teeth of a large herbivorous dinosaur in Sussex, England. Charles Lyell published the first volume of his *Principles of Geology*, which revealed the Earth to be older than any biblical calculations, in 1831, the year Darwin set off on the *Beagle* on a voyage that would change the way human beings think about life in time. In 1841, the British anatomist Sir Richard Owen coined the term *dinosaur*, meaning "terrible lizard." The first American dinosaur fossil was excavated near

Haddonfield, New Jersey, in 1858, and just a year later there appeared Darwin's *Origin of Species*, which authoritatively removed human beings from any Garden of Eden. Karl Marx was already at work on *Das Kapital*, the great synopsis of history's material (and secular) laws. In this context, the dinosaurs testified to the reality of a world that had disappeared an incomprehensibly long time ago but was still somehow present. Human beings were latecomers, backward-gazers on events not of their making. Nature was capable of shuffling the deck thoroughly—indeed, of clearing the table and beginnning a new game.

Yet the fascination with dinosaurs did not take hold immediately. When Philadelphian Charles Willson Peale and later the Englishman Waterhouse Hawkins put dinosaurs on display in the early and mid-nineteenth century, both drew large crowds at first. The public, however, soon lost interest. These monsters seemed mere antediluvian curiosities. Dinosaurs only caught on after the turn of the century, when the American Museum of Natural History began to reconstruct them from its fossil bone pile, which was the largest in the world. The Museum gave the world its first view of *Tyrannosaurus*, *Apatosaurus* (formerly *Brontosaurus*), and *Stegosaurus*, among others, with a lifelike art never before seen. By the 1930s, the Museum's dinosaur expeditions were so famous that newspaper articles about curator Barnum Brown's discovery of a trove of fossils on a remote ranch in Wyoming drew hundreds of visitors to the site each week. The bones tell a story—the only story that has come down to us—about life in the past. That story has

been revised considerably in the retelling over the last few decades, but the creatures have only strengthened their grip on the collective imagination. With dinosaurs, knowledge seems only to deepen wonder.

Bones of Contention

Fossil bones are the major source of information about dinosaurs and extinct mammals. Since dinosaurs thrived for at least 160 million years (they did not all die out) and ranged from the Arctic Circle to Antarctica, there are plenty of bones lying around. The Museum contains by rough estimate 50 million bones of all kinds, many of which are dinosaur and mammal fossils. The Earth continues to give up its primordial dead in remote places such as the southern Sahara of Africa and the Gobi of Mongolia (see page 71) Yet what scientists have gathered in this and all museums around the world is only a small fraction of what once lay underground, just as the six hundred-plus species so far identified merely hint at the probable diversity of dinosaurs. To come down to us, the bones must have been captured in layers of sediment that under pressure from subsequent deposits eventually hardened into rock. In the process, calcium phosphate in bone was replaced by minerals, especially silica. Left uncovered and exposed to

water and air, the bones would have disintegrated. They must also have survived geological instability, which can expose, scatter, and smash them beyond hope of reconstruction.

It may seem self-evident, but it is worth pointing out that the older a dinosaur, the less likely that its bones have survived. That skews knowledge and chastens scientists' interpretation of the so-called fossil record. The three ages of dinosaurs—the Triassic (245–208 million years ago); the Jurassic (208–145 million years ago, the period of huge four-footed creatures); and the Cretaceous (165–45 million years ago, the age of *Tyrannosaurus*)—span an immense period. Museums have lots of Cretaceous fossils, fewer but spectacular ones from the Jurassic, and almost none from the most important period when dinosaurs emerged. Miraculously, a few dinosaur bones

have turned up in peat bogs, not yet fossilized.

The other problem for students of fossils is access. One might find dinosaur bones in the rain forest, but the effort to get at and retrieve them would not likely be worth the trouble. The promising areas, where the strata of hundreds of millions of years lie exposed, are broadly known. The Earth's geology displays a wonderful consistency, enabling scientists to "read" sites in diverse and distant locations based on known formations of rock strata. Productive sites can attract crowds, and in the past this has led to claim and counterclaim. The Museum's

collection of dinosaur fossils was born in such rivalry, but the area soon proved rich enough to bury all the bones of contention.

Principals of the duel were two of the greatest paleontologists, Othniel C. Marsh and Edward Drinker Cope, and the "second" left standing after the combatants had fallen was the future president of the American Museum of Natural History, Henry Fairfield Osborn. Both Marsh, a Yale professor, and Cope, a wealthy Philadelphian, were driven scientists who used their fortunes to seek and secure fossils. Some they collected themselves; some they obtained with the help of

To prospect for fossils along the Red Deer River in Alberta, Canada, in 1911, paleontologist Barnum Brown had constructed a barge twelve by thirty feet. It could carry eight tons and was steered by two oars. Loaded with bones, boats were often in a precarious position when the river ran fast. From a hand-colored lantern slide by Barnum Brown

paid fossil collectors—entrepreneurs who moved from site to site, digging for any institution or person willing to pay. Not only did these hired hands do the prospecting and spadework, but some, such as David Baldwin and John Bell Hatcher, possessed considerable acumen in identifying dinosaur species. They knew what to look for. With their help, Cope and Marsh amassed collections that ultimately formed a foundation for two museums: Yale's Peabody Museum of Natural History and the American Museum of Natural History. They classified hundreds of species and genera of dinosaurs and extinct mammals. Cope alone published fourteen hundred scientific papers.

Their rivalry had personal roots: professional posturing by both quickly dissolved a tentative early friendship. Marsh, for example, took barely concealed pleasure in pointing out to the scientific community that one of Cope's reconstructions, of an extinct marine reptile (reconstructed on paper, that is, for displays were rare), sported a head at the end of its tail. Cope, on the other hand, bought a controlling interest in a scientific journal in order to rush his names and descriptions of fossil animals into print first.

Territory touched off the tinder of competition. In 1871 Marsh traveled into the Bridger Basin of southwestern Wyoming and Utah and unearthed remains of an impressive creature from the early age of mammals, the uinathere. Cope followed in 1872 and set up camp in the region. The pattern would be repeated with obsessive regularity. The two acted a similar scene, in reversed roles, near Carson City, Colorado, with the remains of Jurassic dinosaurs as the prize. Neither man ever

Mr. Frick's Mammals

Think of the paleontologist as a modern Noah. When he lowers the gangplank of his ark, which is the ancient Earth, out walks a gallery of creatures saved from the Flood. Included are dinosaurs, to be sure, but just as strange and compelling are the fun house–mirror versions of our own fauna, the extinct mammals—great-tusked mastodons, huge-fanged cats, diminutive tapir-like horses, heavy-headed wolves, and polyglot creatures like the Hemicyon, *with the proportions of a tiger and the teeth of a dog. Of all the Noahs at the American Museum of Natural History, Childs Frick built the biggest ark.*

Son of Henry Clay Frick, who gave New York City the fabulous Frick Collection of art, Childs Frick was the family black sheep. Instead of going into business and increasing the family fortune, he spent it studying extinct mammals and collecting their remains. The Museum's reputation in vertebrate paleontology rests as much on its collection of mammals as on its dinosaurs, and Frick, quietly, patiently, became the most important single figure behind the mammal fossil collection. In 1909 and 1911, the recent Princeton graduate led game-hunting expeditions to Africa to collect specimens for the Carnegie Museum and the National Museum of Natural History. On those trips he glimpsed an important truth: the animal forms we see today are the living expressions of a vast and varied past. He gave up hunting and started digging.

The people from whom he could learn the most were at the Museum—Osborn, Granger, Matthew, and Brown. Beginning in 1916, Frick began to sponsor expeditions to the western United States and to lead his own. The itinerary soon expanded to India, Burma, South America, and eventually China, where Frick arranged for collecting after Roy Chapman Andrews had given up. On some expeditions, he took his entire family. He hired astute collectors, who worked with him for

owned any of the land he worked; their sense of field decorum was highly subjective.

In the late 1870s, they both turned their attention to a rock outcrop in southeastern Wyoming called Como Bluff. It is part of a larger geological formation known as the Medicine Bow Anticline. Union Pacific workers had found fossils there and sent specimens to Marsh. Typically, Marsh swore them to secrecy and sent in crews. Secrecy was a vain hope;

Cope himself soon followed and set up camp only a few hundred yards away. Cope tried to hire Marsh's collectors and went so far as to invade his digs, or so Marsh insisted. The site was certainly worth fighting for: Como Bluff turned out to be a mother lode of early mammals and Jurassic dinosaurs, yielding the plated *Stegosaurus*, the long-necked *Diplodocus*, and the fierce *Allosaurus*.

One of Cope's acolytes and de-

decades. In 1931, no fewer than seven Museum expeditions occupied the field under his sponsorship.

The invaluable collections poured in. Frick established a laboratory at the Museum, studied the fossils, and wrote about them. He was even made an honorary curator of vertebrate paleontology. Yet Frick, who was also an active conservationist, kept such a low profile that many in the Museum did not recognize him. In 1937, when Frick's wife felt that road traffic made commuting to New York City too dangerous, he built a laboratory on his Long Island estate, where he could work on specimens transported from the Museum. After his death in 1965, one of the greatest private fossil collections ever assembled was officially donated to the Museum, where most of it already resided. Frick's legacy endures in other ways. When the team from the Museum returned to the Gobi of Mongolia in the 1990s, it relied on support from an endowment created decades before by the gifted amateur, who would have enjoyed the bone hunt.

Marsh's position with the Survey.[2]

If this seems a bit sordid for science, it conveys the flavor of the time. Marsh, Cope, and the anatomist Joseph Leidy, who had begun to identify dinosaurs well before the two competitors, created a scientific discipline, but they did not establish its etiquette. It is no wonder that fossil hunting—and fossil naming—was territorial. For one thing, the Wild West was still wild, and collectors could find their lives on the line. When Marsh went west in 1870, he was escorted part of the way by Buffalo Bill Cody, who listened to his campfire stories of extinct life with interested skepticism. When Cope went west in 1876, he was informed en route of the Battle of Little Big Horn but proceeded undaunted.

Intense competition persisted for decades. In 1910, Barnum Brown led a Museum expedition into the fossil-rich cut of the Red Deer River in Alberta, Canada, which had been prospected by the Canadian Geological Survey decades before. The Canadian National Museum, annoyed at being "scooped," responded by sending an entire family of famous collectors, the Sternbergs, to the site. Although the official version is one of friendly competition, Brown and Osborn were furious and redoubled their efforts to secure the best possible specimens. Turnabout is fair play, however, and the American Museum of Natural History was happy to purchase from the

fenders was young Henry Fairfield Osborn, who had visited the scientist while still a Princeton undergraduate. In 1890, as a new department chairman at the Museum, Osborn bought from his ill and destitute mentor Cope's priceless collection of fossil mammals. Cope had lost his fortune to bad investments and retreated from the fossil-hunting field, but not from the war. He was engaged in his last skirmish with Marsh, conducted largely in the

press. Marsh proved the Pyrrhic victor, using his position with the U.S. Geological Survey to cut off publication funds to Cope and then to deny him access to fossils he had collected. Osborn resolved to pick up where Cope had left off, in more ways than one. Osborn escalated the war with Marsh, attempting first to hire away one of the best of his disgruntled collectors, John Bell Hatcher, discoverer of *Stegosaurus*, and later to sabotage

Sternbergs one of the prize trophies of that war, a nearly complete skeleton of the tyrannosaur-like *Albertosaurus*.

Today the procedures of scientific publication, discussion, and collaboration are codified, but with new knowledge reopening nearly every question about dinosaurs, from their color to their intelligence (or presumed lack thereof), debates have sometimes taken on an in-your-face quality that would not have surprised Osborn and Brown.

After acquiring Cope's collection, the ambitious Osborn planned a program to collect fossils. He sought first of all mammals from the Cretaceous, rare trophies from the final period of dinosaur dominance, when mammals were small. Dinosaurs were a secondary priority. The first expedition, launched in 1897, headed straight for Como Bluff, Wyoming—Marsh's territory. Appropriately, it was led by a former Cope collector, Jacob L. Wortman, who already had directed successful Museum searches for fossil mammals. The revolving crew of Wortman's early expeditions to Wyoming reads like a *Who's Who* of modern paleontology: Osborn and Wortman, of

course, but also Walter Granger, Albert Thomson, and Peter Kaisen, a trio who later won fame with Museum expeditions to Mongolia, and a young man who eventually earned the nicknames "Mr. Bones" and "the Dinosaur Finder"—Barnum Brown.

All these men were gifted and to some degree eccentric (the word is redundant when applied to paleontologists). Granger never finished high school and was always ready to put down his pick to go duck hunting, but he discovered tiny fossil skulls in Mongolia that hold a key to understanding the evolution of mammals. Wortman left the Museum in 1899 to take the second most important fossil job (after Osborn's), as head of vertebrate paleontology at Pittsburgh's Carnegie Museum. When he left that job, it was to run a drugstore. Brown's sartorial fastidiousness—he was always impeccably turned out at a dig; he even wore a fur coat—might make him appear a figure of fun to modern eyes, but he was a great fossil hunter and leader, and he continued to make discoveries throughout his long life. He also unearthed the Museum's first dinosaur fossil: at the end of a lean initial summer at Como

Bluff, Osborn and Brown were prospecting together when they struck paydirt, the vertebrae of a gigantic *Diplodocus*. With this discovery, a new age had begun for the Museum and for the imagination of the American public— the Age of the Dinosaurs.

The success proved deceptive; Como Bluff had given up all its easy treasures to Marsh and Cope. The group prospected farther north along the Medicine Bow Anticline. Here they discovered a site of which legends are made. A sheepherder had built a hut entirely of gigantic dinosaur bones, and the fossils poked out of the ground like strange blooming plants. They called their dig Bone Cabin Quarry. This and another nearby Medicine Bow quarry yielded hundreds of tons of bones. Granger unearthed one of the most complete *Apatosaurus* skeletons ever found. The harvest proved so rich that the Museum needed railroad cars to cart it back. Trustee J. P. Morgan obliged with two. As a participant in the Marsh-Cope feud, Osborn prudently left someone behind to "winter over" and guard the site.

The process of retrieving fossils is by turns arduous, tedious, and delicate. First, the fossils have to be found. Then the topsoil (called overburden) must be removed—either by whisk broom or by bulldozer, if a rock layer intervenes. The top surfaces of the protruding brittle bones are shellacked to insure they do not splinter, swathed in paper, cloth, or burlap, and coated with plaster. Then the hard part begins: a block containing the fossils must be freed from the underlying stone. Excess is chipped away until the block resembles a stone mushroom. The "stem" is cut and the whole slab flipped over. After this side receives its plaster jacket, the

whole is then packed for shipment. When Granger finished unearthing the *Apatosaurus* thigh bone, it weighed five hundred seventy pounds. (The mule and horse teams pulling the wagons in early photographs do not look at all pleased to be furthering the cause of science.)

Museum teams worked the Medicine Bow quarries for six years, sometimes well into the winter, when temperatures dropped to −40°F and snow buried the fossils. Such rigors, however, could not extinguish the romance of this pioneering work. Forty years later, when Brown revisited Como Bluff with his junior colleague Roland T. Bird, he wistfully recalled how he looked forward to the passing of the Union Pacific train. "Every day the engineer on the morning train threw off my mail as he went by. He'd always toot to let me know he was coming."[3]

While Museum crews were digging at Medicine Bow, at the turn of the century, Cope died, and Osborn purchased the second part of his collection, of fossil reptiles. Added to the material arriving from the West, the Cope collection made the Museum a great fossil repository. Marsh had

already reconstructed dinosaurs with great accuracy, but only on paper. Osborn used the Museum's financial resources to add the other two dimensions. "What you have seen is not Fine Paleontology but Fine Art,"[4] objected the head of the National Museum of Natural History to Osborn's earlier restoration of a fossil mammal. To the contrary, Osborn's goal went beyond aesthetics or entertainment.

In the Museum's reconstruction of *Apatosaurus*, completed in 1905, the public could see the concrete state of current scientific knowledge. It was daring for scientists as sober as Osborn, William Diller Matthew, and Granger to present their ideas in so public an arena. Moreover, it was expensive, requiring artists, preparators, cast makers (most dinosaur exhibits are made of casts, not real bones), and workmen. Extracting the *Apatosaurus* bones from the matrix of rock and plaster, reassembling them, and preparing them for mounting took two years. Laboratory work presented its own pitfalls. As a young Museum staff member, R. T. Bird was lending a hand in turning over a gigantic pelvis so it could be cleaned when the matrix split, sending bone fragments all over the floor. The paleontologists frantically swept up the pieces and hid them in drawers. Over the next few months, they cleaned the pieces and glued them back together. Barnum Brown apparently never found out.

The Carnegie Museum unveiled its *Diplodocus* mount in 1904, actually beating New York to the punch. Yet none could match the scale of the New York museum's display halls. It had amassed such a collection that it was able to trade or sell fossils to obtain missing bones or casts. The

"A Continuous Creation"

It is impossible to understand fully the development, substance, impact, and authority of the American Museum of Natural History without coming to terms with the equivocal figure of its president for twenty-five years, Henry Fairfield Osborn. Osborn was born in 1857 in New York City to wealthy parents. He attended Princeton, and in 1876, when he and a group of friends were puzzling over William Paley's Natural Theology, *someone suggested, "Let's go West and collect fossils." Osborn made his first fossil-hunting trip after graduation, to Wyoming. It was partly a game of playing frontiersman, but the satisfaction of bringing back the Princeton Museum's first fossils set him on his course.*

Like the Museum itself, Osborn was a Victorian on the cusp of historic change, which he promoted and resisted simultaneously. A devout Christian, he was committed to scientific inquiry as a means of understanding the natural world. A defender of evolutionary theory, he dogmatically opposed many of its most revolutionary ideas, especially in the emerging domain of genetics. Evolution embodied a purpose, he felt, not simply the soulless recombination of chemicals. He made a number of famous scientific enemies, including the paleontologist O. C. Marsh and the Nobel laureate and genetics pioneer Thomas Hunt Morgan. Osborn spoke the language of his patrons, however, and his will shaped the Museum's scientific study, as well as its exhibition halls and its moralizing education programs.

*History is unkind to those who stand in its way. By 1920, Osborn had become one of the leading scientific figures in America, yet few of his nine hundred forty articles and books are still read, and the most important of them—*The Proboscidae *and his long monograph on ancient rhinoceros-like animals called titanotheres—were written largely by Museum staff. Some, such as* The Evolution of Life, *are so vague and idiosyncratic that even Osborn's most loyal staff members were mystified. Since his death in 1935, everything from his political attitudes to his operating budgets have been questioned. Yet his reputation will likely outlive the criticism because the Museum is still his. He hired one of the finest scientific staffs outside a major university. William Diller Matthew, George Gaylord Simpson, William K. Gregory, and Barnum Brown, among others, elevated vertebrate paleontology into a premier discipline. The fossils they collected have educated millions of people about life before humankind and supplied the current generation of Museum scientists with material to unravel evolutionary mysteries. Above all, Osborn made the Museum a center for the study of evolution, which represented for him the primary scientific challenge of our time. He called it "a continuous creation of life fitted to a continuously changing world. . . . The spiritual principle of evolution is the evidence of beauty, of order, and of design in the daily myriad miracles to which we owe our existence."*

Museum's adult *Barosaurus* is just such a composite, from many sources. Its composition is distinctive; 80 percent is fossil bone. As R. T. Bird once remarked, "If you get enough odds and ends, you can make a dinosaur."[5]

"The Holy Ground"

In contrast, the most famous dinosaur in the Museum, *Tyrannosaurus rex*, is a singular trophy. A large part of it came out of the ground at a place appropriately named Hell Creek. Complete dinosaur skeletons are rare, for time scatters old bones. Carnivorous dinosaurs are especially rare, comprising fewer than three percent of all the dinosaurs found. Only a dozen tyrannosaurs have been discovered, and most are mere fragments. Barnum Brown found two spectacular exceptions. Long ago, the Hell Creek region of the Missouri River in east central Montana lay on the edge of a vast sea that stretched

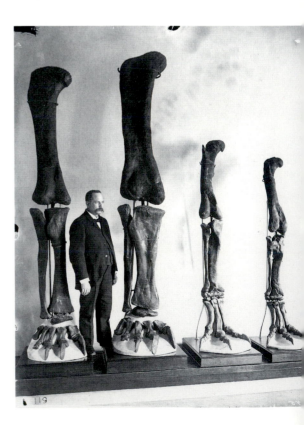

from Canada to Mexico. Many dinosaurs died there, including the horned *Triceratops*, the duck-billed *Anatotitan*, and the king of the tyrant lizards. Brown had received a report of fossils from a highly reliable source, the zoologist W. T. Hornaday, who had been hunting in the area and pho-tographed them. In 1902, Brown went to investigate the site, one hundred thirty miles from the nearest railhead: "Judging by your reports," wrote Osborn, "you are in what Marsh used to call the 'The Holy Ground'; and there is every reason to think . . . you may find something of real value."[6]

Brown searched for more than a month, without much luck, and was nearly ready to give up when he decided to try one more day. The human imagination is richer as a result: "Quarry No. 1 contains the femur, pubes, part of the humerus, three vertebrae, and two indeterminate bones of a large carnivorous dinosaur, not described by Marsh," Brown wrote to Osborn in August. "I have never seen anything like it from the Cretaceous."[7] Three years later, when Osborn published Brown's findings, it was the first time the creature had been completely described.

Brown found the other specimen at Hell Creek six years later. It was not as well preserved as the first, with one exciting exception—it included the finest skull of a carnivorous dinosaur ever found and provides a wealth of information on how these dinosaurs hunted and consumed their prey. The creature was buried deep in the ground. Brown removed it with the only tools he had: pick-axes, brushes, and dynamite.

Hell Creek provided the Museum with samples from both

ends of the fossil spectrum—the familiar as well as the extraordinary. Remains of the horned dinosaur *Triceratops* were everywhere. Over seven years, Brown estimated that he found parts of at least five hundred skulls and countless other bones. Perhaps the name Hell Creek is misleading after all. The diversity of dinosaur remains indicates that the region was more like Eden. Indeed, its fossil record is rich in every kind of primordial creature, from crocodiles and turtles to mammals from the Cretaceous, including marsupials and rodent precursors called multituberculates. Thus, scientists seeking to understand the environment of dinosaurs and mammals at the time of the great dinosaur extinction needed only to go to Hell Creek. Unfortunately, they can no

longer make the trip, for the area now lies under the waters of a reservoir.

Jurassic Park

Museum teams collected steadily, limited only by season and, of course, sponsorship. Barnum Brown was on the move almost constantly for sixty years, and, although expeditions are identified by particular locations, Brown usually directed teams at several sites simultaneously. He was always thinking of the places he wished to visit or return to, and the cross-country car trips to the sites offered plenty of opportunities for digression. Thus, the story of how Brown discovered a "Jurassic park" in 1934 really began many years before and

miles away. In 1927, while Brown was prospecting the Plains states, he and Peter Kaisen traveled along the Big Horn River in south central Montana to the Crow Indian reservation. There he found a small skeleton of a plant-eating dinosaur, *Tenontosaurus*. He returned to the site each year for the next several years, and he and Kaisen unearthed some of the most spectacular and important dinosaurs, including *Microvenator* and *Deinonychus*. The latter was a small, bipedal flesh-eater from the Cretaceous period. It is a treasure because it is small, and small bones rarely survive, and because, on the second toe of its foot, it also sports a raptorial claw, designed for seizing prey. This and other features have led scientists to conclude that it very

likely represents a stage in the evolution of modern birds.

Brown found the creature but never had time to name and describe it officially. This is, alas, a common situation. Preparing and establishing the lineage of a dinosaur can take far longer than excavating it. When the Museum purchased Cope's collection, many of the specimens had never been unwrapped. Important dinosaurs such as *Ornitholestes*, another birdlike creature, nest on the cold shelves in the Museum's basement, awaiting study. As Museum paleontologist Mark Norell remarked, "We have more than we can study, but you can't stop collecting when you have questions that might be answered by specimens you haven't found yet."

Brown would have agreed. While working on the Crow reservation, he was already thinking about another location he wanted to visit in northern Wyoming. In 1932, Brown and company followed the Cretaceous formation down to the edge of the Big Horn Basin. They had heard about a ranch owned by one Barker Howe, whose corral had a gatepost propped up with a bone—a very large bone. Howe took them up a hill behind the house. Poking up through a thick stratum of sandstone were well-preserved parts of what appeared to be two sauropod dinosaurs—not Cretaceous predators but older, four-footed giants from the Jurassic period. They appeared to represent a new species, but there was not enough

Opposite: Hauling out fossils from the Sand Creek area of the Red Deer River, 1914. The undulating plains of Canada's grain belt near Alberta give little hint of the rugged badlands along the river. Photograph by Barnum Brown

time to uncover them before winter set in.

The Great Depression had begun to deplete the Museum's resources, and in order to return, Brown had to scramble for support. He found it with the Sinclair Oil Company. Oil is associated with fossil deposits, albeit fossils of animals much smaller than dinosaurs, and Harry Sinclair was only too glad to supplement his usual prospecting crew with someone as geologically astute as Brown. In return for support, Brown agreed, among other things, to help direct an extensive aerial survey in the company airplane *Diplodocus*, replete with the Sinclair logo—a modified *Apatosaurus*!

When Brown returned to the Howe Ranch in June 1934, "it soon became apparent that, instead of two skeletons, there was a veritable herd of dinosaurs," he wrote, "their skeletal remains crossed, crisscrossed, locked and interlocked, in a confused and almost inextricable manner. To one not acquainted with such deposits, it seemed a bewildering and hopeless confusion."[8] Fully excavated, Howe Quarry yielded more than four thousand bones, comprising at least twenty dinosaurs. Most of them were large sauropods—*Barosaurus*, *Apatosaurus*, and *Camarasaurus*. Retrieving them proved a herculean task. Many of the bones had been shattered, and had they been embedded in hard sandstone rather than clay, some of them would still be there. Articles in newspapers as far away as New York brought hundreds of carloads of visitors each week from all over the United States. Some availed themselves of specimens, at least one of which was returned by the guilt-ridden thief.

The bones lay in such a heap

that it was clear they had not been washed up there from some other location. The animals seemed to have died one on top of another. Scientists still are not certain what happened at Howe Ranch 150 million years ago, just as they are puzzled by other extensive "death assemblages" in Canada and New Mexico. Brown believed that the climate may have changed and begun to dry the vast continental wetlands. Dinosaurs in search of water may have been trapped in the thick, fine-grained mud, and their weight doomed them. Howe Quarry held, in addition, one final treasure—extensive impressions of dinosaur skin.

How R. T. Bird Brought the Brachiosaur Out of the Water

At Howe Quarry, an eager neophyte fossil hunter from Rye, New York, suggested that reconstructing the dinosaurs might be easier if someone made a detailed chart of the quarry. It took Roland T. Bird much longer to complete his voluntary task than he had imagined—more than a month—but it earned him a place as Barnum Brown's protégé. He amply confirmed Brown's confidence. Among other accomplishments, Bird helped bring the sauropods out of the water, where nearly everyone had assumed they lived, and set their feet on land.

All R. T. (as he was called) ever wanted to be was a paleontologist. The younger brother of Museum archaeologist Junius Bird, he was aided and abetted by his father, an accomplished entomologist who spent most of his spare time with the scientists at the Mu-

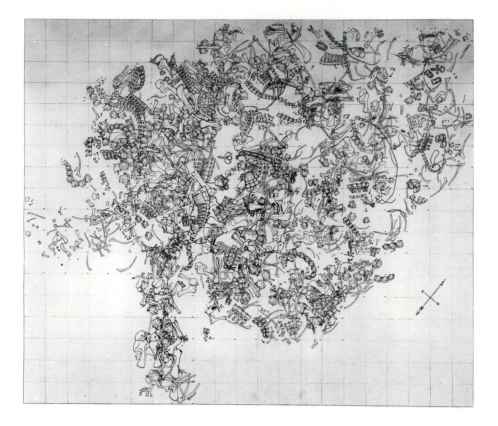

seum. Henry Bird did not bat an eye when, instead of enrolling at college, R. T. chose to ride west on a Harley-Davidson motorcycle outfitted with a makeshift camper. Bird knew next to nothing about geology or fossils in 1932, but he was where he wanted to be—the Petrified Forest of Arizona—and who knew what might turn up:

A clay apron reached out from the base of the nearest butte; it was from such clays as these that the logs of the Petrified Forest had weathered out. I could still see in my mind's eye the great boles lying everywhere, scattered like logs in an old mill pond, truly an Enchanted Forest, showing jasper and quartz and agate interiors, flashing colors of a shattered rainbow. "These trees," the park ranger said, casually as if talking about breakfast, "were alive 200 million years ago. They grew away back in the Age of Reptiles . . . the days of the dinosaurs."

To think that dinosaurs had known the world I could see cross-sectioned in the faces of the weathered buttes! I knew little enough about the great beasts, but the ranger's words . . . I

called to mind the great skeletons in New York's American Museum of Natural History which I had known as a boy; then they weren't associated with anything in the land of the living. But I was *here* now . . . where *they had* been! I looked about, half expecting to find bones lying about.[9]

Bird parked his motorcycle, walked into the Painted Desert, and came out with half of a rare fossil skull. When he could not find the other half, he began to realize how big the desert is. He sent the piece to his father, who took it to Barnum Brown, who said, "Great. A new genus and species of giant amphibian. Where is the other half?" Six months later, Bird went back and, amazingly, found it. For the next year, he crossed Brown's trail in the West, finally ending up at Howe Ranch, where he, too, marveled at the gate prop. Bird did not meet Brown on that trip; he was finally introduced to the paleontologist in New York and, a few months later, in the spring

of 1934, was invited to go digging.

Bird dug dinosaurs with Brown until World War II, some of that time at Howe Quarry, some in Colorado and Wyoming along a geologic formation known as the Mesa Verde, where they hoped to discover elusive dinosaurs from the Triassic. He also helped direct the excavation of a set of dinosaur footprints from the roof of the States Mine in western Colorado. The miners there told him of an abandoned mine nearby that contained a single room covered with fossil impressions of ancient plants. The impressions were so spectacular that the miners called the chamber the "Picture Room." Bird convinced them to take him into the old mine, only to discover that the room had caved in. One beautiful palm impression remained, however, and when Brown heard about it, he insisted, "R. T., we have to have it." Bird talked the miners into helping him excavate the impression, at enormous personal risk. He himself barely avoided a cave-in.

By the end of the 1938 season, however, everyone was frustrated with the poor results of the Mesa Verde search. Bird spent the end of the fall chasing after several chimeras, including another set of dinosaur footprints that turned out to be fakes. His route back to New York took him near the town where the fakes had been purchased, Glen Rose, Texas, and he decided to stop. Real dinosaur footprints were very much in evidence; one was even incorporated into the town bandstand.

Whenever Bird came to a town where there might be fossils, the first thing he did was talk to people. Townspeople in Glen Rose directed him to Ernest Adams, a Rhodes Scholar and local lawyer who was supposed to know about fossils. Adams amused Bird by flaking perfectly shaped glass arrowheads from the bottom of a medicine bottle while they talked. He told Bird that there were many dinosaur tracks along the nearby Paluxy River and recommended a particular stretch of the bank. Sure enough, tracks in the hard limestone ran clearly along and into the river, but Bird was somewhat disappointed. They were from a three-toed dinosaur and not especially rare. As he cleaned the prints, he tossed the river muck into nearby potholes. He had paid no attention to them because they were so large— nearly a yard long. Suddenly, he realized he was looking at an entirely different set of prints, of a huge sauropod.

The Paluxy trackway is one of the most important set of footprints ever discovered, and it continues to provoke creative debate. For one thing, it demonstrated beyond doubt that the very large plant-eaters—Bird thought the tracks were made by an *Apatosaurus*, but *Brachiosaurus* is a better candidate—spent at least part of their time on dry land. Not only could they walk, they could move at a smart pace. It had become almost a dogma that such creatures needed water to support their enormous bulk, and Bird continued to believe they spent most of their lives partially submerged. Such thinking, however, assumes that nature pays more attention to compensating for disadvantages than to testing possible advantages. The trackway helped scientists begin to see sauropods for the marvels of natural engineering they were, with a light, flexible, and strong vertebral structure balanced on four columnar legs, much as a roadway is balanced between the pilings of a suspension bridge.

The path led into a river that regularly rose as much as twenty feet. The Museum had to join forces with the Texas Geological Survey and several other institutions to excavate the site. First a dike was constructed and the water pumped out, widening the riverbank. That revealed even more sauropod footprints, so the crew moved the dikes again. They divided the trackway into sections and chiseled the footprints from the underlying stone. The Museum received the largest

section, seven tons' worth, but it was not reassembled until after World War II. Bird's health had deteriorated by then, but he returned to the Museum to direct the reconstruction.

A compelling moment from 107 million years ago emerged. A herd of a dozen sauropods appeared to have been pursued by at least three carnivores, perhaps allosaurs. So Bird believed, although the carnivores may actually have come hours or even days later. One idea that did not occur to Bird was that the sauropods moved in an organized formation. Just after he discovered the Paluxy tracks, Bird examined another important sauropod trackway, at the Davenport Ranch near San Antonio. In the late 1960s, at the end of Bird's life, the iconoclastic paleontologist Robert Bakker suggested the Davenport group was organized as a true herd, similar to elephants, with younger members on the inside and elders on the outside for protection. A growing body of evidence suggests that the social behavior of dinosaurs is more complex than had been suspected. "A possible point I had never thought of,"[10] remarked Bird, who helped dinosaurs walk out of the past and into the American Museum of Natural History.

The Little Dinosaurs of Ghost Ranch

Modern paleontologists are ancestor worshipers. In trying to establish dinosaur family ties, they seek to identify not only the similarities among coeval groups but, more tellingly, evidence of descent from a common ancestor. Dinosaurs are members of a group called archosaurs, which also includes crocodiles. They are not lizards and probably were not "cold-blooded"—in short, nothing like the familiar picture of sluggish, splay-footed overgrown Gila monsters. The archosaurs began to diverge from so-called reptiles, including lizards and snakes, more than 250 million years ago. Evidence of an archosaur ancestor is the X on a paleontologist's treasure map, but almost as elusive are fossils of the earliest true dinosaurs, from the Triassic period. These fossils can tell us much about the most basic characteristics of dinosaurs, but not many have survived. In 1947, at a place called Ghost Ranch, a team from the American Museum of Natural History found the largest trove ever uncovered.

Arthur Pack's ranch in northern New Mexico, near Abiquiu, took its name from legend. A half-century before, a Spanish sheepherder claimed he had seen coiled on a cliff, waiting to strike, a rattlesnake of thirty feet or more—a ghost reptile, he averred. The true ghosts of Abiquiu, however, proved to be of another kind. In the 1870s, a collector for both Cope and Marsh, David Baldwin, had found bones of a small primitive dinosaur he named *Coelophysis*. So fragmentary were his specimens that scientists have since disputed his claim to have identified anything from them. Yet as late as 1947, they still constituted the only evidence of the "pocket-sized" dinosaur. Brown and Bird had had little success finding Triassic dinosaurs, but Edwin Colbert, Brown's successor at the Museum, thought he might have more luck if he followed Baldwin's lead in New Mexico, especially since a team visiting the ranch from the University of Chicago had found a phytosaur, a large crocodile-like archosaur from the Triassic.

At first Colbert had no luck. Then his colleague George Whitaker found a handful of tiny claws. As with the mammal teeth found in the Gobi, it is amazing the small bits of bone survived or were recognized. The topsoil layer proved so thick, however, that Pack agreed to lend the team a bulldozer and a crew to plow it away. "When the entire bone layer within the limits of the quarry was exposed, we were stirred with mixed emotions," wrote Colbert, "joy at such a rich deposit and dismay at the prospect of trying to get the material out of the quarry and to the Mu-

seum. The bone layer was almost a solid mass of dinosaurs."[11]

During the seasons of 1947 and 1948, the Museum team unearthed more than a dozen intertwined skeletons of *Coelophysis bauri*, in a remarkable state of preservation for Triassic fossils. Represented were adults and juveniles, an entire life progression, ranging in size up to six feet long. The sharp-toed, two-legged walker resembled a large ground bird, an analogy that points up how long and continuous may have been the path of avian evolution. No other kinds of fossils were found nearby. This group more than likely died together and in isolation, possibly near a stream-

bed. What killed them so suddenly? Had they massed together, panicked, and drowned? Deposits of other dinosaurs in Canada and Africa show similar patterns of assembly and mortality. Had a volcano's gases suffocated them? Did they die by disease? Like so many other questions about dinosaurs, scientists still do not have answers.

Open Questions

Dinosaurs lived and died so long ago that the evidence is frustratingly sketchy. The blanks leave considerable room for speculation. Yet we know far more about dinosaurs than ever before, as knowledge from a wide range of fields, from ecology to infectious diseases to genetics, is being brought to bear on the study of fossils. The results are eye-opening. The Museum's reconstruction of an eighty-foot *Barosaurus lentus*, installed in the Theodore Roosevelt Rotunda in 1991, does something that would have surprised Osborn and Brown. It rears up on its hind legs to protect its young from attack. Although there is no way of knowing whether the dinosaurs behaved this way, the display reflects changes in thinking about dinosaur physiology and social behavior. The American Museum of Natural History has emerged as both a provocative and a circumspect authority, insisting on the necessity of hard evidence, discouraging wild scenarios, but encouraging imaginative conclusions.

This has been the Museum's educational role from the time of its first dinosaur exhibit. Nearly a century ago, a Museum artist, Charles R. Knight, depicted a rearing sauropod in one of his most famous paintings, and the Museum mounted the carnivo-

rous *Albertosaurus* not as a tail-dragging Frankenstein but as a swift-running predator. In its recent Museum reconstruction, *Tyrannosaurus* has been similarly liberated.

The dawn of a new day for dinosaurs sheds a bright light on perennial questions. The result is not always certainty, but always a richer image of life's complexity. To take the most obvious example, we do not know what dinosaurs looked like. In 1908, the Museum purchased a rare dinosaur mummy of *Edmontosaurus* from the collector Charles Sternberg. Even with its fossilized skin, scientists still can only guess about such features as musculature and skin color. Here the dinosaur family tree becomes very important. Old genealogies placed dinosaurs closer to lizards, and analogy doomed them to sartorial dullness—browns, greens, and grays. As early as 1860, however, scientists recognized skeletal similarities between some dinosaurs and birds, and recent discoveries by the Museum, most notably in the Gobi, have reinforced the connection. Such a lineage suggests the possibility of a wide range of color schemes, since color would likely have been important both for species and mate recognition. Circumstantial evidence is suggestive: the location of eye sockets clearly indicates that some dinosaurs saw in stereo, as do birds and people. Birds also see in color. If, as scientists believe, some dinosaurs had brains similar to those of modern birds, they recognized colors, too. It is unlikely that so important a capability served no purpose or had no colorful object to recognize.

Dinosaurs have been popularly thought of as intellectually handicapped. Enormous bodies and small heads seemed to equal terminal stupidity. Some paleontolo-

The Name Game

The Dinosaur Encyclopedia *lists more than one hundred names no longer in use. This does not mean that creatures have disappeared from museums; rather, many specimens once thought to be dinosaurs have been reclassified, and many legitimate dinosaurs have had their names altered. This name game reflects, above all, the changing face of knowledge about a field where much is still unknown.*

There are rules, of course. All names have two parts; the first denotes a genus, the second the particular species. The names are usually derived from Latin or Greek roots, and the person who first describes a new kind of fossil has the privilege of naming it. A name without a published description is not an official name. Barnum Brown did not have time to publish descriptions of many fossils he discovered and named, including an important birdlike dinosaur "Daptosaurus." The serviceable appellation was elbowed aside decades later by John Ostrum's Deinonychus anthiroppus. *Names may describe a significant feature of the creature, the place where it was collected, or more imaginative attributes—* Tyrannosaurus rex, *for example, means "king of the tyrant lizards." Dinosaurs (and new species of all other creatures) may also bear the name of the discoverer. Dinosaurs and extinct mammals have been named after Roy Chapman Andrews, Edwin Colbert, Walter Granger, and Peter Kaisen, among other Museum scientists.*

The name game has produced some notable losers. In 1877, paleontologist O. C. Marsh described a specimen of a gigantic four-footed herbivorous dinosaur, which he called Apatosaurus. *Two years later, he described another similar giant,* Brontosaurus *(thunder lizard). They turned out to be the same species, so the later name was stripped of its italics and demoted to the popular lexicon, where it has persisted because of its descriptive élan. Indeed, the learned doctors often disagreed about nomenclature, as revealed in the following missive of December 16, 1924, from William Diller Matthew to his boss Osborn:*

gists thought that dinosaurs such as *Stegosaurus* must have had second brains in their tails and that their lack of mental capacity prevented them from "adapting" to a changing environment. The relation of brain size to body size, however, is not an infallible measure of neurologic capability. Nor can scientists confidently calculate either body size or brain size from fossils. Many dinosaurs might have been smaller and their brains larger than is generally thought. When such ratios are revised more realistically it turns out that, with some notable exceptions, dinosaurs probably did not have unusually small brains. The question then becomes, What could dinosaur brains think about? The braincases of some dinosaur families—dromaeosaurs, for instance—suggest that what they

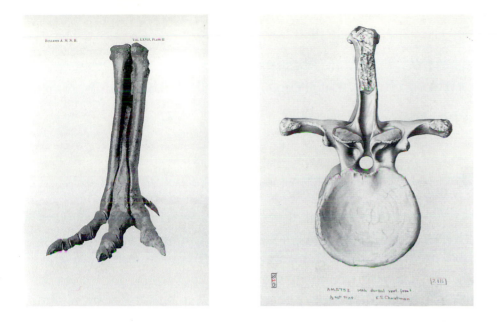

At the luncheon the other day you happened to allude to your new genus Velociraptor as meaning "swift seizer," or words to that effect. May I suggest that the meaning as thus compounded would be "seizer of the swift." Swift seizer would be Raptor velox,—not compounded. I do not think it would be good Latin to compound it; the language does not lend itself to compounds of this type with the facility that Greek does. There is somewhat of a parallel difference between English and German; the latter compounds terms much more fluently. As a consequence the Englishman, when he wants to compound words, is very apt to resort to a foreign language for his roots and then anglicize them,—e.g., telephone. The German uses his own language,—Fernsprecher. Similarly, the Latin writer who desired to coin a new term by compounding roots, was very apt to turn to Greek for his roots and then latinize the resultant compound.

The conventions regarding scientific names date back, as you know, to a time when scientific descriptions were written in Latin as the common language of the learned. The convention that the generic name should be derived from Greek roots rests, so far as it is sound, upon the above relations of the two languages. It is far from being an universal convention; nevertheless, it does have some application in the case of Velociraptor, which probably is the reason why Doctor Bather instinctively took exception to the name, and then, I suppose, cast about for a reason, which he intimates himself is not a very strong one.

Of course, the name is perfectly sound according to the rules of nomenclature. But this little kink rather interested me when I came to think it over. The way the matter came up at the luncheon, I thought it not quite courteous to make the comment just then.

contained were similar in complexity to the brains of primitive modern birds.

Beginning in the early 1970s, the idea of "warm-blooded" dinosaurs began to gain ground and now threatens to become a new dogma. Evidence is stubbornly inconclusive. Lizards and crocodiles are amazingly frugal users of energy. They vary their body temperature according to their activity level and derive heat energy from their environment (ectothermy). By contrast, "warm-blooded" (endothermic) animals such as birds keep a constant body temperature, dependent on their internal chemical activity, their metabolism. Birds may have achieved endothermy before they became feathered, but thus far, scientists do not know when. Analysis of fossil-bone structure reveals that many dinosaurs may have been endothermic, but others appear to have been more like lizards. Scientists also deduce endothermy from inferred levels of dinosaur activity, in behaviors such as hunting, herding, and migration. With high metabolic rates, endotherms such as mammals are active. So, too, are birds. The physiology of some birdlike dinosaurs suggests they were very active. More definitive statements than these, however, are pure speculation.

The transcendent question is not about dinosaurs but rather their disappearance. Dinosaurs as we know them first appeared on Earth at least 225 million years ago. For the next 160 million years they diversified and dispersed over the globe. They swam, walked, ran, and flew, nibbled the tops of trees, and swiped small eggs. They herded together and probably hunted together. In terms of biological success, they did, indeed, rule the Earth. Then, 65 million years ago, dinosaurs ceased appearing in the fossil record. No one knows exactly why they disappeared, but for as long as people have been studying them, they have been blaming the dinosaurs for their own demise. Antievolutionists of an earlier century saw in patterns of extinction God's rough drafts, crumpled and tossed aside until He got it right and produced a world fit for human beings. Some scientists, including Henry Fairfield Osborn, insisted that species and even genera had life spans, eventually growing "old" and losing the ability to adapt and compete. In a more sophisticated version of this idea, dinosaurs were said to be "overspecialized," that is, so closely fitted to particular environments that any change could prove fatal.

Dinosaurs were the most successful large animals the Earth has ever seen and admirably adaptive. To kill them off must have taken a truly cataclysmic event. Or did it? Assuming that dinosaurs are the direct ancestors of modern birds, they are still very much with us in more than ten thousand bird species. Yet somehow this fact fails to satisfy. The more scientists seek an explanation for the disappearance of nonavian dinosaurs, however, the more elusive becomes the catastrophe. For one thing, the "great dying" may have taken as long as 10 million years, a span in which slow developments such as the depletion of particular dinosaur populations could have occurred. Flying reptiles and sea creatures were especially hard hit, but that may have happened 8 million years before the end of the Cretaceous dinosaurs. Moreover, the true giants such as *Apatosaurus* had already died out in the Jurassic period, 210 million years ago. Perhaps the Cretaceous "catastrophe" was a gradual change in the position of the continents, the retreat of the seas, and an intolerable change in temperature. If so, then temperature-sensitive creatures such as turtles and frogs should also have died, but there is no evidence they did.

Volcanoes present an attractive villain, but they, too, would have killed with less discrimination.

The American Museum of Natural History in the Field:
Dinosaurs and Fossil Mammals

Bridger Basin Expedition—1902   *In the 1870s and 1880s, E. D. Cope and O. C. Marsh collected and described extinct mammals from the early age of mammals, the Eocene period. Especially fascinating to Museum scientists were the titanotheres, which evolved from doglike creatures to massive rhinoceros relatives. No one, however, had systematically described the strata in which these or other mammal fossils appeared. The Museum sent Walter Granger and William Diller Matthew into the Bridger Basin of Wyoming to collect specimens and place them in geologic time. Based on their detailed work, Henry Fairfield Osborn was able to publish correlations between fauna and the known geologic horizons, in effect providing paleontologists a handbook for determining the distribution of species in time.*

Egypt Expedition—1907–8   *Henry Fairfield Osborn became interested in reports that British colleagues had unearthed bones of animals new to science in the desert of Fayum, west of Cairo and one hundred miles south of the Mediterranean. The area had once been the shore of the sea, and, even earlier, it had been underwater. Many of the discoveries were of ancient sea creatures. With the diplomatic assistance of President Theodore Roosevelt, an expedition led by Walter Granger was welcomed in Cairo. Excavations in the Fayum produced some of the most unusual fossils ever seen. The upper strata, 35 to 38 million years old, held the skull of the earliest known elephant,* Moertherium, *and an unknown rhino-like animal with huge horns, which was named* Arsinoitherium, *after an Egyptian queen. At a deeper level, representing the first period of the age of mammals, the team found primitive whales, indicating that long ago, mammals had already adapted to watery environments.*

Alberta, Canada, Expedition—1910–15   *The Red Deer River cuts a gorge through central Alberta exposing some of the richest fossil-bearing strata in the world. The wealth and variety of its dinosaurs is breathtaking. Here, Museum expeditions led by Barnum Brown found an almost perfect specimen of an ostrich-like* Struthiomimus, *and a spectacular horned dinosaur* Styracosaurus, *of which the Museum has the only mounted specimen. A* Corythosaurus *came out of the ground with some fossilized skin and tendons preserved. Although dinosaurs were discovered along the river in the 1880s, the true wealth of the region was unknown until a Canadian rancher visiting the Museum convinced Barnum Brown that there were tons of bones to be found.*

They were not easy to retrieve, however. Most of them were weathering out of steep river canyons and in nearby badlands that had

In 1912, at a spot three hundred feet above the Red Deer River in Alberta, Canada, the Museum team found a skull of the armored dinosaur Ankylosaurus, indicated by the pickax. To get at the rest of the skeleton, they had to blast away the side of the hill. From a hand-colored lantern slide by Barnum Brown

scarcely been explored. Brown, Peter Kaisen, and an intrepid group of paleontologists mounted the first dinosaur expedition to the region. They prospected along the river in a flat-bottomed boat, powered only by two oars, stopping to excavate promising sites. The teams worked under harsh conditions, sometimes on impossibly steep inclines. Floods inundated various digs, yet they managed to excavate so many fossils that at times the boat was in danger of sinking.

The astonishing state of preservation went hand-in-hand with a mystery Brown was to confront several times in his career: the apparent mass death of a large number of dinosaurs. It remains an enigma to scientists today.

Chinese Academy of Sciences–American Museum of Natural History Joint Research Venture—1982–91 *The desire to reestablish joint work in China motivated the Institute of Vertebrate Paleontology and Paleoanthropology (IVPP) of the Chinese Academy of Sciences to visit the American Museum of Natural History in 1980. The two institutions found they both had collections from the Shanxi Province and a common interest in reinvestigating a region that had yielded a spectacular four-million-year record of mammalian history, which included the initiation of bipolar glaciation and the Ice Age cycles. Led by Richard Tedford of the Museum and Zhanxiang Qui (IVPP), parties of U.S. and Chinese scientists and students were in the field for four seasons. They acquired many new fossils, conducted geological work, and used paleomagnetic techniques to date the deposits. The fossil record showed the response of the fauna to climatic change, including extinction, evolution, and the immigration of foxes, wolves, horses, camels, and mastodons from North America into eastern Asia. The new collections are the property of China but are on loan for study to the Museum.*

The high content of the radioactive element iridium in the boundary clay marking the end of the dinosaur age has suggested to many scientists an extraterrestrial culprit, a meteorite crashing into the Earth, kicking up dust, darkening the sun, wiping out plants, chilling the air—a nuclear winter without the bomb. Scientists think they have identified the crater, a vast depression called Chixulub, discovered in the early 1990s off the Yucatán peninsula of Mexico. Perhaps it was not a meteorite but a comet, or a barrage of comets, that caused the cataclysm, or did disease turn the Earth into a "hot zone" for dinosaurs, as Robert Bakker believes?

The insoluble problem is that the fossil record is not very precise. Even the fossil sequences nearest in time and most clearly defined offer a record as difficult to read as the want ads of a newspaper from the opposite side of a gymnasium. The Cretaceous strata define intervals of millions of years when the events may have taken place within only a thousand years, or a hundred, or even fewer. This poor resolution spurs scientists to return to the field, to what R. T. Bird once called the "fascinating boredom" of fossil hunting. Just as they seek the first dinosaur, they seek also the last, and the next to last. Paleontology is a remarkable act of contrition and homage to species that had to vanish before their chroniclers and eulogizers could come into being.

Biodiversity and Evolution:
A Knowledge Divine

When I affirm that the knowledge of beasts is divine, I mean no other than the right and perfect description of their names, figures, and natures.
 —Edward Topsell, *The History of Four-Footed Beasts* (1607)

For all that moveth doth in change delight.
 —Edmund Spenser, "Cantos of Mutabilitie" (1595)

And I brought you into a plentiful country, to eat the fruit thereof and the goodness thereof; but when ye entered, ye defiled my land and made mine heritage an abomination.
 —Jeremiah 1:6

View from the Emergency Room

HUMAN BEINGS have split the atom, walked on the moon, and deciphered the code of their own origins. All around them, however, in the narrow zone they share with other forms of life, something is going terribly wrong:

• When young Frank Chapman, later curator of birds at the American Museum of Natural History, began studying the bird life of Florida in 1886, the state was "the Mecca of American ornithologists . . . possibly not equalled [in interest] by that of any other part of the world."[1] In 1904, Chapman had the cheerless privilege of viewing perhaps the last wild band of Carolina parakeets, a group of thirteen in a nest near Lake Okeechobee. The parakeet had been hunted by orchard keepers as a pest, by bird catchers, plumage sellers, and sportsmen, and its extinction had long been predicted. By 1914, it was gone for good.

• When Leo Miller traveled through the lake region of western Argentina in 1916, "there were ducks everywhere," he wrote. "Black-headed gulls flew back and forth overhead, and cormorants stood on snags, drying their outstretched wings. To shoot birds under such circumstances would be mere slaughter, and the number one can kill is limited only by the amount of ammunition at hand. The natives kill four or five hundred ducks each day during this season, and have done so for years."[2]

• Herbert Lang, one of the leaders of the Museum's Lang-Chapin Expedition (see page 104), spent most of his life in Africa. In an article for a special Africa issue of *Natural History* in 1924, he estimated that the number of elephants killed for ivory between 1913 and 1923 was more than 630,000. He noted that one of the greatest protectors of Africa's game was the tsetse fly, which carries a parasite causing sleeping sickness. Disease alone limited the human presence. Yet this protection proved illusory, for it prompted a call for the extermination of all game that might carry disease-producing microorganisms. As Lang wrote, "The reign of terror came with overwhelming force. A cause that was apparently in the interest of humanity was able to enlist the support of the fanatic."[3] Only strenuous conservation efforts have managed to save elephants and many other African mammals, but they are still threatened by poachers in their preserves.

• When Lamont Curator Lester Short was in Malaysia seeking bird specimens for the Museum in the early 1970s, he came to a state forest where hunting was strictly prohibited. He was unable to secure an exemption as a scientist, and when he next visited the forest, months later, it was gone—burned and clear cut. A few of the woodpeckers he had come to study were still there, however, perched on smoldering stumps, looking for homes that no longer existed.

• Museum entomologist Norman Platnick, one of the world's foremost experts on spiders, had a similar experience. Since the 1970s, he has studied the spiders of temperate forests in Chile, a species-rich habitat that rarely receives publicity as a haven for biodiversity. For the last fifty years, those forests have been destroyed at an alarming rate, including ones where the identifying specimens of several species had been found. "On some occasions, I have had the unpleasant experience of trying to re-collect, at some of my type localities, species I had taken just a few years earlier, only to find that what had been pristine *Nothofagus* [southern beech] forests were just piles of smoking embers."[4]

In the attempt to conserve species, we face, in Norman Platnick's words, a triage situation. So many species in so many different areas of the world are being threatened by so many economic pressures that it is not possible to preserve every species. It is possible to imagine—indeed, it has even been proposed—that scientists might create species banks, in which DNA of a vast variety of living things would be stored, to be reintroduced at some future time to begin the repopulation of previously compromised locales. Life, however, is greater than the sum of its parts.

Saving such groups will not restore biodiversity. Indeed, species cannot be saved except as parts of larger assemblages—their habitats. The losses are mounting; the thirteen parakeets in Chapman's nest can stand for a Noah's ark of lost life. Natural-history museums, however, possess the knowledge to maintain a biodiversity triage desk, essential for sound and economically realistic conservation priorities. The role is implicit in the work they have been doing for more than a century.

The long view is sobering. Like the end of the nursery rhyme about the crooked man, life seems to lead only to "death and death and death indeed." Scientists estimate that 99 percent of all species that have ever lived on Earth are no longer alive. Geology reveals the true dimension of the process of extinction. In the eighteenth century, fossils in the ground hinted at evidence of the world before the biblical Flood;

in the nineteenth century, of a sequence of catastrophes whose profligate wasting of creatures could only be redeemed by the appearance of human beings, the ne plus ultra of creation. In the twentieth century, extinction and the pulse of life's diversification have shown themselves to be inextricably linked. Dates and durations remain sketchy, but what Niles Eldredge, curator of invertebrates at the Museum, calls "biotic Armageddon" has been

going on for at least 500 million years, when 50 percent of all trilobites, the primitive precursors of crustaceans, disappeared from the seas. After that came five more major extinction events, including the decimation of an estimated 96 percent of all species at the end of the Permian period, 245 million years ago, and the demise of all nonavian dinosaurs, 65 million years ago. In addition, at the end of the Eocene epoch, 35 million years ago, a "minor" extinction cleared the table of many mammal forms and other species, and a series of mammalian extinctions beginning with the Ice Age, 1.2 million years ago, introduced the fauna we see today.

There appears to be a catastrophe in every species' future. Some crucial differences, however, divide past events from today's headlines. Ancient extinctions were not tied to human intervention and, as Museum curator emeritus Norman Newell, the dean of extinction studies, has pointed out, most of them

took a very long time, perhaps as long as 10 million years. Our future appears quite different. Human beings—bipedal primates—are making the extinction clock run faster than it has ever run in Earth's history. Harvard entomologist and Museum trustee Edward O. Wilson has estimated that "human activity has increased the extinction between 1,000 and 10,000 times over this level [the natural "background" extinction rate] in the rain forest by reduction in area alone. Clearly we are in the midst of one of the great extinction spasms of geological history."[5]

Noah's Auk

It is common for evolutionary biologists today to say that they study "systems" or "populations," and terms such as *deme*, *taxon*, *aggregate*, and *clade*, to select a few at random, make their view of life seem coldly abstract. Yet the majority of biologists at the American Museum of Natural History were and are naturalists in the old-fashioned sense. They have pursued knowledge because of their fascination with particular life forms—cichlid fishes, for example, or spiders that weave orblike webs, or trilobites. Their knowledge of species loss is intimate, and their involvement in conservation has been almost inevitable from the beginning.

In 1883, a group of scientists met in the library of the Museum to form an organization that would change the practice of conservation. That group called itself the American Ornithologists Union, and it included Spencer Baird, the secretary of the Smithsonian Institution, and Daniel Giraud Elliott, who would lead the Museum's first expedition, to the American West. The first presi-

dent was Joel Asaph Allen, soon to become the Museum's chief scientist. The A.O.U. adopted as its symbol and the title of its journal the Great Auk, a large flightless seabird that had been hunted to extinction by 1844. The A.O.U.'s mission was to promote scientific study, especially bird identification, but, under Allen's direction, it soon aligned itself against the wholesale slaughter of birds to supply the millinery and taxidermy trades. The A.O.U. took the first direct action by ornithologists on behalf of an imperiled species by appointing a committee for bird protection and drawing up the first model bird-protection law, which became the prototype for bird legislation throughout the nation. One of its most active members was George Bird Grinnell, for several years a Museum associate, who sponsored a pledge drive to discourage the wearing of feathers. This initiative led to the creation of the Audubon Society. Although the A.O.U. soon left the work of conservation largely to the Society, the Museum had entered the thick of the fight.

President Henry Fairfield Osborn used the Museum and *Natural History* magazine as platforms for conservation education. In 1921, he and mammalogist Harold Anthony asked in an article typical of the period, "Can we save the mammals?" They insisted their question was "not the cry of the alarmist; it is the expression of an actual and most melancholy fact, namely, that the glorious AGE OF MAMMALS is closing, that man will soon be alone amid the wreck of creation."[6] Frank Chapman's popular bird handbooks began to turn attention away from hunting birds to watching them. In the 1920s, Carl Akeley spurred the

creation of Africa's largest gorilla sanctuary (see page 117). Conservationists and big-game hunters made uneasy alliances as Theodore Roosevelt and other wealthy members of the Boone and Crockett Club put their considerable financial muscle behind efforts to create wilderness preserves, including national parks. Roosevelt was strongly influenced by Chapman and Sierra Club founder John Muir, who nevertheless failed to convince the president to "get beyond the boyishness of killing things."

Today, advocacy and science go hand in hand. The greatest contribution Museum scientists can make to the protection of species is knowledge. Conservationists have identified some eighteen global hotspots as havens of biodiversity, but no one knows the true range of species that live there. Other areas might also be rich in species. In any case, not all such areas can be preserved. Are the small forests of central Chile more important than the western slopes of Ecuador? Which areas of the arid Gran Chaco, the second largest ecosystem of South America, should be singled out?

Most of the Museum scientists practice *systematics,* the classification of species and the tracing of their lineages. This discipline, which has existed since the time of Aristotle, has become highly specialized. Mammalogist Guy Musser's description of a new species of Celebes rodent, for example, comprises mostly photographs taken with a scanning electron microscope and detailed comparisons of tiny teeth and jaws. Herpetologist Charles Myers's classification of a new species of poison-dart frog from Colombia depends nearly as much on molecular biology as on the naked eye, for the chemical

composition of the poison is a distinguishing characteristic. To identify a species and place it in a lineage, the systematist must also know its range and distribution. Systematists are biogeographers, and preservation priorities often depend on biogeography. Remarked entomologist David Grimaldi, "Official protection is afforded to species and subspecies, and defining them is the core of what we do."

One of the first tasks of systematists is to clarify the meaning of biodiversity. If, for example, only the number of species in an area matters, arthropods (including insects and spiders), whose species vastly outnumber those of mammals and birds, must be the measuring stick. (Microorganisms might be, but identification of them lags far behind.) Sheer numbers, however, may be the wrong criterion. Should an area that contains three thousand species be maintained over one that contains only five hundred if all the species in the first are represented elsewhere in the world while none in the second are? This argument for preserving *endemism* —concentrations of unique native species—has placed some overlooked habitats on the triage list. Moreover, species diversity itself is not the only, or perhaps even the chief, concern. Higher classifications—genera, orders, and families—play a part. Some scientists may deplore a "save the mammals" bias in conservation, yet few would argue that we should give up mammals in order to preserve, say, a far greater vari-

ety of nematodes (a class of parasitic worms). In practical terms, the mammals act as preservation umbrellas for a wide variety of other types of creatures. As a rule of thumb, Platnick proposes conserving the maximum number of endemic species in the minimum area. This requires that the inventory of species be global and comparative.

Melanie Stiassny, ichthyologist at the American Museum of Natural History, has suggested another dimension. Suppose there existed, in a ramshackle local library in an out-of-the-way town, the only remaining copy of a book containing information available nowhere else. Suppose the book could not be removed from the library, the knowledge might be of enormous significance, and the cost of maintaining the library prohibitive. That is more or less the situation of cichlid fishes on the island of Madagascar, off the southeastern coast of Africa. This family of freshwater fishes, which includes tiny dwarf species as well as the large and economically important tilapias, are distributed throughout Africa, South America, and southern India. In Madagascar, however, they have been developing in isolation for tens of millions of years. In the Madagascan waterways, evolution has proceeded slowly, yielding only nine distinct species—hardly hotspots compared to mainland African lakes, which harbor hundreds of species each. These nine species, however, have diverged little from the ancient ancestral stem and have retained many primitive characteristics. They afford a rare glimpse of the evolutionary past and provide a yardstick for measuring genetic and behavioral innovation in the more common species. Each species is a page in the rare book that can be read nowhere else.

If this seems a highly particular measure of "diversity," conservation decisions already depend on even more elaborate ones. Is the spotted owl endangered in the southwestern United States, where it dwells on mountaintops? That was the question the U. S. Forest Service asked Museum ornithologist George Barrowclough. A particular population of owls might be endangered, but did it constitute a separate species, or was there gene flow among different, widespread mountaintop groups? Barrowclough has applied a variety of measures, including analysis of DNA sequences of owl populations, but the answer has not resolved conservation issues. The owls appear to be members of the same species, although each group is genetically distinct enough to betray its geographic home. If the owls disappear in one place, might others eventually take their place, or is this a de facto extinction? The research has raised questions about how much habitat needs protecting in order to preserve a species. Perhaps all the mountain ranges should be managed as a unit. Science may sharpen policy questions but cannot necessarily resolve them.

Signs of Life

For biogeographers and systematists confronting such issues, the overwhelming fact is that of their own ignorance. A reasonable estimate of the number of species alive today is 12.75 million, of which only 10 percent have been described. This casts the time problem in rather stark relief, considering Edward O. Wilson's proposed rates of extinction. Systematists are being mobilized to conduct species inventories of areas that are either unknown or in peril or both. Scientists from the American Museum of Natural History have joined teams around the world to conduct a variety of such studies. One of the most important focuses on Cuba.

As early as 1972, Lamont Curator Lester Short had sought permission to enter Cuba to study the Cuban green woodpecker and search for the ivory-billed woodpecker. Every year he was turned down until, in 1985, he was hastily invited. He spent three weeks in the field in Cuba and repeated the visit in 1986 and 1987. He observed what may have been the last ivory-billed woodpecker on the island and paved the way for a historic collaboration.

In 1990, Museum mammalogist Ross MacPhee visited Cuba for what might seem an unlikely conference—on speleology, or cave exploration. He had been invited by Gilberto Silva Taboada,

Hot Zone—40,000 B.C.

Nearly twenty-five hundred years ago, human beings arrived on the island of Madagascar. By 1000 A.D. most of the larger vertebrates had disappeared. Seven thousand years ago, human beings came to the islands of the Caribbean. Soon after, many kinds of mammals and other species began to decline rapidly toward extinction. Twelve thousand five hundred years ago, human beings first made their way into North America. Fewer than two thousand years later, the New World suffered more than eighty-five extinctions. The breadth of the loss was staggering: mammoths, American horses, ground sloths, saber-toothed cats, and dozens of other large mammals were among the disappeared.

The last forty thousand years have seen repeated bursts of extinction, most visibly among nonhuman mammals and birds. These events have occurred around the globe, wherever human beings arrived on the scene. Dating the catastrophes remains problematic and evidence of direct links is circumstantial, but it appears that human beings have been one of nature's more destructive forces for a long time. Scientists have pointed the finger at hunting and habitat destruction, but curator Ross MacPhee believes there may be another factor, one that humans could not control: disease.

Above: Descending into a cave in search of clues to primate extinctions in the Caribbean island of Anguilla, 1989. Photograph by Ross MacPhee

Below: Prospecting caves on the Caribbean island of Anguilla, 1989. Photograph by Ross MacPhee

"Evidence suggests," says MacPhee, "that the period of first contact, to the degree we can pin it down, was the most deadly. After that, the rates of extinction drop off." The pattern is hard to explain by hunting and habitat destruction but is consistent with effects of hypervirulent disease. Other scientists have taken a hard look at the hunting hypothesis and found that there is little empirical evidence to support it. According to MacPhee's theory, either human beings, their domesticated animals, or creatures that accompanied them, were walking "hot zones," reservoirs of viruses and microorganisms that could jump to other hosts. Humans often were acclimated to these agents, but the mammals they encountered in their migrations out of Africa were not.

Examples of the lethal impact of hypervirulent diseases pepper the landscape of life, from tuberculosis to the measles that decimated North American Indian populations when the disease arrived with Europeans. The natural history of AIDS and many other emerging diseases reveals the ways in which viruses jump from one type of animal to another, leaping across species, families, and even orders. Nor do all the members of a group have to be killed for the group to be effectively wiped out. When a population is drastically reduced, it becomes more vulnerable to other forces affecting its viability.

To test the disease theory, MacPhee and his colleagues must search for telltale pathogens in bones or other tissues from an extinct species at the probable point of its contact with humans. Viruses and bacteria contain genetic material (DNA), and their DNA should be detectable in well-preserved tissues of animals they infected. This DNA (or, in some viruses, RNA) can be identified only by comparison with appropriate modern viruses, and the match may be far from identical. The intricate process is like searching for a smoking gun when the only hint of a crime is the faintest smell of powder in the air.

Top left: A sky-blue anole lizard, of a species yet unnamed, discovered on the combined American Museum of Natural History–Museo Nacional de Historia Natural biological survey, 1991. Photograph by Alfonso Silva Lee, Museo Nacional de Historia Natural, Havana

Top right: Iguana (Leiocephalus carinatus) at Cayo el Ingles, Cuba, 1991. Photograph by Alfonso Silva Lee, Museo Nacional de Historia Natural, Havana

Above left: A tiny Cuban emerald hummingbird (Chlorostilbon ricordii). Photograph by Alfonso Silva Lee, Museo Nacional de Historia Natural, Havana

Above right: Greta cubana, one of only two species of clear-winged butterflies in the Greater Antilles. Photograph by Alfonso Silva Lee, Museo Nacional de Historia Natural, Havana

one of the founders of the Cuban National Museum of Natural History. MacPhee, however, was less interested in caves than in what they contained. In one cave, explorers had found the remains of an ancient extinct monkey, a kind not thought to have been present in the Greater Antilles (the largest Caribbean islands, including Cuba). These and other fossils indicate that some 80 percent of all the native mammals disappeared from the Greater Antilles, perhaps when human beings first arrived. MacPhee went to Cuba to investigate the cause of that extinction and to study the current fauna.

Cuba is perhaps the most geo-logically and biotically diverse island of the Greater Antilles group, but scientific information there is scanty. The Cuban and U.S. museums agreed to mount a joint biological survey, extending over several years, to help Cuba identify and manage its rare bio-logical resources. Currently two hundred varieties of Cuban plants and animals are on the United Nations list of endangered species. Remarked icthyologist Michael Smith, who has been a member of the Museum's Cuba team, "It is chilling to realize that as fast as we are discovering spe-cies, they may be disappearing."

The survey has revealed a gar-den of hitherto unknown de-

lights. In short order, the teams discovered previously unidentified species: the delicately hued sky-blue anole (a tiny lizard), three fish species, new cacti, and ground spiders. Yet new species are not the only mark of Cuba's splendor. It can be seen in a hummingbird no larger than a thumbnail and through the transparent wings of the *Greta cubana,* one of only two species of clear-winged butterflies in the Greater Antilles. Sometimes it cannot be seen: the secretive almiqui, a foot-long relative of the shrew and one of Cuba's few remaining land mammals, has not been sighted for a decade. Only reports of its scent indicate that it still exists.

Surveys do not always follow a strict conservation itinerary: systematists usually seek answers to questions about species relatedness, not about habitats per se or the interactions among all the life forms within them. Most questions about communities of different organisms are the domain of the ecologist. Even with limited objectives, however, Museum scientists inevitably possess a great deal of on-the-ground ecological knowledge and can make unexpected contributions to broader conservation discussions. In 1994, Melanie Stiassny and David Grimaldi joined a team from the Wildlife Conservation Society (formerly the New York Zoological Society) to make an inventory of species in Tanzania's Tarangire National Park. They were also asked to help develop the expertise of African systematists and students. Stiassny sought to understand the spread and diversification of cichlid fishes throughout the lakes and rivers of East Africa.

The Tarangire River system is seasonal. In the rainy season, the river feeds a great swampy lake. In summer, lake and river nearly dry up, save for spring-fed pools, which become a lifeline for an array of animals, from insects to elephants living on the Masai Steppe. The park officials wanted to know what fauna the park supported.

Above: Local collector Alawi R. M. Msuya on Lake Manyara, a "soda lake," during the dry season, Tanzania, 1994. Photograph by Melanie Stiassny

Opposite: When Museum scientists arrived at Tarangire National Park, Tanzania, in 1994 to conduct a biological survey, they found the rivers and swamps nearly dried up and the lake beds littered with the bones of large catfish. Photograph by David Grimaldi

Grimaldi and Stiassny arrived in the midst of a severe drought. Tarangire's swamp was almost completely dry, and many of the pools had all but disappeared. The skeletons of large catfish lay baking on the parched beds. They soon recognized, however, that something other than climate had gone wrong. In order to encourage ecotourism, a large lodge had been built within sight of the pools and their spectacular wildlife. Wells sunk into the aquifer were tapping the same water that fed local springs, threatening to break a living chain of the region's precious fish resources. The discovery has sounded an alarm for water conservation in the park.

The ultimate fate of all habitats threatened by human modification, from Florida to the Himalayas, is symbolized by Madagascar, the largest noncontinental island on Earth, whose once verdant hills are nearly nude for mile upon mile and whose unique wildlife has been reduced to a vestige of its former richness. It is in places like Madagascar where both the fragility and the fecundity of life are cast in dramatic relief. Stiassny recalled her first visit to Madagascar, on a journey in search of cichlids: "Coming in by airplane, you fly over a panorama of devastation. On the river, you travel through it. The rivers themselves have become turbid and choked from the erosion caused by deforestation. Finally, you arrive at a place where the forest still exists. Suddenly, life is there in all its profusion—not just a fragment of it but its myriad forms together. Such an oasis contains all our hope for our collective future."

Family Matters and "Just-So" Stories

Definitions of biodiversity rest on the identification of species. What, however, is a species, and how do scientists know one when they see one? Carolus Linnaeus, the Swedish botanist who introduced the convention of naming species with two Latin terms, questioned his students to distraction about how they classified various creatures in order to demonstrate that nothing was so difficult as calling a thing by its right name. Georges Cuvier, a leading biologist of the late eigh-

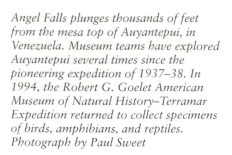

Angel Falls plunges thousands of feet from the mesa top of Auyantepui, in Venezuela. Museum teams have explored Auyantepui several times since the pioneering expedition of 1937–38. In 1994, the Robert G. Goelet American Museum of Natural History–Terramar Expedition returned to collect specimens of birds, amphibians, and reptiles. Photograph by Paul Sweet

species . . . but the amount of difference considered necessary to give to any two forms the rank of species cannot be defined."[8]

Yet they can, in spite of the obvious difficulty posed by a universe of creatures displaying varying degrees of similarity and difference. That is because species do not simply merge into and replace each other like steps up a ladder; rather, they branch and diverge. Two exist where once there was one, and neither is necessarily replaced, although that might be the final outcome. This idea of descent is thornier than it first appears. Conventional drawings of "trees of life" tend to emphasize the vertical and reinforce the idea of simple succession of one species (or even class) by another. We may dismiss the idea that human beings evolved from monkeys, knowing that both evolved from a common apelike ancestor. Both are present in the world today. Yet even the Museum's great expert on vertebrate evolution, William K. Gregory, unintentionally reinforced the idea in the title of his synoptic look at evolution, *Our Face from Fish to Man.* Frustration with this tenacious image of succession has, according to Norman Platnick, provoked some systematic biologists to utter the heresy, "Down with Darwin!"

teenth century, had plenty of confidence in his ability to make the distinctions. The story is told of how one of his students, in an elaborate practical joke, dressed as Satan and burst in on the scientist in his bedroom. "I am the devil and I am going to eat you!" he shouted. To which Cuvier is said to have replied, "Horns, cloven hooves, a tail: herbivore. You can't eat me."[7]

Charles Darwin was considerably less confident. In the very book that promised to answer the question, *The Origin of Species,* he begged it: "Finally, varieties cannot be distinguished from

It is possible to discover whether or not creatures that seem to be alike are members of the same species by referring both to a probable common ancestor and comparing the degrees of similarity. Sharks and porpoises look superficially alike, but they are only distantly related. Their intervening relatives appear totally different. They represent a case of convergent evolution—forms becoming similar over time through adaptation to the same environment. To take a reverse example, lizards look like dinosaurs and birds do not, but birds are more closely related to dinosaurs than lizards are, for birds and dinosaurs share a more recent common ancestor.

Systematists, however, must turn a cold eye not only on similitude but also on adaptive explanations about why things are as they are. Their careful reconstructions of family histories can prevent some embarrassing evolutionary "just-so" stories. Elaborate scenarios have been devised to explain the development of wings and flight, but birds' wings may have served originally not for flight at all but for cooling.

There were many just-so explanations and few rules for determining true relations when Gareth Nelson came to the Museum in the late 1960s. He and a number of other Museum systematists were disturbed by the lack of rigor and method in classifying species. At best, they confronted the system of ornithologist Ernst Mayr, who had left the Museum for Harvard University. Mayr offered a concept of species that included a vast array of subspecies, so many, in fact, that it was hard to tell what the concept of species meant. At the other end of the spectrum was the system of another former Museum scientist,

George Gaylord Simpson, who asserted that classification was as much an art as a science.

The approach developed by Nelson, Museum ichthyologist Donn Rosen, and Norman Platnick, among others, is called *cladistics*, and the family trees are called *cladograms*. Cladistics paid more precise attention to which characteristics of any organism were relevant to its definition. It also provided a more effective method for tracing which characteristics were recent innovations and which were truly primitive. As Platnick has pointed out, the process is much like trying to determine the history of a medieval manuscript. With each new copying of a text, scribes would introduce new errors, or novelties, which later scribes would then transmit, inevitably adding new ones of their own. It is possible to work backward to the original version by noting the cumulative progress of innovations.[9]

Cladistics took rapid, noisy dominion among systematic biologists because it provided a means for resolving many difficult family matters, or at least a standard against which various alternative genealogies might be measured. Aardvarks, for example, still lack a legitimate family coat of arms. Cladistics introduced such criteria for relatedness as the clustering of *synapomorphies*, which are shared characteristics derived from some probable common ancestor. It also provided a framework perfectly suited to make use of one of the most precise tools yet employed in classification, a tool unimaginable to Cuvier or Darwin—the analysis of the very material of inherited traits, DNA.

In the Museum's Molecular Systematics Laboratory, scientists can compare DNA sequences from extant and, if necessary,

extinct creatures—provided they have tissue samples. Several processes for determining similarity exist, and all are complex. One depends on the double-stranded nature of DNA. If DNA from two different samples are split and hybridized, the "fit" of the strands is a measure of similarity. Another approach involves reading the amino-acid sequences of the DNA and looking for matches. As these techniques have become standard, systematists have begun to carry into the field a new tool for collecting—the liquid-nitrogen bottle, used to quick-freeze specimens for the complete preservation of DNA. Indeed, they may not always need to take whole specimens at all but, where it is practical, only small tissue samples.

Clearly, molecular information is not just another characteristic, like eye color. It is far more voluminous. Yet it can be just as self-contradictory and difficult to interpret as traditional sources of evidence. DNA does not fully declare its kinship, and it cannot reveal anything about behaviors that might separate species in the wild. Systematists need not be philosophers in order to join names to things, but they must make judgments. These judgments ultimately depend on how the scientists view the way life unfolds, which has been and continues to be the Museum's enduring preoccupation.

Darwin's Bulldogs

In 1879, Henry Fairfield Osborn traveled to Cambridge University to begin his postgraduate education. That fall, he registered for a class taught by the English anatomist Thomas Henry Huxley, who had resoundingly defended Darwin's theory of evolution on the public platform against Bishop Samuel Wilberforce. Thereafter, Huxley referred to himself as "Darwin's bulldog." In Huxley's laboratory, the young Osborn met Darwin himself, an Olympian figure, with eyes that "seemed to image his wonderfully calm and deep vision of nature and at the same time to emit benevolence."[10] Yet it was Huxley who riveted Osborn's attention: "Huxley comes in as the clock strikes and begins to lecture at once, almost before it ceases. He looks old and somewhat broken, his eyes deeply sunken, but is a lecturer as strong as ever could have been."[11]

Darwin and his fellow naturalist Alfred Russel Wallace had discovered a new intellectual continent—the concept of descent with modification (evolution). Huxley embodied the cost and difficulty of its exploration. Yet he inspired Osborn, who launched the American Museum of Natural History on its own exploration of this continent, and the study of evolution has been the Museum's most important expedition ever since.

As a paleontologist, Osborn could not help confronting what he called "the primary scientific and theological challenge of our age." The story of descent with modification was written in the fossils he studied—of horses, for example, which first appeared as small, three-toed creatures and gradually became the large-hooved animals we know. The idea proposed in Darwin's *The Origin of Species* and in Wallace's "On the Law that has Regulated the Introduction of New Species" is breathtakingly simple, although it arose out of a background of at least a century of thought. In outline, the theory asserts that kinds (or species) of

living things give birth to other kinds through a process of gradual physical modification. In other words, the forms of living things are not immutable. Individuals, whether finches or worms or apes, present attributes to the world. Different individuals present slightly different attributes. The individuals with attributes more advantageous to survival in a particular environment thrive and pass their advantages on; others less well equipped die off. This is the process of adaptation through natural selection. In Darwin's view, change accumulated until a species insensibly became a new species. Life, then, was a steady stream that began with a single common ancestor eons ago and spread across the Earth, changing over time through selection and adaptation.

Darwin had no clear idea how attributes were passed on or how variation might be introduced. (Gregor Mendel identified this mechanism—later called the gene—in 1865, but the significance of his discovery was not grasped for thirty-five years.)

Darwin even thought characteristics acquired in a single lifetime might be passed on. Nevertheless, no natural scientist today doubts that selection is the determining factor in evolution. How new species—and by extension families and orders—arise is another matter; scientists cannot actually see that. For almost a century and a half, the process has been evolutionary theory's "black box." Three Museum scientists, George Gaylord Simpson, Ernst Mayr (now emeritus professor at Harvard University), and Niles Eldredge, have made important attempts to lift the lid and let in some light, both empirical and theoretical.

An Inner Agenda

Osborn would not have agreed with any of their conclusions. As a scientist, he recognized Darwin and Wallace as liberators. The living world had not been set in changeless categories but had evolved in spectacular and interesting profusion according to regular principles, over a span of time far greater than the Bible knew. For Osborn the Christian, these revelations meant that theology and science must harmonize at some other level than the literal. Osborn spent most of his career attempting to demonstrate their mutual compatibility. Osborn put the question this way in 1917: "Our present state of opinion is this: we know to some extent *how* plants and animals and man evolve, we do not know *why* they evolve."[12] The idea of adaptation—successful modifications in response to the environment—enabled him to explain the why of many changes and ultimately to salvage a special destiny for human beings in an otherwise contingent process.

Osborn posited for each species a kind of inner agenda, a potential, carried in the reproductive cell (he later located it in the "aristogene"), activated to some unknown degree by the environment, and expressed through adaptation. It was as if each creature carried the evolutionary mandate "Be all you can be," which time and circumstance would define. Human beings had an aristogene, too, which gradually realized its full potential in, strangely enough, those who occupied the same racial, social, intellectual, and educational rung as Osborn himself. Other races had other aristogenes but with different—and, as he implied, lesser—potentials. Who knew what great developments lay in store for humanity as long as the line with the greatest potential could be nurtured?

This unfortunate conclusion to an untenable theory obscures Osborn's principal motivation: he could not accept the picture of utter contingency that was emerging from evolution's "black box." Instead, naturalists had begun to argue as soon as *The Origin of Species* was published that Darwin had not paid enough attention to the importance of physical isolation as a source of new species, an odd oversight considering Darwin's sojourn in the remote Galápagos Islands. Perhaps species did not emerge only in straight lines from previous species but also as the result of a more disjunctive process, the separation of a population and the subsequent independent development of the groups.

Full recognition of life's complex and multifarious branching all but banishes Osborn's notion of an inner agenda. External, arbitrary circumstances such as the disappearance of a land bridge or a change of climate have more to do with the changing shapes of creatures than some inborn program. What's more, an even greater challenge to Osborn's ideas came from inside living things themselves.

Across the Great Divide

By the beginning of the twentieth century, Gregor Johann Mendel's cross-breeding experiments with peas had been rediscovered, and, soon thereafter, Thomas Hunt Morgan began experimenting in a similar vein with fruit flies. Taken together, these researches confirmed the existence in the cell of a single vehicle of inheritance—genes, which are distributed in offspring according to definite rules. Moreover, variations in traits are the products not of outside influences or some mysterious inner suasion but of alterations in the vehicle itself—

genetic mutations. Osborn maintained that laboratory biologists such as Morgan could not see the forest for the trees; that is, they could not distinguish these probably insignificant variations among individuals from the directional transformations of true evolution. Their theories were too chemical, too random, too Godless. "I am sorry to hear that mammals have not evolved by mutation," Morgan remarked condescendingly. "I cannot but hope that you will relent some day and let us have the mammals back."[13]

As the challenge grew more forceful, Osborn attempted to co-opt the language of genetics and physics, but the handwriting was on the wall. The path to understanding the mechanisms of evolution would lead straight to the microscope and the study, not of fossils and living creatures, but of cells and their chemistry. Nothing would check the ascent of molecular biology, from Morgan's fruit flies to the discovery of DNA's double helix to the recent "selfish genes" proposed by Richard Dawkins. The most radical practitioners of microscope science have attempted to dissolve the world of organisms and species into irrelevance. All that exists, in their view, are groups of mutating genes, determined to replicate themselves, continuously developing ways of exploiting (via bodies) the energy resources of their environment in order to accomplish their goal.

By the late 1930s, biochemists had stopped talking to systematists and paleontologists, even though both sides admitted that what actually happens in evolution was still murky. For instance, mathematician Sewell Wright pointed out that populations of a species are genetically far from

Above: Camp with water bucks, Tarangire National Park biological survey, Tanzania, 1994. Photograph by David Grimaldi

Opposite: Ants attacking a praying mantis, captured in Dominican amber, 25–30 million years ago. The actual length of this piece is only 1.2 inches.

uniform, and some genes are statistically certain to drop out as members die. Genetic drift, as he called the phenomenon, goes almost unnoticed in a large population with much genetic variation, but in small ones, it can radically bias the possibilities for adaptation to environmental change, and it raises yet other questions. How fast, in fact, do species develop adaptations? How often and under what circumstances do they diverge?

Many geneticists retreated to statistical descriptions of changing gene frequencies in populations. As they saw it, that was evolution. They accused the naturalists of attempting, in the words

Through a Glass Darkly

Not far away from the American Museum of Natural History, across the Hudson River in New Jersey, can be found a prehistoric embalming parlor. It is a deposit of amber from the late Cretaceous period, 65 to 95 million years old. Although it contains no saber-toothed cats or mammoths like the tar pits of Rancho La Brea in Los Angeles, it has provided just as revealing a glimpse of lost life on Earth.

Amber is the hardened resin that certain trees exude to protect themselves from invasive insects. Over the course of millions of years, polymerization occurs, and amber becomes an inert substance. The sticky resin may entrap insects, leaves, flowers, pollen, frogs, fur, and feathers, preserving them virtually intact. Although amber can be found all across the globe, certain areas, such as the Baltic region, the Dominican Republic, and Chiapas in southern Mexico are particularly rich.

In the 1980s, Museum entomologist David Grimaldi began collecting amber from sites in New Jersey. Because of his interest, he was directed to a collection of amber stored in the Museum's basement. Rummaging through a box labeled "Kinkora, New Jersey, coll. Alfred C. Hawkins," Grimaldi made an unusual discovery—a large piece of clear yellow Cretaceous amber that contained what looked like a bee. This was puzzling. The earliest known bees dated from the much later Eocene period, 40 million years ago. The specimen was indeed a bee, and a stingless one at that, a specialization that was thought to have developed even more recently. An examination of the amber's chemical properties pinpointed its age at 80 million years and identified the source of the

resin as a conifer. The new species of bee was called Trigona prisca *(meaning ancient* Trigona). *Because this species was already highly specialized, Grimaldi surmised that it may have appeared as long ago as 135 million years. The implications of this discovery are far-reaching, for it means that flowering plants, which provided pollen and nectar for the bee, must have existed far earlier than was generally believed.*

The remarkable embalming characteristics of resin, which dehydrates the specimens it surrounds, means that some of the insect specimens contain actual tissue with genetic material. In September 1992, a team from the Museum's Molecular Systematics Laboratory extracted a fragment of a single gene from a 30-million-year-old extinct termite found in a piece of amber from the Dominican Republic. Grimaldi named this termite Mastotermes electrodominicus. Through the process of polymerase chain reaction, the scientists made thousands of copies of this DNA and were able to identify its genetic sequence and compare it with the DNA of living insects.

This extinct termite has but one living relative, in northern Australia. A comparison of biochemical information from both the living and extinct species and from other living termites, mantises, and roaches, has helped resolve several long-standing questions about the relationship of termites to roaches. Although Grimaldi will never be able to reproduce extinct species, as imagined in Jurassic Park, *comparisons of the DNA sequences of extinct insects with those of living species may one day provide the answers to two fundamental questions: What are the precise mechanisms through which new species emerge on Earth, and why do certain species, and not others, become extinct?*

of paleontologist George Gaylord Simpson, "to study the principles of the internal combustion engine by standing on a street corner and watching the cars whiz by." In truth, the naturalists and paleontologists were interested not in the engine but in how the car got where it was going. In the genetics camp, Theodosius Dobzhansky was an exception; he never lost sight of the organisms carrying the genes. He identified reproductive isolation, even among nearly identical groups, as the hallmark of species. To him species were reproductive communities, collections of DNA adapted to particular circumstances, or they were nothing at all.

Like Darwin's early critics, Dobzhansky recognized that discontinuity was important for the appearance of new species. What imposed or impelled this discontinuity was, first of all, the genes themselves. They produced discrete variations in a group, and some of those variations would be less likely to mate with each other. Other isolating mechanisms could be as dramatic as the rising of the sea, which might suddenly divide a community of lizards, or as subtle as the capacity of a group of rats to digest a certain kind of mushroom growing on a ridge instead of down in the valley crowded with their fellows. "Systematists are inclined to regard the geographical differentiation of a species into local races . . . as the precursor of the formation of new species,"[14] Dobzhansky wrote in 1941.

In a single sentence, Dobzhansky foreshadowed one of the major contributions of Museum ornithologist Ernst Mayr. Mayr, too, sought to bridge the gap between genetics and systematics. From his observations of birds in the South Seas (see pages 181–85) and South America, Mayr understood the importance of geographic separation as a driving force in the origin of bird species. Mutations present genetic variety to the environment, which selects those most favorable. Over a geographic area, Mayr saw this constant process producing a wide range of variations within a species, variations he labeled subspecies. Geographic isolation appeared to be necessary to transform adaptation of random mutations within groups into true reproductive communities.

Yet the closer one looks at Mayr's studies, the less important isolation becomes. Adaptation and natural selection are so powerful and specific that any geographic variation will do. Mayr's gradual process, with all its subspecies becoming species, begins to look very much like Darwin's. Moreover, Mayr could not explain large-scale morphological changes, such as the development of flight or the transition from water to land or the development of backbones, except by extrapolating incremental changes: "There is only a difference of degree, not one of kind, between the two phenomena."[15]

Museum paleontologist George Gaylord Simpson was not so sure. A colleague of Mayr's, he sought to unite knowledge of genetics with fossil evidence of past evolution in a work revealingly titled *Tempo and Mode in Evolution*. Early theological critics had attacked the notion of evolution because it took too long. It required that the Earth be immeasurably older than was projected in the Bible. Simpson observed the earliest appearance of bats and whales in the fossil record and calculated from subsequent rates of change that bats would have had to begin developing from some flightless mammalian ancestor before such mammals existed at all. The vaunted fossil record is often as puzzling as it is illuminating. It offers a series of gaps, interrupted by the appearance of species and higher orders of creatures apparently full blown. Genetics and Mayr's bird studies convinced Simpson that change was gradual, but the absence of gradations was puzzling. In any case, rates of evolution clearly could vary dramatically, and Simpson began to suspect that two different processes were at work.

"Nature Does Not Make Leaps"

For Simpson, the origin of new species was straightforward: the gradual transformation of a lineage. In spite of his respect for Mayr, he paid little heed to splitting models of speciation. Simpson's model represented the main mechanism of evolution, much as Darwin had described it. The fossil record was not likely to preserve all evidence of the process but only of those adaptations that succeeded and endured. Nevertheless, the larger leaps remained. Earlier biologists had insisted, "Nature does not make leaps." Simpson developed a radical idea to explain how such leaps could occur: quantum evolution.

In quantum evolution, certain members of a species might actually be *preadapted* for future change; that is, they might possess characteristics of little importance to their immediate situation but of potentially great importance to a different one. Moreover, as a result of genetic drift, they might also lack some current adaptations. Compared to their fellows, they were generalists, able to respond to a broad or dramatic change in the environment. The more significant the preadaptations and the more dramatic the changes, the faster new forms might appear and evolve.

Simpson was roundly criticized for this view of population genetics, even though geneticists knew that genetic fit, or adaptation, of organisms to environments was often much looser than they pretended in their "just-so" stories. Everything in nature was not a miracle of congruent engineering. Simpson, however, retreated to the position that quantum evolution was, after all, just speciation on a larger scale, speeded up, perhaps as a result of more extreme conditions. Yet the problem of evolutionary jumps would not go away, just as it would not for Darwin.

It was still there in 1972 to confront Museum scientist Niles Eldredge, a specialist on invertebrates, and Harvard's Stephen Jay Gould. Together, they proposed a new description of evolutionary events called punctuated equilibria. Eldredge has been exploring the implications of that insight ever since.

Eldredge studies trilobites, primitive invertebrate sea creatures that thrived until 200 million years ago; or rather, like Simpson, he studies fossils, and fossils reveal one salient fact about trilobites: over time spans of up to 10 million years, individual species virtually did not change. In the absence of some strong stimulus, their adaptations were stable and did not evolve, nor did they split very often into new species. Eldredge and Gould concluded that this pattern was true for all species. Evolution—*both* the splitting off of new species and the transformation of a single species through adaptation—happens over comparatively short periods of time, in bursts or punctuations. Such periods are succeeded by longer intervals of stability.

The stimulus for change is nature itself. As Dobzhansky, Mayr, and Simpson all recognized, environmental alterations produce both reproductive isolation and new adaptations—as well as extinction. In the face of change, the first response of most populations, whether fishes or birds or prehuman primates, is to move—if they can—in search of familiar conditions. If they succeed, they will remain much the same, but they are not always successful, especially if the changes are drastic or extensive. Habitat disruption tends to promote movement, fragmentation of already genetically diverse groups, speciation, and rapid new adaptations. Suddenly, there may be many new species, each seeking a slightly different foothold. According to Eldredge, all will have at least a brief moment, but the larger principle of selection, the unforgiving rule of a process without conscience, will assert itself. Many species will not survive, and their sojourn on Earth will be too brief for the rocks to record.

Far from being an exception to mutability's jurisdiction on the Earth, human beings exemplify the punctuating process, for, as Darwin wrote, "Man is a species produced like any other—lawfully."

Nearly 4 million years ago, the first human ancestors to walk upright left footprints in the soft earth and volcanic ash of Laetoli, Africa. This is a cast of the original footprint of Australopithecus, *created for the Museum's Hall of Human Biology and Evolution in 1991.*

The Enigma of Our Arrival

Five million years ago, central Africa endured a prolonged cold snap. It lasted not for a few weeks or a season, but long enough to rearrange a vast array of habitats. To the north, the Mediterranean Sea retreated dramatically. On all the continents forests died back and were replaced by thousands of miles of savanna. For certain tree-dwelling primates living in the dwindling African forests, it was time to move—to "track their habitat," as scientists term it. It must have been a hard transition, for their legs were short and moving across open ground was dangerous. But they were anatomically capable of walking upright and did. Perhaps their posture enabled them to keep cool on the arid plains and extended their vision, helping them detect predators, prey, and carrion, a compensation for their slow speed.

Probably some did not walk as efficiently, and they survived only briefly. The walkers left footprints in the volcanic soil of Laetoli, Tanzania, 3.5 million years ago, and the death of one bequeathed to the present a small skeleton near Hadar, Ethiopia—Lucy.

The arrival of early human ancestors and, later, of modern human beings, demonstrates that there are no exceptions to Darwin's "descent with modification," only marvelous fulfillments. Human beings are not different in essence from other creatures, only in attributes and circumstance. In his study of human evolution, Museum anthropologist Ian Tattersall has brought a naturalist's perspective to this often wildly speculative field. Consider Piltdown Man, a bold forgery that was clearly intended as a joke but not dismissed for decades. There is also the cautionary example of Nebraska Man—*Hesperopithecus haroldcookii*—America's own "missing

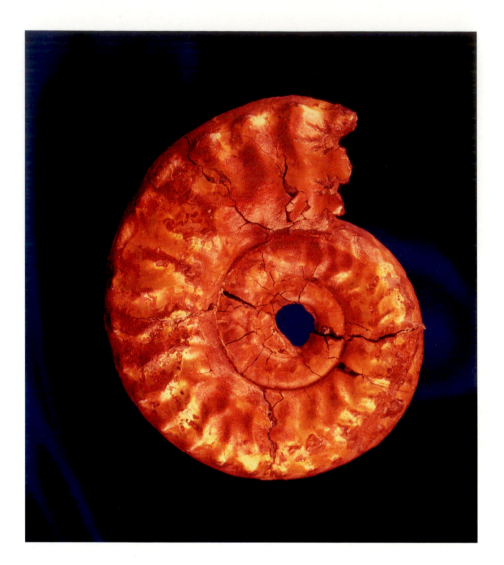

link," described enthusiastically by Osborn from a single tooth. The tooth was later found to belong to a species of pig.

Ironically, the speculation about human descent has tended to reduce the variety of the human story. Tattersall, an expert on lemurs, who discovered a new species in Madagascar, has sought to restore that variety. In preparing the Museum's Hall of Human Biology and Evolution, he surveyed all the fossil evidence—"the fossil trail," he calls it—and found familiar evolutionary patterns. For nearly a century, since the first prehuman remains were discovered in Java, hypothetical lineages have emphasized a Darwinian progress—gradual direct transformation and replacement of one group by another, from *Australopithecus afarensis* (Lucy), to *Homo erectus*, to (it was once believed) *Homo neanderthalensis* to *Homo sapiens*. A steady accumulation of fossils, cladistic rigor, and closer application of evolutionary theory has shown, instead, the consistent play of new species at every stage of prehuman evolution. As with lemurs, so with human ancestors.

In Tattersall's scheme, Lucy's line persisted relatively unchanged until another cooling, 2.5 million years ago, initiated more discontinuity and a wave of speciation into at least two major lines, followed by more splitting. One stem divided into several species, including the "robust" group, with sloping brows and projecting faces. The other line eventually produced the famous "Turkana boy," who was recognizably modern from the neck down and, about half a million years ago, the common ancestor that led to both modern humans and what we now call Neanderthals.

Calling Neanderthals a separate species acknowledges the likelihood of many contemporary species of near humans at any given time. Two million years ago, for example, several species in at least two genera coexisted, and all may have been using primitive tools. By ninety thousand years ago, anatomically modern humans ranged widely, from Africa (their probable direct origin) to the Middle East. So did the unmodern but large-brained Neanderthals, and, in some areas, these groups may have existed together for as long as fifty thousand years. Intriguingly, the two appear to have lived very similarly until about fifty thousand years ago, when, as Tattersall has remarked, "*Homo sapiens* stopped simply looking modern and began to behave in a modern fashion."[16] There is no evidence of the Neanderthal "bear clans" imagined in popular fiction, whereas there is plenty of evidence that *Homo sapiens* created art, notation, and even music. Perhaps humans were doing things differently much earlier, but those traces have been lost. Still, the great leap forward seems to have happened independently of any anatomical change. In a sense, then, *Homo sapiens* arrived twice, first physically, then culturally. The reason remains a mystery.

Having arrived, will we continue to evolve? Henry Fairfield Osborn thought so. That would, however, require discontinuity and isolation, the twin products of habitat disruption. For 3.5 billion years, some forms of life have always passed through the bottleneck of extinction to continue their divergent transformations. With the next great disturbance, the reproductive success of humans thus far does not guarantee that we will be among the survivors.

The American Museum of Natural History in the Field: Biodiversity and Evolution

Molecular Systematics—1990   *In 1990, the American Museum of Natural History established a Molecular Systematics Laboratory to bring a new and definitive tool to the study of phylogeny (the descent of species). Comparative studies of genetic material are being used to determine similarities among contemporary species and to unravel species' histories. Directed by invertebrate specialist Ward Wheeler and entomologist Robert DeSalle, the laboratory has conducted studies on a wide range of subjects, from the natural history of arthropods to the conservation genetics of endangered beetle species. The laboratory is equally important for advancing analytical techniques, including the recovery of DNA from fossil bones and the identification of matching gene sequences in comparative DNA samples.*

French Guiana Survey—1991–94   *How many species really do live in a rain forest? No current list of fauna approaches comprehensiveness because few systematic inventories have been made. That was the situation confronting mammalogists Robert Voss and Nancy Simmons. In response, they conducted the most intensive survey to date of the mammals of a neotropical rain forest. This survey represents an important step in answering fundamental questions about these rain forests—whether, for example, geographic patterns of diversity and endemism are the same for both plants and animals. Moreover, Voss and Simmons sought to predict where high and low levels of diversity would occur. Inventories are the key to understanding these complex communities of organisms and determining what is at stake in their protection.*

Vietnam Institute of Archaeology–American Museum of Natural History Joint Research Venture—1992–94   *To draw a more complete picture of primate evolution at the time that humankind was emerging, curator of anthropology Ian Tattersall began a collaboration with scientists in Vietnam to search for fossils in the limestone caves north of Hanoi. In a second field visit, the group was joined by paleontologist James Clark, who sought fossil evidence of the ancestors of crocodiles. Tattersall and his Vietnamese colleagues identified remains of previously unknown species of primates, which indicate that early man had many contemporary ecological competitors, especially a large extinct ape called Gigantopithecus.*

Notes

Preface

1. Roy Chapman Andrews, *Ends of the Earth* (New York: G. P. Putnam's Sons, 1929), 332–35.
2. Robert Cushman Murphy, "Increasing Knowledge Through Exploration," *Natural History*, 30, no. 4 (1930): 468.

Introduction

1. Albert S. Bickmore, autobiography, 1908, 2:80, Archives of the American Museum of Natural History, New York.
2. See Bickmore, autobiography, 1908, and Louis Gratacamp, "History of the American Museum of Natural History," n.d., both in the Archives of the American Museum of Natural History, New York; Joseph Choate, "Reminiscences of a Founder of the American Museum," *The American Museum Journal*, 17, no. 5 (1917); Geoffrey Hellman, *Bankers, Bones and Beetles: The First Century of the American Museum of Natural History* (Garden City: The Natural History Press, 1969); John Michael Kennedy, "Philanthropy and Science in New York City: The American Museum of Natural History, 1868–1968" (Ph.D. diss., Yale University, 1968); Douglas Preston, *Dinosaurs in the Attic* (New York: St. Martin's Press, 1986); and various anniversary and memorial celebrations in *Natural History*.
3. Kennedy, "Philanthropy and Science," 27.
4. Joseph Kastner, *A Species of Eternity* (New York: Alfred A. Knopf, 1977), 121.
5. See Herman Viola and Carolyn Margolis, eds., *The Magnificent Voyagers: The U.S. Exploring Expedition 1838–1842* (Washington, D.C.: Smithsonian Institution, 1985).
6. Bickmore, autobiography, 1:14.
7. Ibid., 1:23.

8. Quoted in ibid., 2:22.
9. Ibid., 2:10.
10. Ibid., 2:15.
11. Albert S. Bickmore to James Dwight Dana, April 29, 1869, quoted in Kennedy, 55.
12. Albert S. Bickmore to William Haines, November 6, 1879, quoted in ibid., 72–73.
13. Ibid., 79.
14. Ibid., 108.
15. Morris K. Jesup to Seth Low, January 17, 1891, quoted in ibid., 111.
16. Albert S. Bickmore to F. W. Putnam, October 7, 1891, quoted in ibid., 112.

The North Pacific

1. Franz Boas to George Hunt, April 14, 1897, Archives, Department of Anthropology, American Museum of Natural History, New York.
2. Annual Report of the American Museum of Natural History, no. 28 (1896).
3. Editorial, *The New York Times*, March 14, 1897.
4. Quoted in Marvin Harris, *The Rise of Anthropological Theory* (New York: Thomas Y. Crowell, 1968), 256.
5. Franz Boas, "The Jesup North Pacific Expedition," *American Museum of Natural History Memoirs*, 2, part 1 (1898): 4.
6. George Hunt to Franz Boas, January 16, 1919, Franz Boas Professional Papers, American Philosophical Society, Philadelphia.
7. Although Boas wanted to preserve accurately the oral traditions of the Indians in their own language and in English translation, at the turn of the century some of the material was considered to be far too sexually explicit to be printed in English in the expedition monographs. Boas got around this problem by translating long passages into Latin.

8. Franz Boas, "The Jesup North Pacific Expedition," *The American Museum Journal*, 3, no. 5 (1905): 82.
9. Quoted in Ronald Rohner, ed., *The Ethnography of Franz Boas: Letters and Diaries of Franz Boas Written on the Northwest Coast from 1886 to 1931* (Chicago: University of Chicago Press, 1969), 215.
10. Dorsey would continue to cause problems for Boas during the ensuing years of the expedition, repeatedly trying to engage the services of both George Hunt and Harlan Smith. In 1899, a man claiming to work for the American Museum of Natural History sought out Hunt in Alert Bay to tell him that Boas would no longer be coming out to the Northwest Coast from New York because of the expense of the trip. This man claimed to be the new representative from the Museum. Although the man refused to identify himself, the suspicion was that it was George Dorsey himself.
11. Quoted in Rohner, *The Ethnography of Franz Boas*, 221.
12. *New York Herald*, October 31, 1897.
13. Quoted in George Stocking, *A Franz Boas Reader: The Shaping of American Anthropology, 1883–1911* (Chicago: University of Chicago Press, 1974), 127.
14. Quoted in Aldona Jonaitis, *From the Land of the Totem Poles* (New York: American Museum of Natural History, 1988), 198.
15. Quoted in Boas, "The Jesup North Pacific Expedition," 97–98.
16. Quoted in ibid., 107.
17. Quoted in ibid., 114.
18. Quoted in ibid., 97.
19. Quoted in ibid.
20. Quoted in ibid.
21. Berthold Laufer to Franz Boas, November 2, 1899, Archives, Department of Anthro-

pology, American Museum of Natural History, New York.

22. Quoted in Boas, "The Jesup North Pacific Expedition," 104.

23. Waldemar Jochelson, "The Yukaghir and Yukaghirized Tungus," *American Museum of Natural History Memoirs*, 9, part 1 (1910): 2.

24. Quoted in Boas, "The Jesup North Pacific Expedition," 109.

25. Quoted in ibid., 113.

26. Quoted in ibid., 114.

27. Preston, *Dinosaurs in the Attic*, 32.

28. Knut R. Fladmark, "Getting One's Berings," *Natural History*, 95, no. 11 (1986).

29. Franz Boas to Waldemar Borgoras, April 22, 1905, Archives, Department of Anthropology, American Museum of Natural History, New York.

30. Borgoras to Boas, November 1905, Archives, Department of Anthropology, American Museum of Natural History, New York.

31. Conversation with Laila Williamson, March 1994.

32. Conversation with Laurel Kendall, April 1994.

33. Gloria Webster, "The Contemporary Potlatch," in Aldona Jonaitis, ed., *Chiefly Feasts: The Enduring Kwakiutl Potlatch* (New York: American Museum of Natural History, 1991), 248.

The Gobi

1. Some recent historians have used the Asian human origins goal as a stick to beat Osborn for his neglect of Africa as a possible site for the beginnings of humankind; see, for example, Ronald Rainger, *An Agenda for Antiquity* (Tuscaloosa: University of Alabama Press, 1991), 99–104. Certainly Osborn's racial attitudes cannot be glossed over, but his theory may prove more durable than its critics. Recent expeditions in China have discovered monkey fossils that are among the oldest remains of primates. According to Richard Kay of the Duke University Primate Center, the site may be "practically the Garden of Eden for primates"; see "Fossils Hint at Primate Garden of Eden," *The New York Times*, April 19, 1994, C12.

2. Roy Chapman Andrews, *On the Trail of Ancient Man* (New York: G. P. Putnam's Sons, 1926), 216–17.

3. Ibid., 83.

4. Ibid., 78.

5. Edwin Colbert, *Men and Dinosaurs* (New York: E. P. Dutton, 1968), 201.

6. D. R. Barton, "The Way of a Fossil Hunter," *Natural History*, 47, no. 3 (1941): 174.

7. Charles Berkey, "Geological Reconnaissance in Central Mongolia," *Natural History*, 24, no. 2 (1924): 172–73.

The Poles

1. Quoted in Wally Herbert, *The Noose of Laurels* (New York: Atheneum, 1989), 51.

2. Quoted in Evan S. Connell, *A Long Desire* (New York: Holt, Rinehart and Winston, 1979), 128.

3. Quoted in ibid., 128.

4. Quoted in John Edward Weems, *Race for the Pole* (New York: Henry Holt and Company, 1960), 29.

5. Introduction to Josephine Diebitsch Peary, *My Arctic Journal* (New York: Contemporary

Publishing, 1893), 3–5.

6. Robert E. Peary, *Northward over the "Great Ice"* (New York: Frederick A. Stokes, 1898), 1: 343–44.

7. Ibid., 2:146.

8. Ibid., 2:568.

9. Ibid., 2:572.

10. Ibid., 2:584.

11. Ibid., 2:592.

12. Robert E. Peary, *Nearest the Pole* (New York: Doubleday, 1907), 51.

13. Ibid., 308.

14. Ibid., 207.

15. Quoted in Roy Chapman Andrews, *Beyond Adventure* (New York: Duell, Sloan and Pearce, 1954), 44–45.

16. George Borup, *A Tenderfoot with Peary* (New York: Frederick A. Stokes, 1911), 145.

17. Peary, *Nearest the Pole*, 145.

18. Robert E. Peary, *The North Pole* (New York: Dover Publications, 1986), 281.

19. Ibid., 316.

20. Weems, *Race for the Pole*, 133.

21. Andrews, *Beyond Adventure*, 74.

22. Donald MacMillan, *Four Years in the White North* (New York: Harper and Brothers, 1918), 80.

23. Ibid., 87–88.

24. Ibid., 313.

25. Lincoln Ellsworth, *Beyond Horizons* (New York: Doubleday, Doran and Company, 1938), 10–11.

26. Quoted in Harold T. Clark, "Inspiration: The True Story Back of Lincoln Ellsworth's Polar Achievements," *Natural History*, 29, no. 4 (1929): 38.

27. Quoted in ibid., 38.

28. Ellsworth, *Beyond Horizons*, 124.

29. Ibid., 192.

30. Ibid., 158–59.

31. Ibid., 164.

32. Ibid., 168.

33. Ibid., 212.

34. Ibid., 214.

35. Ibid., 222.

36. Ibid., 333.

37. Ibid., 235.

38. MacMillan, *Four Years in the White North*, 321.

Africa

1. Georg Schweinfurth, *The Heart of Africa: Three Years Travels and Adventures in the Unexplored Regions of Central Africa from 1868 to 1871* (New York: Harper and Brothers, 1874), 2:42–43. The passage is quoted in Enid Schildkrout and Curtis Keim, *African Reflections: Art From Northeastern Zaire* (New York: American Museum of Natural History and University of Washington Press, 1990), 143. Discussion of the Lang-Chapin expedition, including its origin, itinerary, photographic record, and ethnographic importance, relies extensively on the research and writing of Schildkrout and Keim in their landmark volume.

2. Herbert Lang, "Famous Ivory Treasures of a Negro King," *American Museum Journal*, 18, no. 7 (1918): 532.

3. James Chapin, "Pursuit of an African Star," autobiographical reminiscence, n.d., p. 11, Archives, Department of Ornithology, American Museum of Natural History, New York.

4. James Chapin, Reminiscences, recorded by E. T. Gilliard, n.d., reel 4A, transcript p. 5.

Archives, Department of Ornithology, American Museum of Natural History, New York.

5. Ibid., reel 2A, p. 16.

6. James Chapin, "Profiteers of the Busy Bee," *Natural History*, 24, no. 3 (1924): 329.

7. Lang, "Famous Ivory Treasures," 532.

8. James Chapin to Dee Streeter, December 29, 1957, Archives, Department of Ornithology, American Museum of Natural History, New York.

9. Ibid.

10. Carl Akeley, *In Brightest Africa* (New York: Doubleday, Page & Company, 1924), 252.

11. Ibid., 101–2.

12. Delia Akeley, *Jungle Portraits* (New York: The MacMillan Company, 1930), 73.

13. Carl Akeley, Uganda Journal, 2, quoted in Penelope Bodry-Sanders, *Carl Akeley: Africa's Collector, Africa's Savior* (New York: Paragon House, 1991), 138.

14. Delia Akeley, *Jungle Portraits*, 250.

15. Bodry-Sanders, *Carl Akeley*, 265.

16. Ibid., 262.

17. Quoted in Colin M. Turnbull, *Man in Africa* (Garden City: Anchor Press/Doubleday, 1976), 109.

18. Colin M. Turnbull, *The Mountain People* (New York: Simon and Schuster, 1972), 73.

19. Colin M. Turnbull, "Children of the Forest," *Natural History*, 69, no. 7 (1960): 25.

20. Ibid., 24.

21. Colin M. Turnbull, "A People Apart," *Natural History*, 75, no. 8 (1966): 10.

22. Turnbull, *The Mountain People*, 251.

23. Ibid., 222.

24. Colin M. Turnbull to Harry Shapiro, February 20, 1966, Archives, Department of Anthropology, American Museum of Natural History, New York.

25. Colin M. Turnbull, *The Human Cycle* (New York: Simon and Schuster, 1972), 266.

Early Americans

1. Carl Lumholtz, "My Life of Exploration," *Natural History*, 21, no. 3 (1921): 226.

2. Carl Lumholtz, "Report on Explorations in Northern Mexico," *Bulletin of the American Geographical Society*, 26, no. 3 (1891): 388.

3. Carl Lumholtz, "Among the Tarahumaris," *Scribner's Magazine* (July 1894): 34.

4. Lumholtz, "Report on Explorations in Northern Mexico," 394.

5. Ibid., 395.

6. Ibid., 401–2.

7. Lumholtz, "My Life of Exploration," 231.

8. Carl Lumholtz, "The American Cave-Dwellers: The Tarahumaris of the Sierra Madre," *Bulletin of the American Geographical Society*, 26, no. 3 (1891): 302–3.

9. Carl Lumholtz, "Tarahumari Life and Customs," *Scribner's Magazine* (September 1894): 301.

10. Lumholtz, "The American Cave-Dwellers," 303–4.

11. Carl Lumholtz, "The Huichol Indians of Mexico," *Bulletin of the American Museum of Natural History*, 10 (1898): 10.

12. Ibid., 1.

13. Fernando Benítez, *In the Magic Land of Peyote*, transl. John Upton (Austin: University of Texas Press, 1975), xxv.

14. Carl Lumholtz, *Unknown Mexico* (New York: Charles Scribner's Sons, 1902), 1:358.

15. Ibid., 2:469.

16. Quoted in Robert H. Lister and Florence C. Lister, *Chaco Canyon* (Albuquerque: University of New Mexico Press, 1936), 23.
17. Quoted in ibid., 10.
18. Edgar L. Hewett, *The Chaco Canyon and Its Monuments* (Albuquerque: University of New Mexico Press), 11.
19. Clark Wissler, "How Science Deciphers Man's Past," *Natural History*, 51, no. 3 (1943): 120.
20. Earl Morris to Clark Wissler, 1922, Archives, Department of Anthropology, American Museum of Natural History, New York.
21. Quoted in Robert H. Lister and Florence C. Lister, *Earl Morris & Southwestern Archaeology* (Albuquerque: University of New Mexico Press, 1968), 7.
22. Ibid., 50.
23. Earl Morris to Clark Wissler, April 26, 1921. Archives, Department of Anthropology, American Museum of Natural History, New York.
24. Earl Morris, "Excavations in the Aztec Ruin," *Anthropological Papers of the American Museum of Natural History*, 26 (1928): 420.
25. Quoted in Lister and Lister, *Earl Morris & Southwestern Archaeology*, 112.
26. Quoted in ibid., 159.
27. Clark Wissler, "Twilight of the Old West," *Natural History*, 39, no. 5 (1937): 307.
28. Clark Wissler, "The Indian and the Supernatural," *Natural History*, 42, no. 2 (1938): 124.
29. Ibid., 125.
30. Ibid., 154.
31. Clark Wissler, "Smoking-star, a Blackfoot Shaman," in Elsie Clews Parsons, ed., *American Indian Life* (New York: The Viking Press, 1925): 61–62.

South America

1. Arthur Conan Doyle, *The Lost World* (New York: Looking Glass Library, 1959), 86.
2. Quoted in Gordon Willey, "Biographical Essay," in Junius Bird, *Travels in Archaeology in South Chile* (Iowa City: University of Iowa Press, 1988), xxviii.
3. Quoted in Adolph F. Bandelier, *The Islands of Titicaca and Koati* (New York: Hispanic Society of America, 1910), 316.
4. Charles Lummis, "In Memory," introduction to Adolph Bandelier, *The Delight Makers* (New York: Dodd, Mead and Company, 1960), xv.
5. Quoted in Craig Morris and Adriana Von Hagen, *The Inka Empire and Its Andean Origins* (New York: American Museum of Natural History and Abbeville Press, 1993), 98.
6. Wendell Bennett, "Archaeological Hikes in the Andes," *Natural History*, 33, no. 2 (1933): 169.
7. Frank Chapman, *Autobiography of a Bird Lover* (New York: D. Appleton-Century Company, 1933), 219.
8. Leo E. Miller, *In the Wilds of South America* (New York: Charles Scribner's Sons, 1918), vii–viii.
9. George K. Cherrie, *Dark Trails* (New York: G. P. Putnam's Sons, 1930), 123.
10. Claude Lévi-Strauss, *Tristes Tropiques* (New York: Atheneum, 1974), 18.
11. Miller, *In the Wilds of South America*, 207.
12. Ibid., 241–42.
13. Theodore Roosevelt, Jr., *Through the Brazilian Wilderness* (New York: Greenwood Press, 1969), 259.
14. Cherrie, *Dark Trails*, 293.
15. Roosevelt, *Through the Brazilian Wilderness*, 285.
16. Cherrie, *Dark Trails*, 309.
17. Kermit Roosevelt, introduction to ibid., vi–vii.
18. Arthur Conan Doyle, *The Lost World*, 47–49.
19. Frank M. Chapman, "The Phelps Venezuela Expedition," *Natural History*, 40, no. 5 (1937): 760.

The South Pacific

1. Robert Cushman Murphy, "The Whitney South Sea Expedition," *Natural History*, 24, no. 5 (1924): 539.
2. Rollo Beck, "The Voyage of the 'France,'" *Natural History*, 23, no. 1 (1923): 39.
3. Ernst Mayr, "A Tenderfoot Explorer in New Guinea," *Natural History*, 32, no. 1 (1932): 91.
4. Ernst Mayr, "Birds of Paradise," *Natural History*, 54, no. 6 (1945): 264.
5. Peter Matthiessen, *Under the Mountain Wall* (New York: Viking, 1962), xi.
6. Richard Archbold and A. L. Rand, *New Guinea Expedition* (New York: Robert M. McBride and Co., 1940), 22.
7. Ibid., 196.
8. Richard Archbold, "Unknown New Guinea," *National Geographic*, 79, no. 3 (1941): 319.
9. Matthiessen, *Under the Mountain Wall*, xiv.
10. Margaret Mead, *Letters from the Field 1925–1975* (New York: Harper & Row, 1977), 1.
11. Margaret Mead, "Samoan Children at Work and Play," *Natural History*, 28, no. 6 (1928): 625.
12. Margaret Mead, *Letters from the Field*, 47.
13. Margaret Mead, *Coming of Age in Samoa*, in *From the South Seas: Studies of Adolescence and Sex in Primitive Societies* (New York: William Morrow, 1939), 157.
14. Margaret Mead, "Living with the Natives of Melanesia," *Natural History*, 31, no. 1 (1931): 63.
15. Margaret Mead, *Growing up in New Guinea*, in *From the South Seas*, p. 4.
16. Ibid., 11.
17. Ibid., 260.
18. Mead, *Letters from the Field*, 103.
19. Margaret Mead, *Sex and Temperament in Three Primitive Societies*, in *From the South Seas*, xiv.
20. Margaret Mead, *Letters from the Field*, 130.
21. Margaret Mead, *Blackberry Winter: My Earlier Years* (New York: William Morrow, 1972), 204.
22. Mead, *Sex and Temperament*, 167.
23. Ibid., 173–74.
24. Gregory Bateson and Margaret Mead, *Balinese Character: A Photographic Analysis* (New York: Academy of Sciences, 1942), xii.
25. Ibid., 1.
26. Mead, *Blackberry Winter*, 237–38.
27. Margaret Mead, *New Lives for Old: Cultural Transformation—Manus, 1928–1953* (New York: William Morrow, 1956), 21.
28. Mead, *Letters from the Field*, 248.
29. Ibid., 283.

Dinosaurs and Mammals

1. William Diller Matthew, "The Value of Paleontology," *Natural History*, 25, no. 2 (1925): 167.
2. Rainger, *An Agenda for Antiquity*, 82–83.
3. Roland T. Bird, *Bones for Barnum Brown* (Fort Worth: Texas Christian University Press, 1985), 115.
4. Hellman, *Bankers, Bones and Beetles*, 134.
5. Bird, *Bones for Barnum Brown*, 111.
6. Henry Fairfield Osborn to Barnum Brown, June 25, 1902, Archives, Department of Vertebrate Paleontology, American Museum of Natural History, New York.
7. Barnum Brown to Henry Fairfield Osborn, August 12, 1902, Archives, Department of Vertebrate Paleontology, American Museum of Natural History, New York.
8. Barnum Brown, "The Sinclair Dinosaur Expedition," *Natural History*, 36, no. 6 (1935): 4.
9. Bird, *Bones for Barnum Brown*, 19.
10. Ibid., 217.
11. Edwin H. Colbert, "The Little Dinosaurs of Ghost Ranch," *Natural History*, 56, no. 9 (1947): 396.

Biodiversity and Evolution

1. Frank M. Chapman, *Camps and Cruises of an Ornithologist* (New York: D. Appleton and Company, 1908), 79.
2. Miller, *In the Wilds of South America*, 419–20.
3. Herbert Lang, "The Vanishing Wildlife of Africa," *Natural History*, 24, no. 3 (1924): 323.
4. Norman Platnick, "Patterns of Biodiversity," in Niles Eldredge, ed., *Systematics, Ecology and the Biodiversity Crisis* (New York: Columbia University Press, 1992), 22.
5. Edward O. Wilson, *The Diversity of Life* (Cambridge: Harvard University Press, 1992), 280.
6. Henry Fairfield Osborn and Harold Elmer Anthony, "Can We Save the Mammals?" *Natural History*, 22, no. 5 (1922): 389.
7. David L. Hull, *Science as a Process* (Chicago: University of Chicago Press, 1988), 90.
8. Charles Darwin, *On the Origin of Species by Natural Selection*, 6th ed. (New York: D. Appleton and Company, 1886), 47.
9. Norman Platnick and H. D. Cameron, "Cladistic Methods in Textual, Linguistic, and Phylogenetic Analysis," *Systematic Zoology*, 26, no. 4 (1977): 380–85.
10. Henry Fairfield Osborn, *Impressions of Great Naturalists* (New York: Charles Scribner's Sons, 1924), 78.
11. Ibid., 58.
12. Henry Fairfield Osborn, *The Origin and Evolution of Life* (New York: Charles Scribner's Sons, 1917), x.
13. Rainger, *An Agenda for Antiquity*, 136.
14. Theodosius Dobzhansky, *Genetics and the Origin of Species*, 2d ed. (New York: Columbia University Press, 1942), 342.
15. Ernst Mayr, *Systematics and the Origin of Species from the Viewpoint of a Zoologist* (New York: Dover Publications, 1964), 291.
16. Ian Tattersall, *The Fossil Trail* (New York: Oxford University Press, 1995), 225.

Bibliography

General History

Allen, Joel Asaph. *Autobiographical Notes.* New York: American Museum of Natural History, 1916.

Bickmore, Albert S. *Travels in the East Indian Archipelago.* New York: D. Appleton and Company, 1869.

_____. Autobiography. 1908. Archives, American Museum of Natural History, New York.

Bruce, Robert V. *The Launching of American Science, 1846–1876.* New York: Alfred A. Knopf, 1987.

Chapman, Frank. *Autobiography of a Bird Lover.* New York: D. Appleton-Century Company, 1933.

Gratacap, Louis. "History of the American Museum of Natural History." No date. Archives, American Museum of Natural History, New York.

Hellman, Geoffrey. *Bankers, Bones and Beetles: The First Century of the American Museum of Natural History.* Garden City: The Natural History Press, 1968.

Kastner, Joseph. *A Species of Eternity.* New York: Alfred A. Knopf, 1977.

Kennedy, John Michael. "Philanthropy and Science in New York City: The American Museum of Natural History, 1868–1968." Ph.D. diss., Yale University, 1968.

Peck, Robert McCracken. "The Museum that Never Was." *Natural History* 103, no. 7 (1994).

Preston, Douglas. *Dinosaurs in the Attic.* New York: St. Martin's Press, 1986.

Viola, Herman, and Carolyn Margolis, eds. *The Magnificent Voyagers: The U.S. Exploring Expedition 1838–1842.* Washington, D.C.: Smithsonian Institution, 1985.

The North Pacific

Annual Report of the American Museum of Natural History. No. 28. New York: 1896.

Annual Report of the American Museum of Natural History. No. 29. New York: 1897.

Bancroft-Hunt, Norman, and Werner Forman. *People of the Totem.* Norman and London: University of Oklahoma Press, 1988.

Boas, Franz. "The Jesup North Pacific Expedition." *American Museum of Natural History Memoirs* 2, part 1 (1898).

_____. "The Mythology of the Bella Coola Indians." *American Museum of Natural History Memoirs* 2, part 2 (1898).

_____. "The Jesup North Pacific Expedition." *The American Museum Journal* 3, no. 5 (1903).

_____. "The Kwakiutl of Vancouver Island." *American Museum of Natural History Memoirs* 8 (1909).

_____. *The Mind of Primitive Man.* New York: Macmillan, 1911.

Borgoras, Waldemar. "The Folklore of Northeastern Asia." *American Anthropologist* 4 (1902).

_____. "The Chukchee." *American Museum of Natural History Memoirs* 7 (1904–9).

_____. "Chukchee Mythology." *American Museum of Natural History Memoirs* 12, part 1 (1910).

Cole, Douglas. *Captured Heritage: The Scramble for Northwest Coast Artifacts.* Vancouver: Douglas and McIntyre, 1985.

Fitzhugh, William, and Aron Crowell. *Crossroads of Continents: Cultures of Siberia and Alaska.* Washington, D.C.: Smithsonian Institution Press, 1988.

Fladmark, Knut R. "Getting One's Berings."

Natural History 95, no. 11 (November 1986).

Freed, Stanley A., Ruth S. Freed, and Laila Williamson. "Scholars Amid Squalor." *Natural History* 97, no. 3 (March 1988).

_____. "Capitalist Philanthropy and Russian Revolutionaries: The Jesup North Pacific Expedition (1897–1902)." *American Anthropologist* 90 (1988).

Harris, Marvin. *The Rise of Anthropological Theory.* New York: Thomas Y. Crowell, 1968.

Jochelson, Waldemar. "The Yukaghir and Yukaghirized Tungus." *American Museum of Natural History Memoirs* 9, part 1 (1910).

_____. "The Ethnological Problems of Bering Sea." *American Museum Journal* 26, no. 1 (1926).

_____. *Peoples of Asiatic Russia.* New York: American Museum of Natural History, 1928.

Jonaitis, Aldona. *From the Land of the Totem Poles.* New York: American Museum of Natural History, 1988.

Jonaitis, Aldona, ed. *Chiefly Feasts: The Enduring Kwakiutl Potlatch.* New York: American Museum of Natural History, 1991.

Lévi-Strauss, Claude. "The Art of the Northwest Coast at the American Museum of Natural History." *Gazette des Beaux-Arts* 24 (1943).

_____. *The Way of the Masks.* Translated by Sylvia Modelski. Seattle: University of Washington Press, 1982.

Miller, Thomas Ross, and Barbara Mathé. "Drawing Shadow to Stones: Photographs from the Jesup North Pacific Expedition." In press.

Preston, Douglas. *Dinosaurs in the Attic.* New York: St. Martin's Press, 1986.

Rohner, Ronald, ed. *The Ethnography of Franz Boas: Letters and Diaries of Franz Boas Written on the Northwest Coast from 1886 to 1931.* Chicago: University of Chicago Press, 1969.

Stocking, George W. *A Franz Boas Reader: The Shaping of American Anthropology, 1883–1911.* Chicago: University of Chicago Press, 1974.

Swanton, John. "Contribution to the Ethnology of the Haida." *American Museum of Natural History Memoirs* 5, part 1 (1905).

Teit, James. "The Thompson Indians of British Columbia." *American Museum of Natural History Memoirs* 2, part 4 (1900).

Wardwell, Alan. *Objects of Bright Pride: Northwest Coast Indian Art from the American Museum of Natural History.* New York: Center for Inter-American Relations and the American Federation of Arts, 1978.

The Gobi

Andrews, Roy Chapman. "In Search of the Most Ancient Man." *Natural History* 20, no. 4 (1920).

_____. *Across Mongolian Plains.* New York: Blue Ribbon, 1921.

_____. Notebook entry. June 14, 1923. Archives, American Museum of Natural History, New York.

_____. *On the Trail of Ancient Man.* New York: G. P. Putnam's Sons, 1926.

_____. *Ends of the Earth.* New York: G. P. Putnam's Sons, 1929.

_____. "The Fate of the Rash Platybelodon." *Natural History* 31, no. 2 (1931).

_____. "J. McKenzie Young." *Natural History* 32, no. 3 (1932).

_____. *New Conquest of Central Asia.* New York: American Museum of Natural History, 1932.

_____. *Under a Lucky Star.* New York: Viking, 1943.

Barton, D. R. "Gambler on the Gobi." *Natural History* 45, no. 2 (1940).

_____. "The Way of a Fossil Hunter." *Natural History* 47, no. 3 (1941).

Berkey, Charles. "Geological Reconnaissance in Central Mongolia." *Natural History* 24, no. 2 (1924).

Bolitho, William. *Twelve Against the Gods.* New York: Simon and Schuster, 1929.

Colbert, Edwin. *Men and Dinosaurs.* New York: E. P. Dutton, 1968.

"Field Notes." *Natural History* 31, no. 1 (1931).

"Fossils Hint at Primate Garden of Eden." *The New York Times,* April 19, 1994.

Granger, Walter. "Camp Life on the Gobi Desert." *Natural History* 31, no. 4 (1931).

_____. "The Story of the Dinosaur Eggs." *Natural History* 38, no. 6 (1936).

Matthew, William Diller. *Climate and Evolution.* 2d ed. New York: New York Academy of Sciences, 1939.

McKenna, Malcolm. "Early Relatives of Flopsy, Mopsy and Cottontail." *Natural History* 103, no. 4 (1994).

Morden, William J. *Across Asia's Snows and Deserts.* New York: G. P. Putnam's Sons, 1927.

Norell, Mark, Luis Chiappe, and James Clark. "New Limb on the Avian Family Tree." *Natural History* 102, no. 9 (1993).

Novacek, Michael. "A Pocketful of Fossils." *Natural History* 103, no. 4 (1994).

Osborn, Henry Fairfield. *Men of the Old Stone Age.* New York: Charles Scribner's Sons, 1915.

_____. "American Men of the Dragon Bones." *Natural History* 23, no. 4 (1923).

_____. "The Discovery of an Unknown Continent." *Natural History* 24, no. 2 (1924).

_____. Introduction to Hugo Obermiller, *Fossil Man in Spain.* New York: Hispanic Society of America, 1924.

Perkins, John. *To the Ends of the Earth.* New York: Pantheon, 1981.

Pope, Clifford. "Hainan—An Island of Forbidding Reputation." *Natural History* 24, no. 2 (1924).

Rainger, Ronald. *An Agenda for Antiquity.* Tuscaloosa: University of Alabama Press, 1991.

Shapiro, Harry L. *Peking Man.* New York: Simon and Schuster, 1974.

Wilford, John Noble. *The Riddle of the Dinosaur.* New York: Alfred A. Knopf, 1986.

_____. "Gobi Diary: A Sedimental Journey." *The New York Times Magazine,* November 10, 1991.

_____. "Treasure Trove of Fossils Turns Up in the Gobi." *The New York Times,* April 5, 1994.

The Poles

Amundsen, Roald, and Lincoln Ellsworth. *First Crossing of the Polar Sea.* New York: Doubleday, Doran and Company, 1928.

Andrews, Roy Chapman. *Beyond Adventure.* New York: Duell, Sloan and Pearce, 1954.

Anthony, H. E. "To the Arctic for Walrus." *Natural History* 29, no. 1 (1929).

Borup, George. *A Tenderfoot with Peary.* New York: Frederick A. Stokes, 1911.

Bridgman, Herbert L. "Three Polar Expeditions, 1913–1916." *The American Museum Journal* 16, no. 5 (1916).

Clark, Harold T. "Inspiration: The True Story Back of Lincoln Ellsworth's Polar Achievements." *Natural History* 29, no. 4 (1929).

Connell, Evan S. *A Long Desire.* New York: Holt, Rinehart and Winston, 1979.

Ekblaw, W. Elmer. "The Plant Life of Northwest Greenland." *Natural History* 19, no. 3 (1919).

Ellsworth, Lincoln. "To Antarctica Again." *Natural History* 34, no. 4 (1934).

_____. "Ellsworth's Own Diary." *Natural History* 37, no. 5 (1936).

_____. *Beyond Horizons.* New York: Doubleday, Doran and Company, 1938.

Green, Fitzhugh. "The Crocker Land Expedition." *Natural History* 28, no. 5 (1928).

Herbert, Wally. *The Noose of Laurels.* New York: Atheneum, 1989.

Hobbs, William Herbert. *Peary.* New York: MacMillan, 1936.

Jackson, Donald Dale. "Lincoln Ellsworth, the Forgotten Hero of Polar Exploration." *Smithsonian* (October 1990).

Lore, David. "Polar Dreams, Polar Nightmares: The Quests of Lincoln Ellsworth." *Timeline* (December 1988/January 1989).

MacMillan, Donald B. "Food Supply of the Smith Sound Eskimos." *The American Museum Journal* 18, no. 3 (1918).

_____. *Four Years in the White North.* New York: Harper and Brothers, 1918.

_____. "Scenes from the Eastern Arctic." *The American Museum Journal* 18, no. 3 (1918).

Murphy, Robert Cushman. "A Desolate Island of the Antarctic." *The American Museum Journal* 13, no. 6 (1913).

Peary, Josephine Diebitsch. *My Arctic Journal.* New York: Contemporary Publishing, 1893.

_____. *The Snow Baby.* New York: Frederick A. Stokes, 1901.

_____. *Children of the Arctic.* New York: Frederick A. Stokes, 1903.

Peary, Robert E. *Northward over the "Great Ice."* 2 vols. New York: Frederick A. Stokes, 1898.

_____. *Nearest the Pole.* New York: Doubleday, 1907.

_____. *The North Pole.* New York: Dover Publications, 1986.

Perkins, John. *To the Ends of the Earth.* New York: Pantheon, 1981.

Rainey, Froelich G. "Mystery People of the Arctic." *Natural History* 47, no. 3 (1941).

Stefansson, Vilhjalmur. "By Air to the Ends of the Earth." *Natural History* 28, no. 5 (1928).

_____. "The Theoretical Continent." *Natural History* 29, no. 5 (1929).

_____. *My Life with the Eskimo.* New York: MacMillan, 1951.

_____. *Discovery.* New York: McGraw-Hill, 1964.

Weems, John Edward. *Race for the Pole.* New York: Henry Holt and Company, 1960.

Africa

Akeley, Carl. *In Brightest Africa.* New York: Doubleday, Page & Company, 1924.

Akeley, Delia. *Jungle Portraits.* New York: The MacMillan Company, 1930.

Akeley, Mary L. Jobe. *Carl Akeley's Africa.* New York: Blue Ribbon Books, 1929.

_____. "King Albert Inaugurates the Parc National Albert." *Natural History* 30, no. 2 (1930).

Andrews, Roy Chapman. "Carl Akeley." In *Beyond Adventure.* New York: Duell, Sloan and Pearce, 1954.

Bodry-Sanders, Penelope. *Carl Akeley: Africa's Collector, Africa's Savior.* New York: Paragon House, 1991.

Chapin, James. "Profiteers of the Busy Bee." *Natural History* 24, no. 3 (1924).

_____. "The Crowned Eagle, Ogre of Africa's Monkeys." *Natural History* 25, no. 5 (1925).

_____. "Climbs in the Kivu Volcanoes." *Natural History* 32, no. 4 (1932).

_____. "In Pursuit of the Congo Peacock." *Natural History* 40, no. 5 (1937).

_____. Unpublished reminiscences. 1960. Tape transcript, Archives, Department of Ornithology, American Museum of Natural History, New York.

Heine, Bernd. "The Mountain People: Some Notes on the Ik of Northeastern Uganda." *Africa* 55, no. 1 (1985).

Johnson, Martin. *Above African Jungles.* New York: Harcourt, Brace and Company, 1935.

Johnson, Osa. *I Married Adventure.* Philadelphia: J. B. Lippincott Company, 1940.

Lang, Herbert. "Famous Ivory Treasures of a Negro King." *American Museum Journal* 18, no. 7 (1918).

Mark, Joan. *The King of the World in the Land of the Pygmies.* Lincoln: University of Nebraska Press, 1995.

Raven, H. C. "Gorilla: The Greatest of All Apes." *Natural History* 31, no. 3 (1931).

Sanford, Gertrude, and Sidney LeGendre. "In Quest of the Queen of Sheba's Antelope." *Natural History* 30, nos. 1, 2 (1930).

Schildkrout, Enid. "Young Traders of Northern Nigeria." *Natural History* 90, no. 6 (1981).

Schildkrout, Enid, and Curtis Keim. *African Reflections: Art from Northeastern Zaire.* New York: American Museum of Natural History and University of Washington Press, 1990.

Schweinfurth, Georg. *The Heart of Africa: Three Years Travels and Adventures in the Unexplored Regions of Central Africa from 1868 to 1871.* New York: Harper and Brothers, 1874.

Turnbull, Colin. "Children of the Forest." *Natural History* 69, nos. 7, 8 (1960).

――――. *The Forest People.* New York: Simon and Schuster, 1961.

――――. "A People Apart." *Natural History* 75, no. 8 (1966).

――――. *The Mountain People.* New York: Simon and Schuster, 1972.

――――. *Man in Africa.* Garden City: Anchor Press/Doubleday, 1976.

――――. *The Human Cycle.* New York: Simon and Schuster, 1983.

――――. Letters. Archives, Department of Anthropology, American Museum of Natural History, New York.

Early Americans

Benítez, Fernando. *In the Magic Land of Peyote.* Translated by John Upton. Austin: University of Texas Press, 1975.

Ceram, C. W. *The First American: The Story of North American Archaeology.* New York: Harcourt Brace Jovanovich, 1971.

Cook, Harold. "New Geological and Paleontological Evidence Bearing on the Antiquity of Mankind in America." *Natural History* 27, no. 3 (1927).

Douglass, A. E. "Dating Our Prehistoric Ruins." *Natural History* 21, no. 1 (1921).

Duel, Leo. *Conquistadors without Swords.* New York: St. Martin's Press, 1967.

Figgins, J. D. "The Antiquity of Man in America." *Natural History* 27, no. 3 (1927).

Freed, Stanley A., and Ruth S. Freed. "Clark Wissler and the Development of Anthropology in the United States." *American Anthropologist* 85, no. 4 (1983).

Hewett, Edgar L. *The Chaco Canyon and Its Monuments.* Albuquerque: University of New Mexico Press, 1936.

Kidder, A. V. "The Museum's Expedition to Cañon de Chelly and Cañon del Muerto, Arizona." *Natural History* 27, no. 3 (1927).

Lister, Robert H., and Florence C. Lister. *Earl Morris & Southwestern Archaeology.* Albuquerque: University of New Mexico Press, 1968.

――――. *Chaco Canyon.* Albuquerque: University of New Mexico Press, 1981.

Lumholtz, Carl. "Report on Explorations in Northern Mexico." *Bulletin of the American Geographical Society* 26 (1891).

――――. "Letter from Mr. Carl Lumholtz, in Northern Mexico." *Bulletin of the American Geographical Society* (1893).

――――. "The American Cave-Dwellers: The Tarahumaris of the Sierra Madre." *Bulletin of the American Geographical Society* 26, no. 3 (1894).

――――. "Among the Tarahumaris." *Scribner's Magazine,* July 1894.

――――. "Tarahumari Life and Customs." *Scribner's Magazine,* September 1894.

――――. "The Huichol Indians of Mexico." *Bulletin of the American Museum of Natural History* 10 (1898).

――――. *Unknown Mexico.* 2 vols. New York: Charles Scribner's Sons, 1902.

――――. "My Life of Exploration." *Natural History* 21, no. 3 (1921).

Morris, Earl. "Discoveries at the Aztec Ruin." *Natural History* 17, no. 3 (1917).

――――. "An Unexplored Area of the Southwest." *Natural History* 22, no. 6 (1922).

――――. "Excavations in the Aztec Ruin." *Anthropological Papers of the American Museum of Natural History* 26 (1928).

Nelson, N. C. "Chronology of the Tano Ruins, New Mexico." *American Anthropologist* 18, no. 2 (1916).

Roberts, David. " 'Reverse' Archaeologists Are Tracing the Footsteps of a Cowboy-Explorer." *Smithsonian* 24, no. 9 (December 1993).

Thomas, David Hurst. *Archaeology.* Fort Worth: Holt, Reinhart and Winston, 1989.

Wissler, Clark. "A Page of Museum History." *Natural History* 13, no. 3 (1913).

――――. *The American Indian.* New York: Douglas C. McMurtrie, 1917.

――――. "Dating Our Prehistoric Ruins." *Natural History* 21, no. 1 (1921).

――――. "Smoking-star, a Blackfoot Shaman." In *American Indian Life,* edited by Elsie Clews Parsons. New York: The Viking Press, 1925.

――――. "Twilight of the Old West." *Natural History* 39, no. 5 (1937).

――――. "The Indian and the Supernatural." *Natural History* 42, no. 2 (1938).

――――. *Indian Cavalcade.* New York: Sheridan House, 1938.

――――. "How Science Deciphers Man's Past." *Natural History* 51, no. 3 (1943).

Wissler, Clark, ed. "Sun Dance of the Plains Indians." *Anthropological Papers of the American Museum of Natural History* 16 (1921).

South America

Bandelier, Adolph F. *The Islands of Titicaca and Koati.* New York: The Hispanic Society of America, 1910.

Bennett, Wendell. "Archaeological Hikes in the Andes." *Natural History* 33, no. 2 (1933).

Bennett, Wendell, and Junius Bird. *Andean Culture History.* New York: American Museum of Natural History, 1949.

Bird, Junius. *Travels in Archaeology in South Chile.* Iowa City: University of Iowa Press, 1988.

Chapman, M. Frank. "The Andes: A New World." *Natural History* 24, no. 4 (1924).

――――. *Autobiography of a Bird Lover.* New York: D. Appleton-Century Company, 1933.

――――. "The Phelps Venezuela Expedition." *Natural History* 40, no. 5 (1937).

Cherrie, George K. "To South America for Bird Study." *The American Museum Journal* 17, no. 4 (1917).

――――. *Dark Trails.* New York: G. P. Putnam's Sons, 1930.

Conan Doyle, Arthur. *The Last World.* New York: Looking Glass Library, 1959.

Dennison, L. R. *Devil Mountain.* New York: Hastings House, 1942.

Donnelly, Maureen A., and Charles W. Myers. "Herpetological Results of the 1990 Venezuelan Expedition to the Summit of Cerro Guaiquinima, with New Tepui Reptiles." *American Museum Novitates,* no. 3017 (June 28, 1991).

George, Uwe. "Venezuela's Islands in Time." *National Geographic* 175, no. 5 (1989).

Gilliard, E. Thomas. "Unchallenged Champion." *Natural History* 46, no. 3 (1940).

Lévi-Strauss, Claude. *Tristes Tropiques.* New York: Atheneum, 1974.

Lummis, Charles. "In Memory." Introduction to Adolph Bandelier, *The Delight Makers.* New York: Dodd, Mead and Company, 1960.

Mayr, Ernst, and William R. Phelps, Jr. "The Origin of the Bird Fauna of the South Venezuelan Highlands." *Bulletin of the American Museum of Natural History* 136, article 5 (1967).

Miller, Leo E. *In the Wilds of South America.* New York: Charles Scribner's Sons, 1918.

Morris, Craig, and Adriana von Hagen. *The Inka Empire and Its Andean Origins.* New York: The American Museum of Natural History and Abbeville Press, 1993.

Murphy, Robert Cushman. *Oceanic Birds of South America.* 2 vols., New York: American Museum of Natural History, 1936.

Roosevelt, Theodore, Jr. *Through the Brazilian Wilderness.* 1914. Reprint. New York: Greenwood Press, 1969.

Simpson, George Gaylord. *Splendid Isolation: The Curious History of South American Mammals.* New Haven: Yale University Press, 1980.

――――. *Attending Marvels, A Patagonian Journal.* Chicago: University of Chicago Press, 1982.

Tate, George H. H. "Through Brazil to the Summit of Mount Roraima." *National Geographic Magazine* 58, no. 5 (1930).

――――. "A New Lost World." *Natural History* 42, no. 2 (1938).

Tate, George H. H., and C. B. Hitchcock. "The Cerro Duida Region of Venezuela." *Geographical Review* 20 (1930).

The South Pacific

Archbold, Richard. "Unknown New Guinea." *National Geographic* 79, no. 3 (1941).

Archbold, Richard, and A. L. Rand. "With Plane and Radio in Stone Age New Guinea." *Natural History* 60, no. 3 (1937).

――――. *New Guinea Expedition.* New York: Robert M. McBride and Co., 1940.

Bateson, Gregory, and Margaret Mead. *Balinese Character: A Photographic Analysis.* New York: New York Academy of Sciences, 1942.

Beck, Rollo. "Ten Days in Tahiti." *Natural History* 20, no. 6 (1920).

――――. "Bird Collecting in Polynesia." *Natural History* 22, no. 6 (1922).

――――. "The Voyage of the 'France.' " *Natural History* 23, no. 1 (1923).

_____. "A Collector in the Land of the Birds of Paradise." *Natural History* 29, no. 6 (1929).

Chapin, James. "Through Southern Polynesia." *Natural History* 37, no. 4 (1936).

Gilliard, E. Thomas. "In Quest of Birds of Paradise." *Natural History* 63, no. 2 (1954).

_____. "A Stone Age Naturalist." *Natural History* 66, no. 7 (1957).

Lanyon, Wesley. "Ornithology at the American Museum of Natural History." Archives, Department of Ornithology, American Museum of Natural History, New York.

LeCroy, Mary. "A Wing for the Birds." *Natural History* 98, no. 9 (1989).

Matthiessen, Peter. *Under the Mountain Wall.* New York: Viking, 1962.

Mayr, Ernst. "A Tenderfoot Explorer in New Guinea." *Natural History* 32, no. 1 (1932).

_____. "A Journey to the Solomons." *Natural History* 52, no. 1 (1943).

_____. "Birds of Paradise." *Natural History* 54, no. 6 (1945).

Mead, Margaret. "Samoan Children at Work and Play." *Natural History* 28, no. 6 (1928).

_____. "Living with the Natives of Melanesia." *Natural History* 31, no. 1 (1931).

_____. *From the South Seas: Studies of Adolescence and Sex in Primitive Societies.* New York: William Morrow, 1939.

_____. *New Lives for Old: Cultural Transformation—Manus, 1928–1953.* New York: William Morrow, 1956.

_____. *Blackberry Winter: My Earlier Years.* New York: William Morrow, 1972.

_____. *Letters from the Field: 1925–1975.* New York: Harper & Row, 1977.

Minor, Roy Waldo. "Pearl Divers." *Natural History* 47, no. 5 (1941).

Murphy, Robert Cushman. "The Whitney South Sea Expedition." *Natural History* 24, no. 5 (1924).

Musser, Guy. "The Mammals of Sulawesi." In *Biogeographical Evolution of the Malay Archipelago,* edited by T. C. Whitmore. Oxford: Clarendon Press, 1987.

Musser, Guy G., and Marion Dagosto. "The Identity of *Tarsius pumilus,* a Pygmy Species Endemic to the Montane Mossy Forests of Central Sulawesi." *American Museum Novitates,* no. 2867 (1987).

Rand, A. L. "The Courtship of the Magnificent Bird of Paradise." *Natural History* 65, no. 3 (1940).

Richards, Guy. "Trails and Tribulations of Bougainville." *Natural History* 31, no. 2 (1931).

Shapiro, H. L. " 'Robinson Crusoe's Children.' " *Natural History* 28, no. 3 (1928).

_____. "Mystery Island of the Pacific." *Natural History* 35, no. 5 (1935).

Sprecht, Jim, and John Fields. *Frank Hurley in Papua.* Bathhurst, Australia: Robert Brown and Associates, 1984.

Wallace, Alfred Russel. *The Malay Archipelago.* New York: Harper and Brothers, 1869.

Dinosaurs and Mammals

Barton, D. R. "The Way of a Fossil Hunter." *Natural History* 47, no. 3 (1941).

Bird, Roland T. "A Dinosaur Walks into the Museum." *Natural History* 47, no. 2 (1941).

_____. "Did Brontosaurus Ever Walk on Land?" *Natural History* 53, no. 2 (1944).

_____. *Bones for Barnum Brown.* Fort Worth: Texas Christian University Press, 1985.

Brown, Barnum. "Fossil Hunting by Boat in Canada." *American Museum Journal* 11, no. 8 (1911).

_____. "The Sinclair Dinosaur Expedition." *Natural History* 36, no. 6 (1935).

_____. "The Mystery Dinosaur." *Natural History* 41, no. 3 (1938).

Colbert, Edwin H. "The Little Dinosaurs of Ghost Ranch." *Natural History* 56, no. 9 (1947).

_____. *The Age of Reptiles.* New York: W. W. Norton, 1965.

_____. *Men and Dinosaurs: The Search in the Field and Laboratory.* New York: E. P. Dutton, 1968.

Desmond, Adrian J. *The Hot-Blooded Dinosaurs: A Revolution in Paleontology.* New York: Dial Press, 1976.

Eldredge, Niles. *Fossils: The Evolution and Extinction of Species.* New York: Harry N. Abrams, 1991.

Frick, Childs. "Prehistoric Evidence." *Natural History* 26, no. 5 (1926).

Galusha, Theodore. "Childs Frick and the Frick Collection of Fossil Mammals." *Curator* 18, no. 1 (1975).

Hellman, Geoffrey. *Bankers, Bones and Beetles: The First Century of the American Museum of Natural History.* Garden City: The Natural History Press, 1969.

Matthew, William Diller. "Fossil Animals of India." *Natural History* 24, no. 2 (1924).

Norell, Mark A., and Michael J. Novacek. "Congruence between Superpositional Phylogenetic Patterns: Comparing Cladistic Patterns with Fossil Records." *Cladistics* 8 (1992).

Norell, Mark, Eugene S. Gaffney, and Lowell Dingus. *Discovering Dinosaurs.* New York: Alfred A. Knopf, 1995.

Norman, David. *Dinosaur!* New York: Prentice Hall, 1991.

Rainger, Ronald. *An Agenda for Antiquity.* Tuscaloosa: University of Alabama Press, 1991.

Wilford, John Noble. *The Riddle of the Dinosaur.* New York: Alfred A. Knopf, 1985.

Biodiversity and Evolution

Darwin, Charles. *On the Origin of Species by Natural Selection.* 6th ed. New York: D. Appleton and Company, 1886.

Dawkins, Richard. *The Selfish Gene.* New York: Oxford University Press, 1976.

Dobzhansky, Theodosius. *Genetics and the Origin of Species.* 2d ed. New York: Columbia University Press, 1942.

Eldredge, Niles. *Unfinished Synthesis, Biological Hierarchies and Modern Evolutionary Thought.* New York: Oxford University Press, 1985.

_____. *The Miner's Canary.* New York: Prentice Hall, 1991.

_____. *Reinventing Darwin.* New York: John Wiley and Sons, 1995.

Gregory, William K. *Our Face from Fish to Man.* New York: G. P. Putnam's Sons, 1929.

Grimaldi, David. "Forever in Amber." *Natural History* 102, no. 6 (1993).

Hull, David L. *Science as a Process.* Chicago: University of Chicago Press, 1988.

Lang, Herbert. "The Vanishing Wildlife of Africa." *Natural History* 24, no. 3 (1924).

Matthiessen, Peter. *Wildlife in America.* New York: Viking Press, 1959.

Mayr, Ernst. *Systematics and the Origin of Species from the Viewpoint of a Zoologist.* New York: Dover Publications, 1964.

Osborn, Henry Fairfield. *The Origin and Evolution of Life.* New York: Charles Scribner's Sons, 1917.

_____. *Impressions of Great Naturalists.* New York: Charles Scribner's Sons, 1924.

Osborn, Henry Fairfield, and Harold Elmer Anthony. "Can We Save the Mammals?" *Natural History* 22, no. 5 (1922).

Platnick, Norman. "Patterns of Biodiversity." In *Systematics, Ecology and the Biodiversity Crisis,* edited by Niles Eldredge. New York: Columbia University Press, 1992.

Platnick, Norman, and H. D. Cameron. "Cladistic Methods in Textual, Linguistic, and Phylogenetic Analysis." *Systematic Zoology* 26, no. 4 (1977).

Rainger, Ronald. *An Agenda for Antiquity.* Tuscaloosa: University of Alabama Press, 1991.

Simpson, George Gaylord. *Tempo and Mode in Evolution.* New York: Columbia University Press, 1944.

Stiassny, Melanie. "Phylogenetic Analysis and the Role of Systematics in the Biodiversity Crisis." In *Systematics, Ecology and the Biodiversity Crisis,* edited by Niles Eldredge. New York: Columbia University Press, 1992.

Taboada, Gilberto Silva. "The Conservation of Animal Diversity in Cuba." In *Systematics, Ecology and the Biodiversity Crisis,* edited by Niles Eldredge. New York: Columbia University Press, 1992.

Tattersall, Ian. "Human Origins and the Origins of Humanity." *Human Evolution* 7, no. 2 (1992).

_____. *The Fossil Trail: How We Know What We Think We Know about Human Evolution.* New York: Oxford University Press, 1995.

Vrba, Elisabeth. "The Pulse That Produced Us." *Natural History* 102, no. 5 (1993).

Wilson, Edward O. *The Diversity of Life.* Cambridge, Massachusetts: Harvard University Press, 1992.

Index

Photograph Credits

Most of the photographs in this book come from the Museum's Special Collections and individual curators; otherwise, they represent objects, specimens, and expeditions associated with the Museum. Photographs with accession numbers are available from the Library and Special Collections. The authors and publisher are deeply grateful to the staff of Special Collections as well as to the curators, photographers, and institutions who provided photographs for reproduction.

Akeley, Carl: 12 (AMNH #3137), 114 (AMNH #219019), 115 (AMNH #324719), 116 (AMNH #211510).

Alcosser, Murray, permission courtesy Nevraumont Publishing Company: 242.

Anderson, A. E.: 212 (AMNH #35045).

Andrews, Roy Chapman: 60 right (AMNH #251744).

Andrews, Yvette Borup: 56 right.

Bandelier, Adolph; 161 below (AMNH #44185).

Bandelier, Fanny: 161 above (AMNH #44340-A).

Bartlett, Robert: 91 above.

Beck, Rollo: 178 (AMNH #105955), 180 (AMNH #105896), 181 (AMNH #114886).

Beckett, Jackie: 182 above left (AMNH #5404), 239.

Bernheimer, Carl: 145 (AMNH #293808).

Bird, Junius: 7 above, 158, 163 (AMNH #323388).

Bird, Roland T.: 217 (AMNH #324393).

Boas, Franz: 35 (AMNH #328734).

Boltin, Lee: 48 (AMNH #2513).

Borgoras, Waldemar: 49 above (AMNH #22402), 50 (AMNH #2518).

Brass, Leonard: 188 (AMNH #257-20).

Brown, Barnum: 207 below, 213 above (AMNH #19508), 214 (AMNH #19493), 223.

Chapin, James: 192 (AMNH #289223).

Cherrie, George: 164 above (AMNH #235762), 164 below (AMNH #332337), 167 below (AMNH #2591), 168 (AMNH #218623), 171 (AMNH #235806).

Chesek, Craig: 135 (AMNH #K16619), 241 (AMNH #5300).

Clark, James: 71 below (AMNH #265809).

Coles, Charles H.: 156 left (AMNH #287270).

Conrad, Fred R./The New York Times: 68–69 above and jacket back, 68 below, 69 below.

Coxe, J.: 160 and jacket back (AMNH #2253).

Curtis, Edward: 39 (AMNH #34583), 148 (AMNH #324004).

Daher, Joseane: 166.

Dimock, Julian: 153 (AMNH #48244).

Dixon, James: 150–51 (AMNH #324436).

Dossetter, Edward: 41 above (AMNH #44309).

Ellison, Michael: 71 above (AMNH #2A21321).

Ellsworth, Lincoln: 93 (AMNH #2A5282), 97 below (AMNH #337261).

Finnin, Denis: 218, 221 right (AMNH #338546).

Ford, Linda S.: 177.

© Frances, Scott/Esto Photographics: jacket front.

Gardiner, Lynton: 33 above (AMNH #45779 and #45778), 106 below right (AMNH #3894).

Gilliard, E. Thomas: 173, 182 above right (AMNH #5238), 183.

Goldberg, Peter: 27.

Granger, Walter: 57 (AMNH #253482), 61 below (AMNH #108720), 209 (AMNH #18517).

Grimaldi, David: 224–25, 227 and jacket back, 233, 238.

Hamerman, Don: 16.

Haring, David/Duke University Primate Center: 229.

Hastings, O. C.: 7 below (AMNH #336108), 37 (AMNH #336118), 41 below (AMNH #334106).

Henson, Matthew: 83 (AMNH #2A11357).

Hollenbeck, Phillip: 130 (AMNH #3408).

Hurley, Captain Frank: 186 below (AMNH #122419).

Courtesy Institute for Intercultural Studies, New York: 196, 201; photograph Gregory Bateson, 202; photograph Reo Fortune, 197.

Jochelson, Waldemar: 30 (AMNH #4169), 42 (AMNH #1604), 43 (AMNH #1573), 47 (AMNH #4194).

Johnson, Martin: 118 below (AMNH #286972), 119 (AMNH #314032).

Jonas, Louis: 20 (AMNH #101864).

Kirschner, Julius: 29 (AMNH #32800), 61 above (AMNH #108777), 74 (AMNH #33758), 205 below (AMNH #314804).

Lang, Herbert: 100 (AMNH #111806), 102 above (AMNH #5264), 102 below (AMNH #5266), 105 (AMNH #221158), 106 above (AMNH #5267), 106 below left (AMNH #5260), 108 (AMNH #36617), 109 (AMNH #225687), 110 above (AMNH #5258), 110 below (AMNH #5268), 111 left (AMNH #5263), 111 right (AMNH #5261).

Lee, Alfonso Silva: courtesy Museo Nacional de Historia Natural, Havana: 231 top left, 231 top right, 231 above left, 231 above right.

Logan, Robert: 22 (AMNH #328715), 149 (AMNH #1902).

Lucas, F. A.: 87 above (AMNH #239462).

Lumholtz, Carl: 131 (AMNH #335871), 132 (AMNH #43241), 133 (AMNH #338174), 134 (AMNH #43769).

MacMillan, Donald: 72–73 (AMNH #4993), 79 (AMNH #233098), 85 (AMNH #331040), 87 below (AMNH #231403), 89 (AMNH #232031), 90, 91 below (AMNH #233531).

MacPhee, Ross: 230 above, 230 below, 236.

Miller, Leo: 169 (AMNH #218722).

Menke, H. W.: 210 right (AMNH #17863), 211 (AMNH #17838).

Meyer, E. M.: 146 below (AMNH #283468).

Morris, Craig: 157 (AMNH #4957).

Morris, Earl: 6 (AMNH #126114), 140 (AMNH #119747), 141 (AMNH #126446), 142 (AMNH #5132); Earl Morris and A. V. Kidder: 146 above (AMNH #126050), 147 (AMNH #126101).

Murphy, Robert Cushman: 94 (AMNH #4988).

Musser, Guy: 8, 187.

Myers, Charles: 226.

Myers, Stephen: 1 (AMNH #3852), 33 below left (AMNH #3836), 33 below right (AMNH #3850), 33 below center (AMNH #3859), 40 (AMNH #3810).

Nelson, N. C.: 137 above (AMNH #4990), 139 above (AMNH #2580), 139 below (AMNH #2593).

Orchard, William: 28 left (AMNH #45087).

Peary, Robert E.: 80 (AMNH #329140), 84 (AMNH #272317).

Pepper, George: 138 above (AMNH #411912), 138 below (AMNH #4632).

© Ranney, Edward: 154.

Schildkrout, Enid: 125.

Schroeder, Eugene: 186 above (AMNH #31825).

Shackelford, James: 2–3 (AMNH #410998), 52 (AMNH #411077), 54 (AMNH #411065), 58 (AMNH # 410955), 59 (AMNH #410767), 60 left (AMNH #4711), 62 left (AMNH #251744), 62 right (AMNH #410737), 63 above right (AMNH #410746), 63 below left (AMNH #258395), 63 below right (AMNH #410761), 64 (AMNH #410783), 65 above (AMNH #410926).

Shapiro, Harry: 193 above (AMNH #337432).

Simmons, Nancy: 243 (AMNH #267108).

Smith, Harlan: 38 (AMNH # 46093).

Courtesy Smithsonian Institution, National Anthropological Archives: 34, 44, 49 below.

Stefansson, Vilhjalmur: 77 (AMNH #15270).

Stiassny, Melanie: 232.

Sweet, Paul: 234.

Tate, George H. H.: 167 above (AMNH #2586), 174 above left (AMNH #2584), 174 above right (AMNH #2585), 174 below (AMNH #2588), 175 above, 175 below.

Taylor, John Bigelow: 156 right (AMNH #5003).

Thomson, Albert: 65 below (AMNH #116818), 66 (AMNH #274528), 205 above (AMNH #17905).

Turnbull, Colin: 121 (AMNH #331155); courtesy Joseph Allen Towles Collection, Avery Research Center for African American History & Culture, College of Charleston, Charleston, South Carolina: 122, 123.

Photographer unknown: 4–5 (AMNH #4995), 23 (AMNH #324743), 27 below (AMNH #337389), 46 (AMNH #337173), 56 left, 80 (AMNH #323974), 82 (AMNH #2A9577), 88, 96 (AMNH #324601), 97 above (AMNH #110861), 103 (AMNH #5259), 107 (AMNH #5267), 117 (AMNH #260071), 118 above (AMNH #412166), 128 (AMNH #411866), 137 below (AMNH #412001), 182 below, 190, 191 (AMNH #483), 193 below (AMNH #419), 195 (AMNH #1664), 199 (AMNH #1508), 203 (AMNH #3158), 207 above left (AMNH #312091), 207 above right, 210 left (AMNH #17808), 213 below (AMNH #35424), 216 (AMNH #314524), 219 (AMNH #2421), 221 left (AMNH #337739).